Des is wie mer's saagt in Deitsch

(This is how we say it in Pennsylvania Dutch)

*Lee R. Thierwechter's Responses to
Dr. Ellsworth Kyger's Word Lists*

July 2002

*Center for Pennsylvania German Studies
Millersville University of Pennsylvania
Millersville, PA*

Published by:
C. Richard Beam
406 Spring Drive
Millersville, PA 17551

Second Edition, 2002

Library of Congress Control Number: 2002110688
International Standard Book Number: 1-930353-61-8

Printed by
Masthof Press
219 Mill Road
Morgantown, PA 19543-9516

PREFACE

This compilation of more than 4,000 Pennsylvania German (PG) words in context is an outgrowth of the numerous trips the Center for Pennsylvania German Studies made to the beautiful campus of Susquehanna University in Selinsgrove, Snyder County, PA beginning in the late 1980s when Dr. Susan Johnson was the head of the Department of Modern Languages. As a successor to the late Prof. Dr. Russell W. Gilbert, leading PG poet, who for 40 years was the professor of German, Dr. Johnson invited outstanding PG authorities to come to the campus and meet with a lively group of lovers of things Pennsylvania Dutch.

Among the group of Pennsylvania Germans who had distinguished themselves in many ways [*cf* page v] was a gifted gentleman from Belleville, Mifflin County, PA, Lee R. Thierwechter. We soon learned to appreciate Lee Thierwechter's ability to talk (and write) about his **Leweslaaf** in Pennsylvania Dutch. We look forward to the publication of the story of his life in which he gives a good account of life in Lebanon County—originally the northern extension of Lancaster County.

A few years ago after we had completed combing through M. Ellsworth Kyger's three-volume English - PG dictionary published by the Pennsylvania German Society in 1986 and copyrighted by Prof. Dr. Kyger, we were able to share these word lists/questionnaires with Mr. Thierwechter, who very kindly was able to place over 4,000 of Ellsworth Kyger's dialect words into Lebanon County contexts. Since Dr. Kyger had granted us permission to seek out appropriate dialect settings for his listing of English to dialect terms, Mr. Thierwechter's willingness to search through his experiences and memories proved to be a real boon. It must be underscored that Lee Thierwechter's love of and skills with the Standard German language [*cf* page iv] greatly facilitated his ability to express and record in PG in written form his childhood experiences in and about Mt. Zion, Lebanon County, PA. Thus our special focus in this study is on the PA German dialect of Lebanon County, PA.

It is not often possible to dedicate a volume in our beloved **Mudderschprooch** to such an outstanding personage as Mr. Lee R. Thierwechter. We Pennsylvania Germans have been remiss in such endeavors.

We also thank those co-workers in the Center for Pennsylvania German Studies who have helped to make this volume possible: Rachel Cornelius, Lyndell Wagner Thiessen, Joshua Brown of Emmaus, and most of all, Dorothy Pozniko Beam, whose constant support has made all of this possible. Last but not least, we thank Mrs. Elizabeth Kyger for her continued encouragement before and after the passing of her husband, M. Ellsworth Kyger, on November 30, 2000, at the age of 80.

As we have so many times in our weekly newspaper dialect column, **Es Pennsilfaanisch Deitsch Eck,** we raise our **Deitscher Schtrohhut** in salute to PG writer, poet, historian and teacher, Lee R. Thierwechter.

C. Richard Beam, Director
Center for Pennsylvania German Studies
Millersville University of Pennsylvania
July 12, 2002

Lee R. Thierwechter

A SKETCH OF THE LIFE
OF
LEE R. THIERWECHTER

I was born on a farm near Kimmerlings, Lebanon County, PA, in 1929. My parents were Robert J. and Edna P. (Peiffer) Thierwechter. My grandparents were Cyrus A. and Annie A. (Rutter) Thierwechter and Martin and Sallie A. (Phillipy) Peiffer.

My early recollections centered around my little world at Zoar Evangelical Lutheran Church (**Die Ziegel Kirche**) at Mt. Zion, Bethel Township, Lebanon County, PA. The church owned a little 23-acre farm and we moved there when I was three years old. My folks had the responsibilities of the farm, the church, and the cemetery. Adjacent to our property was the two-story Mt. Zion Grammar School (a public school), where our consistent language of communication was Pennsylvania German. Except for in church and at school, most people spoke in Pennsylvania German. Even the auctioneers at public auctions rattled off prices in Pennsylvania German.

I can still remember Pastor Diehl as we walked into church Sunday mornings saying, "Here come the Gate Keepers." We must remember that pastors were among the few learned people in our communities in those days. Little did I know that Pastor Diehl knew that our last name was originally spelled **Thürwächter**, and that meant gate keepers. With our farm, church and school so close, my family truly served in many ways, which was atypical for that time. Fortunately, my father in particular, was a hard-working, "people" person. Mother was a quiet, hard worker and strong supporter of my father. She loved to cook and sew.

Because of my upbringing in the environs of family love, church and school, the **Pennsilfaanisch Deitsch Mudderschprooch** has become an ingrown part of me. When I started first grade, I could hardly speak any English. My teacher (**die Teachern**) said I needed to learn to say "Tierwechter" or "Dierwechter" like we spelled "Thierwechter." I went home and told my parents and they said, "Oh, Sierwechter."

We resided at the church farm for ten years, and here is an indication of how our home was a home to everyone: the church council decided to begin an annual celebration, to be called "Homecoming." This was to be a Sunday, all-day affair, with the noon meal consisting of members bringing covered dishes. But the only place to have such a sit-down dinner was our kitchen and in the butcher/wash house. The Majestic kitchen range was hardly large enough to provide all the cooking and heating space, so we used the butcher furnace in the butcher/wash house. This event was considered so successful that for the next year, church members enclosed part of the old church horse-and-carriage shed to serve as a kitchen and dining room.

Indeed, this ten-year period seemed to come and go very quickly. My mother was getting tired and her health was failing a bit. To further complicate things, she gave birth to her second son, my brother, Glen in 1935. We were now in the World War II days and in spite of Dad's "busy-ness" he took a night-shift job at the Lebanon Bethlehem Steel Plant. All this was getting to be too much, so we purchased and moved to a several acre place on Race Street in Myerstown, PA. Dad was now primarily a steel worker, but could not totally give up farming. We had a huge garden, a small field of field corn, several hogs, a large flock of chickens, ducks, bantams, pigeons, and rabbits. Of course we still had Spot, our cross-bred hunting dog, and **Schtumpi,** our bob-tailed cat.

The Mt. Zion community missed us and we missed them. Grandpa Martin (**Mordi**) Peiffer continued to be one of the country store keepers there. Just across the road from the store was the old Grumbine residence of Dr. Ezra Grumbine and later that of the son, Thaddeus Grumbine. Soon after we moved to Myerstown, Thad died. The heiresses were in touch with **Mordi** and he pushed Dad and Mom to buy this residence and move back to Mt. Zion. So we moved in March of 1945. The property needed much work. This was once again an exciting time in my life. The place had remained much as it was when the doctor resided there. When Thad died, the heiresses had the large pieces of furniture and other items removed, but much of the small memorabilia remained scattered all over the property. Even the Jenny Lind, the doctor's hard-rubber-tire horse carriage, remained in the doctor's small horse barn.

In the attic were many things, but in particular, there was a copy of ***Der Prahl Hans***, by Dr. Ezra Grumbine. This book remains in my possession to the present day. It is part Pennsylvania German and part English and was published in 1927. There were other "goodies" like little pocket apothecary scales in a walnut wooden case. A woolen, moth-eaten, smoking jacket was also found. I later wore it under my hunting jacket to hunt deer in very cold weather. Certainly German thrift and hard work were always part of my upbringing.

My interest and love for the Pennsylvania German **Mudderschprooch** took off here when a neighbor lady, Alyce Stoever Meyers, taught me how to read the **"Horrich Amohl Boova! Der Alt Bauer Hut Eppes Tsu Sawga"** column in the *Lebanon Daily News* as I was simultaneously studying Standard German at Fredericksburg High School. Had it not been for the influence of several relatives and friends, I probably would have planned a future career in Germanic languages. After high school I headed for Lebanon Valley College, intending to become a veterinarian. My best grades were attained in Biology and German. I just loved German and our German professor, Mari Luise Huth, seemed to enjoy me and my parents. She would even try to hold occasional conversations with us in a dialect similar to Pennsylvania German. Miss Huth, a native German, had served as an interpreter with our Armed Forces after the war and ultimately came to this country, where she embraced the faith of the Society of Friends. The German carry-over that still existed here in Pennsylvania was a delight to her. Several items which were part of the things she brought from Germany were presented to me, including a pair of hand-painted glass goblets and a set of books. In hindsight, I regret not having majored in German.

Attending veterinary school never materialized. I went on to Penn State University and graduated with a degree in Agricultural Education. I graduated *in absentia* in order to marry Neda Kreider of Palmyra, PA, before starting my employment at the Milton Hershey School. After two years at the school, I went to work for the Eastern States Farmers' Exchange, which later became Agway.

Neda and I have three sons, John, David, and Andrew. While they have never become fluent in Pennsylvania German or Standard German, they have shown considerable interest in these languages. After the death of my mother in 1981, I had little opportunity to converse in the dialect. When Agway transferred me to Belleville, in Mifflin County, PA, I found, to my delight, that the Big Valley Amish maintain a language and lifestyle similar to what I knew from my childhood.

Another step up in the **Pennsilfaanisch Deitsch** ladder was when I retired from Agway in 1982, which enabled Neda and me to spend 23 days in Holland, Austria, Switzerland, France, and Germany. It was very interesting to find that the word for railroad track in Holland was **Spoor** and in Germany it was **Gleis**. Certainly, both these terms were familiar to me in our dialect at home, but never in connection with a railroad track. In PG a **Schpur** was like a foot track left in the snow by a deer and a **Glees** was like a rut in a dirt road left by a wagon. Hence, we borrowed from the English this term: **Riggelweg Draeck.**

After our return from Europe, I returned to work and spent the next twelve years working as a District Representative with Aid Association for Lutherans. This is a Fraternal Benefit Society founded by German Lutherans in 1902 in the Midwest.

It was in the late 1980's that I was invited to attend gatherings of Pennsylvania German enthusiasts at Susquehanna University, Selinsgrove, PA. The head of the Department of Modern Languages, Dr. Susan Johnson, was the convener. Approximately 30-40 people attended these meetings. The presenters which she invited to these gatherings were very fluent and prominent Pennsylvania German individuals, such as C. Richard Beam, Allen Musser, Earl C. Haag, (Rev.) Luke Brinker, (Rev.) Frederick S. Weiser, Ivan Glick, Howard Geisinger, John A. Hostetler, Larry Neff, Noah Zimmerman, and others.

These meetings served as my inspiration to begin writing my early autobiography in the Pennsylvania German dialect. I now serve on the board of directors of the Pennsylvania German Society and they have offered to publish my autobiography. A listing of the seventeen chapters follows:

In addition, my manuscript contains six poems as listed:

Die schaenscht I
Die schaenscht II
Kuddelfleck
Die Wutz
Zwee satte Leit
Der aarem "Boots"

* * * * * * * * * *

Kuddelfleck
En Gedicht vun gut Esses un Gschtank, was mer
ghat hot wann mer der Kuddelfleck gekocht hot

Oh Kuddelfleck, oh Kuddelfleck, duhn ich dich awwer arig verlange!
Es is awwer schund so, so lang, hab ich dich net versucht.
Awwer nee, nee mei Appeditt fer dich is mir noch nie net vergange!
Yaahre lang unni dich duh, waar mir schund en grosser Verluscht.

Deel Leit wisse vielleicht net vun was as mir schwetze.
Ya well, wann dir net mit Kuddelfleck uffgwaxe sind,
Denkt dir leichtsinnich, mir sin yuscht am retze.
Saagt dir, "Grunder Welt, dir sind verhafdich blind."

Wann Kuddelfleck zu eich nix mehnt,
Wie kummt's dann as dir hett en Wunner?
Well, wann dir vun Kinner uff, nix meh sehnt,
No kummt der Appeditt fer den Wamper wie's Dunner.

Oh, Kuddelfleck, wie kann mer dich vergesse?
In die Kich dich lang zu koche,
Seller Rindswamper sei Gruch hot em schier verfresse.
Denkt mer an em sei Hunger, no hot mer nix geroche.

Gebunne un gekocht waare die gleene Rolle,
No naus in's Kalde, bis sie schee fescht waare.
Naegscht hot mer sie gschnitte zu gleeni Grolle.
Mei Gedanke fer dich hab ich nie net verlore.

Mit bissel Zucker, Salz, Peffer un Essich aa, oh guder Kuddelfleck!

En Pennsilfaanisch Deitschi Schtimm vum Lee Thierwechter - June 12, 1996

Tripe

A poem about good eating and smells,
what we always got when we cooked tripe.

Oh tripe, oh tripe, you make me long for you!
        It is already so, so long ago since I have tasted you.
But no, no, my appetite for you hasn't gone away yet.
        I have done without you for many years now---That's been a great loss.

Some people might not know what we are talking about.
        Yes, well, if you haven't grown up with tripe,
You are thinking foolishly, I'm just here to tease you.
        You are saying, "My goodness, you are blind indeed!"

If **Kuddelfleck** doesn't mean anything to you,
        How come you are wondering?
Well, if you don't see anymore from childhood on,
        Your appetite for the "maw" will come like thunder.

Oh, tripe, how can we forget you?
        To cook you long in the kitchen.
That beef stomach's smell just about consumed me.
        If we think about our hunger, then we smelled nothing at all!

Bound and cooked are the little rolls,
        Then put them out into the cold until they were nice and stiff.
Next we cut them into little curls.
        I've never lost my thoughts of you.

With a little sugar, salt, pepper, and vinegar too, oh delicious tripe!

Lee Thierwechter - June 12, 1996

* * * * * * * * * *

En Pennsilfaanisch Deitschi Schtimm
vum Lee Thierwechter

Deitsche Schprichwadde mache en latt Verschtand.

Wann dir net wisst, Schprichwatt mehnt "proverb" in Englisch. In dem Zeidingschtick will ich eich drei sadde Schprichwadde gewwe. Die erscht Satt sin die wu

ich schund vun gleenem uff gheert hab. Die zwett Satt sin die wu ich glannt hab wie ich in die Schul gange bin un hab Hochdeitsch glannt, un die dritt Satt sin die as ich glannt hab zidder as ich do in Belleville wuhn. Nau wann dir wisse wett wie die Englische eenich-eens odder all die Sprichwadde saage, dann misst dir mich ewwe wisse losse. Well, do gehne sie:

1. So aarm wie en Karichemaus. Der Appel fallt net weit vum Schtamm. Sie losse's zu eem Ohr nei geh un zum annere naus. Was mer net im Kopp hot, muss mer in d'Fiess hawwe. Er sauft wie en Fisch. Er is ken Schuss Pulfer wert. Geb ihm der glee Finger un er will die ganz Hand hawwe. Wann mer der Esel nennt, kummt er gerennt. Er verdient net sei Salz in d'Supp. Zopp dei eegni Naas. En ungebutzter Seikopp. Mer kann en Gaul net saufe mache. Wer's letscht lacht, der lacht am beschde. Wer net draut, is net zu verdraue. Es zwett dritt sich. Er hot sei Bett gemacht, nau los ihn drin leie. Mariye rot, bis owed Dreck im Kot. Sunneblicker, Rege Schicker. Nasser Abrill un kiehler Moi, bringt viel Frucht un Hoi. Sis ken Haffe so schepp as ken Deckel druff fitt.

2. **Übung macht den Meister** (StG = Practice makes perfect.). **Jugend hat keine Tugend** (PG = Yugend hot ken Tugend). **Jeder Hafen findet seinen Deckel.**

3. En unehrlicher Sent fresst zehe gerechdi. Yeders muss sei Haut zum Garewer draage. Der Dod sett ihn hole. So dod wie en Katz. Er bekimmert sich mehner um die Woll as wie um die Schof. Die Erfaahring is en haddi Schul, awwer die Narre lanne in ken anneri. Es is net dewert as ee Esel der anner lang-ohrich heest. Geb me Kalb genunk Schtrick, un es hengt sich selwert. Was em net brennt, brauch mer net blose. Wer sich in die Gfaahr begebt, kummt drin um. Es Oier lege un's Gaxe sin zwee unerschittliche Sache. Die Fliege hen katzi Beh un laafe sich glei mied. Es kummt net uff die Grees aa, schunscht kennt en Kuh en Haas fange. Wer's Graab graabt fer anneri, fallt selwert nei. Die gleene Dieb hengt mer, awwer die grosse losst mer geh.

Well, bis naegscht Woch un "So aarem wie en Karichemaus," "Die Wunnernaas vun Baricks Co." daed saage, "Nix fer Ungut un gaar nix fer Schpeit, un schreibt mir alsemol."

* * * * * * * * * *

A Pennsylvania Dutch Voice
by Lee Thierwechter

PA Dutch proverbs make a lot of understanding.

For those who don't know, **Schprichwatt** means "proverb" in English. In this article I will give you three lists of proverbs. The first list is from proverbs I've heard ever since I was little. The second list are words that I learned when I went to school and learned Standard German, and the third list are words I've learned since I've lived here in Belleville. Now, when

you want to know the English meanings of one or all the proverbs, then you have to let me know.
Well, here it goes:

1. As poor as a church mouse. The apple doesn't fall far from the tree. She lets it go in one ear and out the other. What we don't have in our heads, we must have in our feet. He drinks like a fish. He's not worth a bit of powder. Give him your little finger and he'll take your whole hand. When you mention the donkey, he comes running. He doesn't earn the salt in his soup. Blow your own nose. An uncouth pig's head. You can lead a horse to water, but you can't make him drink. Whoever laughs last, laughs best. One who does not trust, shouldn't be trusted. That which happens twice, will happen a third time. He made his bed and is now lying in it. Morning a red sky, until evenings dirt in the muck. Sun through the clouds portends rain. A wet April and cool May, brings lots of grain and hay. There isn't a pot so crooked that doesn't have a lid to fit on it.

2. Practice makes perfect. Youth has no virtue. Every pot will find a lid that fits.

3. A dishonest cent consumes ten honest cents. Each takes his own hide to the tanner. Let death take him away. As dead as a cat. He cares more about the wool than he does about the sheep. Experience is a tough school, but the fools don't learn in any other. There is nothing worse than a donkey who calls the others long-eared. Give a calf enough rope and it will hang itself. What doesn't burn, doesn't need to be blown. Whoever doesn't watch out for danger, falls into it. Laying eggs and cackling are two different things. Flies have short legs and are soon tired. It's not a matter of size, otherwise a cow could catch a rabbit. Whoever digs graves for others, falls in himself. We hang the small thieves, but the big ones we let get away.

Well, until next week and "As poor as a church mouse," **"Die Wunnernaas of Baricks Co."** would say, "Nothing was said with an evil intent and nothing at all for spite, drop me a line from time to time." [These were the words G. Gilbert Snyder, **Die Wunnernaas vum Baricks County,"** used at the end of his weekly radio broadcast from Robesonia, PA.]

[August 19, 1998 column]

Lee writes this weekly column, **En Pennsilfaanisch Deitschi Schtimm vum** Lee Thierwechter, every week for the [Mifflin] *County Observer,* published in Yeagertown, PA. His first column appeared on June 28, 1995 and he continues writing today. By the end of April 2002, he had already published over 350 columns!

A GUIDE TO PRONUNCIATION

Vowels

A vowel is long when doubled. A vowel is long when followed by an h. Almost without exception a vowel is short when followed by two consonants.

Vowel	Pennsylvania Dutch	Engl Approximation		
a (short)	*Sache* (things)	a	in	what
aa (long)	*Aag* (eye)	aw	in	saw
ae (long)	*Baer* (bear)	ea	in	bear
ae (short)	*Maetsch* (match)	a	in	match
	Paesching (peach)	a	in	match
a(r) (long)	*darf* (may)	a	in	father
e (long)	*geht* (goes)	a	in	gate
	weech (soft)			
e (short)	*fett* (fat)	e	in	get
i (long)	*ihn* (him)	ee	in	see
	Biewel (Bible)			
i (short)	*bin* (am)	i	in	pin
	Biwwel (Bible)			
o (long)	*rot* (red)	oa	in	boat
u (long)	*Blut* (blood)	oo	in	moon
u (short)	*dumm* (stupid)	oo	in	cook
	kumm (come)			

Dipthongs

Dipthong	Pennsylvania Dutch	Engl Approximation		
au	*laut* (loud)	ow	in	cow
ei	*leicht* (light)	i	in	pine
oi	*Roi* (row)	oy	in	boy
	Moi (May)			
	Hoi (hay)			

Consonants

Most of the consonants of Pennsylvania German are pronounced much like they are in American English *(b, p, d, t, k, ck, f, h, l, m, n, s* and *w)* - Some of them are associated with letters which occur in English but with different sounds (v in PG = *f, sch* in PG = sh; *z* in PG = ts in English). Some do not occur in American English *(ch (ich), ch (ach),* and *r* (in certain positions)).

Consonant	Pennsylvania Dutch	Engl Approximation		
b	*Bank* (bench)	b	in	bank
	ab (off, away)	p	in	bump
ch (always follows a vowel)	*ich* (I)	(Sound not in Engl)		
	mache (to make)	(Sound not in Engl)		
ck	*packe* (to pack)	ck	in	picky
	Pack (pack)	ck	in	pack
d	*Daal* (valley)	d	in	dog
	Dodder (egg yolk)	dd	in	buddy
	Dod (death)	d	in	dot
f	*finne* (to find)	f	in	find
	hoffe (to hope)	f	in	huffy
	Schof (sheep)	f	in	hoof
g	*Geld* (money)	g	in	gold
	Grischt (Christian)	g	in	ground
	Regischder (register)	g	in	regulate
g (between vowels only)	*Aage* (eyes)	(Sound not in Engl)		
g (in final position)	*Aag* (eye)	k	in	kick
h	*Hut* (hat)	h	in	hat
h (silent)	*Uhr* (clock)			
k	*Keenich* (king)	k	in	king
l	*Leicht* (funeral)	l	in	light
	Millich (milk)	ll	in	silly
	Schlingel (rogue)	l	in	single
m	*Mann* (man)	m	in	man
	Besem (broom)	m	in	broom
n	*Not* (need)	n	in	not
	Menner (men)	nn	in	banner
	in (in)	n	in	in
ng	*Ring* (ring)	ng	in	ring
nk	*genunk* (enough)	nk	in	sink
p	*Parre* (pastor)	p	in	pastor
	Lumpe (rag)	b	in	number
pp	*Kopp* (head)	p	in	hep
	roppe (to pick, pluck)	bb	in	robber

r (Some native speakers of Pennsylvania German employ an American *r* in certain positions. Others use a slightly trilled *r* in an initial and medial position. The final *r* is very close to the StG final *r*.)

s, ss	*sadde* (sort of)	s	in	sort
	Kissi (cushion)	ss	in	sissy
	Boss (kiss)	ss	in	boss
sch	*Schul* (school)	sh	in	shop
t	*Tee* (tea)	t	in	tea
	Text (text)	t	in	next
	datt (there)	t	in	debt
v	*verrickt* (crazy)	f	in	for
w	*Wasser* (water)	w	in	water
x (Sometimes *chs)*	*Hex* (witch)	x	in	ax
	waxe, wachse (to grow)	x	in	ax
y	*Yung* (young)	y	in	yard
z	*Zucker* (sugar)	ts	in	hats

ABBREVIATIONS

acc	accusative
adj	adjective
adv	adverb
art	article
Bk.	Bucks County
Bs.	Berks County
cf	compare
Cl.	Clinton County
Cn.	Carbon County
Cr.	Center County
comp	comparative
conj	conjunction
CRB	C. Richard Beam
dat	dative
decl	declension
def	definite
def art	definite article
dem	demonstrative
dim	diminutive
Dn.	Dauphin County
E.	East
Engl	English
e.g.	exempli gratia, for example
ex.	example
f	feminine
gen	genitive
i.e.	id est, that is
ibid	ibidem, in the same place
imp	imperative
indef art	indefinite article
ind	indicative
indecl	indeclinable
inf	infinitive
insep	inseparable
interr	interrogative
KYG	M. Ellsworth Kyger
Lh.	Lehigh County
Ln.	Lebanon County
Lr.	Lancaster County
LRT	Lee R. Thierwechter
m	masculine

Me.	Monroe County
Mn.	Mifflin County
My.	Montgomery County
n	neuter
N.	North
Nd.	Northumberland County
NHG	New High German
Nn.	Northampton County
nom	nominative
num	numeral
PA	Pennsylvania
pers	person
PG	Pennsylvania German
pl	plural
poss	possessive
pp	past participle
pred	predicate
pref	prefix
prep	preposition
pres	present
pron	pronoun
refl	reflexive
rel	relative
S.	South
SE	southeast
sg	singular
SGrove	Sugar Grove, West Virginia
Sl.	Schuylkill County
Sr.	Snyder County
StG	Standard German
subj	subjunctive
sup	superlative
SW	southwest
Un.	Union County
W.	West
Yk	York County
~	key word
✪	place name

aa, *prep* - unto. **Es is ~ en Latt Gfraes an dem Weg nooch.** There too is a lot of trash along this road. LRT. *cf* **bis, dezu, zu.** KYG2114.

aa wann, *adv* - **1** though. = **obschon, doch, ewwe, wann. 2** even though. = **wann aa, aa, iewen wann.** KYG2002

aabappe - to stick on, paste on. **Guck mol datt, die Zeiding is an's Dischduch aagebappt, ich denk's waar Melassich datt.** Look, the newspaper is stuck to the tablecloth, I guess there was molasses there. LRT

aabasse - to palm off on. **eeni ~ -** to tell a lie. = **liege, eeni aahenke.** KYG1980

aabefehle - to warn. *cf* **sich bewanne, maahne, verwanne, wanne.** KYG2165

aabiede, *pp* **aagebodde** - to offer. **Er hot mir aagebodde fer mir alles fer nix gewwe.** He offered to give me everything for nothing (free). **Er hot mir aagebodde fer mir helfe mei Haus aaschtreiche.** He offered to help me paint my house. LRT

aabiede - to tender. KYG1984. **Was hen sie dir aagebodde fer selli Flint?** What did they offer you for that gun? LRT

aabinne, *pp* **aagebunne** - to tie up a horse. **Eb'd ins Haus kummscht, binn dei Gaul aa.** Before you come into the house, tie up your horse (to the hitching post). LRT **Hoscht du dei Gaul aagebunne?** Did you tie (fast) your horse? LRT. = **feschtbinne. Du kannscht dei**

Gaul do an den Baam ~. You can tie (tether) your horse here at this tree. LRT

Aabinngwicht, *n* - iron weight (for hitching horses). LRT

Aabinnrieme, *m* - tie strap. KYG2015. **Seller ~ is zu leicht.** That tie strap is too light (weak). LRT

aabohre - to tap. = **aazappe, abzappe, rauszappe, zappe.** KYG1971

aabrenne - to set fast in cooking. *cf* **Dreh selli Hitz nunner, die Grummbiere sin am ~.** Turn down the heat, the potatoes are setting fast. LRT

aabrode - to stick to a pan in frying. KYG1878. **Dreh die Hitz nunner, es Fleesch is am ~.** Turn the heat down, the meat is sticking fast to the frying pan. LRT

aabrowiere - to try on. KYG2071. **Browier selli Schuh mol aa un seh mol wie sie fidde (basse).** Try on those shoes and see how they fit. LRT

Aadler[1], *m* - turkey buzzard, vulture, eagle. (Yk) *Cathartes aura septendrionalis. cf* **Bossart, Geier, Luderaadler** (Bs,Lr,Ln), **Ludergrapp** (Lr), **Luderwoi** (Lh), **Ooshaahne** (Bs), **Oos-grapp, Ooshaahne, Ooshinkel** (Lh,Bx,Yk), **Oose,** *pl* (Lr), **Oosvoggel** (Lr), **Ooswoi** (Lh), **Welschhinkelgeier, Welschhaahnegeier.** KYG2075

Aadler[2], *m* - **1** whole kernel of a walnut. **2** half a kernel. KYG2161. **Glopp die Walniss**

net so hatt, mir welle e latt scheeni ~ hawwe. Don't hammer the walnuts so hard, we want a lot of nice whole walnut halves. LRT

aadreffe - to meet. **Ich hab mei Amischer Freind, der Schteffi, aagedroffe an die Vendu.** I met my Amish friend, Steffie, at the sale. LRT

aadrehe - to turn on (of a spigot)(of a light). KYG2077. **Kannscht du's Wasser ~?** Can you turn on the water (faucet)? LRT

aadresche - to begin thrashing. KYG2006

aaduh, *pp* **aageduh** - to dress. **Duh dei Hut aa!** Put on your hat! = **gleede, schee aageduh =** prettily dressed. = **schee gegleed.** LRT

aafaahre, *pp* **aagfaahre** - to turn the first furrow. KYG2077. **2** to speak gruff. **Uff ee mol is er ihm aagfaahre mit me heftiche grosse Maul.** All of a sudden he blasted him with a violently big (and vulgar) mouth. LRT

aafaule, *pp* **aagfault** - to begin to rot. **Wann die Grummbiere mol aagfault sin, no is net viel as mer meh duh kann.** Once the potatoes have begun to rot, there is not much one can do. LRT

aafechde - to tempt (by the devil). KYG1983

aafeichde - to moisten. KYG1237. *cf* **aaschpritze** - to sprinkle wash for ironing. LRT

aafiehle - to touch. *cf* **aafingere, aarege, aariehre, befiehle, fiehle, sich rege.** KYG2041

Aafiehles, *n* - sympathy. **Mer muss ~ hawwe fer sie; sie hen ewwe nau Schund vier Kinner verlore.** One must feel sorry for them; now they have already lost four children. LRT

Aag, *n, pl* **~e** - eye. **Sie kann grossi ~e mache, wann's aa nix mehnt.** She can make out surprised (make big eyes) even if it means nothing. LRT

aageh - to take fire. **Sell is graad was mir welle, es Holz im Offe is am ~.** That's just what we want, the wood in the stove is taking fire. LRT

aagenehmt, *adj* - honored, respected. **Die Nochbersfamillye is mir arig ~.** I have great respect for the neighbor family. LRT

Aagewasser, *n* - tears. **Es ~ is net kumme.** He was tearless. = **Draen.** KYG1976. **Sie hen all gsaat wie hatt as er gheilt hot, awwer ich hab nie ken ~ gsehne ghat.** They all said how hard he cried, but I never saw any tears. LRT

aagewwe, *pp* **aagewwe** - to declare. **Er hot ~ er daed uns immer helfe.** He declared he would always help us. LRT

Aagezaah, *m* - canine tooth (in people). KYG2035. **Wie seller Balle ihn gedroffe hot, hot's sei rechtser ~ abgebroche.** When the ball hit him, it broke off his right eye tooth (canine tooth). LRT

Aagezwidderes, *n* - twitching of the eyelids. KYG2084

aaglewe - to fasten on by sticking. KYG1878.

aagnippe - to tie on. KYG2015

aagsehne, *adj* - respected. **gut ~** - well respected. **Dir kennt eich datt druff verlosse, seller Mann is gut ~.** That man is well respected, you can depend on that. LRT

aagucke - to look at. **Ya, guck mich yuscht aa, ich hab gemehnt was ich gsaat hab.** Yes, just look at me, I meant what I said. **Do guck mich mol aa, ich will dich besser sehne.** Here, look at me, I want to get a better look at you. LRT

aagwaxe, *adj* - liver-grown. **Mir nemme dich zum Braucher, du bischt ~.** We're taking you to the powwow doctor. You are liver-grown. LRT

aahacke - to chop into. **Duh mol seller Block ~.** Chop into that log. = **eihacke.** LRT

aahariche - to take advice. **Harich ihm net aa.** Don't take his advice. LRT

aahelfe - to help a person put on clothes. **Kann ich dir ~?** May I help you get dressed? LRT

Aahenglichkeit, *f* - tenacity. KYG1984. **Unser Maad hot gsaat ihre Beau sei ~ is zu viel fer sie.** Our maid said her boyfriend's tenacity is too much for her. LRT

aahenke, *pp* **aaghenkt** - **1** to hang on to. **epper eppes ~** - to sell by persuasion. **Er hot mir paar geyuusdi Tires aaghenkt, awwer ich waer besser abgwest, wann ich, "Nee," gsaat hett, "Du kannscht sie bhalde!"** He talked me into buying a pair of used tires, but I would have been better off if I had said, "No, you can keep them." LRT. **Sie hen net uffgewwe bis sie ihm's aaghenkt ghat hen.** They didn't give up until they talked him into buying it. LRT. **2** to hook onto. **Schpann mol die Geil an selli Eehg aa.** Hitch the horses onto that harrow. LRT. **3** to yield. **Des waar en schlecht Yaahr fer die Grummbiere, sie henke yuscht leicht aa.** This was a poor year for potatoes, their yield is light. LRT

aahenkisch, *adj* - tenacious. = **aahengend.** KYG1983. **Ihre Hund is zu ~ fer mich, er will yuscht uff meim Schooss rumrutsche.** Their dog is too tenacious for me, he just wants to crawl around on my lap. LRT

aahewe - to hold on. **Hebt aa, Buwe, mir gehne nunner!** Hold on, boys, we're going down. **Wann du der Hiwwel nunner gehscht uff em Schlidde, muscht gut ~, schunscht rollscht runner.** When you go down the hill on the sled, you must hold on well, or you will roll off. LRT

aahitze - to warm up. = **uffwareme.** KYG2164. = **uffhitze.** LRT

aakumme[1] - to get along with. **Wie kummscht aa mit die Nochbere?** How are you getting along with the neighbors? LRT

2

aakumme² - to depend. **Es kummt druff aa, wie kalt as es is, eb's schneet odder net.** It depends on how cold it is, as to whether it snows or not. LRT

aalaafe, *pp* **is aagloffe - 1** to form mist on surface. **Sell Wasser muss awwer kalt sei; guck mol, wie die Glesser aagloffe sin.** That water must really be cold; look how the tumblers are covered with condensate. **Die Fenschdere sin alles aageloffe.** The windows are all misted shut. LRT. **2** to rise (of flooding river). **De Mariye waar die Grick aagloffe.** This morning the creek was swollen. LRT

aalege - to place grain in a place for thrashing. KYG2006

aalosse - to pretend. **Loss net aa, as du alles weescht.** Don't pretend that you know everything. LRT

aamache - to build a fire. **Kannscht du's Feier ~ mariye frieh?** Can you start the fire [in the stove] tomorrow morning? LRT

aamache, *refl* - to get along (with folks). **Er kann sich net mit Leit ~.** He cannot get along with people. KYG2112. **Er kann sich besser ~ mit d'Hund as wie mit d'Leit.** He can get along better with the dogs than with the people. LRT

aamesse - to take a person's measurements. **Kumm mol doher, ich will dich ~ fer sehne was fer Grees Gleeder as du brauchscht.** Come here once, I want to take your measurements to see what size clothes you

need. LRT

Aametfeld, *n* - two-crop hayfield. KYG2085. = **Uhmetfeld.** LRT/Leb.

aanemme¹ - to take on. **Wer schunscht daed so'n Arewet ~?** Who else would take on such a piece of work (responsibility)? LRT

aanemme² - to accept, put up with. **Sell Geblauder nemm ich net aa.** I'll not put up with (accept) that kind of talking. LRT

aanemme, *refl, pp* **aagenumme** - to take on. **Er hot sich zu viel Arewet aagenumme.** He took on too much work. LRT

aaraffe, *pp* **aageraft** - to tackle something with might and main. **Der Hund hot die Katz wiescht aageraft.** The dog tackled the cat nastily. LRT

aaranke, *refl, pp* **aagerankt** - to take hold (by means of tendrils). KYG1985. **Die Arebse hen sich an die Hecke aagerankt.** The peas have taken hold of the sticks (by means of their tendrils). LRT **Die Drauweschteck hen sich gut ans Grischt aagerankt.** The grape vines have attached themselves to the trellis well. LRT

aarege - to touch. **Ich hab dir gsaat, du sollscht sell net ~.** I told you, you are not supposed to touch that. LRT

aareisse - to tear into. KYG1976

aareiwe - to ignite by rubbing.

Schtreichhelzer dutt mer ~ bis mer die Flamm seht. One rubs matches until they ignite and one sees the flame. LRT

aarem, *adj* - poor. **~i Leit verfehle en latt Sache, as die Reiche net duhne.** Poor people miss a lot of things that the rich (people) do not. LRT

aarichde - to stir up. *cf* **aaschtarre, nuffschtarre, rumriehre, rumschtarre, schtifde, uffhetze, uffpoke, uffrege, uffriehre, uffschtarre, uffschtachle.** KYG1882

aariehre - to mix by stirring. = **aaschtarre, verriehre.** KYG1882. **Do sin die Oier, die Millich, der Zucker, un's Mehl; duh sie gut zammerriehre.** Here are the eggs, the milk, the sugar and the flour, stir them together. LRT

Aarmehaus, *n* - poor house. **Ich hab do katzlich gsehne im e alde Parres Daagbuch, as en Thierwechter Weibsmensch im ~ gschtarewe is.** Recently I saw in an old pastor's diary that a Thierwechter woman died in the poor house. LRT

aarmseelich, *adj* - poor, needy. LRT

Aarsch, *m* - ass. **Du settscht dich in dei ~ neischemme.** You should be thoroughly ashamed of yourself. KYG2001. **Sei ~ Backe sin schwatz un bloh.** His buttocks are black and blue. LRT

Aart, *f* - sort. **Yunger, sell hot die ~, sell is was ich gleich zu sehne.** Young man, that is of real excellency, that is what I like to see. = **Saart, Sart, Satt.** LRT

aasaage - to bring word. **Buwe, ich will eich ~, so Sache dutt mer net.** Boys, I want to bring word to you, such behavior is unacceptable. LRT,4/11/2000

Aaschein, *m* - plausibility. **Was fer'n ~ is mer dann sell?** What does that mean anyway? LRT

aaschiesse, *pp* **aagschosse** - to wound. **Die Schitz hen der Hasch aagschosse, awwer er is ihne weckkumme.** The hunters wounded the deer, but he got away (from them). LRT,4/18/2000

Aaschleeg, *pl* - pranks. **~ fresse** - to gape, to wonders (ironically). **Er will sei ~ fresse, so as mer net wisse soll, was er am duh is.** He wants to gape (and pretend he's tired from overwork) and hide from his pranks and silly actions. LRT,4/11/2000

aaschmeechle, *refl* - to coax by soft words. **Du kannscht dich yuscht browiere ~, awwer's batt dich nix.** You can just keep trying to ingratiate yourself, but it will do you no good. LRT

aaschmeechlich, *adj* - ingratiating. **Sie is en ~ Ding, awwer no eb mer's wees sin sie un ihre Mann widder am fechde.** She is an ingratiating character, but before one knows it, she and her husband are fighting again. LRT

Aaschmeiss, *m* - first throw in game of quoits. **Yunger, sell waar en guder schmiss.** Young man, that was a good throw. *cf*

Schmeiss, Schmiss. KYG2009

aaschnarre, *pp* **aagschnarrt** - to speak roughly to. *cf* **gnoddere, gnuddere, abmaule. Der Weg wie er sie aagschnarrt hot, hot sie gwisst as sei Antwatt "nee" waar.** The way he snapped her off, she knew his answer was "no." **Sie hot ihn aagschnarrt wie en beeser Hund.** She snapped at him like an angry dog. LRT

aaschneide - to trim (a horse's hoof) = **der Huf ~.** KYG2061. **Schneid mol sell Schtick Gwalle-Fleesch aa.** Take (the first) a slice of that piece of dry beef. LRT

aaschpanne - **1** to stretch taut. KYG1973. **2** to hitch a horse to something. LRT

aaschpelle - to pin on. **O, guck mol, ich duh mei Gaund verschlappe; ich muss en Schatz ~.** Oh look, I am messing up my dress; I have to pin on an apron. LRT

aaschpritze - to sprinkle. **Heit duhne mir die Wesch ~ un mariye duhne mir sie biggle.** Today we sprinkle the wash and tomorrow we iron it. LRT

aaschpruchlos, *adj* - unostentatious. KYG2109

Aaschprung, *m* - short run before a jump. **Wann du so hoch tschumbe witt, dann musscht du's erscht en ~ mache.** If you want to jump so high, then you must first take a short run. LRT

aaschtecke, *pp* **aagschteckt** - to light, set on fire. **Er hot die**

Ladann aagschteckt. He lit the lantern. LRT. **Die Buwe hen die Welschkannlaabschack aagschteckt.** The boys set the corn fodder shocks on fire. LRT

aaschteh - to appeal to. **Sell schteht mir aa.** That appeals to me. LRT

aaschtelle, *refl* - to act stupidly. **Er dutt sich dumm ~.** He acts stupidly. LRT

aaschtickere - to add pieces. **Des Haus is nau gross genunk, mir schtickere nix meh aa.** This house is large enough now, we'll add nothing more. LRT

Aaschtifdes, *n* - machination. **Sei ~ waar fer de Nochbere ihre Hund dodmache.** His (evil) scheme was to kill the neighbor's dog. LRT

aaschtimme - to strike up (a hymn). **Blos die Peif so as mir ~ kenne.** Let's have the pitch pipe so we can strike up the song. LRT

Aaschtooss, *m* - scandal. *cf* **Schand.** LRT

aaschtoosse - to touch glasses (in drinking toast). KYG2041

aaschwelle - to begin to swell. **Was is letz, dei Gnechel sin am ~?** What is wrong, your ankles are swelling? LRT

Aasehnes, *n* - respect. **Sei ~ mehnt en Latt zu mir.** The respect that is shown to him means a lot to me. LRT

aasetze - **1** to take aim. **2** to sew onto. **Mamm, mei Gaund is zu katz, kannscht du mir noch**

drei **Zoll vun dem blohe Duch ~?** Mother, my dress is too short, can you sew three inches of this blue fabric on for me? LRT

aaverdraue - to put in trust in something. KYG2070

aawatzle - to take root. **Mer muss geduldich sei; ebmols nemmt's ordlich lang fer die Blanze ~.** One must be patient; sometimes it takes pretty long for these plants to take root. LRT

aawickle - to begin to wind on a reel. **Kannscht du den Bendel uff der Haschbel ~?** Can you start this string on the reel? LRT

aazaahme - to tame an animal. **Es hot sie net lang genumme fer seller Hutsch ~.** It didn't take them long to tame that colt. LRT

Aazeeche, *n* - token. = **Zeeche.** KYG2031

aazettle - to put warp on loom for weaving. KYG2165

aaziehe[1], *pp* **aagezoge** - to pull on clothes. **Duh dei Gleeder ~.** Put on your clothes. LRT

aaziehe[2], *pp* **aagezoge** - to become moist through the absorption of moisture. **Wann's so feicht is draus, duhne em sei Gleeder Wasser ~.** When it's so damp outside, our clothes absorb moisture. LRT

aaziehe[3] - to tighten. = **eischnalle, fescht mache.** KYG2016

abbatzle - to tumble off.

KYG2073. **Sell Kind is vum Wagge abgebatzelt.** That child tumbled off the wagon. LRT

abbinne - to remove a wart (by tie a string around the base of a wart). KYG2166. **Der bescht Weg fer en Waarz los warre is fer sie ~.** The best way to get rid of a wart is to tie it off. LRT

abbliehe - to stop blooming. *cf* **verbliehe.** KYG1889

abbloge, *refl, pp* **abgeblogt** - to exhaust oneself by overworking. **Er hot sich abgeblogt bis er nimmi schaffe hot kenne.** He exhausted himself until he could no longer work. **Er hot sich abgeblogt, bis er schier umgfalle is.** He worked and worked until his almost fell over. LRT,4/11/2000

abblose, *refl, pl* **abgeblose** - to vent ones opinions or feelings. **Die Balledixleit hen ihn verzannt, no hot er (sich) abgeblose wie en Schtieminschein.** The politicians angered him, then he blew off like a steam engine. LRT,4/11/2000

abbreche, *pp* **abgebroche** - to break off, snap in two. KYG2085. **Die Geil hen der Poschde abgebroche.** The horses broke off the post. LRT

abbumpe - to remove by pumping (so as to get cold water). **Du muscht Weil ~ , bis es Wasser kalt watt.** You will need to pump off some water until it gets cold. **Duh's leppisch Wasser ~ bis du frisch Wasser grickscht.** Pump off the stale water until you get fresh water. LRT

abbutze, *pp* **abgebutzt** - to wipe off. **Die Fraa hot der Disch abgebutzt.** The wife wiped off the table. LRT

Abbutzlumbe, *m* - towel for drying dishes. KYG2043. **Sis Zeit fer seller ~ in die Wesch schmeisse.** It's time to throw that dish towel in the laundry. LRT

abdecke, *pp* **abgedeckt - 1** to unroof. KYG2111. **Sell alt Haus hen sie abgedreckt, nau gebt's en nei Dach.** They took the roof off that old house, now there will be a new roof. LRT. **2** to uncover. = **uffdecke.** KYG2094. **Sie hen em Henner sei Graab abgedeckt. Sie welle ihn ammenents schunscht vergraawe.** They uncovered Henner's grave. They want to bury him somewhere else. LRT

abdetschle - to touch base (in hide and seek). KYG2041

abdowe, *pp* **abgedopt,** *refl* - to run to exhaustion. **Er hot sich abgedopt bis er umgfalle is.** He ran and raged until he dropped. LRT

Abdraag, *m* - **1** tax. = **Tax.** KYG1973. **2** something carried off. LRT

abdrehe, *pp* **abgedreht - 1** to turn off.= **zudrehe.** KYG2077. **Hoscht du der Kicheoffe abgedreht?** Did you turn off the kitchen range? LRT. **Des Wasser misse mir ~.** We must turn off this water. LRT. **2** to turn on a lathe. KYG2078. **3** to twist off. KYG2084

abdrenne, *pp* **abgedrennt** - to unrip, unseam. KYG2111. **Die Weibsleit hen all selli Blumme**

vun sellem Deppich abgedrennt. The women ripped all the flowers off that quilt. LRT. **Wann du seller Sack vun deim Gaund abdrennscht, guckt er viel besser.** If you rip that pocket off your dress, it will look much better. LRT. = **abrippe**

abdresche, *pp* **abgedrosche - 1** to thrash with a flail or a machine. KYG2006. **Well, die Aern is abgedrosche fer des Yaahr.** Well, the harvest (grains) are all thrashed for this year. LRT. **2** to thrash soundly. = **darichleddere.** KYG2003. **Was gebt's mit sellem Buh, der Weg wie er schund abgedrosche is warre?** What will become of that boy, the way he has been beaten already. LRT

abdricke - to pull the trigger. = **losdricke.** KYG2061. **Datt is en Haas, (du) muscht ~!** There's a rabbit, pull the trigger! LRT

Abdrickellumbe, *m* - towel. *cf* **Handduch.** KYG2043

abdrilliere - to trill. **es Lied ~ -** to trill off a song. KYG2061

abdrumpe - to trump. KYG2068

abduh - 1 to take off. **2** to postpone. **Des duhne mir ab bis mariye.** We will postpone this until tomorrow. LRT

abfaahre, *pp* **abgfaahre -** to drive away. **~ losse -** to slam. **Er hot sellem Mann eens uff der Kopp abgfaahre glosst.** He gave that man a blow to his head. LRT

abfaddiche - to finish off. **Du**

muscht der Bull ~. Schlack ihn noch eemol uff der Kopp. You must finish off the bull. Hit him on the head one more time. LRT

Abfall, *m* - trimming around hard soap. = **Brockeldings.** KYG2062. **Der Schinnerhannes dutt der ~ vum Butschere weck faahre.** The rendering man hauls away trimmings from the butchering. LRT

Abfallbax, *f* - refuse box. **Die ~ is voll, leer sie aus.** The refuse box is full, empty it. LRT

Abfalleise, *n* - scrap iron. = **Brucheise, alt Eise. Wann mer en neie Kaer seht, is es net en Wunner as sie mol en Haufe ~ waar?** When one sees a new car, isn't it a wonder that it was once a pile of scrap iron? LRT

abfaule - to rot off. **Wann mol alles verfault is, no is nix meh as ~ kann.** Once everything has rotted, then nothing more can rot off. LRT

abfeddre, *refl* - to molt (of fowl). **Es gebt net viel Oier die Woch; die Hinkel sin sich hatt am ~.** There will be few eggs this week; the hens are in a heavy molt. LRT

abfege, *pp* **abgfegt -** to scrub or scour off. **Sie hot selli wieschde Messere un Gawwle schee abgfegt.** She scoured those ugly knives and forks nicely. LRT,4/11/2000. **Sell Messer hot Roschtblacke, kannscht du sie ~?** That knife has rust spots, can you scour them off? LRT

abfixe - to give tit for tat. *cf*

vergelde. KYG2026

Abfluche, *n* - a string of profanity. **Mer hot gemehnt er daed net faddich warre mit seim ~.** One would think he'd not get finished with his string of profanity. LRT

abfroge, *pp* **abgfrogt - 1** to question someone about something. KYG1540. **2** to ask permission not to do something that was expected of one. **Ich hab yuscht abgfrogt.** I just asked to be let off or excluded. LRT

abgarewe - to thrash. = **dresche, drexle, lause, verschimpfe.** KYG2003

abgawwle, *pp* **abgegawwelt -** to unload (grain) with a fork. KYG2107. **Die Buwe hen's Hoi vum Wagge vun Hand abgegawwelt.** The boys forked the hay off the wagon by hand. LRT

abgekocht, *adj* - mulled (of cider). **Geschder hen die Nochbere ihre Lattwarick ~.** Yesterday the neighbors mulled their apple butter. LRT

abgewwe, *refl* - to associate with. **Er hot sich net ~ mit ihne.** He didn't associate with them. KYG2116

abgezehrt, *adj* - thin. **~i Luft -** thin air. = **darr, dinn, schneckerich.** KYG1997. **Guck yuscht mol wie sie ~ is, sie hot 30 Pund verlore.** Just look at how she has thinned down, she has lost 30 pounds. LRT

abgnewwle, *pp* **abgegnewwelt -** to tie bundles of rye-straw with a

Gnewwel, *qv*. KYG2015. **Ya, mir hen die Garwe all abgegnewwelt.** Yes, we have tied up all the sheaves. LRT

abgnippe - to tie a knot in yarn. **Kannscht du sell Gaarn ~?** Can you tie a knot in that yarn? LRT,4/18/2000

abgnippe - to unbutton. = **uffgnippe, uffgneppe.** KYG2092. **Yarick, du dei Rock uffgneppe.** George, unbutton your coat. LRT

abgraawe - to remove by digging. **Sie hen seller Barig gedichdich ~ fer Route 322 breeder mache.** They drastically dug away at that mountain to make Route 322 wider. LRT

abgratze - to scrape off. **Wann du sell Eis vum "Windschield" abgratzscht, dann kannscht du besser sehne.** If you scrape the ice off the windshield, then you can see better. LRT. = **abschwaawe.**

abgreische, *pp* **abgegrische** - to scream at. **sich der Hals ~** - to scream oneself hoarse. **Er hot sich der Hals schier abgegrische, awwer sei Kind is ewwe doch verbrennt.** He almost screamed himself hoarse, but his child burned to death anyway. LRT

abgritzle - to scribble a copy. **Dapper duh des, was es saagt uff dem Brief, ~.** Quickly scribble a copy of what it says on this letter. LRT

abgscharre - to unharness (a horse). **Datt schtehne die Geil un sie sin noch net abgscharrt,** oh yeh, nochemol! There stand the horses and they haven't had their harnesses removed, oh my! LRT. = **abscharre.** KYG2104.

abgscheppt, *adj* - skimmed. **Ich gleich ~i Millich; sie is gut fer eem.** I like skimmed milk; it is healthful. LRT

abgschmackt, *adj* - tasteless. = **leppisch.** *cf* **abschteh** - to become tasteless. KYG1972

abgschtanne, *adj* - unthrifty. **Selli Tomaetsblanze gucke ~.** Those tomato plants look sick (unthrifty). LRT. = **abschtennich**

abgschtumpt, *adj* - worn off. **Sell Messer is awwer ~.** That knife is really worn off (or dulled). LRT,4/18/2000

abgucke - to observe. **Wann du des lanne witt, dann guck's ab.** If you want to learn this, then observe well every detail. LRT

abhalde, *pp* **abghalde** - to hold off, prevent. **Des Kinnerhawwe hen mei Eldre zehe Yaahr abghalde, no endlich hen sie mol mich ghat un no sex Yaahr schpaeder hen sie mei Bruder ghat.** This matter of having children was prevented by my parents for 10 years and then finally they had me and 6 years later they had my brother. LRT

abhaschble - to unreel (yarn, fishing line, etc.). KYG2110

abheele, *pp* **abgheelt** - to heal up. **Dei Gritzer sin schier abgheelt.** Your scratches are almost healed up. LRT

abheere, *refl, pp* **abgheert** - to shed a coat of hair. **Die Katz hot sich abgheert.** The cat shed a coat of hair. LRT. = **abhaare.**

abhengisch, *adj* - sloping. **Eier Gaarde is awwer ~.** Your garden is really sloped. LRT

abhenke[1] - to be out of plumb. **Mer kann gut sehne as seller Poschde abhenkt.** One can easily see that that post is leaning, *i.e.* is out of plumb. LRT

abhenke[2] - to unhinge. **sell Dierli ~** - to unhinge that little door. KYG2104. **Sis Butscherzeit, mir misse sell Dierli ~, sis zu unhendich wann mir net duhne.** It's butcher time, we must unhinge that door, it's too inconvenient if we don't. LRT

abhewe - to take off. **Seller Fettkessel misse mir ~ vum Feier.** We must lift that lard kettle from the fire. LRT

abhowwele, *pp* **abgehowwelt** - to plane off. **Sell rauh Holz hot er alles schee glatt abghowwelt.** He planed off nice and smoothly that rough wood. LRT

abkehre, *pp* **abgekehrt** - to sweep off. **Der Danksaagungsmunet is eppes; ee Daag hab ich der Hof gemaeht und der naegscht Daag hab ich Schnee vun die Bortsch abgekehrt.** This November weather is something; one day I mowed the lawn and the next day I swept snow from the porch. LRT

abkeime - to remove sprouts

from a potato. **Du kannscht selli Grummbiere ~, awwer so gleeni zammer-gerunzeldi Dinger gebt mer die Sei.** You can remove the sprouts from those potatoes, but such little wrinkled things one only gives to the pigs. LRT

abkeppisch, *adj* - thoughtless. = **gedankelos, leichtsinnich, noochlessich, unbedenkt, unvorsichdich, unbedacht.** KYG2002. **Er is immer so ~.** He is always so inconsiderate. LRT

ablaade, *pp* **abgelaade** - to unload. *cf* **auslaade.** KYG2107. **Buwe, hett dir der Wagge abgelaade?** Boys, did you unload the wagon? LRT. **Well, der Wagge is abgelaade, sis Zeit fer esse!** Well, the wagon is unloaded, it's time to eat. LRT

Ablaaf, *m* - overflow. **Der ~ Kandel an sellem Dach is darich geroscht.** The rain spout at that roof has rusted through. LRT

ablaafe, *pp* **is abgloffe** - **1** to turn aside. = **auswenne. 2** to turn out. **gut ~** - to turn out all right. KYG2077. **Es Wasser is recht gut vum Feld abgeloffe.** The water drained off of the field real well. LRT. **Es Wasser is vum Feld abgeloffe.** The water ran off of the field. LRT. *cf* **fattlaafe. 3** to run off. *cf* **abrinne, darichgeh, verlaafe. Drick der Lumbe bis es Wasser ablaaft.** Squeeze the rag until the water comes out. LRT. **4** to walk away. **~ mit** - to walk off with. KYG2158.

ablause, *pp* **abgelaust** - to gain by sharp practice. **Der Tschann**

hot sei Bauerei nimmi; sei Buwe hen ihm sie abgelaust. John doesn't have his farm anymore; his sons took it from him through illegal practices. **Sie hen ihm sei Flint abgelaust, nau kann er nimmi yaage geh.** They craftily took his gun from him, now he can't go hunting anymore. LRT

ableedre - to take off ladders from a wagon. KYG1962. **Wann der Hoiwaage abgleedert is, is er ken Hoiwaage meh.** If the hay wagon has its ladders removed, it is no longer a hay wagon. LRT

ablege, *pp* **abgelegt** - to lay off (from work). **Sie hen ihn abgelegt vun seine Arewet.** He has been laid off from his work. LRT

ablese - to read off. **Les mer selli Nummere ab!** Read those numbers to me! **Ich les dir die Sache ab was du duh muscht.** I'll read off (to you) the things you will need to do. LRT

abmadde - to tire oneself out. KYG2025

abmaehe - to mow off. **Do in dem heese Summer waxt des Graas net viel, yuscht der Schpitzewettrich un den misse mer allegebott ~.** Here in this hot summer the grass doesn't grow very much, only the narrow-leafed plaintain and this we need to mow off every now and then. LRT

abmesse - to measure off. **Kannscht du uns zwee Acker Land ~?** Can you measure off two acres of land for us? LRT

abmoschdre - to tap off

vinegar. KYG1969

abnemme - 1 to take off. **Ich hab paar Daag ~ misse, weil ich grank waar.** I had to take off several days (from) work because I was sick. LRT. **sei Sach ~** - to take one's wraps off. KYG1960. **2** to make a photograph. **Wann du selli Blumme gleichscht, dann nemm sie ab.** If you like those flowers, then take a picture of them. LRT. KYG1961. **3. an sich selwer ~** - to take on basis one's personal experience. KYG1962

Abnemmer, *m* - photographer. **Mir hen der ~ an die Schul ghat heit.** We had the photographer at school today. *cf* **Abnemmern.** LRT

Abnemmerei, *f* - photograph business. **Selli Abnemmer an die Schmutzer ~ verschtehne ihre Bissniss.** Those photographers at the Schmutzer Photography understand their business. LRT

Abnemmeslicht, *n* - waning moon. **Der Muun is im ~.** The moon is in its waning stage. LRT

Abnemmetlicht, *n* - the waning moon. KYG2162

abpaare, *pp* **abgepaart** - to pair off. **Sie hen die Geil abgepaart.** They paired off the horses. LRT

abpetze - 1 to pinch off. **Ich brauch paar Schticker Droht; kannscht du sie mir ~?** I need several pieces of wire; can you pinch them off for me? **2 eppes ~** - to take a nip. KYG1961

abraahme, *pp* **abgeraahmt -** 1 to redd off. **Die Mamm hot endlich die Schenk abgeraahmt (ausgeraahmt) heit.** Mother finally redd off the cupboards today. = **ausraahme.** LRT. 2 to take cream off milk. KYG1960. **Millich ~ kann mer duh vun Hand odder mit re Maschien.** Milk can be separated (cream from milk) by hand or with a machine. LRT

abranke - to clean superfluous shoots from vines. **Mer hen die Grummbiere abgerankt, un die naegscht Woch duhne mir sie ausmache.** We have de-vined the potatoes, and next week we will dig them out. LRT

abrechle, *pp* **abgrechelt -** to square accounts. **Vun deine Rechning hen mir abgrechelt was du uns geschder gewwe hoscht.** From your account, we accounted for what you gave us yesterday. LRT

abreisse - 1 to tear apart. = **vunnanner verreisse, verroppe. 2** to tear down. = **nidderreisse, nunnerreisse, runnerreisse, rumreisse, umreisse, zammereisse. 3** to tear off. KYG1976. **Sie hen's Dach vun sellem Haus abgerisse.** They tore the roof from that house. LRT

abrenne - to knock off in running. **Schpring net so naegscht an die Blumme, du rennscht sie ab.** Don't run so close to the flowers, you'll knock them off. LRT

abrichde - to teach an animal tricks. KYG1975

Abrill´, *m* - April. **Ich hab ihn**

in der **~ gschickt.** I made an April fool of him. LRT

abriwwle - to form roll of dirt on body. **Wann do so gschwitzt bischt, kann mer der Dreck yuscht vun deim Buckel ~.** When you are so perspired, one can just roll the dirt off of your back. LRT

abrolle - to roll from. **Kannscht du mir en Schtick Waxbabier vun selle Roll ~?** Can you roll a piece of wax paper from that roll for me? LRT

abrunde - to round off. **Wann du den eckiche Disch net gleichscht, dann kenne mir dir en ~.** If you don't like this table square, then we can round it off for you. LRT

abrutsche, *pp* **abgerutscht -** to wear the napp off. **Guck yuscht mol, du hoscht dei Hosse awwer abgerutscht.** Just look, you have really worn the napp off of your pants. LRT

absaage, *pp* **abgsaat -** to refuse. **Sell hab ich ihm abgsaat.** I told him "No!" LRT. **Sie hen mei Kaer kaafe welle, awwer ich hab's ihne abgsaat.** They wanted to buy my car, but I said, "No," to them. LRT

absaddle - to unsaddle. KYG2111. **Der Gaul is mied, sis Zeit fer'n ~.** The horse is tired, it's time to unsaddle him. LRT

Absatz, *m, pl* **Absetz -** step from one floor to another. **Geb acht, datt im dunkle Gang, datt is en diefer ~.** Be careful, there in the dark hall, there is a step down. LRT

abschaame - to take scum from liquid.

abschaele, *pp* **abgschaelt -** to peel, shave, off. **Mir hen die Rinn abgschaelt.** We shaved off the bark. LRT

abschaffe - to work off. KYG2246. **Er hot sell gross Esse ~ misse.** He had to work off that big meal. LRT,4/11/2000

abscharefe, *pp* **abgschareft -** to taper. *cf* **abschlaamse.** KYG1969. **Der Blaeckschmitt hot mir mei Grubbax abgschareft.** The blacksmith tapered my pick axe. LRT

abscharre[1] **-** to scratch off. = **abgratze.** KYG1687

abscharre[2]**,** *pp* **abgscharrt -** to take harness from horse. **Yunger, hoscht du die Geil abgscharrt?** Young man, did you take the harnesses off of the horses? = **abgscharre.** KYG1961

abscheppe - to skim milk. LRT

abschere - to trim off with scissors. **Kannscht du die Fransele bissel ~?** Can you trim off the fringes a bit? LRT

abschicke, *pp* **abgschickt -** to send off. **Vanne in de 1940 Yaahre hen en latt Eldere ihre Buwe abgschickt in der Grieg.** In the early 1940's, a lot of parents sent their sons off to war. LRT

abschiesse - 1 to shoot off (one's mouth). **Seller yung Mann waar datt drunne bei de Buwe, am sei Maul ~.** That young man was down there with the boys shooting off his mouth. LRT. **2** to tell someone off. KYG1981

abschiewe, *pp* **abgschowe** - **1** to postpone, put off action on a certain issue. **Des Graas maehe un Hoi mache hen mir abgschowe bis die naegscht Woch.** We've postponed this grass mowing and hay making until next week. **2** to push a sheaf from the dropper (on reaper). KYG1531 LRT. = **nausschiewe.**

abschinne, *pp* **abgschunne** - to scuff. **Er hot sei Schuh abgschunne.** He scuffed his shoes. LRT

abschittle - to shake off (a rug). **Kannscht du selli Eppel vun sellem Nascht ~?** Can you shake those apples from that branch? LRT

abschlaamse - to slope or taper. **Seller Hiwwel dutt ordlich hatt ~.** That hill has a pretty good slope. LRT

abschlaecke - to slacken up. **Wann die Kaere do darich des Wasser faahre, duhne sie ~.** When the cars drive through this water, they slow up. LRT

abschlagge - to strike off. **Summerflecke ~ -** to wash one's face in dew on May first (to remove freckles). KYG2167

abschmeisse, *pp* **abgschmisse** - to throw off. KYG2009. **Macht schur as dir der Mischt all vum Wagge abgschmisse hett.** Be sure you've thrown all the manure off of the wagon. LRT

abschnalle - to unbuckle. KYG2092 = **los-schnalle, uffmache, uffschnalle.** KYG2092

abschnappe - **1** to give a curt reply. **Wann du mich so ~ witt, dann kannscht du yuscht heemgeh.** If you want to snap at me like that, then you can just go home. LRT. **2** to lose the trend of thought. KYG2002. **Sis mir wennich zu schnell abgschappt.** I spoke before I should have. LRT

abschneide, *pp* **abgschnidde** - **1** to cut one short in an argument. **Er hot eppes saage welle, awwer sie hen ihn abgschnidde.** He wanted to say something, but they cut him off. **2** to overtake by a short-cut. LRT. **3** to trim off. **es Fett ~ -** to trim fat off meat. KYG2061. **Sie hen seine Fraa die zwee Fiess abgschnidde.** They amputated his wife's two feet. LRT

abschnelle - to let fly. **Er gleicht sei "Sling-Shot" ~.** He likes to let things fly with his sling shot. LRT

abschpalde - to split off. **Seller Block is zu gross, mir misse bissel ~.** That log is too big, we need to split some off. LRT

abschpiele, *pp* **abgschpielt** - **1** to shirk (duties). **Der Weg wie du ~ duscht, verdienscht ken Geld.** The way you goof off, you will earn no money. = **sich raus-scheele.** LRT. **2** to play truant. **Er hot abgschpielt.** He played hooky. KYG2067. **Er waar net in d'Schul, net weil er grank waar, awwer weil er abgschpielt hot.** He wasn't in school, not because he was sick,

but because he played hooky. LRT

Abschpiele, *n* - truancy. KYG2066

abschpinne - to spin off. **eens ~** - to tell a yarn. KYG1981

abschpringe - to run away (of horses). **Wann die Geil ~, un sie sin in en Wagge gschpannt, sell kennt en wieschder Unfall mache.** If the horses run away, and they are hitched to the wagon, that could cause a bad accident. LRT

abschrauwe - to unscrew. = **losschrauwe.** KYG2111

abschrecke - to scare off. **sich net leicht ~ -** to not scare easily. **Es kann niemand ihn ~!** No one can scare him off! LRT

abschridde - to step off, *i.e.* to measure by stepping. **Wann du wisse witt was die Leng is vun sellem Gebei, dann muscht's ~.** If you want to know the length of that building, you'll have to step it off. LRT

abschtaawe - to remove dust from. **Du kannscht mei Fedderwisch yuuse fer dei Sache ~.** You can use my feather duster to dust off your things. LRT

abschteh, *pp* **abgschtanne** - to become rancid. **Selli Millich schmackt bissel abgschtanne.** That milk tastes a bit tainted. LRT. **Die Ess-Sache schmacke abgschtanne.** These foods have lost their taste. LRT. KYG1972.

abschtelle - to turn off (a switch or electric appliance). =

abdrehe. KYG2077

abschtempe - to stomp off. **Schnee ~ -** to stomp off snow. KYG1886. **Eb'd in's Haus kummscht, duh der Schnee vun deine Schtiffel ~.** Before you come into the house, stomp the snow from your boots. LRT

abschtennich, *adj* - non-thriving plants. **Selli Blanze gucke mir bissel ~.** Those plants look a little sick to me. LRT. KYG2007. = **abgschtanne.** LRT

abschtickle, *pp* **abgschtickelt** - to stake off. **Geschder hen sie die Lott abgschtickelt wu sie ihre Haus baue welle.** Yesterday they staked off the lot where they want to build their house. LRT

abschtoppe (an) - to stop in. *cf* **reikumme.** KYG1889. [A modernized context of both these words: **Wann'd im Schteddel bischt, dann schtopp rei.** If you are in town, stop in (to see us). LRT]

abschtricke - to rope off. **Sell Loch misse mir ~.** We must rope off that hole. LRT

abschwaarde, *pp* **abgschwaart** - 1 to cut slabs from logs. **Sie hen die Bleck all abgschwaart.** They cut the slabs from all of the logs. 2 to take a rind from pork. **Deel Leit gleiche wann ihre Schunke abgschwaart sin.** Some people prefer hams with the rind removed. LRT

abschweere, *pp* **abgschwore** - to renounce. **Ich hab abgschwore, ich daed sei Lewe nix wie sell duh.** I swore I

would never do anything like that. LRT. **Er hot abgschwore, er daed sei Lewe nimmi drinke.** He swore that never in his life would he drink again. LRT

abschwenke, *pp* **abgschwenkt** - to rinse. **Mach schur as du die Seef vun deine Haar abgschwenkt hoscht.** Be sure that you have rinsed the soap from your hair. LRT

absenke - to singe off. **Die feine Feddere kann mer ~.** The fine feathers can be singed off. LRT

absettle, *pp* **abgesettelt** - to make a settlement. **Sie hen Vendu ghat, es Haus is verkaaft un nau is alles abgsettelt.** They had a sale, the house is sold, and now settlement has been made of everything. LRT

absetze, *pp* **abgsetzt** - to set off. **Deinemeit ~ -** to set off dynamite. **Sie hen der ganz Hiwwel weckgeblose wie sie der Deinemeit abgsetzt hen.** They blew the whole hill away when they set off the dynamite. LRT

absinge - to sing off. **eens ~ -** to sing a tune. KYG2074

abtrimme - to trim off. = **abdrimme.** KYG2062. **Sie hen die Paschingbaem abgetrimmt.** They pruned the peach trees. LRT

abverdiene, *pp* **abverdient** - to work off an obligation. **Er hot sei Koscht meh wie abverdient.** He worked more than he was required to pay for his room and board.

LRT,4/11/2000

abverkaafe, *pp* **abverkaaft** - to sell off. **Die Bauerei is yuscht meh halwer so gross as sie waar, sie hen die Helft vum Land abverkaaft.** The farm is only half the size that it was, they sold off half the land. LRT

abwaarde[1] - to wait at a table. **Sie gleicht die Disch ~ an sellem Essblatz.** She likes to wait on tables at that restaurant. LRT

abwaarde[2] - to serve. **Wann mer die Kinner zu viel ~ dutt, dann kann mer sie vergwehne.** If one waits on the children too much, one can spoil them. LRT

abwaere, *pp* **is abgewore** - to wear off. **Die Fareb uff d' Bortsch is abgewore.** The paint on the porch floor is worn off. LRT,4/18/2000

abwanne, *pp* **abgewannt** - to warn to keep away. KYG2165. **Er waar abgewannt, awwer er hot sich doch in die Gfaahr grickt.** He was warned to keep away but he endangered himself anyway. LRT

Abwax, *m* - undergrowth. = **Unnerhecke.** KYG2096

abweede - to crop a pasture close. **Wann's schier alle Daag reggert, is es hatt fer die Felder ~.** When it rains almost every day, it is hard to graze the fields down close. LRT

abweise[1] - to show off. **Die Abweiser duhne ~.** The poseurs are show offs. LRT

abweise[2] - 1 to turn away. **epper**

~ - to turn someone away. = **epper abschicke.** KYG2077. **2** to show off. **Er will sei zaahmi Haase ~.** He wants to show off his domesticated rabbits. LRT

abwelke - to wither and fall off. **Die Blumme sin all abgwelkt.** The flowers have all wilted and fallen off. LRT

abwennisch, *adj* - uninterested. KYG2105. **Die ganz Zeit as mir gschwetzt hen, waar er ~.** The whole time that we talked, he was uninterested. LRT. = **abwennich**

abwickle - **1** to uncoil, unfurl. KYG2093. **der Schtrick ~** - to uncoil the rope. KYG2095. **2** to unfold. KYG2102. **Eb mir Hoi nuff in der Borer ziehe kenne, muss der Schtrick losgewickelt sei.** Before we can pull hay up into the mow, the rope will need to be unraveled. LRT. *cf* **uffwickle** - to wind up.

abwische, *pp* **abgewischt** - to wipe off. **Sie hot die Grimmle vum Schelf abgewischt.** She wiped (brushed) the crumbs off the shelf. LRT

Abwischer, *m, pl* ~ - wiper. **Sei** "windshield" **hot drei ~.** His windshield has three wipers. LRT

abyoche - to unyoke. **Die Buwe duhne immer die Oxe ~.** The boys always unyoke the oxen. LRT. *cf* **aus-schpanne.** KYG2116.

abzaahme - to unbridle. KYG2092. **Tschecki, kannscht du die Geil ~ un ihre Halfdere aaduh?** Jaky, can you unbridle the horses and put their halters on? LRT

abzaahne - to lose (one's) teeth. = **em sei Zaeh verliere.** KYG1979. **Er is an die Elt wu er sei Millichzaeh ~ meecht.** He is at the age where he may be shedding his baby teeth. LRT

abzackere, *refl, pp* **abgezackert** - to wear oneself out. **Er hot sich schteewens abgezackert.** He slaved away terribly. LRT. **Sie hen sich awwer abgezackert, bis sie selli Kuh gemolke ghat hen!** They were really frazzled until they had finally milked that cow! **Er hot sich abgezackert bis er ken Odem meh ghat hot.** He plugged along until he was out of breath. LRT

abzanke, *pp* **abgezankt** - to upbraid. *cf* **vorhalde, zanke.** KYG2117. **Der Yarick hot sei gleener Bruder wieschderlich abgezankt.** George upbraided his little brother very badly. LRT

abzappe - to tap off. KYG1969. **Do, ich duh dir en Glaas Wasser ~.** Here, I'll tap a glass of water for you. LRT

abzehre - to become thin. KYG1997

abzettle, *pp* **abgezeddelt** - to fill up with. KYG2117. **Sie hen heit abgezeddelt fer die Schmitte Bauerei.** Today they settled (the purchase) for the Smith farm. LRT

abziehe - to skin. **Mir kenne der Bull net ~ bis er dod is.** We can't skin the bull until he's dead. LRT

achtgewwe - **1** to pay attention.

Sie hen gsaat, es fehle paar Graabschtee, awwer ich hab ken ~ ghat. They said there are a few tombstones missing, but I had not noticed it. LRT. **2** to take care. **Geb Acht uff dich!** Take care of yourself! KYG1960

achtnemme, *pp* **achtgnumme** - **1** to take notice. **Hoscht du achtgnumme wie viel Veggel as do verbeigfloge sin?** Did you notice how many birds flew by here? LRT **2** to take care.

achtsam, *adj* - **1** thoughtful. *cf* **bedenklich, diefsinnich, gedankevoll.** KYG2002. **Yunger, du muscht ~ sei.** Young man, you must be heedful and attentive. LRT. **2** wary. = **vorsichdich.** KYG2166. **Yunger, wann du seller hoch Baam graddelscht, dann witt du awwer ~ sei.** Young man, if you climb up that high tree, you will want to be careful (wary). LRT

Achtzehhunnertzwelfgrieg, *m* - War of 1812. KYG2163. **Der ~ waar vor meinere Zeit.** The War of 1812 was ahead of my time. LRT

Addning, *f* - order, discipline. **Der Schulmeeschder hot ken ~ in der Schul halde kenne.** The schoolmaster could not keep order in his school. LRT

Aeddemsschteddel, *n* - ✪ Adamstown, northern Lanc. Co, PA. KYG2267

Aerbiereboi, *m, f* - strawberry pie. = **Arebelepei.** LRT/Leb

Aerbierekosdert, *m* - strawberry custard. =

Arebelekosdert. LRT/Leb

Aerbieretschelli, *m, f* - strawberry jelly. = **Arebeletschelli.** LRT/Leb

aerdlich, *adj* - worldly. KYG1988. **Sell is zu ~ fer deel Leit.** That is too wordly for some people. LRT

Aerdscholle, *m* - lump of earth. **Die ~ sin schier so hatt wie Felse.** The lumps of earth are nearly as hard as rocks. LRT

Aerebgrind, *m* - tetter. *cf* **Grind, Koppgrind, Millichgretz, Millichgrind, Millichgruscht, Zedder.** KYG1990

Aereblosser, *m* - testator. *cf* **Aereblosserin.** KYG1989

Aern, *f* - harvest. **Des Yaahr hen mir en gudi ~ ghat.** This year we had a good harvest. LRT, 4/21/2000

aernschthaftlich, *adj* - sincere. **Mir gleiche Leit as ~ sin.** We like people that are sincere. = **aernschtlich, uffrichdich.** LRT

aernschtlich, *adj* - unfeigned. KYG2102. **Sie is immer en ~i Fraa.** She is always a sincere woman. LRT

Affegsicht, *n* - ugly monkey face. = **Frees, Gfress, Riewegsicht.** KYG2088

Affregaa - ✪ Africa. KYG2267

affrigaa´nisch, *adj* - African. KYG2267

all zamme, *adv* - all at one time. KYG2018. **Mit die Gedanke ~,**

Gott is der Harr. With all thoughts combined, God is Lord. LRT

allegebott, *adv* - every now and then. = **allgebott, alligebott.** KYG1993. **~ sett mer frischi Luft eihauche.** Every now and then one should breath in fresh air. LRT

allemnooch, *adv* - it would seem. = **scheins. ~ hen sie die Schul frieh ausgelosst heit, do kummt yo schund die Bus.** It would seem that school has been dismissed early today, here comes the bus already. LRT. **~ is des die letscht Zeit as mir heere vun dir.** It would seem that this is the last time we will hear from you. LRT,4/18/2000. = **allemno**

aller-aermscht, *superl adj* - poorest of all. **Die ~e Leit sin ewwe, die wu gaar nix hen.** The poorest of all people are those who have absolutely nothing. LRT

allerarigscht, *superl adj* - worst of all. **Sell waar die ~ Breddich, as mir noch gheert hen.** That was the worst of all sermons that we ever heard. LRT,4/18/2000

allererscht, *superl adj* - very first. **Des waar's ~ Mol, as er in re Karich waar.** This was the very first time he was in a church. LRT

allerhand, *adv* - all sorts of, generally. **~ waare sie all zufridde.** Generally they were all satisfied. LRT

allerwiescht, *superl adj* - ugliest of all. KYG2088

alleweil, *adv* - right now. **~ sin die Weezepreise hoch.** Right now the wheat prices are high. LRT

allgebreichlich, *adj* - universal. = **allgemei(n).** *cf* **iwwer die ganz Welt** - all over the world. KYG2106

allgemee, *adv* - universally. = **allgemei(n).** KYG2106

allimunet, *adv* - monthly. **Deel vun de Pennsilfaanische Deitsche hen ~ Versammlinge.** Some of the PA Germans (groups) have monthly meetings. = **munetweis.** LRT

allmenanner, *adv* - all together. *cf* **gemeeschefdich, vereenicht.** KYG2106. **Uff ee Mol ziehe mir ~.** At one time we all pull together. LRT. **Die Familye, ~ waare datt an die Versammling gewest.** The family, all together, were at the gathering. LRT

allzamme, *adv* - in unison. KYG2105. **Mir hen ~ gsunge.** We all sang in unison. LRT

als dann, *adv* - then. *cf* **dann, dennoch, do, derno, dezu mol, no, dennoch, nort, not, numme, selle mol(s).** KYG1993

altbekannt, *adj* - known for many years. **Sell is awwer en ~ Singschtick.** But that is an old familiar song. LRT,4/18/2000

Altlicht, *n* - the last phase of the moon. **Die alde Deitsche hen der letscht Vaddel vum Muun es ~ gheese.** The old Germans called the last quarter of the moon "the old light," es ~. LRT

Altweiwersglaawe, *m* - superstition. **Deel vun denne ~ kann ich yuscht net glaawe.** Some of these superstitions I just cannot believe. LRT

Amerikaa - ☺ The United States of America. KYG2268,LRT

Amerikaa´ner, *m* - an American. KYG2268,LRT

amerikaa´nisch, *adj* - American. KYG2268,LRT

ammenents, *adv* - somewhere. **Es is ~ eppes letz do.** Somewhere here, there is a problem. = **aeryets, aryets, ariyets.** LRT

andeweil, *adv* - just now. **~ lest mer net viel Gudes in de Zeiding.** Just now one does not read many good things in the newspaper. LRT

Angel[1]**,** *f, pl* **Angle** - sting of an insect. = **Gixer, Schtachel, Schtecher.** KYG1880

Angel[2]**,** *f, pl* **~e** - **1** fish hook. LRT. **2** warble fly. KYG2166

angelbissich, *adj* - of stock bitten by the warble fly. KYG2166

Angscht, *f* - fear, fright. **Sie waar voll ~.** She was filled with fear. LRT

anne, *adv* - thither. = **dattanne, datthie, dohie, hie.** KYG2000. **Schtell's yuscht datt ~.** Just send it (down) there. LRT

anne-schtrecke, *pp* **anne-gschtreckt** - to stretch out. **Hot er dir die Hand gewwe? Ya,** er hot mir sie annegschtreckt. Did he extend his hand to you? Yes, he stretched out his hand. LRT

anneduh - to take over (deliver). **Du kannscht's Geld datt ~.** You can put the money there (on the counter). LRT

annereide - to ride to a place. **Fer den Blatz sehne, hen sie ~ misse.** To see the place they had to ride there (on their horses). LRT

anneschmeisse - to throw down. = **hieschmeisse, nunnerschmeisse, runnerschmeisse, umschmeisse, zammeschmeisse.** KYG2009. **Schmeiss die faule Eppel datt anne.** Throw the rotten apples down there. LRT

anneschpringe, *pp* **is annegschprunge** - to run to a certain point or location. **Er is dapper datt annegschprunge.** He ran quickly to that location. LRT

Antlaa´ni, *f* - ☺ Ontelaunee Creek, Lehigh Co., PA. KYG2278

Antwaddes, *n* - response. **Sei ~ hot niemand verschteh kenne.** No one could understand his response. LRT

antwattlich, *adj* - responsible. **Die Kinner sin ~ zu ihrem Daadi.** The children are responsible to their father. LRT

Appeditt, *m* - appetite. **der ~ nemme** - to take one's appetite. KYG1960. **Seller G(e)ruch nemmt em der ~.** That odor takes one's appetite. LRT

Appelschtengel, *m* - stem of apple. **Die menscht Zeit kann mer en ~ rausroppe.** Usually an apple stem can be pulled out. LRT

Arebschaft, *f* - patrimony. **Er hot en grossi ~ grickt.** He got a large inheritance. LRT

Arebse, *pl* - peas. **Wann mer die ~ ken Hecke odder Droht gebt, lege sie sich yuscht hie, un sell is nix waert.** If one doesn't give peas, sticks or wire, they just lie down, and that's not good. LRT

Arebsehecke, *pl* - sticks to support pea vines. [We cut small branches from the trees in the nearby woods.] LRT

Arewet, *f* - work. **Selli Yunge wisse was ~ is.** Those young men know what work is. LRT. **Sei ~ mehnt en Latt zu ihm.** His work is very important to him. LRT, 4/11/2000

arig, *adj* - terrible. **Der Wind hot ~ wiescht geblosse.** The wind blew terribly. LRT. = **arich.** *cf* **baremlich, en(t)setzlich, erbaremlich, erschrecklich, farichderlich, greisslich, greisselbaarisch, grisslich, grisselmeesich, hesslich, schauderhaft, schauderhafdich, schauderlich, schreckeldaanisch, schreckelballich, schrecklich, scheisslich.** KYG1988

ariyer, *comp adj* - worse. **De lenger as es geht, de ~ as es waert.** The longer it goes, the worse it gets. LRT,4/18/2000

ariyets, *adv* - somewhere. **Wann du's net gleichscht do, dann kannscht yuscht ~ schunscht hiegeh.** If you don't like it here, then you can just go somewhere else. LRT

as, *conj* - that. **Es dutt sieme, ~... -** It seems that.... KYG1992. **Was is es ~ dich so schtolz macht?** What is it that makes you so proud? LRT

aus, *prep* - out. **Er is ~ seim Kopp.** He is (acting) out of his mind. **Yunger, du bleibscht ~ em Weg.** Young man, you stay out of the way. **~ Fix -** out of fix. **Was macht dich widder so ~ Fix?** Why are you so upset again? LRT

aus sei - to be on bad terms. KYG1987

aus-daa-e - to thaw out. = **aus-schleffle.** KYG1992. = **ausschlafde.** LRT/ Leb. Co.

aus-iewe - to carry out. **sei Schpeit ~ -** to take out one's spite. KYG1962

aus-schleffle - to thaw. *cf* **daa-e, schleffle, schmelze, uff-daa-e, uffgeh, verschmelze.** KYG1992. **Die Wasserpeif is zugfrore; mir misse sie ~.** The water pipe is frozen; we've got to thaw it out. LRT

aus-schpanne - to unhitch (horses from a wagon). KYG2104. **Sis Owed un Zeit fer die Geil ~.** It's evening and time to unhitch the horses. LRT

aus-schtrecke, *refl, pp* **ausgschtreckt -** to stretch oneself out. **Guck mol, er hot sich ausgschtreckt.** Look, he

stretched himself out (taking a nap). LRT

aus-schtrecke - to stretch out. **Sache duhne viel lenger aushalde wann mer sie bissel aus-schtreckt.** Things last much longer if one conserves a bit. LRT

aus-schwemme - to wash away (by force of water). *cf* **nauss-schwemme, schwemme, weck-schwemme.** KYG2167

aus-schwitze, *pp* **ausgschwitzt -** to sweat it out. **Sie hen der Dischbedaat ausgschwitzt.** They sweated out the dispute. LRT

ausaarde, *pp* **is ausgaard -** to not produce true to kind. **Des Siesswelschkaann muss ausgaard sei mit Feldwelschkaann, es schmackt net recht.** This sweet corn must be crossed with field corn, it doesn't taste right. LRT

ausbeisse, - to oust by bitting. **Beiss seller schlecht Blacke aus dem Appel.** Bite that bad spot out of this apple. LRT

ausbiggle, *pp* **ausgebiggelt -** to iron out. **Biggel selli Runzle aus.** Iron out those wrinkles. LRT

ausblanze - to set out. *cf* **naussetze. Mer muss waarde bis die Reife verbei sin, eb mer die Tomaets ausblanzt.** One must wait until the frosts are over to plant out the tomato plants. LRT

ausblaudre, *refl, pp* **ausgeblaudert -** to talk to one's heart's content. KYG1964.

Bischt du ausgeblaudert? Can you say more? LRT

ausbluge - to plow out potatoes. LRT

ausbrowiere - to try out. KYG2071. **Tscheck, browier mol die zwee Geil aus.** Jake, give these two horses a try. LRT

Ausbrowiering, *f* - tryout. KYG2071. **Heit is die ~ fer sehne wie schtarick as die Buwe schpringe kenne.** Today is the tryout to see how fast the boys can run. LRT

ausdenke - to think out. = **aussinne.** KYG1998

ausdiene - to serve one's time. KYG2019

ausdinne - to thin out. *cf* **dinnere, dinn mache.** KYG1997. **Mir misse unser Welschkann ~, sis zu dick geblanzt.** We will need to thin out our corn, it is planted too thickly (close). LRT

ausdowe, *refl, pp* **ausgedopt -** to give free course to one's energy (passions). **Die Buwe hen sich ausgedopt, bis sie schier nimmi laafe hen kenne.** The boys vented their rage until they could hardly walk. LRT

ausdrehe, *pp* **ausgedreht -** 1 to turn out. **Kens vun selle Buwe hen gut ausgedreht.** None of those boys turned out well. LRT. **schlecht ~ -** to turn out badly. KYG2077. **Selli Yunge sin schlecht ausgedreht.** Those youngster turned out badly. LRT 2 to wring. **Wesche, schwenke, un ~ —sell is wie mer's dutt.** Wash, rinse and wring—that's

how it is done. LRT,4/18/2000.
3 to turn out (a wheel on a lathe). KYG2077. **4** to extinguish. **Sie hen's Licht ausgedreht.** They turned out the light. LRT

ausdreiwe, *pp* **ausgedriwwe** - to drive out. **Die Hund hen die Hinkel all aus em Gaarde gedriwwe ghalde.** The dogs kept all the chickens driven out of the garden. LRT

ausdresche - **1** to thrash out. = **rausdresche.** *cf* **aus-schaffe. 2** to finish thrashing. = **rausdresche.** KYG2006

ausdricke, *pp* **ausgedrickt** - to squeeze out. **~ is es flissich Fett aus die gleene gebrodne Seifettschticker (was mer Griewe heest) griege. Mer yuust en Fettbress fer des duh.** ~ is separating the liquid fat from the small fried pieces of hog fat (called cracklings). One does this with a lard press. **Mir hen die Brieh aus die Kasche gedrickt fer Wei mache.** We squeezed the juice out of the cherries to make wine. LRT

ausduh - to unrobe. KYG2111. **Kind, duh dei Gleeder aus.** Child take your clothes off. LRT **Ich muss mei Gleeder ~, so as ich mich baade kann.** I must take off my clothes so I can take a bath. LRT. = **ausziehe, schtrippe.** KYG2100.

ausenannernemme - to take apart. **Mir welle die dod Katz ~.** We want to dissect the dead cat. LRT. = **ausennermache, drenne.** KYG1962

Ausfarichde, *n* - making rows for planting. **Es ~ is faddich,**

mir kenne die Grummbiere blanze. The rows have been made, we can plant the potatoes. LRT

ausfariche, *pp* **ausgfaricht** - to make rows (prior to planting). **Hett dir's Grummbiereschtick ausgfaricht?** Did you make the furrows for the potato patch? LRT

ausfechde - to settle (a difference). **Du kannscht saage was du witt, awwer mir duhne des Ding ~.** You can say what you want, but we're going to settle this thing. LRT

ausfeddle - to unstring. KYG2113. **Ich daed gleiche wann dir all die Gwiltnodle ~ daede.** I'd like if you would unthread all the quilt(ing) needles. LRT

ausfege, *pp* **ausgefegt** - to clean out thoroughly. KYG2001. **Der Kessel muss gut ausgefegt sei, er is alles eigegruscht.** This kettle must be scoured out well, it is all encrusted. LRT

ausfiehre - to perform. **Mir breiche en Mann, as all die Arewet ~ kann.** We need a man who can manage the completion of all this work. LRT

ausfille, *pp* **ausgfillt** - to fill up. KYG2117. **Die Fuderseck sin all ausgfillt.** The feed sacks are all filled up. LRT

ausfinne, *pp* **ausgfunne** - to find out. **Darich sei Leses hett er en latt neie Sache ~ selle.** Through his reading he should have learned (found out) many new things. LRT

ausfische - to spy out. **Er hot viel gfrogt---schur er waar am ~.** He did lots of asking---sure he was spying. LRT

ausfranzle, *pp* **ausgfranzelt** - to unravel. **Du muscht seller Gaund naehe; datt um dei Aermel is es alles ausgfranzelt.** You'll have to sew your dress. It is all frayed around your sleeve. LRT

ausfroge, *pp* **ausgfrogt** - to question. **Hoscht du ihn nau ausgfrogt?** Have you interrogated him now? LRT

ausgangs, *adv* - toward the end of. **~ Matz** - toward the end of March. KYG2042. [We always said **hinne im Munet** - toward the end of the month. LRT]

ausgedient, *adj* - having become unfit. KYG2102

ausgeh, *pp* **ausgange** - **1** to take a walk. KYG1962. **2** to go out, die out. **Es Feier is ausgange.** The fire went out. LRT

ausgelegt, *adv* - laid out. **Innewennich is sell Haus schee ausgelegt.** That house is laid out nicely inside. LRT

ausgelosse, *adv* - unruly. *cf* **schtippich, trotzich, unbennich, ungebascht, ungezoge, wiescht, wild.** KYG2111

ausgewwe, *pp* **~ 1** to be compelled to stop. KYG1889. **2** to be compelled to stop work (from exhaustion). **Er hot gschafft bis er ~ hot.** He worked until he was completely exhausted. LRT. **Sei Grefde hen ewwe ~.** His strength failed him. LRT,3/11/2000

ausgfeddelt, *adj* - unthreaded. ~ **warre** - to become unthreaded. KYG2113

ausgritzle, *pp* **ausgegritzelt** - to scribble over. **Sie hen alles ausgegritzelt ghat, mer hot nix lese kenne.** They had scribbled all over everything, one could not read a thing. **Was es saagt datt is net recht, duh's ~.** What it says there is incorrect, scribble it out. LRT

ausgschpielt, *adj* - played out. **Er is ~, mer kann sell gut sehne.** He is played out---one can well see that. LRT

ausgucke, *refl, pp* **ausgeguckt** - **sich die Aage ~** - to look until one is tired. KYG2025. **Mir hen uns die Aage schier ausgeguckt un hen's doch net gsehne.** We almost looked our eyes out and still didn't see it. LRT

aushalde - **1** to withhold. **Wann er net so viel ~ daed, hedde mir blendi.** If he hadn't withheld so much, we'd have plenty. LRT. **2** to be true to one's experiences. KYG2068. **Sie hen sehne welle wie lang as er ~ kann.** They wanted to see how long he could endure. LRT

aushenke - to unhook. KYG2104. **Kannscht du seller Hoke vun sellem Ring ~?** Can you unhook that hook from that ring? LRT. **= abhenke**

auskehre, *pp* **ausgekehrt** - to sweep out. **Die Maad hot die Kich ausgekehrt.** The maid swept out the kitchen. LRT

auskitsche - to rake out ashes with a **Kitsch,** *qv.* **Daedscht du der Offe gut ~?** Would you rake out the ashes from the stove? LRT

auskumme - to live on good terms (with). KYG1987. **Sie is zimmlich gut ~.** She had pretty good results. LRT

auskunsiddere - to consider thoroughly. KYG2001

auslaafe - to terminate. *cf* **End mache; zum End bringe.** KYG1988. **Am Schtor hen sie gsaat sie sin aus gekaendi Tomaets geloffe.** At the store they said they ran out of canned tomatoes. LRT

ausleere - to empty. **Es hot gereyyert bis die Kiwwel voll waare, no hoscht du sie ~ kenne.** It rained until the buckets were full; then you could empty them. LRT

ausleffle, *pp* **ausgeleffelt** - to lift out with a spoon. **Walniss ~** - to hull a walnut. KYG2161. **Sie hot mir'n Schissel voll Supp ausgeleffelt.** She spooned out a bowl full of soup for me. LRT

Ausleger, *m* - **1** undertaker. = **Begraawer, Begreewer, Dode-ausleger, Dodefleger, Dodemann, Dodesversaryer, Eibalsemierer, Laademacher, Laademann, Laademesser, Leichtbeschteller, Leichtmann, Leichtversariyer.** KYG2098. [These terms do not all mean undertaker. LRT]. **2** one who buries. LRT

ausleinisch, *adv* - out of line. **Schick dich net so ~ aa!** Don't

act so "out of line," wacko! LRT. *cf* **halbleinisch**

ausmauere, *pp* **ausgemauert** - to line with a wall. KYG2160. **Sie hen sei Graab ausgemauert mit Backeschtee.** They lined his grave with a wall of brick. LRT

ausmelke, *pp* **ausgemolke** - to drain a cow of her milk. **Wie mir Kinner am lanne waare melke, is die Mamm immer hinnenoochgange un hot die Kieh ausgemolke.** When we children were learning to milk, mother always followed us and milked the cows dry. (When you milk, make sure you pull the teats dry.) LRT

ausmischde, *pp* **ausgmischt** - to clean out the stable. **Der Geilsschtall muss alle Woch ausgemischt sei.** The horse stable must be cleaned out each week. LRT

ausnaehe, *pp* **ausgenaeht** - to stitch. *cf* **naehe, flicke, reihe, schteppe.** KYG1882. **Die Weibsleit hen scheeni Blumme uff seller Deppich ausgenaeht.** The women embroidered pretty flowers on that quilt. LRT

ausnemme, *pp* **ausgenumme** - **1** to take out in trade. KYG1962. **2** to gut. **Ich hab der Hasch ausgenumme.** I gutted the deer. LRT

auspacke - to unpack. KYG2109. **Mir hen immer en grossi Zeit, wann mir unser Grischtkindlin ~.** We always have a great time when we unpack (unwrap) our Christmas gifts. LRT

ausraahme - to clear of rubbish. **Den Schank misse mir mol ~.** We just need to tidy up this cupboard. LRT

ausraawe, *pp* **ausgeraawe** - to rob (of everything). *cf* **beraawe, schtehle, raawe. Sie hen ihn ausgeraawe bis er nix meh ghat hot.** They robbed him of everything he had. LRT

ausrechle - **1** to figure out. **Wann du mich net glaabscht, dann rechel's aus fer dich selwert.** If you don't believe me, then figure it out for yourself. **2** to solve a math problem. LRT

ausreisse - to tear out. = **nausreisse, rausreisse.** KYG1976. **Sie welle die Wend im Sundaagschulgebei ~.** They want to tear out the walls in the Sunday School building. LRT

ausreiwe - to erase, to rub out. LRT

Ausrett, *f* - excuse. **Yunger, du hoscht widder geduh was ich dir gsaat hab as du net duh sollscht, was is dei ~ dessemol?** Young man, again you did what I told you not to do, what is your excuse this time? LRT

ausrolle, *pp* **ausgerollt** - to roll out thin. **Mer muss der Deeg recht dinn ~ fer Sandtart-kichlin.** One must roll the dough out really thin for sand tart cookies. LRT. **Fer sand tarts mache muss der Deeg recht dinn ausgerollt sei.** To make sand tarts the dough needs to be rolled out real thin. LRT

ausruge, *refl, pp* **ausgerugt** - to get a thorough rest. KYG2001. **Bischt du nau gut ausgerugt?**

Now are you thoroughly rested? LRT. **Der Weg wie du gschafft hoscht heit, daedscht dich mol besser gut ~.** The way you worked today, you'd better take a good rest. LRT

aus-schaffe - to work out (a problem). **Des is en verhuddelt Wese, des misse mir browiere ~.** Tis is a mixed up mess, we'll need to try and work it out. LRT,4/11/2000

aus-scheppe - to scoop out. LRT

aus-schiddle - to shake out. **Schiddel die Feddere aus sellem Koppeziech.** Shake the feathers out of that pillowcase. LRT

aus-schiesse, *pp* **ausgschosse** - to send forth shoots. **Die Zwiwwle sin ausgschosse.** The onions have gone to seed. = **ausschlagge.** LRT

aus-schlagge, *pp* **ausgschlagge** - **1** to send forth sprouts, germinate. **Ya, es Welschkann is am ~.** Yes, the corn is germinating. LRT. **2** to stun. **Der Hund waar ausgschlagge gwest, awwer er is widder zu Lewe kumme.** The dog was stunned (knocked out), but he came to life again. LRT. **3** to strike, beat. **fehl ~ -** to turn out unsuccessfully. KYG2077. **Der bescht Balleschpieler waar's erscht fer ~.** The best ballplayer was the first one to strike out. LRT. **Sie hen uns reaus-gschlosse.** They locked us out. LRT

aus-schliesse - to lock out, exclude. LRT

aus-schpodde - to taunt. = **bschimbe, schmeeche, schpettle, wiescht stumbiere.** KYG1973. **Ich gleich net as sie immer Leit ausschpott wehe ihre Gleeder.** I don't like that she is always taunting people on account of their clothes. LRT. **Yunger, sell settscht du net duh, so epper ~; sell waar net schee.** Young man, you should not do that, mimic someone like that; that was not a nice thing to do. LRT

aus-schtambe - to stamp out. **Mir duhne der Dreck aus sellem Karebet schtambe.** We'll stamp the dirt out of that carpet. LRT. **Kannscht du sell Feier ~?** Can you stamp out that fire? LRT

Aus-schteene, *n* - removing (cherry) stones. **Wann du Kaschepie backe witt, dann daede mir besser an's ~ geh.** If you want to bake cherry pies, then we had better get to stoning the cherries. LRT

aus-schteh, - 1 to be outstanding. **2** to suffer, bear, tolerate, withstand. **Die Sache was der Zaahdokder geduh hot heit, hab ich yuscht schier net ~ kenne.** The things the dentist did today I could hardly bear. LRT. **Selli laut Musik kann ich yuscht nimmi ~.** I just can't stand (endure) that loud music anymore. LRT. *cf* **baschde, dulde, geh, leide, verdraage, verschmatze, uffduh mit.** KYG2031. **Ich wees net wie er sell ~ kann.** I don't know how he can tolerate that. LRT

aus-schtehlich, *adj* - tolerable. *cf* **basslich, leidlich,**

middelmaessich, zimmlich. KYG2031

aus-schtoosse - to exclude or oust. **Er hot Ruus aus em Offerohr gschtoosse.** He thumped the soot out of the stove pipe. LRT

aus-schtrecke, *refl, pp* **ausgschtreckt** - to stretch (oneself) out. **Er hot sich ausgschtreckt un hot sich flach uff der Grund gelegt.** He stretched himself out and lay flat on the ground. LRT. **Er is ausgschtreckt uff em Grund.** He is lying flat on the earth. KYG1511

ausschwenke, *pp* **ausgschwenkt** - to rinse out. **Die Weschgleeder sin ausgschwenkt.** The wash clothes are rinsed out. LRT

ausse, *adv* - on the outside. **Wann du in die Kich geh witt, dann geh yuscht ~ um seller Portscheposchde.** If you want to go into the kitchen just go around that porch post. LRT

ausserum, *adv* - around the outside. **Du muscht ~ geh fer die hinnerscht Dier finne.** You will need to go around the outside to find the back door. LRT. **Dei Schuh sin zu dreckich, du muscht ~ geh.** Your shoes are too dirty (muddy), you must go around the outside. LRT

aussewennich[1]**,** *adj* - outside. LRT

aussewennich[2]**,** adv - by heart. **Kannscht du sell ~ saage?** Can you say that from memory? LRT

Aussicht, *f, pl* **~e** - prospect. **Was fer ~e hett dir mit eirem Suche fer en Dokder fer eier Schtadt?** What kind of prospects do you have in your search for a physician for your town? LRT

aus-suche, *pp* **ausgsucht** - to search out, search thoroughly. **Du hoscht der ganz ewwerscht Schpeicher ausgsucht, un du hoscht nix wie sell gfunne, is sell recht?** You searched through the whole attic and you found nothing like that, is that right? **Unser Hund hot sell glee Feld gut ausgsucht.** Our dog searched out that little field really well. LRT

ausverkaafe, *pp* **ausverkauft** - 1 to sell out. **Sis alles ausverkaaft.** Everything is sold (out). LRT. 2 to sell by forced sale. **Mir hen ken Brofitt mache kenne, no hen mir ausgemacht, mir daede alles ~.** We couldn't make a profit, so we decided we would sell out everything. LRT

auswaere, *pp* **is ausgewore** - to wear out. **Yunger, dei Schuh sin ausgewore.** Young man, your shoes are worn out. LRT,4/18/2000

auswaxe, *pp* **ausgewaxe** - to outgrow. **Yunger, du hoscht dei Gleeder all ausgewaxe.** Young man, you have outgrown all your clothes. LRT

ausweiche - to turn out (evade). KYG2077

Auswenger, *m* - a turn (in plowing) at end of field. KYG2076

auswesche, *pp* **ausgewesche** - to wash out. *cf* **rauswesche.** KYG2167. **Hoscht du dei dreckichi Gleeder ausgewesche?** Did you wash out your dirty clothes? LRT

auswessere - to place in water to remove salt. **Fer lenger hen deel Penn. Deitschi eigsalzni Fisch gekaaft fer esse mit ihrem Mariye-esse, awwer eb sie sie gebrode hen, hen sie sie ~ misse.** Years ago some Pennsylvania Germans bought salted fish to eat with their breakfasts, but before they fried them, they had to soak them in water to remove the salt. LRT

auswinne, *pp* **ausgewunne** - to triumph. **~ iwwer epper** - to triumph over someone. KYG2063. **Er hot meh verkaaft as eenich-epper schunscht, un sell hot gemehnt as er ausgewunne hot.** He sold more than any one else, and that meant that he won. LRT

auswische, *pp* **ausgewischt** - to wipe out. **Yunger, du grickscht dich ausgewischt.** Young man, you are going to get a swatting. LRT

auszaahne - 1 to finish teething. 2 to put a tooth in a rake. KYG1979

Auszehring, *f* - tuberculosis. **Heidesdaags heert mer net viel vun die ~.** Now-a-days one doesn't hear much about tuberculosis or consumption. LRT/Leb. Co. **Er hot der Aafang vun ~.** He is tubercular. KYG2072. **Die ~ hot ihn gfixt (dod gemacht).** Tuberculosis fixed him (killed him). LRT

ausziehe, *pp* **ausgezoge - 1** to remove clothing. **Zieg dei Gleeder aus.** Take your clothes off. LRT. **Zieg dei Schtrimp aus, sie schtinke.** Pull off your stockings, they stink. LRT. **2** to withdraw, evacuate. **Die Maad un der Gnecht sin ausgezoge.** The maid and the hired man moved out. LRT. **3** to trim. *cf* **bsetze, drimme.** KYG2061.

ausziehe, *refl* - to take off one's clothes. **Yunger, duh dich ~!** Young man, take off your clothes. LRT. = **sich schtrippe.** KYG1962

autsche - to give evidence of soreness. **Dutt dei Fuuss noch ~?** Does your foot still hurt? LRT

awwer dann, *adv* - but then. KYG1993.

awwer nau - 1 but now. **Es hot fer wochelang net gereyert, ~ hen mir meh as mir breiche.** It didn't rain for weeks, but now we have more than we need. LRT. **2** There now! KYG1994

awwerglaawisch, *adj* - superstitious. **Sie is en ~i Fraa.** She is a superstitious lady. LRT

Baaligaul, *m, pl* **-geil** - horse with white forehead. **Em John sei paar -geil gucke immer so schee.** John's pair of horses (with a white forehead) always look so nice. LRT

Baartzer(t), *m* - fowl without tail.

Baartzerthaahne, *m* - tailless rooster. **Mir sedde seller Baartzerthaahne schlachde fer's Sundaagmiddaagesse.**

We should kill that rooster without a tail for Sunday dinner. LRT

Babbelmaul, *n* - talkative person. KYG1965

babble - 1 to tattle. **2** to talk incessantly. KYG1964. **Sie dutt nix as wie ~.** She does nothing but talk incessantly. LRT = **belle, blatsche, retsche, Neiichkeede draage.** KYG1972. **~ so viel as du witt, awwer ich glaab dich net.** Babble as much as you want, but I don't believe you. LRT

Babbles, *n* - idle talk. = **Geblapper.** KYG1964

babblich, *adj* - talkative. **Oh, sie is ~!** Oh, she is talkative! = **blaudrich, gackrich, gaxich, schnepperich, schwetzich, vergaxt, verschnawwelt, windich, windisch.** KYG1965

Babierli, *n* - *dim* of **Babier.** little piece of paper. LRT/Leb.Co.

Backe, *pl* - cheeks. **Ihre ~ waare wennich rot.** There was a tinge of red in her cheeks. KYG2022

Backe, *m* - jaw of tong. KYG2033

Backebuch, *n* - pocketbook, purse. **Muscht ihn froge, er hot's ~.** You'll have to ask him, he controls the purse strings. LRT

backeschteenich, *adj* - brick. **Heidesdaags baue sie wennicher ~e Heiser.** Now-a-days they build fewer brick houses. LRT

Backeschtreech, *pl* - slap on the cheek. **Du griegscht ~ wann du net achtgebscht.** You will get slapped on the cheek if you are not careful. LRT

Backezaah, *m* - **1** lower canine tooth. = **Maagezaah.** KYG2035. **2** molar. LRT

Backmollgratzer, *m* - scraper used in kneading dough. **Der ~ is ausgwore, mir breiche en neier.** This scraper is worn out, we need a new one. LRT

badde, *pp* **gebatt** - to give relief. **Hot selli Medizin gebatt?** Did that medicine give relief? LRT

Baddibaesk, *m* - underwaist. KYG2098

badei'isch, *adj* - unreasonable. *cf* **unvernifdich, unverschtennich.** KYG2110

Baehn, *f* - trail. **Die Buwe hen en ~ darich der Busch gebroche.** The boys broke a trail through the woods. LRT

Baenkglarick, *m, pl* **~** - teller. *cf* **Glarick.** KYG1981. **Unser ~ mache ganz wennich Fehler.** Our bank tellers make very few mistakes. LRT

Baerick, *m* - castrated hog. **Hett dir yuscht ~ im Seischtall? Nee, mir hen aa Loose un Ewwer datt drin.** Do you have only castrated hogs in the pig stable? No, we also have sows and boars in there. LRT

Baert - *<Engl* part. **sei ~ nemme** - to take one's part. = **sich sekendiere.** KYG1961. = **Batt**

ballaad'sche - to talk in a long tiresome manner. KYG1964

Balle, *pl* - testicles. = **Ballicks, Glicker, Hode.** KYG1989.

Balle, *m* - ball of the thumb. KYG2010

Ballhoke, *m* - **1** common teazel. *Dipsacus sylvestris (Tourn) L.* = **Kaardedischel, Bollhoke, Bullhoke (Ln). 2** wild or Fuller's teazel. KYG1977

Balsamdramm, *m* - tincture of balsam (poplar) steeped in spirits. KYG2022

Balwier′messer, *n* -straight razor. LRT

bamblich, *adj* - wobbly. **Der Hund is awwer ~ iwwer der Hof gloffe.** The dog walked wobbly across the yard. LRT

Bandwarem, *m* - tapeworm. = **Mitesser.** KYG1970

Bangichkeit, *f* - timidity. = **Faricht, Farichtsamkeet.** KYG2021

Bannwill - ✪ Bernville, Berks Co. PA.

bappich, *adj* - **1** pasty. **Der Kuche is noch net faddich gebacke, der Zaehblicker is noch ~.** The cake is not finished baking, the toothpick is still pasty. LRT. **2** sticky. = **gammich, aahenkisch, glebich, schtickich.** *cf* **schmierich.** KYG1879. **Melassich is ~.** Molasses is sticky. LRT

bapple, *pp* **gebappelt** - to reveal a secret. **Es hett niemand's gwisst, awwer seller Mann**

hot's gebappelt. No one would have known it, but that man tattled. **Er kann sei Maul net halde, er bappelt alles as er wees.** He can't keep his mouth shut, he tells everything he knows. LRT

Bapplebaam, *m* - tulip tree. *Liriodendron Tulipifera L.* = **Dollebohnebaam, Gehlbapple** (My), **Hickribapple** (My), **Weissbapple** (My). KYG2073

Bappler, *m* - rattle-brain. **Glaab ihm nix, er is yuscht en ~!** Don't believe him; he is just a rattle-brain! LRT

Barchet, *m* - **1** twill calico. KYG2083. **2** double thread of the warp. KYG2165

Baremhatzichkeit, *f* - kindliness. **Wie die Scheier nunnergebrennt is, hot mer en latt ~ gsehne.** When the barn burned down, we saw lots of kindliness. LRT

Baricks Kaundi - ✪ Berks Co., PA. **In ~ is en Ladann en Lutzer.** In Berks County a lantern is a **Lutzer.** LRT,4/21/2000

Baricks - tick. **uff ~ -** on tick. KYG2013

baschde, *pp* **abgebascht** - to scrub. **Mir hen die dreckich Bortsch gut abgebascht.** We scrubbed down the dirty porch really well. LRT

Baschdert, *m* - swamp with bushes, used for pasture. **Sie duhne ihre Rinner uff em ~ bhalde.** They keep their heifers on the scrub pasture. LRT

Baschthelzel, *n* - wooden shucking pin (used in cornhusking). **Ich hab en ~, as mol em Dr. Ezra Grumbeh** (Grumbine) **seins waar.** I have a wooden husking pin that once belonged to the late Dr. Ezra Grumbine. LRT,4/11/2000. = **Baschtholz, Schtrippholz**

Basshann, *n* - tuba. KYG2071. **Wann's Maulschtick zu glee is an seim ~, dann sett er zum annere End neiblose.** If the mouth piece is too small on his tuba, then he should blow in the other end. LRT

Batt - <*Engl* part. **Yunger, nemm dei eeye ~!** Young fellow, you take your part (or: Stand your ground! Defend yourself!) LRT

Batzel, *m* - **1** tumble. = **Schtatz.** KYG2073. **2** back, rump. **Ich hab Schmatze im ~.** I have pain in my (lower) back. LRT

Batzelbaam, *m* - somersault. **Er hot paar mol ~ gschlagge.** He performed a few somersaults. LRT

batzich, *adv* - pertly, saucy. **Seller Yung schtratzt so ~, wie en Pohaahne.** That young man struts as pertly as a peacock. **Was sol mer duh mit so'm ~e yunge Ding?** What should one do with such a saucy young guy? LRT

batzle - to tumble. *cf* **dappe, falle, nidderschlagge, iwwerschlagge, schtatze, umschtatze, Batzelbaam schlagge.** KYG2073. **Er is vum Hoiwagge runner gebatzelt.** He tumbled down off the hay wagon. LRT

Bauchgatt, *f* - surcingle. **Selli ~ fitt seller Gaul net.** That surcingle does not fit that horse. LRT

Bauchrieme, *m* - belly strap. **En Geilsgscharr hot en ~.** A horse harness has a belly strap. LRT

Bauchschmatze, *pl* - stomach cramps. *cf* **Bauchweh** [Leb. Co., LRT], **Gramp, Gramph, Grampschmatze, Leibgriwwles, Leibschmatze, Maagegramp, Maageweh, Maageschmatze, Windkollick.** KYG1885. [For all the PG words used here, "sick to the stomach" would be a better translation. LRT].

Bauchwehdroppe, *pl* - stomach ache drops. KYG1885

Bauchwehmedizin - stomach ache medicine. **Mei ~ is roher Gnowwlich un roh Graut.** My stomach ache medicine is raw garlic and raw cabbage. LRT

Bauchwehpill, *f* - stomach ache pill. KYG1885

Bauchzuwwer, *m* - tub for pickling meat. KYG2071

Bauer, *m* - farmer. **der recht ~** - trump jack. = **der Recht.** KYG2069. **Er hot meh Kieh wie eenich annerer ~.** He has more cows than any other farmer. LRT

Bauer(e)schtack, *m* - stock (on a farm). KYG1883. **Sie hen Vendu vum ganze Bauereschtack.** They are having sale of the whole (total) farm stock. LRT

Bauersleit, *pl* - farm folk. LRT

Baugeld, *n* - money to repair/remodel church building. **Viel Kariche hen ~ weckgschpaart.** Many churches have a building fund set aside. LRT

Bauholz, *n* - timber. **Der Barig is gelaade mit gut ~.** The mountain is loaded with good timber. LRT. **Eeche is sei ~.** Oak is his (preferred timber). LRT. *cf* **Bleck.** KYG2018.

beant´wadde - to answer a question. **Wie kann ich dich ~, wann ich net wees, was du wissse witt?** How can I answer you, if I don't know what you want to know? LRT

Becker, *m* - salesman who delivers bread to the house. **Unser ~ is immer zweemol die Woch kumme.** Our baker (truck) always came twice a week. LRT

Becki, *f* - *dim* of Rebecca. **Unser Suhnsfraa heest ~.** Our daughter-in-law's name is Becky. LRT,4/21/2000

Beckmoos, *n* - peck measure. LRT

Bedaerf´ - want. **Der Harr is mei Schofhieder, ich hab ken ~.** The Lord is my shepherd, I shall not want. LRT

bedan´ke, *refl* - to thank. **Ich bedank mich widder.** Thank you again. = **Dank saage; Dank abschtadde.** KYG1990. **Ya, ich bedank mich fer den scheene Schunke.** Yes, I thank you for this nice ham. LRT

bedar´efe - to want. = **brauche, breiche, mangle.** *cf* **verlange,**

winsche. KYG2163

bedau´(w)erlich, *adj* - sorrowful, pitiful. **Sell waar ~ wie ihre Haus nunnergebrennt is.** That was pitiful when their house burnt down. **Der Weg wie sie sell Kind uffziehe is awwer ~.** The way they are rearing that child is pathetic. LRT

bedenk´lich, *adj* -thought-provoking. **Fer die Waahret zu saage, sell is es ~ Ding fer duh.** To say the truth, that is the wise thing to do. LRT. **Sis ~ wann's so Sache gebt.** It's thought-provoking when such things occur. LRT

beden´ke, *pp* **bedenkt** - to think about. *cf* **draadenke.** *cf* **Denk dewehe!** Think about it! KYG1998. **Wer hett sell bedenkt?** Who would have thought about that? LRT

bedin´ge, *pp* **bedingt** - to stipulate. *cf* **aushalde, ausbhalde.** KYG1882. **Ich hab sell all bedingt ghat.** I had stipulated all of that. LRT

bedisch´dere - to pacify. LRT

bedrach´de - to survey. **Hett dir bedracht was am aageh waar?** Did you observe what was going on? LRT

bedriebt´-guckich, *adj* - troubled looking. KYG2065. **Sie is arig ~.** She is very troubled (sad) looking. LRT

bedrie´ge - to swindle. = **bscheisse**

bedrie´we, *refl* - to sadden. **Iwwer was duhscht du dich immer so ~?** What is causing you to always be so sad? LRT

bedrun´ke, *adj* - tipsy. = **benewwelt, gschwewwelt, gsoffe.** KYG2025

bees, *adj* - angry. **Sie is ~ warre, weil er ihr ken Geld gewwe hot.** She got angry because he didn't give her any money. LRT. **Uff-ee-mol waar sie so ~ wie en Hummler.** All of a sudden she was as angry as a bumblebee. LRT

Beesfiewer, *n* - typhoid, typhus fever. *cf* **Frissel, Narefefiewer, hitzichi Granket.** KYG2087

befrie´diche - to satisfy. **Dutt sell dich ~?** Does that satisfy you? LRT

Begleed´ing, *f* - trimming. = **Besetzing, Drimming, Trimming, Verziering.** KYG2062. **Ihre ~ macht sie reich gucke.** Their clothing (the way they dress) makes them look rich. LRT

Begraawer, *m, pl* **Begreewer** - one who buries. LRT

begree´me, *refl* - to complain. **Er dutt sich immer ~.** He is always complaining. LRT

begreif´lich, *adj* - understandable. = **verschtendlich.** KYG2098. **Des is mir gaar net ~.** I just don't comprehend this. LRT

begrei´fe - to understand. = **eisehne, ergreife, kenne, neisehne, vernemme, verschteh.** *cf* **heere saage.** KYG2097. **Des kann ich gaar net ~.** I just can't understand this. LRT

beguc´ke - to look at, examine. **die Guckbax ~** = to watch television. KYG1980. **Daedscht du gleiche die Pickders ~?** Would you like to look at these pictures (photographs)? LRT

Beh, *n, pl* **~** - leg. **Sei ~ sin grumm, vielleicht is sei Naame Grummbeh (Grumbine).** His legs are bowed, perhaps his name is Grumbine. LRT

behaap´de, *refl, pp* **behaapt** - to maintain. **Er hot sich behaapt as er recht waar!** He maintained that he was correct! LRT

behatz´iche - to take to heart. KYG1962

behel´fe, *refl, pp* **beholfe** - 1 to help oneself. **Es macht nix aus was as es is, er kann sich ~.** It doesn't matter what the situation, he can help himself. LRT. **2** to makeshift. **Sie hen sich beholfe un hen en Zelt uffgschtellt.** As a makeshift, they set up a tent. LRT

beheng´e, *refl* - to put on (jewelry). **Sie behengt sich mit Sache as mer net oft seht.** She wears (puts on) jewelry that one rarely sees. LRT

behen´ke, *refl* - to put on trinkets. KYG2062. **Der Weg wie sie sich behenkt, guckt sie wie en Grischtdaagsbaam.** They way she overdoes trinkets and jewelry makes her look like a Christmas tree. LRT

Behie´de(r)s! - by thunder! = **Galli! Bigatt! Beihieders! Hol's der Deiwel! Hol's der Schinner!** KYG2011

beifaahre - to convey thither in a vehicle. KYG2000

beifalle, *pp* **is beigfalle** - 1 to recollect. 2 to come to (mind). **Heit is es mir beigfalle.** Today it popped into my mind. LRT. **Sis mer ~.** The thought came to me. LRT

beikumme - to come from. **Wu kummscht du bei?** Where did you come from? LRT

beinanner, *adv* - together. = **anenanner, beisamme, menanner, mit(e)nanner.** *cf* **inanner, nanner, sammt, zamme, zamme-nanner.** KYG2030. **Wuhne selli zwee noch ~?** Do those two still live together? LRT

Beint, *m,n* - <*Engl* pint. **Alle zwee Munet geb ich en ~ Blut.** Every two months I give a pint of blood. LRT

Beintblech, *n* - 1 tin cup. = **Drinkblech.** KYG2022. **Sell ~ is awwer roschdich.** My, that tin cup is rusty. LRT. **2** tin pint measure. KYG2023

Beintbusch, *m* - ✪ Pine Grove, PA.

Beintholz, *n* - pine wood. **Mer kann scheeni Benk mache vun ~.** One can make beautiful benches from pine wood. LRT

Beintrassem, *m* - pine rosin. LRT

Beintsaft, *f* - pine sap. **Selli ~ is awwer bappich.** That pine sap is sticky. LRT

Beintschtumpe, *m* - pine tree stump. LRT

beiricke - to take a seat nearby. KYG1961

beirufe, *pp* **beigerufe** - to call near. **Er hot sich so en ordlichi Drupp Leit zammer beigerufe ghat.** He had called together quite a group of people. LRT

beischleefe - to drag up to. KYG2117. **Mer wees nie net was die Katze ~ meechde.** One never knows what the cats might drag in (or up). LRT

beischpiellos, *adj* - without examples. KYG2101

beischpringe, *pp* **beigschprunge** - to run up to. *cf* **zuschpringe. Ich waar leenich datt im Dunkele un er is beigschprunge kumme.** I was alone there in the dark and he came running by. LRT. **Die Yunge sin iwweraal beizuschpringe kumme.** The youngsters came running up from all directions. LRT

Beiss, *m* - bite, snack. **en ~ Kaes** - a snack of cheese. **Nemm en ~, du muscht den Kuche versuche.** Take a bite, you have to try this cake. LRT

beisse - to bite (a physical discomfort, such as an itch or a sting). LRT

beissich, *adj* - itchy. **Des Hemm macht mei Buckel ~.** This shirt makes my back itchy. LRT. **Deel sadde Gleeder mache em ~.** Some kinds of clothes make one itchy. LRT

Beisszang, *f* - 1 pinchers. **En ~ kann mer yuuse fer em Gaul sei Huf nunnerschneide .** A pinchers can be used to cut back

the hoof of a horse. **2** pinchers. **Deheem hen mir immer en ~ ghaat.** At home we always had an (all-purpose) pinchers. LRT

bekannt´mache - to announce, publish. **Allegebott duhne die Amische en Hochzichdaag ~.** Every now and then the Amish publish a wedding day. LRT

bekim´mere, *refl* - to be concerned. **sich net ~** - to be unconcerned. KYG2094. **Er bekimmert sich net iwwer sei Hund.** He has no concern for his dog. LRT

belaa´yere - to complain unceasingly. KYG2093

belei´diche - to torment. **Tschonni, beleidich selli Katz net.** Johnnie, don't torment that cat. LRT

belie´ye - to lie to. **Nau du daedscht mich net ~, daedscht du?** Now you wouldn't lie to me, would you? *cf* **wiescht liege** - to drastically lie. LRT

Bell, *f, pl* **~e** - **1** bell. **2** school bell. **die aerscht ~** - the first ringing of the school bell. **die zwett ~** - the second ringing of the school bell. KYG1683. **Die Schulmeschdern, die Marcella Schlaebach Beam, hot schun die zwett Bell grunge.** The school teacher, Marcella Slabach Beam, has already rung the second school bell. CRB

belle, *pp* **gebellt** - **1** to ring the bell. = **die Bell ringe. Sie hen lang gebellt.** They rang the bell for a long time. LRT. **2** to toll. = **tohle. die Glock tohle** - to toll the bell. KYG2031. **3** to tell stories. = **gaffe.** KYG1964

Belle, *pl* - King and Queen of Trumps (in game of **Dadde**). KYG2069

Belleschtrick, *m* - bell rope. **An die Mt. Zion (Leb. Co., PA) Schul sin mol zwee Buwe nuff in der Belletarn gegraddelt un hen der ~ abgschnidde. Un no wie der Schulmeeschder, Edward Wenger, die Bell ziehe hot welle is der Schtrick runner kumme un die Bell hot net gerunge. Sell hot ihn awwer bees gemacht!** At the Mt. Zion school two boys crawled up into the belfry and cut off the bell rope. And then as the schoolmaster, Edward Wenger, wanted to ring the bell, the rope came down and the bell did not ring. That made him angry! LRT

belu´xe - to kid. **Du kannscht mich net ~!** You can't kid me (I don't believe anything you say). LRT

belze, *pp* **gebelzt** - to wallop. KYG2160. **Er hot ihn gebelzt bis er en bludichi Naas ghat hot.** He beat him until he had a bloody nose. LRT

belzich, *adj* - pithy. **Die Riewe sin awwer ~.** The turnips are pithy. LRT

Belznickelnacht, *f* - Twelve Tide. = **Belznickelzeit.** KYG2082

bemar´icke, *pp* **bemarickt** - **1** to remark. **Hett dir sell gwisst? Ya, er hot vun sellem bemarickt.** Did you know that? Yes, he had remarked about that. LRT. **2** to take heed. KYG1961. **3** to take notice, observe. **Ya, der hot's bemarickt.** Yes, he observed (noticed) that. LRT

bemieh´e, *refl* - to go to trouble. KYG2065

benae´me - to give a name. LRT

Bendel, *m* - string. **Nemm den ~ un binn sellem Haahne sei Beh zamme.** Take this string and tie that rooster's legs together. LRT

Bendelschatz, *m* - tie apron. KYG2015. **En halwer ~ is besser wie ken Schatz.** A (half) tie apron is better that no apron. LRT

Benderschteddel, *n* - ✪ Elizabethville, Dauphin Co., PA. = **der Greizweg.** KYG2271

Bengel, *m* - stout lad. **Seller Yunger is en ~.** That young guy is a whopper (extraordinarily large). LRT

Bennel, *m* - tape. = **Bendel.** KYG1969.

Benzepetzer, *m* - penny pincher. **~ sin die menscht Zeit ken Geldschwetzer.** Penny pinchers are usually not boasters of money (wealth). LRT

bero´de - to take counsel. KYG1960

Beschdelschapp, *m* - tinker's shop. KYG2023

beschtell´e, *pp* **beschtellt** - **1** to do odd repairing jobs. **2** to order. **Mir hen die Versammling beschtellt fer der dritt Yuni.** We have planned the meeting for the third of June. LRT

beschtle - to tinker. **im Schapp ~** - to tinker around the shop. *cf* **schpengle, zimmere.** KYG2022

Beschtler, *m* - tinkerer. *cf* **Kesselflicker, Schpengler.** KYG2023

besser, *comp adj* - better. **so viel de ~** - so much the better. **De meh as sie mir gewwe, so viel de ~.** The more they give me, so much the better. LRT. **~ duh** - to surpass. **Mer kann ~ duh wann mer will.** One can do better if one wants to. LRT. **Uff en scheener kiehler sunnicher Daag was ~ kann mer duh as wie fische geh?** On a nice cool day what better can one do than to go fishing? LRT

Betkapp, *f, pl* **~e** - prayer covering. **Die bleeni Weibsleit hen ~e aa.** The plain women are wearing prayer coverings. LRT

Betschtund, *f* - prayer meeting. LRT

bettgrank, *adj* - sick in bed. *cf* **Er is grank im Bett.** He is sick in bed. LRT

Bettlaadgranz, *m* - trim on a bed. KYG2061

bettle - to beg. **en Reit ~** - to thumb a ride. KYG2010. **Es waar en Mann an de Dier, er hot gsaat er is am ~ fer bissel eppes zu esse.** There was a man at the door, he said he is begging for a little something to eat. LRT

Bettleedel, *n* - trundle bed. = **Rollbett, Schiebbettche, Schiebbettleedche, Schiewerli, Schiewesbett, Trondelbett, glee Bett.** KYG2069

Bettsach, *f, pl* **~e** - sheeting. **Des waar en langer Daag, sie hot all die ~e gewesche un gedrickelt.** This was a long day, she washed and dried all the bedding. LRT

Bettziech, *pl* - sheets. **Unser ~ hen Lecher, mir misse neie griege.** Our bed sheets have holes, we need to get new ones. LRT

bewee´were - to ward off. = **weckhalde.** KYG2164

bewe´ge - to stir. *cf* **nuffschtarre, poke, riehre, rumriehre, schtarre, schtuppe, sich mucke, sich rege, sich vermucke, sich verrege.** KYG1882

bewogt´, *adj* - thriving. KYG2007

bezaah´le - to pay. **Du hoscht schund so viel gschafft, ich will dich ~.** You have worked so much; I want to pay you. **Sie hen mich immer gut bezaahlt.** They always paid me well. LRT. **Schick dich yuscht so aa; du bezaahlscht noch devor.** Just act like that; you will pay for it yet. LRT

bezei´ye - to testify. = **Zeichniss (ab)gewwe, Zeige gewwe.** KYG1989

bflecke - to taint. KYG1960. *cf* **verflecke**

bicke, *refl* - to stoop. KYG1889. **Der Dokder hot gsaat, ich misst mich ~ so as er mei Arschloch sehne hot kenne.** The doctor said I had to stoop over so he could see my anus. LRT

Bidderkasch, *f* - wild cherry. LRT

Bierebaam, *m* - pear tree. LRT

Biggelbord, *n* - ironing board. **Geb Acht, du schmeischt des Biggeleise vum ~.** Be careful, you'll knock the iron off the ironing board. LRT

Biggeleise, *n* - sadiron. = **Gletteise. Geb Acht, sell ~ is hees.** Be careful, that iron is hot. LRT

Bindli, *n* - a small package. LRT

binne - to tie. **Hand un Fuuss ~** - to tie hand and foot. KYG2015. **Kannscht du den Schtrick an em Gaul sei Halfter ~?** Can you tie this rope onto the horse's halter? LRT

bis, *conj* - until. **Bleib do, ~ er kumme is.** Stay here until he has arrived. KYG2114. **Du kannscht waarde ~ die Kieh heemkumme.** You can wait until the cows come home. LRT

bis, *adv* - by the time that. KYG2018. **En latt Wasser geht iwwer der Damm ~ sell Zeit.** A lot of water will go over the dam (breast) by that time. LRT

Bischli, *n* - small woods. **Sell ~ hot awwer grossi Eeche drin.** That little woods has huge oak trees in it. LRT/Leb,4/11/2000

Bissel, *n* - a short while. **Kannscht du en ~ waarde?** Can you wait a short while? = **en Bissli.** LRT

bissi, *adj* - <*Engl* busy. **Er hot sich der ganz Daag ~ ghalde.** He kept himself busy all day.

LRT

Bisskatzehaut, *f, pl* -**heit** - skunk hide. **Die -heit sin es menscht waert wann sie net viel weiss hen.** Skunk furs are the most valuable when they don't have much white. LRT

Bisskatzenewwel, *m* - skunk fog. **Des is en ~ Mariye.** This is a skunk fog morning. LRT

Bixschloss, *n* - safe of a gun. **Der Weg wie er schiesst, glaab ich net as er wees was en ~ is.** The way he shoots, I don't believe he knows what the safe of a gun is. LRT

Blaatzinn, *n* - tinfoil. = **Blattzinn.** *cf* **Silwerbabier.** KYG2022

Blacke, *m, pl* ~ - small piece of cloth. **Des nemmt hunnerts vun ~ selli Greess, fer en Deppich mache.** It will take hundreds of patches that size to make a quilt. LRT

blackeweis, *adv* - here and there. **So ~ hen sie schund der Hawwer gaernt.** Here and there they have already harvested the oats. LRT

blaecke, *pp* **geblaeckt** - < *Engl* to black. **sei Schuh ~** - to shine one's shoes. **Hoscht du dei Schuh geblaeckt?** Did you black your shoes? = **Schuh scheine.** LRT

blaeckgaerde - to tease. <*Engl* to blackguard. *cf* **bloge, hensle, ausschpodde, necke, nexe, reiwe, retze, rumzarre, utze, verargere, zarre.** KYG1977. **Hot er dich geblaeckgaerdt?** Did he tease you? LRT

Blanke, *pl* - planks. LRT

blanze, *refl, pp* **geblanzt** - to plant oneself. **Ich hab mich graad datt in die Mitt vun all selle Leit hie geblanzt, un ich bin die ganz Daag datt gebliwwe.** I planted myself right in the middle of all those people, and I stayed there all day. LRT

Blanzet, *f* - planting. **Des waar die greescht ~ as mir noch gmacht hen den Friehyaahr.** This was the largest planting that we made this spring. LRT

blappere - to talk fast. KYG1964

Blarr - bleat. **Der Schofbock hot en ~ gemacht.** The male sheep let out a bleating cry. LRT, 4/18/2000

blarre - to low. **Was is dann letz, die Kieh sin am ~ der ganze Daag?** What is wrong, the cows are lowing all day? LRT

blaschdere, *refl, pl* **geblaschdert** - to plaster oneself. **Was fer'n Granket hot er dann? Er hot sich yo geblaschdert vun Kopp zu Fuuss!** What kind of a disease does he have? Why, he is plastered from head to foot! LRT

Blatsch - stigma. KYG1879

blatsche, *refl, pp* **geblatscht** - to slump (into a chair). **Er hot sich datt in der Schtuhl geblatscht.** He slumped down into the chair. LRT

blatsche - to clap. **Duh dei Hend ~.** Clap your hands. LRT

Blatscher, *m* - **1** tale-bearer. *cf* **Neiichkeitdraeger, Ohreblatscher, Ohrebloser, Retsch, Retscher.** KYG1964. **2** wearisome talker. KYG1965. **3** tattler

Blatz, *m* - room, place. **Kennt dir ~ mache fer 12 Leit?** Can you provide (make place) for 12 people? LRT. **Sie hen ihn in sei ~ geduh.** They put him in his place. LRT. **Wann epper sich in die Ruh setzt, muss epper schunhscht sei ~ nemme.** If someone goes into retirement, someone else has to take his/her place. LRT

blatzweis, *adv* - scatteringly. = **bletzweis. ~ hen sie schwerer Rege ghat. ~** they had heavy rain. LRT

blauderich, *adj* - sociable. **Er is en ~er Mensch.** He is a sociable person. LRT

Blaumebaam, *m* - plum tree. LRT/Leb.Co.

Blech, *n* - tin. **iwwergezinnt ~ -** thin plate of iron covered with tin. KYG2021. **Aluminum hot en latt ~ sei Blatz genumme.** Aluminum took the place of a lot of tin. LRT

Blechbrick, *f* - tin bridge. KYG2021

Blechdach, *n* - tin roof. = **bleche Dach.** KYG2023. **En ~ hebt lang uff.** A tin roof lasts a long time. LRT

bleche, *adj* - tin. = **blechich, zinne, zinnich.** KYG2021

Blechhann, *n* - tin horn. KYG2022

blechich, *adj* - thin sheet of iron covered with tin. **Ihre Haus hot en blechich Dach.** Their house has a tin roof. LRT

Blechscheer, *f* - tin shears. KYG2023. **Mer kann aa Kupper schneide mir re ~.** One can also cut copper (sheeting) with tin sheers. LRT

blechschmidde - 1 to do the work of a tinsmith. **2** to work as a tinsmith. **3** to follow trade of a tinsmith. *cf* **schpenglere.** KYG2023

Blechschmidde, *n* - tinsmithing. KYG2024. **~ mehnt en Mensch muss en latt sadde Blecharewet duh kenne.** Tin smithing means a person must be capable of doing lots of kinds of tin work. LRT

Blechschmidt, *m, pl* **~** - tinner, tinsmith. *cf* **Schpengler, Weissschmidt.** KYG2023. **Yaahre zerick hen die ~ als en latt Kichlimoddle gemacht.** Years ago, the tin smiths used to make a lot of cookie molds. LRT

Blechvoll, *n* - tin cupful. KYG2022. **Ich hab en ~ Wasser gedrunke.** I drank a tin cupful of water. LRT

Bleckli, *n* - *dim* of **Blacke.** small patch. LRT/Leb.Co.

bleech, *adj* - pale, sallow. **Buwli, du guckscht awwer arig ~.** Little boy, you look very pale. LRT. **Selli Fareb guckt ~.** That paint looks pale. LRT

bleeche, *pp* **gebleecht** - to bleach. **Ich hab paar Hemmer as gebleecht sei sedde.** I have a few shirts that should be bleached. LRT

bleed, *adj* - **1** retiring. **2** shy. **Sei Buh is awwer ~.** His son is shy. LRT. **Sell Buwli is en Farichbutzli!** That little boy is a "scardy cat"! LRT. **3** timid. = **bang, eigezoge, farichtbutzich, farichtsam, schichder, schichderich, schichdich, schneckerich, verzaagt, verzacht.** KYG2021.

Bleedel, *n* - tongue of mouse or rat trap. = **Schlegger** (*facet.*) KYG2034

blehe - to bleach clothes by using wash bluing. KYG2167. = **bleeche**

Blenzli, *n, dim* of **Blanz.** little plant. LRT/Leb

Bleschderer, *m, pl* **~** - plasterer. **Die alt Satt ~ sin raar heidesdaags.** The old type of plasterers are scarce now-a-days. LRT

Bleschdering, *f* - plastering. **Oh, yeh nochemol, unser ~ is runnergfalle.** Oh my, our plastering has fallen down! LRT

Bleschderkell, *f, pl* **~e** - trowel. *cf* **Mauerkell.** KYG2066. [Not one and the same: **Bleschderer** is a plasterer and **Mauerer** is a stone mason. LRT]

Blessier', *f* - pleasure. **~ dreiwe** - to have a (pretty) good time. = **sich blessiere, en scheeni Zeit hawwe.** KYG2018. **Waar sell en ~ fer noch Hershey Park geh?** Was it a pleasure to go to Hershey Park? LRT

bletsche, *pp* **gebletscht** - to paddle, spank, strike with the open hand. **Wann du sell net schtoppscht, grickscht du dich gut gebletscht.** If you don't stop that you are going to get a good paddling. **Du grickscht dich gebletscht, wann du dich net bedraagscht.** You will get a spanking if you don't behave yourself. LRT

Bletsching, *f* - paddling. **Wann du dich net bedraagscht, grickscht en gudi ~.** If you don't behave, you'll get a good paddling. LRT

Blettli, *n* - saucer. **En ~ muss sei Koppli hawwe.** A saucer needs its cup. LRT

blettre - to turn pages (of a book). *cf* **darichblettre, rumblettre.** KYG2077. **Er hot darich's Buch geblettert bis er gfunne hot was er am Suche waar.** He paged through the book until he found what he was looking for. LRT

Bletzli, *n* - *dim* of **Blatz.** small place. LRT

bletzweis or **blatzweis,** *adv* - at places. **Geschder hot's awwer runnergschitt so ~.** Yesterday it poured down at places. LRT

Blickbuhn, *f, pl* **~e** - shell bean. **Mir fralicke denowed un gewwe Acht uff die ~e.** We will frolic tonight and take care of the shell beans. LRT

blicke - to shell. **Arebse ~** - to shell peas. **Ich gleich Arebse ~.** I like to shell peas. LRT

Blicki, *n* - a small tin cup or dish. = **Blechli.** LRT

Blog, *f* - ailment. **Sell Kind hot**

die alt satt **~.** That child has the old time ailment. LRT

bloge, *refl* - to drudge. **Er blogt sich immer zu hatt.** His drudgery is always too extreme. LRT, 4/11/2000

Blogsack, *m* - a child annoyingly desiring something. **Yunger, sei net so en ~!** Young man, don't be so annoyingly desirous of something! LRT

Blohbarig, *m* - ✿ Blue Mountains, the most prominent physical feature in SE PA.

Blohbarigtee, *m* - Blue Mountain tea. = **Barigtee, Blohbariyertee.** KYG1974

Blohbariyer[1], *pl* - inhabitants of the Blue Mountains (PA) region. KYG2269

Blohbariyer[2], *adj* - Blue Mountain. **Ich bin daschdich fer ~ Tee.** I'm thirsty for Blue Mountain tea. LRT,4/21/2000

Blohbariyertee, *m* - Blue Mountain tea. [Leb. Co.]. **Es verschtaunt mich, wie viel Leit as net wisse was ~ is.** I'm astonished at how many people don't know what Blue Mountain tea is. LRT. **~ schmackt bissel wie** licorice. Blue mountain tea tastes a bit like licorice. LRT = **Blohbarigtee, Barigtee.**

Blohfaadem, *m* - blue thread. KYG2003. **Seller ~ uff sellem Gaund sett net datt sei.** That blue thread on that dress should not be there. LRT

Blosbaligbumper, *m* - person who pumped the bellows of pipe organ. LRT. = **Blosbaligzieher**

blose, *pp* **geblose** - to blow. **der Kopp voll ~** - to blow the head full of stories. KYG1964. **Ya, well, sie hen ihm ewwe der Kopp voll geblose.** Yes, well, they have blown his head full of stories (lies). LRT

blottkeppich, *adj* - uncovered. **Sis zu kalt fer ~ nausgeh.** It's too cold to go outside bare-headed. LRT

blotze, *refl, pp* **geblotzt** - to be jolted. **Fer uff sellem Weg faahre, grickt mer sich gut geblotzt!** If you drive on that road, you'll be well jolted! LRT

Blotzer, *m* - **1** Thank-you-man. = **Abweiser, Ablos.** KYG1991. **2** jolt (in the road). **Well, sell waar en ~!** Boy, that was a jolt (in the road)! LRT

Blug-grendel, *m, pl* **~** - plow beam. **Die recht alde ~ waare gemacht vun Holz.** The real old plow beams were made of wood. LRT

Blugschtrang, *m, pl* **-schtreng** - plow trace. LRT

Blummegaarde, *m* - flower garden. **Selli Fraa hot en scheener ~.** That woman has a nice flower garden. LRT,4/18/2000. = **Blummehof**

Blummering, *m* - wreath of flowers. **Sie hot en scheener ~ an die Dier ghenkt.** She hung a pretty wreath of flowers on the door. LRT,4/18/2000

Blummeschtrauss, *m, pl* **-schtreiss** - stalk with flower. **Selli Soldaade -schtreiss sin wunnderbaar schee rot.** Those scarlet sage plants are a beautiful red. LRT. *cf* **Soldaade-Blummeschtrauss**

Blump! - thud (*onomat.*) = **Bump! Plump!** KYG2010. **Wie seller Sement Sack vum** truck **gefalle is, hot er en rechter ~ gemacht.** When that cement sack fell of the truck, the sound was quite a thud. LRT

Blumpsackschpielerei, *f* - plump sack game. **Lenger zerick hot alle Bauerevendu en ~ ghat fer die Yunge.** Years ago every farm sale had a plump sack game for the young men. LRT

Blut, *n* - blood. **~ schtille** - to stop bleeding. KYG1889. **Alle 58 Daage kann ich en Beint ~ gewwe.** Every 58 days I can give a pint of blood. LRT

Blutbezwinger, *m* - tourniquet. KYG2042

Blutsuckler, *m* - tick (insect). *cf* **Schoflaus, Zeck.** KYG2013

blutwaarem, *adj* - tepid. = **lauwaarem.** KYG1987

Blutwatzel, *f* - tumeric root. *Hydrastis canadensis L.* KYG2076

bocke - to rut. **Die Maerr is am ~, wann du gern en Yunges witt, dann daede mir besser en Hengscht do beigriege.** The mare is in heat, if you want a young one, we had better bring in a stallion. LRT

Bockseckel, *m* - buck's scrotum. **en ~ (Bock) aahenke** - to take all the tricks (in cards). KYG1962

boddelos, *adj* - without sure footing. **Er is ~ in die Heh gfloge.** He lost his footing and flew into the air. LRT

Boddemriege!, *m, pl ~* - bottom rail of a worm fence. **Die ~ sin ewwe die erschde as verfaule an re Schtaakefens.** The bottom rails of a worm fence are indeed the first ones to rot. LRT, 4/18/2000. = **Boddemriggel**

Bohrmaschien, *f* - tenon boring machine. KYG1986

Bolleryockel, *m* - stickweed. *Ambrosia spp.* = **wilder Warmemet.** KYG1878

Bollwarick, *n* - tow of the first hackling (in flax work). KYG2042

boppere, *pp* **geboppert** - to evince unrest. KYG2110. **Er hot geboppert bis niemand eppes meh saage hot welle.** He carried on until no one would say another word. LRT

Bordgewesche, *n* - washing on a board. KYG2168

Bortschebank, *f* - porch bench. LRT

Bortschegelender, *n* - porch banister. LRT

Botschdaal, *n* - ✪ Budge Valley. KYG2269

Bottli, *n* - *dim* of **Boddel.** small bottle. **Sell alt Avon ~ is en latt Geld wert.** That little old Avon bottle is worth a lot of money. = **Boddelche**

Brand, *m* - **1** gangrene. LRT. **Der ~ , sell waar meine**

Gremmemm ihre Dod, hen sie gsaat. Gangrene, that was the cause of my grandmother's death, so they said. LRT **2** smut on corn. **Sell Welschkann hot der ~.** That corn has smut. LRT. **3** sepsis. **Er hot der ~.** He has sepsis. LRT. **4** Saint Anthony's fire. = **heeser ~, feierich Ros, Rotlaafe, Wildfeier**

Brandeweifass, *n* - toper, *lit* brandywine barrel.. = **Drammratt, Drinker, Kaschefanger, Sauflodel, Siffer, schwerer Drinker.** KYG2038

brandich, *adj* - infected. **Er hot en Gritzer im Gsicht ghat, as ~ is warre.** He had a scratch in his face that became infected. LRT, 4/18/2000

brechdich, *adv* - superbly. **Ihre Kuche hot ~ gut gschmackt.** Her cake tasted wonderfully good. LRT

Breddich, *f* - sermon. **en auserlesni ~** - an especially good sermon. **Der Parre Diehl hot die ~ gewwe.** Pastor Diehl delivered the sermon. LRT

Breem, *m, pl* **~se** - warble fly. **Die Breemse sin am brumme.** The warble flies (horse flies) are humming. LRT

Breem(s), *f* - twitchel, thong. KYG2084. **Es nemmt en guder ~ fer en wilder Gaul benniche.** It takes a good thong to subdue a wild horse. LRT

Breemser, *m* - warble fly. = **Warewel.** KYG2166

Breetlatz, *m* - broad front flap

of trousers. KYG2065. **Die Amische Mannsleit hen noch Breetletz uff ihre Hosse.** The Amish men still have broad front flaps on their trousers. LRT

Brennessel, *m* - stinging nettle. = **Brenneesel.** KYG1881. **Net lang zerick hab ich en gleener Buh gsehne as am heile waar, er hot ~ iwwer sei bloddi Beh geriwwe grickt; sie waare rot, hen gebrennt, un waare wesserich.** Not long ago, I saw a little boy, who was crying, he had stinging nettles rubbed over his bare legs; they (the legs) were red, stinging, and were watery (oozing). LRT

Brennhaus, *n* - still house. = **Brennheisli.** *cf* **Brennerei.** KYG1880

brennsich, *adj* - pungent (of smell or taste). **Selli alt satt Sen-Sen schmacke ~.** That old fashioned sen-sen has a pungent taste. LRT

Bressentkieper, *m* - turnkey. KYG2079

Briam'bel, *m* - preamble, long-winded talk.= **Gebreddich.** KYG1964

briehe - to scald. **Mer brieht die Sei so as mer die Baschde losgratze kann.** One scalds the hogs so that one can scratch the bristles off. LRT

Briehgluck, *f, pl* **~e** - brood hen. **Die ~e dutt mer setze mit dreizeh Oier.** The brood hens are set with thirteen eggs. = **Briehhinkel.** LRT

Briehkett, *f* - scalding chain.

Die ~ schafft net so gut wann die Gleecher glee sin. The scalding chain doesn't work so well when the links are small. LRT

Briggel, *m* - piece of wood. **'me Schtick Vieh was immer darich die Fens geht, will mer en Kett um der Hals duh un en ~ draahenge.** On the cattle that always break through the fence, one puts a chain around their neck and fastens a piece of wood. LRT

Briggelholz, *n* - stick wood. KYG1878. **~ macht gut Feierholz.** Stick wood makes good kindling. LRT

Briggelsupp, *f* - wallop. (*facet*). *cf* **Schtreech.** KYG2160. **Yunger, du hoscht dich awwer in die ~ grickt.** Young man, you got yourself in for a real flogging. LRT

Britischer, *m, pl* **Britische** - British. = **Englischer.** KYG2269

Britsch, *f* - paddle. **Is dei ~ die Satt as Micke britsche kann wann sie hocke bleiwe?** Is your paddle the kind that can swat flies when they sit still? LRT. **Seller Buh hot die ~ uff sei Hinnerdeel grickt.** That boy got the paddle applied to his hind end. LRT,4/11/2000

Briwwi, *n* - outdoor toilet. = **Scheissheisli.** KYG2031 **Der Dokder Ezra Grummbeh in Mt. Zion, Leb. Co., PA hot en fancy ~ ghat. Die Wend innewennich waare babiert un die Holzarewet waar dunkel-rot aagschtriche.** Dr. Ezra Grumbine of Mt. Zion, Leb. Co.,

PA, had a fancy outdoor toilet. The inside walls were wallpapered and the wood work was painted dark red. LRT

Brobezeit, *f* - time of testing. KYG1989

brofitt'lich, *adv* - profitable. LRT

Brofitt', *m* - profit. **en ~ mache** - to return a profit. **Fer Bissniss im Gang halde, muss es en ~ mache.** For a business to keep going, it must make a profit. LRT

Brophet', *m* - prophet. LRT

browie're - to strive. **Ich will ~ sell geduh griege.** I want to try and get that done. LRT

Bruchbenner, *pl* - hernia trusses. **Mer heert nimmi viel vun ~.** One doesn't hear much about hernia trusses anymore. LRT

Bruchkarich, *m* - car used in quarrying stone. KYG1886. **En ~ is en notwennich Ding.** A quarry cart is a necessary thing. LRT

brummle, *pp* **gebrummelt** - to grumble in an undertone. KYG2098. **Er hot gebrummelt un ich hab ken Watt verschtanne.** He grumbled and I understood not a word. LRT

Brunne, *m* - shaft (in a well). **Wie dief is dei ~?** How deep is your well? LRT

Bruschtkann, *n* - sweetbread. **~ un Hann mache gut Esses.** Fried sweetbread and brain make good eating. LRT

brutze - to threaten rain. KYG2004. **Mir breiche Rege, es sett meh duh as wie yuscht ~.** We need rain, it should do more than just threaten to rain. LRT

Brutzeck, *n* - pouting corner. **Yungi, geh in dei ~!** Little girl, go in your pouting corner! LRT

brutzich, *adj* - pouty. **Wann du so ~ sei witt, gehscht in dei Brutzeck.** If you want to be that pouty, you go to your pouting corner. LRT

bsaufe, *refl, pp* **bsoffe** - to become intoxicated. LRT

bscheisse, *pp* **bschisse** - to swindle, cheat. **Er hot sei Bruder bschisse.** He cheated his brother. LRT

bschenke, *pp* **bschenkt** - to present. **Des hen sie mir bschenkt.** They presented this to me. LRT

bschlagge - to shoe a horse. **Lee, kannscht du der Nick un der Prince nuff an der Schmittschapp nemme fer sie ~ losse?** Lee, can you take Nick and Prince up to the smith shop to have them shod? LRT

bschmeisse - to throw at. KYG2009

bschpanne, *pp* **bschpannt** - to string (an instrument). **Er hot sei Geig bschpannt grickt.** He had his violin stringed. LRT

bschtennich, *adj* - steady. **Nau sei ~.** Now you be steady (consistent). LRT

bschtohle, *adj* - of a thieving nature. KYG1997. **Sell waar ihne ~ gewest.** That was taken from them in a thieving manner. LRT

bschur, *adv* - surely. **Ei ~, kannscht du sell duh.** Surely, you can do that. LRT

Bschwaerde, *pl* - trouble. *cf* **Elend, Lumperei, Mieh, Moleschde, Rupps, Sarig, Schtrapatze, Verleyyenheit, Yammer.** KYG2065

bschwaerlich, *adj* - troublesome. = **druwwelsam, hinnerlich, iwwerleschdich, verdriesslich.** KYG2065

bsetze - to trim a dress. KYG2061

bsinne, *refl, pp* **bsunne** - to think, come to a conclusion. KYG1998. **Er hot sich recht gschwind bsunne.** He decided very quickly. LRT. **Hoscht du dich bsunne?** Did you make up your mind (decide)? LRT. = **iwwerdenke**

Buch, *n* - book. **Dies ~ lest von so Sache.** This book tells of such things. KYG1981

Bucherdaal, *n* - ✪ Denver, Lanc. Co., PA.

Buckel, *m* - back. **sei ~ uff der anner Weg drehe** - to turn one's back the other way. KYG2078. **Er hot sei ~ uff uns gedreht.** He turned his back on us. LRT. **Er hot en grosser ~.** He can tolerate a lot. LRT

buckere, *pp* **gebuckert** - to pester. **Sie hen ihn gebuckert, bis er heemgange is.** They pestered him until he went home. LRT

bucklich, *adj* - **1** stoop-shouldered. KYG1889. **Selli aarem alt Fraa is awwer ~.** That poor old lady is really stoop-shouldered. LRT. **Sis bedauerlich wie ~ as seller alt Mann laaft.** It's pitiful how stoop-shouldered that old man walks. LRT. **2** uneven. = **dumbich, hopprich, hupperich, hulprich, ruppich, rupplich, unewe.** *cf* **ungraad.** KYG2101

buddere - **1** to butter. **Duscht du dei Brot ~?** Do you butter your bread? LRT. **Gleichscht du dei Weck ~?** Do you like to butter your buns? LRT. **2** to turn to butter. KYG2078

Budderziwwerli, *n, pl* **~n** - tub in which butter is worked. KYG2071. **Heidesdaags sin selli gleene ~n en latt Geld wert.** Now-a-days those little butter tubs are worth a lot of money. LRT

Buh, *m* - boy. **Seller ~ is en rechter Gnopp.** That boy is a real stout chap. LRT

Buhn, *f* - bean. **Du hoscht recht, er is ken hohli ~ waert.** You are correct, he is not worth a hollow bean. LRT,4/18/2000. = **Baahn, Bohn.**

Buhnegreitli, *n* - summer savory. LRT/Leb

Buhneschtengel, *m* - tall, thin person. **Er is en dinner, langer ~.** He is a thin, tall person (string bean). LRT/Leb. *cf* **Buhn, Buhneschtecke**

Bulleballe, *pl* - bull testicles.

Ich hab ee mol gebrodni ~ versucht un sell waar genunk. I once tasted fried bull testicles and that was enough. LRT

Bulledischdel, *f* - common thistle. *Cirsium lanceolatum L.* KYG2000

Bullekalb, *n* - term of contempt (for ignorant bully). KYG1987

Bulleschtall, *m* - stable for bull. **Unser ~ waar im Geilschtall.** Our bull stable was in the horse stable. LRT

Bullhund, *m* - **1** bull dog. LRT. **2** jaws of the stone crusher. KYG1887

Bumbe-schwengel, *m* - pump handle. **Der ~ is verbroche.** The pump handle is broken. LRT

Bumbernickelbrot, *n* - pumpernickel. **Sie saage ~ is en gsund Ding fer esse.** They say pumpernickel is a healthy thing to eat. LRT

bumpe - to thump (of the heart). = **gloppe.** KYG2011

Bumpebett, *n* - pump bed. **Mer will immer em sei ~ in gut Fix halde, weil mer niemand in der Brunne falle losse will.** One wants to keep his pump floor in good condition, because one doesn't want anyone to fall into the well. LRT

Bumpedreeg, *pl* - pump troughs. **~ sin hendich fer Kiwwel neischtelle, wann mer sie voll Wasser bumpe will.** Pump troughs are handy to set buckets in, when one wants to pump them full of water. LRT

Bumpemacher, *m* - **1** pump

maker. **2** pump repairman. **Mei Grossdaadi waar en ~.** My grandfather was a pump repairman. LRT

Bumpeschwengel, *m* - pump handle. LRT

Bumphaus, *n* - pump house. **Datt drunne uff die alt Bauerei waar unser ~, aa unser Millichhaus.** Down there on the old farm our pump house was also our milk house. LRT

Buschland, *n* - woodland. **Ihre Bauerei hot en latt ~.** Their farm has a lot of woodland. = **Holzland.** LRT,4/11/2000

Buschmick, *f, pl* ~e - striped horsefly. **~e sin Blutsuckler.** Horseflies are bloodsuckers. LRT

Buschpaedli, *n* - path through the woods. KYG2242. **Sell ~ is baut en Meil lang.** That path through the woods is about a mile long. LRT/Leb,4/11/2000. = **Buschpaedelche, Buschwegel**

Buschschtick, *n* - piece of land in a wooded area. **Sell ~ is baut zwee Acker gross.** That wooded piece of land is about two acres in size. LRT,4/11/2000

Buschweg, *m* - road through the woods. **Wann mer der ~ nemmt, is es viel naecher.** If one takes the road through the woods, the drive is much shorter. LRT,4/11/2000

butze - to clean. **Baem ~** - to trim trees. KYG2061. **Die Weibsleit duhne's Haus ~ harebschts un friehyaahrs.** The women clean the house in the fall and in the spring. LRT

butzich, *adj* - stringy (of milk). **Sellre Kuh ihre Millich kann net noch Hershey geh, weil sie ~ is.** That cow's milk can not go to Hershey because it is stringy. LRT

Buweschenkel, *pl* - pie made of left-over dough. LRT

Buweschmacker, *m* - tomboy. *cf* **wilder Hummel.** KYG2033

Buweschtofft, *n* - mischievous boys. **des ~** - these naughty boys. KYG1995. **Des ~ sedde mir schtoppe.** We should stop this tomfoolery. LRT. **~ is nix Neies; sie warre mol ee Daag Mannsleit.** Mischievous boys are nothing new; one day they will be men. LRT

Buweschtreech, *pl* - boyish pranks. **Wie sie gheert hot vun selle ~, hot sie sich ganz ver-gnoddelt.** When she heard of those boyish pranks, she became all entangled in frustration. LRT, 4/11/2000

Buwli, *n* - little boy. LRT

Daag, *m, pl* ~, ~e - day. **die letschdi Paar ~e** - the last few days. KYG1992. **Die letschde Paar ~e hot's welterlich geregert.** The last few days it rained terribly. LRT. **heit iwwer varzeh ~** - two weeks from today. KYG2085. **Heit iwwer acht ~ griege mir Bsuch.** A week from today, we are getting visitors. LRT

Daagdieb, *m, pl* -**diewe** - truant. KYG2067

daagenacht, *adv* - continually, day and night. **Er schafft ~.** He works day and night. LRT. **Fer**

achtgewwe uff gleeni Kinner ~, is so'n ordlich G(e)schleef. Caring for small children day and night is quite a drawn-out job. LRT,4/11/2000

daagerdrei, *adv* - three days or so. KYG2004

daaghell, *adj* - daylight. **Mit unsere Arewet kenne mir besser Zeit mache, wann's mol ~ is.** We can make better time with our work once it's daylight. LRT

Daaglennerhaus, *n* - tenant house. KYG1984. **Es ~ brauch en nei Dach.** The tenant house needs a new roof. LRT

Daagloch, *n* - small opening in a wall. KYG2160

Daagwarick, *n* - task. *cf* **Gscheft, Unnernemming.** KYG1972

daag(e)weis, *adv* - a day now and then. **Ich schaff so ~.** I work a day now and then. LRT. *cf* **daagenacht.** KYG1993

daarum, *adv* - therefor. KYG1995. **Ich geb nix ~.** I don't care for this. LRT

Daawid, *m* - David. **Mir hen en Suh, as ~ heest.** We have a son named David. LRT,4/21/2000

Dachkandel, *m, pl* ~ - rain spout. **Die ~ sin verschtoppt mit Schpatzeneschder.** The rain spouts are clogged (shut) with sparrows' nests. LRT

Dachlaade, *m, pl* -laede - hatchway. **Die -laede breiche neie Fenschderscheiwe.** The hatchway shutters need new

window panes. LRT

Dachschtroh, *n* - thatch. *cf* **Schtrohdach.** KYG1992. **Im Yaahr 1982 hab ich un die Fraa Schtrohdecher gsehne driwwe in Holland.** In the year 1982, my wife and I saw straw thatched roofs in Holland. LRT

dadde, *adv* - there (Cbs,Cr,NLr,SELn,NWSl,SEYk ,Elh). = **datt** (elsewhere) *cf* **anne, datt hie, hie, da, daar.** KYG1994

Daddeldaub, *f* - turtledove. = **Reggevoggel.** KYG2080. **Selli ~ hot ihre Daubert weckgschosse grickt.** That turtledove had her male mate shot away from her. LRT

Daddeldaubrich, *m* - male turtledove. KYG2080. = **Daubert.** LRT

daer, *m,* **des,** *n,* **die,** *f, demon pron* - this. **Des is der Mann.** This is the man. **des un sell -** this and that. *cf* **des do, des, die, dies.** KYG1999. **~ Mann graad do will ich bezaahle.** This man right here I want to pay (or, I want to pay this man right here). LRT

daher, *adv* - for that reason. KYG1991

Damf, *m* - steam. **Guck mol wie der ~ vun Rewwer kummt.** Look how the steam is coming from the river. LRT

Dank, *m* - thanks. **Nee, ich saag ~.** Thanks, but no thanks. **Wann mer's yuscht wisse daede, alles sett Gott sei ~ sei.** If we only knew it, everything should be thanks to God. LRT. **~ gewwe -**

to give thanks. **~ saage -** to offer thanks. **epper ~ schuldich sei -** to owe someone thanks. KYG1991. = **Denki, Denki aa.** LRT/ Leb. Co.

dankbaar, *adj* - thankful. KYG1990. **Mir sin arig ~ zu eich fer alles as dir geduh hett fer uns.** We are very thankful for everything that you did for us. LRT **Mit all selli Sache was sie uns gewwe hen, waare mir gross dankbaar.** With all those things they gave us, we just had to be thankful. LRT

Dankbaarkeit, *f* - thankfulness. KYG1990

Dankbreddich, *f* - Thanksgiving sermon. KYG1991

Dankdaag, *m* - Thanksgiving Day. = **Betdaag, Dankesdaag, Danksaagungsdaag.** KYG1991. = **Senksgifing.** LRT

Dankdaagzeit, *f* - Thanksgiving time. KYG1991

dankeswaert, *adv* - worth thanking for. KYG1991

Dankfescht, *n* - Thanksgiving feast day. KYG1991

Dankgebet, *n* - prayer of thanks. KYG1991

Danki! - 1 Thank you! **~ saage -** to reply: No thanks! = **Saddi! ~ schee! Ich bedank mich!** I thank you. KYG1990. **2** to reply: No thanks! KYG1991. = **Denki!** LRT/ Leb. Co.

danklos, *adj* - thankless. =

undankbaar, net dankbaar. KYG1991

Danksdaagsmiddaag, *m* - Thanksgiving dinner. KYG1991

Danksdaagwelschhaahne, *m* - Thanksgiving turkey. KYG1991

dann un datt, *adv* - then and there. KYG1993

Dann¹, *n,f* - ton. KYG2033. **Ya, en ~ is 2000 Pund.** Yes, a ton is 2000 pounds. LRT. = **Dunn**

Dann², *f, pl* ~e - thorn. **~ im Aag** - thorn in the eye. **~ im Fleesch** - thorn in the flesh. KYG2001. **Wann du schtill hebscht, nemm ich dir selli ~ aus d'Hand.** If you hold still, I'll take that thorn out of your hand. LRT

Dannefens, *f* - thicket fence. = **Heckefens.** KYG1996

Danneschpell, *f* - thorn of hawthorn. KYG2001

Danneschtock, *m, pl* -schteck - thorn bush. KYG2001. **Ich hass Haase yaage wu die -schteck dick sin.** I hate to hunt rabbits where the thorn bushes are thick. LRT

dannet wann, *adv* - now and then. = **hie un widder.** KYG1993. = **dann un wann.** LRT/ Leb. Co.

dannich, *adj* - thorny, prickly. KYG2001. **Rose waere schenner, wann wie net so ~ waere.** Roses would be nicer if they weren't so prickly (thorny). LRT. = **schtachlich**

dappe - to walk along unsurely.

KYG2113. **Deel vun denne Haschschitz ~ draus in d'Bariye rum bis sie schier verfrore sin.** Some of these deer hunters traipse around in the mountains until they are almost frozen to death. LRT

Dappert - naegscht am ~ - in the nick of time. KYG2018

dappich, *adj* - clumsy, ungainly. KYG2103. **Ich brauch epper as net ~ is fer helfe des Glaas neiduh.** I need someone who is not clumsy to help put this glass in. LRT. **Du bischt awwer en ~er Mensch!** My, but you're a clumsy fellow! LRT

Dappriggel, *m* - <*Engl* top rail. KYG2038

Daremel, *m* - dizziness. **Sei ~ verschreckt em wennich.** His dizziness scares one a bit. LRT

daremlich, *adj* - dizzy. **Zu viel Dramm macht en Mensch ~.** Too much whiskey makes a person dizzy. LRT

darich, *adj* - thorough. = **dichdich, grindlich, darichaus, ~ un ~.** KYG2001

darich un darich, *adv* - through and through. = **darich eweck, gedichdich.** KYG2008. **Ich bin kalt ~.** I am cold (chilled) through and through. **~ hen die Sei gut zugenumme des Yaahr.** On average the hogs grew well all this year. LRT

darich, *prep* - through. **~ all des** - through all this. **~ all die Schtadt** - through all the city. KYG2008. **Die Peife sin zu gfrore un des waar all des d'~ as die Fannes ken Eel ghat**

hot. The pipes froze shut all because the furnace had no fuel oil. LRT. **Sie hen ~'s ganz Haus gschtewwert un hen nix aus em Weg gfunne.** They searched throughout the whole house and found nothing unusual. LRT

darichaus, *adv* - throughout. = **daricheweck.** KYG2009

darichblettre - to turn the pages of a book. **Eb mer die Guckbaxe ghat hot, hot mer die Sears Catalogs ghat fer ~.** Before we had TV, we had the Sears Catalogs to page through. LRT

darichdenke, *pp* **darichgedenkt** - to think through. KYG1998. **Nochdem as sie alles darichgedenkt hen, hen sie ausgemacht, sie daede die Bauerei kaafe.** After they thought everything through, they decided to buy the farm. LRT

darichdrickle, *pp* **darichgedrickelt** - to dry thoroughly. KYG2001. **Die Wesch is all gut darichgedrickelt.** The wash is all dried thoroughly. LRT

daricheweck, *adv* - throughout. **~ hen die Sei gut zugenumme des Yaahr.** On average the hogs grew well this year. LRT

darichkoche, *pp* **darichgekocht** - to cook thoroughly. **Sell Rinsfleesch is net darichgekocht.** That beef is not thoroughly cooked. LRT

darichlaafe, *pp* **darichgeloffe** - to walk through. KYG2159. **Er is darichgeloffe, un's hot niemand gewisst wie er's**

geduh grickt hot. He walked through and no one knew how he did it. LRT. **2** to run through (of liquids). **Selli Grick laaft graad datt middes darich der Busch nunner.** That creek runs right down through the middle of the woods. LRT

darichlese, *pp* **darichgelese -** to read through. **Er hot die Biewel schund paarmol darichgelese.** He has read the Bible through several times. **Seller Buh hot sell ganze Buch darichgelese in yuscht paar Daag.** That boy read through the whole book in just a few days. LRT

darichnanner¹, *adv* - confused, mixed up. **Wann der alt Mann gschwetzt hot, waare sei Gedanke alles ~.** When the old man spoke, his thoughts were all confused (mixed up). **Was is Neies? Es waar un sis aa noch alles ~.** What is new? The situation was and still is all mixed up. LRT

darichnanner², *adj* - topsy-turvy. **~ mache -** to turn topsy-turvy. **= ~ wiehle. = drunnerscht-driwwerscht, drunner-un-driwwer, unnerscht-un-ewwerscht, verkehrt.** KYG2038. **Alles waar so ~, mer hot nix verschtanne.** Everything is so topsy-turvy, nothing was understandable. LRT

darichnannermache - to turn topsy-turvy. KYG2078. **Es hen so viel Leit an dem Wese gschafft ghat, bis sie alles darichnannergemacht ghat hen.** There were so many that worked on this matter until everything was made a total confusion. LRT. **= -wiehle,**

darichwiehle

darichnemme, *pp* **darichgenumme -** to take through (the paces). **Sie hen ihn darich die Hell genumme.** They took him through hell. LRT. **= iwwer die Kohle nemme.** LRT/Leb

darichreide, *pp* **darichgeridde -** to ride through. **Sie is darich der Rege geridde.** She rode through the rain. LRT

darichreisse, *pp* **darichgerisse -** to tear in two. KYG2085. **Der Hund hot sei Kett darichgerisse.** The dog tore his chain in two. LRT

darichrutsche, *pp* **darichgerutscht -** to wear through by rubbing. **Yunger, hoscht du widder dei Hosse darichgerutscht?** Young man, did you wear your pants through again? LRT

darichschaffe, *refl* - to work one's way through. **Loss sell Buwli sich darich selli Peif schaffe.** Let that little boy work his way through that pipe. LRT

darichschaffe, *pp* **darichgschafft -** to work through. KYG2245. **Ya, sell waar en verhunst Wese, awwer mir hen's darichgschafft grickt.** That was a botched affair, but we worked through it. LRT,4/11/2000

darichschaudre - to thrill. KYG2007

darichscheine, *pp* **darichgscheint -** to shine through. **Die Sunn hot schee darich die Schtubb gscheint.**

The sun shone nicely through the room. LRT

darichschiesse - to shoot through. **Die Oschderblumme sin darich der Schnee ruff zu schiesse kumme.** The Easter flowers came shooting up through the snow. LRT

darichschiewe - to push through. **Es Loch is zu glee, mer kann nix ~.** The hole is too small, one can't push anything through it. LRT

darichschneide, *pp* **darichgschnidde -** to cut in two. KYG2085. **Sie hot des Schtick Ledder darichgschnidde.** She cut this piece of leather in two. LRT

darichschnuffle, *pp* **darichgschnuffelt -** to snoop through, rummage through. **Well, du hoscht darichgschnuffelt, hoscht eppes gfunne?** Well, you snooped through, did you find anything? LRT. **Sis yuscht net schee fer darich alles schnuffle.** It just isn't nice to rummage through everything. LRT

darichschteche - to puncture. **Wann mer'n Nodel darich's Ledder schtecht, no hot mer ewwe en Loch neigemacht.** When one sticks a needle through the leather, then one has made a hole in it. LRT

darichschtewwere, *pp* **darichgschtewwert -** to search every part. **Sie hen iwwerall darichgschtewwert un hen nix gfunne.** They searched everywhere and found nothing. LRT

darichsehne - to see through. **Sellem Buh sei Schularewet kann ich gaar net ~.** I just can't see through that boy's schoolwork (homework). LRT

darichseihe - to strain through. **Was grewwer is wie Wasser un Brieh kann mer net ~.** What is coarser than water and juice cannot be strained through. LRT

darichsuche - to search through. **Du kannscht selli Schupplaad ~, awwer ich saag dir, es is ken Geld datt.** You can search through that drawer, but I tell you, there is no money there. LRT

darichwiehle, *pp* **darichgewiehlt** - to rummage through. **Ich hab darich alles gewiehlt, un was ich am suche waar, waar net datt.** I rummaged through everything and what I was looking for, was not there. LRT

darichziehe, *pp* **is darichgezoge** - to get well again. **Er waar arig grank, awwer er is verhafdich darichgezoge.** He was very ill, but indeed he is well again. LRT

darichzucke - to twitch. *cf* **verzucke, zucke, zwicke.** KYG2084

Darichzug, *m, pl* **-zieg** - girder, main beam. **Der ~ in unserem Keller is en eechner Block.** The main girder(beam) in our cellar is an oak log. LRT. **Seller ~ is awwer schtandhaft.** That main beam is indeed sturdy. LRT

darigle - to reel, stagger. **Er darigelt do rum wie en**

Gsoffner. He staggers around here like a drunk. LRT

Darrbabier, *n* - tar paper. **Dir Mannsleit, kennt dir sell ~ uffreisse?** You men, can you tear up that tar paper (from the roof)? LRT,4/18/2000

Darrbeidel, *m* - tar keg. = **Darrfass, Darrlodel, Darrlokel, Darryokel.** KYG1971

Darrbendel, *m* - tarred twine. KYG2083. **Die Meis gleiche net an ~ kaue.** The mice do not like to chew on tarred twine. LRT

darre, *pp* **gedarrt** - **1** to dry (fruit). **2** to tar a road. **Sie hen der Weg gedarrt.** They tarred the road. LRT. **epper ~ un feddere** - to tar and feather someone. KYG1970. **Der Wegmeeschder hot gholfe der Weg ~ heit.** The township (road) supervisor helped to tar the road today. LRT

Darrebedien, *m* - turpentine. **Veneedischer ~** - Venice turpentine. KYG2080. **Langi Yaahre zerick hen deel Leit en Grie Blaschder gemacht, un ~ waar eens vun die Sache as sie neigeduh hen.** Many years ago some people made a green salve and turpentine was one of the ingredients. LRT

Darrebedienboddel, *f, pl* **~e** - turpentine bottle. KYG2080. **~e sin nix abaddichs.** Turpentine bottles are nothing special. LRT

darrebediene - to apply turpentine. **en Hund ~** - to apply turpentine to a dog's posterior. KYG2080

Darrfass, *m, pl* **-fesser** - tar keg. **Die -fesser sin zu glee.** The tar kegs are too small. LRT

Darrschtrick, *m* - tar rope. KYG1971

Darrseef, *f* - tar soap. KYG1971

Darrwagge, *m* - wagon greased with tar. KYG1970

Dasch, *f* - the core of a cabbage head. LRT

daschderich, *adj* (Dn,Nd) - thirsty. = **daschdich** (elsewhere). KYG1999

daschdich, *adj* - thirsty. **Wann du ~ bischt, settscht du bissel Genswei (Wasser) drinke.** If you are thirsty, you should drink some goose wine (water). LRT. = **daschderich**

Dascht, *m* - thirst. **~ leide** - to suffer from thirst. KYG1999. **Er hot e grosser ~ fer Schnaps.** He has quite a thirst for whiskey. LRT

Daschthunger, *m* - extreme thirst. **Ich hab ~.** I am extremely thirsty. KYG1999

datt nunner, *adv* - down there. *cf* **datt darich nunner, datt darich runner (hie).** KYG1994. **Wann du ~ gehscht, vergess net selli Fuderseck zerick bringe.** If you go back down there, don't forget to bring those feed sacks back. LRT

datt draa hie, *adv* - along there. = **datt draa naus, datt her.** KYG1994

datt draa naus, *adv* - along there. **Sie sin datt am Barig**

draa naus gange bis sie deel Hasch gfunne hen. They went out along the mountain until they found some deer. LRT. = **datt draa hie, datt her**

datt naus, *adv* - out there. KYG1994

datt (hie) newe, *adv* - along the side there. KYG1994. **~ am Haus hen sie scheeni Blumme.** There at the side of the house they have pretty flowers. LRT

datt zerick, *adj* - back there. KYG1994. **~ hinnich d'Dier waar en grossi dodi Ratt.** Back there behind the door was a big dead rat. LRT

datt, *adv* - elsewhere. **Schtell der Schtuhl ~ anne.** Set the chair there. LRT

datt-darich, *adv* - through there. KYG2008. **~ nunner (runner)** - down through there. **~ nei** - in through there. = **~ rei. ~ naus** - out through there. = **~ raus. ~ niwwer** - over through there. KYG2009. **~'s Gross Daal seht mer as sie schund en latt Hoi am mache sin.** Throughout the Big Valley, one sees that already they are making a lot of hay. LRT

dattdarich nei, *adv* - in through there. = **datt darich rei.** KYG1994. **~ gehe die Schtadt waar der Weg noch arig zugeblose.** In through there toward town, the road was still badly blown shut (with snow). LRT

dattdarichnuff, *adv* - up through there. KYG2117. **Wann mer ~ faahrt, seht mer en latt Hasch.** If one drives up through

there, one sees a lot of deer. LRT

dattdebei, *adv* - thereby. KYG1994. **Sie hen alles ~ ghat.** They had everything included there. LRT

dattdedarich, *adv* - therefore. **Der Mann un sei Aldi hen en Fecht ghat un ~ hot sie ihn verlosse.** The husband and his wife had a spat and therefore she left him. LRT

dattdegehe, *adv* - against that. KYG1992. **Fer die Kinner die Freiheit gewwe fer eenich ariyets in die Schul geh, datt bin ich ~.** I oppose giving the children the freedom to attend school anywhere. LRT

dattdehinner, *adv* - behind that, back of that. KYG1992. **Fer Andacht hawwe un die Biewel lese in unser Schule, datt bin ich dehinner.** I support having devotions and reading the Bible in our schools. LRT

dattdevun, *adv* - from that. KYG1992. **Sell is Seifleesch un Sauergraut, gell? Ich hett gern ~.** That's pork and sauerkraut, isn't it? I'd like some of that. LRT

dattdraanuff, *adv* - up along there. KYG2116. **Selli Giftranke sin datt am Baam draanuff gegraddelt.** Those poison (ivy) vines grew up along the tree. LRT

dattdrin, *adv* - therein. KYG1995. **Sie halde die Vendu ~ im Haus.** They are holding the sale there in the house. LRT. **~ in d'Schtubb sin paar Schtiel.** In there in the room are a few

chairs. LRT. *cf* **dattnei**

dattdrowwe, *adv* - up there. = **dattdruff, dattnuff, datthowwe.** KYG2117. **~ am Kandel henke Eiszappe.** Up there are icicles hanging from the spouting. LRT

dattdruff', *adv* - thereupon. = **graad-eweck.** KYG1995

dattdrum, *adv* - thereabout. = **dattrum.** KYG1994

dattdrunne(r), *adv* - under that, thereunder. KYG2095. **~ is eppes Dodes, mer kann's rieche.** Under there is something dead, one can smell it. LRT. **~ in Florida griege sie ganz wennich Schnee.** Down there in Florida, they get very little snow. LRT

datthie, *adv* - thence. **~ schleppe** - to drag thence. = **vun dann.** KYG1993. **Bis ~ hen sie genunk Geld ghat.** To that point they had enough money. LRT

datthinnrizus, *adv* - back in that direction. KYG1991. **~ gehe Glappbordschteddel is en gross Hiwwelfeld.** Back in that direction towards Clapboardstown, there is a big field on a hill. LRT

dattnauszus, *adv* - out in that direction. KYG1991. **~ gehe die Scheier is Ungraut as rausgeroppt sei sett.** Out in that direction toward the barn are some weeds that ought to be pulled out. LRT. **Der Wind hot hatt geblose ~.** The wind blew hard out in that direction. LRT

dattnei, *adv* - thereinto.

KYG1995

dattnuffzus, *adv* - up in that direction. KYG2116. **~ gehe Harrisbarig seht mer en latt neie Heiser.** Up there towards Harrisburg, one can see a lot of new houses. LRT

dattrei, *adv* - from that direction. KYG1991. **Seid dir datt darich selli Dier reikumme?** Did you come in through that door? **Hett dir die Kieh gsehne wie dir ~ kumme seid?** Did you see the cows when you came in from that direction? LRT

dattreizus, *adv* - in that direction. KYG1991. **Hett dir die Kieh gsehne wie dir ~ kumme seid?** Did you see the cows when you came in from that direction? LRT

dattruffzus, *adv* - up that way. KYG2117

dattvarrizus, *adv* - up front there. KYG2116. **Yuscht ~ vun sellem gleene Schteddel is die greescht Bauerei im ganze Kaundi.** Just in front of that little town is the largest farm in the whole county. LRT

dattzu, *adv* - thereto. = **dezu.** KYG1995

Daume, *m* - thumb. **~ suckle** - to suck one's thumb. **~ schpiele** - to twiddle the thumbs. = **schwillere.** KYG2010. **Seller glee Buh schiebt sei ewwerschdi Zaeh raus mit seim ~ suckle.** That little boy will cause his upper teeth to protrude with his thumb sucking. LRT

Daumenaggel, *m* - thumbnail. KYG2011. **Er muss sich uff sei Daume gschlagge hawwe, sei ~ is ganz schwatz.** He must have hammered his thumb, his thumbnail is all black. LRT

Daumeschraub, *f* - thumbscrew. KYG2011

daumesdick, *adj* - thick as a thumb. KYG1996

Daumesuckler, *m* - thumb-sucking child. KYG2011

Daumling, *m* - **1** covering to protect the thumb. KYG2010. **2** thumbstall. = **Deimling.** KYG2011

Dauschper, *m* - twilight. **halwer ~** - half twilight. = **Demmering, Duschper, Duschder, Oweddunkel.** KYG2082

dausendfach, *adv* - thousand-fold. KYG2003. **Die Taxe waare en ~ zu hoch.** The taxes were too high by a thousand fold. LRT

Dausendfiessiger, *m* - milliped. **Guck mol datt, datt is widder en ~ im Baadzuwwer.** Look there, there is a milliped in the bathtub again. LRT

dausendmol, *adv* - 1,000 times. *cf* **dausendewichmol.** KYG2002. **Sie waare denk en ~ in die Karich gange bis sie gewisst hen, was Gnaade sin.** I think they went to church a thousand times before they knew what Grace is. LRT

Dauwegropp, *m* - pigeon's crop. **Die Dauwe duhne ihre Yunge fiedere mit Millich aus**

ihrem Gropp. The pigeons feed their young with milk from their crop. LRT

Dauwemillich, *f* - "pigeon's milk." LRT

Dauwli, *n* - young pigeon. LRT/Leb.Co.

Daxi, *m* - "Shorty." **Mer muss lache iwwer seller glee ~.** One must laugh at that little "shorty." LRT

daxich, *adj* - stooped. *cf* **gedaucht, grummbucklich.** KYG1889

da´!, *exclam.* - there! = **nard!** *cf* **~ hoschdes!** There, take it! There, you have it! KYG1994

debei, *adv* - among that, along with that, by that. KYG1992. **Ee doder Hund waar genunk, awwer no noch ~ waare aa zwee dodi Katze.** One dead dog was enough, but along with that there were two dead cats. LRT

debei´bleiwe - to stick to. = **dezuschticke, henke, schticke, zuschticke.** KYG1878. **Du kannscht ~ wann du witt.** You can stick to it if you want to. LRT

debei´schteh, *pp* **debeigschtanne** - to stand up for one's contentions. **Wann sie net debeigschtanne hedde, dann waer alles futsch gange.** If they had not stood by, everything would have failed. LRT

decke, *pp* **gedeckt** - **1** to top. KYG2037. **Mir hen der Kuche gedeckt mit "icing."** We topped the cake with icing. LRT. **2** to

38

thatch. KYG1992. **Es Dach decke mit nei-ie Schindle waar notwennich.** Covering the roof with new shingles was necessary. LRT

Deckelglaas, *n* - tankard. = **Deckelkann, Henkeglaas.** KYG1967

Decker, *m, pl* ~ - roofer. **Die Arewet as die ~ mache is bissel gfaehrlich.** The work that the roofers do is a bit dangerous. LRT

deheem, *adv* - at home. **sich ~ mache** - to make oneself at home. **Kummt rei un macht eich ~.** Come in and make yourselves at home. LRT

Deichli, *n* - *dim* of **Deich.** a little ravine. LRT/Leb.Co.

Deihenker, *m* - deuce. **Der ~ is los!** There is the devil to pay! KYG1994. **Was der ~ is los do?** What the deuce goes on here? LRT

deimele - to press with the thumb. KYG2010

deiner, *m,* **dei (deine),** *n,* **deini,** *f, poss pron.* - thine. KYG1997. **Waar selli Schrotflint deini?** Was that shotgun yours? LRT

deines gleiche, *adv* - such as you. **Er hot gsaat zu ihre, "Es is niemand ~!"** He said to her, "There is no one such as you!" LRT,4/21/2000

Deitsch, *adj* - German. **Kannscht du ~ schwetze?** Can you speak German? LRT. **Ich bin ~ gebore.** I have a German ancestry. LRT,4/21/2000. **Deitschi Nuss** = English walnut.

= **Deitschi Walniss.** KYG2161

Deitschland, *n* - Germany. **Im Yaahr 1982 waare die Fraa un ich im alde Land.** In 1982 my wife and I were in the old country, Germany. LRT. 4/21/2000. = **es alde Land**

Deiwel, *m* - tempter. *cf* **Vordraager, Verfiehrer, Versucher.** KYG1983. **Der ~ gebt ewwe net uff.** The devil never quits. LRT

deiwelaanisch, *adv* - devilishly. **~ bees** - terribly angry. KYG1988. **Buwe, schickt eich net so ~ aa.** Boys, don't act so devilishly. LRT. = **deiwelisch**

Deiwelsschtreech, *pl* - devilish pranks. **Selli Yunge sin immer am ~ abziehe.** These boys are always pulling off some devilish pranks. LRT

deiwelswiescht, *adj* - ugly as the devil. KYG2088

Deixel, *m* - 1 wagon tongue. **2** deuce. **Was der ~ geht aa do?** What the deuce (heck) is going on here? LRT

Deixelnaggel, *m* - thill pin. KYG1997

delkich, *adj* - 1 soggy. **2** doughy. **Die Kichlin hette laenger gebacke sei selle, sie sin noch ~.** The cookies should have been baked longer, they are still a bit doughy. LRT

Deller, *m* - plate. **zinner ~** - tin-plate. KYG2023. **Wann die ~ gewesche sin, no sin mir faddich uffschpiele.** When the plates are washed, the dish washing is finished. LRT

demariye, *adv* - this morning. = **den Mariye.** KYG2000. **~ sin mir frieh uffgschtanne.** This morning we got out of bed (aroused) early. LRT

demit′, *adv* - therewith. KYG1995

Demmedifeld, *n* - timothy field. KYG2021. **Sell ~ macht gut Geils Hoi.** That timothy field produces good horse hay. LRT

Demmedisume, *m* - timothy seed. = **Demmedisaame.** KYG2021. **~ is net recht deier.** Timothy seed is not real expensive. LRT

demmid′daag, *adv* - today (at) noon. KYG2030. **~ hen mir Oischdersupp fer esse.** This noon we have oyster stew to eat. LRT

Demmidihoi, *n* - timothy hay. = **Feldhoi, Geilshoi.** KYG2021

dene′wekumme, *pp* ~ - to miss out (an opportunity). **Er hot gemehnt, er daed reich warre, awwer er is ~.** He thought he would become rich, but he missed his chance. LRT

dengle - to sharpen a scythe (by hammering). **Deitschi Sense dutt mer ~ uff em Dengelschtock.** German scythes are sharpened by hammering them on the **Dengelstock,** *qv.* LRT

denkbaar, *adj* - thinkable. KYG1998. **Sell is gaar net ~.** That is totally unthinkable. LRT

denke - to think. **~ an** - to think of, about. **Denk an sell!** Think about that! **Ich hett sell ~ selle.** I might have thought of that. **Ich daed so ~.** I would think so. **meim Weg zu ~** - according to the way I think. **Mir sedde ~.** We ought to think. KYG1998. **Wann so Sache aa gsehne, wees mer net was mer ~ sett.** When such things happen, one doesn't know what to think. LRT. **Well, ich denk awwer aa, sell is so!** Well, I'm sure that is so! LRT. *cf* **aahne**

Denker, *m* - thinker. KYG1998

denneweg, *adv* - after this fashion. KYG2000. **Yunger, guck mol do, mer dutt des ~.** Young man, look here once, one does this in this way. LRT

denno´, *adv* - **1** thereafter. = **daarnoch, dart dennoch, dennoch, dennort, vun sellem ab.** KYG1994. **2** according to this. = **dennooch.** KYG1999

dennoch´, *adv* - thereafter. **glei ~** - shortly thereafter. = **katz druff.** KYG1994. **Glei ~ as mir datt drunne waare is ihre Scheier nunnergebrennt.** Soon after we were down there, their barn burnt down. LRT

dennoot´, *adv* - after that. = **no, not, noot, dennort, nochdem, derno, no dennoch.** KYG1992. = **nochdehand.** LRT

dennowed, *adv* - this evening. KYG2000. **Yunger, ~ bleibscht du deheem!** Young man, this evening you are staying home! LRT

Dennwand, *f* - boarded-up sides of the thrashing floor. KYG2006. **Die ~ is zu hoch fer die Yunge driwwer tschumpe.** The boarded-up sides of the

threshing floor are too high for the youngsters to jump over. LRT

desde - the more. **De mehner Leit as in unser Karich kumme, ~ besser.** The more people that come to our church the better. LRT

desdebesser, *adv* - so much the better. **wie greesser ~** - the bigger the better. KYG1992. **D'meh Geld as sie uns gewwe, ~.** The more money they give us, so much the better. LRT. = **de greesser de besser**

desgleiches, *adv* - the likes. KYG1992

desmol, *adv* - this time. = **dessemol.** *cf* **sellemol.** KYG2000

dessemol, *adv* - this time. KYG2019. **Yunger, ~ grickscht du Schlaeg.** Young man, this time you are getting a whipping. LRT. **~ waar alli-epper eiglaade.** This time everyone was invited. LRT. = **desmol**

desweh´e, *adv* - therefore, on that account, for that reason. KYG1991. **Was sett mer duh ~?** What should one do about it? LRT. = **dewehe**

detschle - to pat. **Ich gleich immer gleeni Kinner bissel ~.** I always like to pat little children a bit. LRT

devun´kumme, *pp* **is ~** - to survive. **Sie waar arig grank, awwer sie kummt widderdevun.** She was very sick, but she'll survive. LRT

devun´nemme - to take away

from. KYG1962. **Sie hen gwisst wie Sache ~, so as niemand's sehne hot kenne.** They knew how to take things away, so that it was not detected. LRT

devun´, *adv* - about, of that. KYG1992. **Ich will nix heere ~.** I don't want to hear anything about it. LRT. **Ich hab nix gewisst ~.** I knew nothing about it. LRT

devun´geh, *pp* **is devunange** - to walk off. KYG2158. **Wie er sell gsehne hot, is er devunange.** When he saw that, he walked away. LRT

dewaert´, *adv* - worth it. **Es waar schier net ~, as mir gange waare.** It was hardly worth it that we had gone. LRT,4/18/2000

dewed´derkumme, *pp* **is ~** - to run into a wall. KYG2160. **Allimol as er datt ~ is, hot er gegrische.** Every time he came up against it, he screamed. LRT

dexle - to trim down. KYG2062

dezu´duh - to put in addition, add to. **Wann ich Hinkel- un Welschkannsupp mach, gleich ich bissel Gnowwlichpulwer ~.** When I make chicken corn soup, I like to add a little garlic powder. LRT. **Kannscht du noch bissel Geld do ~?** Can you add a little money to this sum? LRT. **Wann sie noch en hunnert Daaler ~ kennde, sell daed helfe.** If they could add another 100 dollars, that would help. LRT

dezu´kumme, *pp* **is ~** - to arrive unexpectedly. KYG2101. **Zu dem Geld is noch $500 ~.** To

40

this fund came $500 unexpectedly. LRT

dezu′rechle - to include, add into. LRT

dezu′, *adv* - to that. KYG1992

dezu′schtecke - to stick to it. **Du muscht ~ bis die Arewet faddich is.** You must stick to it until the work is finished. LRT

dezwi′sche-darich, *adv* - through the midst of it. KYG2008. **Die Katz is datt ~ gschprunge.** The cat ran through the midst of it. LRT

Dicher, *m* - tiger. KYG2016

Dicherlilye, *f* - tiger lily. = **Kaisergrone, scheckichi Lilye.** KYG2016

dick, *adj* - thick. = **dicht, dicklich.** KYG1995. **darich ~ un dinn** - through thick and thin. **~ mache** - to thicken. **~er mache** - to make thicker. **~ warre** - to become thick. **Mach's ~er.** Add thickening (in a recipe). KYG1996. **Sell Welschkann is zu ~ geblanzt.** That corn is planted too thickly. LRT

Dickhals, *m* - swelling of the throat. KYG2008

dickhaudich, *adj* - thick-skinned. = **dickheidich.** KYG1996

Dickicht, *n* - thicket. = **Heck, Heckes.** *cf* **Hasch-schtall.** KYG1996

Dickimillich, *f* - thick or fermented milk. **~ is besser fer mich.** Thick milk is better for

me. LRT

Dicking, *f* - thickness. KYG1996. **Die ~ vun sellem Deppich is graad recht fer den Winder.** The thickness of that quilt is just right for this winter. LRT

dickkeppich, *adj* - self-willed, blockheaded. KYG1996. '**Die Ludderisch sin ~ un die Reformierde sin leffelverschmiert.**' 'The Lutherans are self-willed and the Reformed are a bit confused [facetious saying used in Lebanon County, PA].' LRT. **Seller alt Gees is immer so ~.** That old goat is always so blockheaded. LRT

Dickkopp, *m* - blockhead. KYG1996. **Du witt ken ~ wie sell froge.** You don't want to ask a blockhead like that. LRT

dickseckich, *adj* - paunchy. LRT

Diddi, *m* - titty. KYG2027. **Boppli, is es Zeit fer bissel ~ hawwe?** Baby, is it time for a little titty (nursing)? LRT. = **Dittli, Ditz, Schtrich(e).** KYG1978

Diebschtaahl, *m* - theft. = **Raawerei.** KYG1993

Dier, *f* - door. **mit epper an die ~ geh** - to see someone to the door. **Wann die ~ gschlosse is, no bleibt mer haus.** If the door is locked, then one stays out(side). LRT

Diereschwell, *f* - door sill, threshold. **Die ~ is am weckfaule.** The door sill is rotting away. **Die ~ is**

kallickschteenich. The doorsill is of limestone. **Sell is en kallickschteenichi ~.** That is a limestone doorsill. **Ihre ~ is am ausfaule.** Their threshold is rotting out. LRT

Dimmelwedder, *n* - thunderstorm. = **Dunnerwedder** [A cuss word in Leb. Co. LRT], **Gewidder, Gewidderschtarem, Grutze-schtarem, Wedder.** KYG2012

dimmle - to thunder (if far away). *cf* **dunnere** (if close). *cf* **gewittre, schuere.** KYG2011

Dindebiere, *pl* - ink berries. Leb Co/LRT

Ding, *n, pl* **~e** - thing. **~e mache** = to tell jokes, stories. KYG1980. **Ich will noch ee ~ saage.** I want to say one thing yet. LRT

Dingel, *n* - *dim* of **Ding.** little thing. = **Dingelche.** KYG1997

dingle - to tinkle. *cf* **glingle, rapple.** KYG2023. **Die Dierebell is am ~.** The door bell is tinkling (ringing). LRT

dinn, *adj* - thin. **darich dick un ~** - through thick and thin. KYG1997. **Mir misse net vergesse: ~ is net Fett!** We must not forget: thin is not fat! LRT

dinnleiwich, *adj* - diarrhea or loose bowels. **Ken Wunner bischt du widder so ~; was hoscht du widder gesse?** No wonder you have such loose bowels again; what did you eat again? LRT

dinnschaalich, *adj* - thin-

41

shelled. *cf* **dinnleiwich.** KYG1998. **Die Hinkel breiche meh Oischderschaale, ihre Oier sin zu ~.** The chickens need more oyster shells, their eggs are too thin-shelled. LRT

Dinschde, *pl* - services. **Sei ~ sin deier.** His services are expensive. LRT

dir-selwer, *reflex.* or *emph. pron.* - thyself. = **dich-selwer.** KYG2012. **Du gebscht acht uff dich selwert.** You look out for yourself. LRT

Dischbedaat, *m* - dispute. **Sell waar en ~ (Schtreit), as net weckgeh hot welle.** That was a dispute that wouldn't quit (go away). LRT,4/18/2000

Dischbeh, *n, pl* ~ - table leg. **Sell sin dicki ~.** Those are big table legs. LRT

Dischdelflaum, *m, pl* ~e - thistledown. KYG2000. **Guck yuscht mol, die ~e sin am fliege wie Schnee.** Just look, the thistle down is flying like snow. LRT

dischdere - to soothe. **Hoscht du ihn ~ kenne?** Could you soothe him? LRT

Dischdlenescht, *n* - thistle patch. KYG2000

Dischdleschtock, *m, pl* -schteck - thistle stalk. KYG2000. **Du muscht Hensching aaduh fer die -schteck roppe.** You will need to wear gloves to pull the thistle plants. LRT

Dischdlesume, *m* - thistle seed. KYG2000. **Der ~ bleibt net deheem, er hot Fliegel.** Thistle

seed doesn't stay put, it has wings. LRT

Dischduch, *n, pl* -dicher - tablecloth. **Die Fraa hot scheeni -dicher.** The Mrs. (my wife) has nice tablecloths. LRT

Discheck, *n* - table corner. **Wann die yungi Leit kumme, duhne sie sich immer ins ~ hocke.** When the young people come, they always sit in the table corner (around the table). LRT

Discheelduch, *n* - table oilcloth. **Es ~ is alles verschprunge.** The table oilcloth is all cracked. LRT

Dischgawwel, *f, pl* ~e - table fork. **Ihre ~e sin Silwer.** Their table forks are silver. LRT

Dischschubblaad, *f, pl* ~e - table drawer. **Die ~e mache die alde Disch meh hole an die Vendue.** The table drawers make old tables bring more at the auctions. LRT

dischtlich, *adj* - full of thistles. **Ihre Grummbiereschtick is arig ~.** Their potato patch is full of thistles. LRT

Dittli, *n* - tit, teat. = **Ditz.** KYG2026

Ditz, *m, pl* ~e - teat. **Die Kuh hot grossi ~e.** The cow has large teats. **Selli Kuh hot yuscht drei ~.** That cow has only three teats. LRT

Ditzboddel, *f* - baby's bottle. **Geb em Boppli sei ~, no schtoppt's sei Heiles.** Give the baby his bottle, then it will stop its crying. LRT

do, *adv* - here. **~ druff hie** - on the strength of this. KYG1999. **Do in daere Bax sin en latt Sache.** Contained here in this box are a lot of things. LRT

do-hinnri-zus, *adv* - back in this direction. KYG2000. **~ wuhnt mei Schweschder.** My sister lives back in this direction. LRT

do-raus-zus, *adv* - out this way. KYG2000. **~ hen mir zwee Kariche.** Out this way we have two churches. LRT

do-ruff-zus, *adv* - up this way. KYG2000. **~ hen mir en latt Bauereie.** Up this way we have a lot of farms. LRT

do vergange, *adv* - some time ago. KYG2019. = **do fer weil zerick.** LRT

dobbmeisich, *adj* - not talkative. = **schweigsam.** KYG1965

dobleiwe - to stay here. **Ich will hawwe as sie ~ bis die Kieh heemkumme.** It's my desire that they stay here until the cows come home (forever). LRT

doch, *adv* - yet. **Der Tschann hot uns bsuche welle, awwer er is ~ net kumme.** John wanted to visit us and yet he didn't come. LRT,4/21/2000

Dochdermann, *m* - son-in-law. **Ihr ~ is gutguckich.** Their son-in-law is handsome. = **Schweyersuh, Schwiegersuh.** LRT

Dod, *m, f,* ~e - **1** remains [corpse]. **2** death. **Mir mache so fatt bis zum ~e.** We will continue until death. LRT

42

dodarich, *adv* - through this section. **~ die Mitt vun die Schtadt mache die Yunge blendi Druwwel.** Through the center of town, the young guys are causing plenty of trouble. LRT

dodarich, *adv* - through this, through here. **~ nunner (runner)** - down through here. = **dodedarich.** KYG2008. **~ naus** - out through here. = **~ raus. ~ riwwer** - over through here. **~ nuff** - up through here. KYG2009. **Des waar ken Nutz ~ zu niemand.** No one benefitted through this. LRT

dodarichnuff, *adv* - up through here. = **dodarichruff.** KYG2116. **~ gehe Germania sin die Bledder immer so schee harebschts.** Up through here toward Germania, the foliage is always so nice in the fall. LRT

Dode-ausleger, *m* - one who prepares the dead one for viewing and burial. LRT

dodebei, *adv* - **1** present. **Bleib ~, mir breiche dich.** Stay with us, we need you. LRT. **2** by this. KYG1999

dodedarich, *adv* - through this. KYG1999

Dodemann, *m* - dead man.

Dodepfleger, *m* - one who cares for the dead. LRT

Dodeschtreech, *m* - toll of church bell announcing a death. KYG2031

Dodesversarger, *m* - one who cares for, provides for the dead. LRT

dodewehe, *adv* - about this. **Ich wees net was zu duh ~.** I don't know what to do about this. LRT

dodgebore, *adj* - still-born. KYG1880. **Sell waar ihre dritt Kind as ~ waar.** That was their third child to be still-born. LRT

dodmache, *pp* **dodgemacht** - to kill. **Der Mann hot Leit yuscht so dodgemacht.** He killed the people wantonly. KYG2163

Dodmacher, *m* - death maker. **Langi Yaahre zerick waar mol en Dokder as gsaat hot, wann epper schlimm grank waar, "Der ~ schafft an dir."** Many years ago there was a doctor who said when somebody was seriously ill, "The death maker is working on you." LRT

dodmied, *adj* - dead tired. KYG2025. **Ich waar ~ gewest un ich bin ins Bett gange.** I was dead tired and I went to bed. LRT

dodraa, *adv* - at this. KYG1999. **~ an die Kett kannscht du dei Hund fescht binne.** You can tie your dog to this chain. LRT

dodrowwe, *adv* - up here. = **dohowwe, doruff, donuff.** KYG2116.

dodrunner, *adv* - under this. KYG2095. **~ is eppes as net datt sei sett.** Under this is something that should not be there. LRT

dodschiesse - to shoot dead. **Sell sin Fensemeis, schiess sie net dod, sie sin zu schee.** Those are chipmunks, don't shoot them (to death), they are too nice. LRT

dodschlagge - to slay. **Fer Haase esse muss mer sie's erscht schiesse odder ~.** In order to eat rabbits one must first shoot them or strike them dead. = **dodmache.** LRT

dodzeidich, *adj* - dead ripe. **Die Kasche sin ~.** The cherries are dead ripe. LRT

Dohick, *f* - ✪ Tohick Creek. KYG2281

dohie, *adv* - to this place. KYG2000. **Hock dich ~.** Sit at this place. LRT

dohiwwe, *adv* - on this side. **~ hen mir vum beschde Siesswelschkann as mer finne kann.** Over here we have the best sweet corn one can find. LRT

Dohl, *n* - underground conduit (for water). KYG2096. **Es waare paar dodi Ende in's ~ kumme un sell hot's verschtoppt.** A few dead ducks got into the water pipe and stopped it. LRT

dohowwe, *adv* - up here. **~ uff em Hiwwel im e helle Daag kann mer fer Meile sehne.** Up here on the hill, on a clear day, one can see for miles. LRT

Dokdersach, *f* - medicine from the physician. **Deel ~ mache em granker, as mer waar eb mer zum Dokder gange is.** Some doctor's medicine makes you sicker than you were before you went to the doctor. LRT

Dollbehocke, *f* - ✪ Tulpehocken Creek. KYG2282. **Wie ich en Yunger waar, hen mir in de Gegend gewuhnt wu die ~ un**

der ~ Paad sin. When I was a young guy, we lived in the area where the Tulpehocken Creek and the Tulpehocken Trail are located. LRT,4/21/2000

domols, *adv* - at that time. *cf* **demols, do zu mol, sellemols.** KYG2019

donaus´zus, *adv* - out in this direction. ~ **waare die Schtrosse all zugeblose.** Out in this direction the roads were all blown shut. LRT

donuff´zus, *adv* - up in this direction. KYG2116. ~ **hen sie en latt Schnee ghat.** Up in this direction they had a lot of snow. LRT

doppellaafich, *adj* - double-barreled. **~i Schrotflint** - double-barreled shotgun. **~i Schrotflinde sin nimmi so aagenehmt as wie sie als waare.** Double-barreled shotguns aren't as popular as they used to be. LRT

doppelschneidich, *adj* - two-edged. **~i Ax** - two-edged ax. KYG2085. **~i Axe kenne bissel gfahrlich sei.** Two-edged axes can be a bit dangerous. LRT

doruff´zus, *adv* - up this way. KYG2117. **Der ganz Weg ~ is es, "Hiwwli nuff un Hiwwli nunner."** The whole way up this way it's "hilly up and hilly down." LRT

Dos, *f* - dose. **en ~ nemme** - to take a dose. KYG1960. **Sie saage immer, "Nemm en ~," awwer wer wees wieviel as en ~ is?** They always say, "Take a dose," but who knows how much a dose is? LRT

dovar´rizus, *adv* - up front there. KYG2116. ~ **vum Glappbordschteddel muss mer iwwer'n Brick geh, wann mer noch Mt. Zion geh will.** Coming front this way from Clappboardstown one has to cross a bridge to get to Mt. Zion. LRT

doyetz´, *adv* - recently. ~ **waar die Mamm kumme uns sehne.** Recently Mom came to see us. LRT

draadenke, *pp* **draagedenkt** - to think of it. KYG1998. **Mir hedde eich geschder bsuche kenne, awwer ich hab net draagedenkt.** We could have visited you yesterday, but I didn't think of it. LRT

draage - to be with young. **Es hot niemand gewisst, as selli Kuh Zwilling am ~ waar.** No one knew that that cow was going to have twins. LRT,4/21/2000

draagend, *adj* - with young. **Sei Fraa is ~ mit Drilling.** His wife is pregnant with triplets. LRT, 4/21/2000

draawelle - to want to get at something. KYG2163. **Er hot abselutt an selli Arewet draa(kumme)welle.** By all means he wanted to get going with that work. LRT

dradde - <*Engl* to trot. **Halt yuscht der Gaul am ~.** Just keep the horse a trotting. LRT

Draenedropp(e), *m* - teardrop. KYG1976. **Guck mol sell glee Maedli; sie het en grosser ~ unnich ihrem linkse Aag.** Look at that little girl; she has a big

tear drop under her left eye. LRT

Draenepeif, *f* - tear duct. KYG1976

Dralli, *m* -<*Engl* trolley. KYG2063. **Yaahre zerick wann mer ken Kaer ghat hot, hot mer die ~ genumme.** Years ago if one had no car (automobile), one took the trolley. LRT

Dralli-faahre, *n* - trolley travel. = **Dralli-gfaahr, Tralli-gfaahr.** KYG2063. **Ich will wedde as ~ en latt Schpass waar.** I'll bet riding in a trolley was a lot of fun. LRT

Dralli-kaer, *m,f, pl* **~e** - trolley car. KYG2063. **Deel ~e waare gschprengt mit Leckdrick.** Some trolley cars were run with electricity. LRT

Dralli-lein, *f* - trolley line. = **Dralli-weg.** KYG2063. **En ~ waar ewwe en satt Riggelweg.** A trolley line was a kind of railway. LRT

Dralli-raad, *n* - trolley wheel. KYG2063. **En ~ is fascht Schtaal.** A trolley wheel is solid steel. LRT

Dramm, *m* - rum or whiskey. LRT

Drammratt, *f* - tippler. = **Lodel, Sauflodel, Siffer, Versaufer.** KYG2025

Drammsupp, *f* - soup with rum or whiskey. LRT

Drang, *m* - tenesmus. *cf* **Zwang.** KYG1985

44

Drangsaal, *m* - torment. *cf* **Gwaal, Pein, Pescht.** KYG2039

Drassem, *m* - unused end of warp (in carpeting). KYG2165

dratsche, *pp* **gedratscht** - to trudge. *cf* **zu Fuuss geh.** KYG2067. **Die Buwe sin darich der Dreck gedratscht.** The boys trudged through the mud. LRT

Dratt, *m* - trot. **Er geht der ~.** He's running at the trot (of a horse). *cf* **en Droll** - an easy trot. KYG2064

Drattgaul, *m* - trotting horse. KYG2064. **Seller ~ is yuscht was mir breiche fer unser Waegli.** That trotting horse is just what we need for our buggy. LRT

Drauerbenk, *pl* - pews at a funeral reserved for mourners. LRT

draus, *adv* - out. **~ im Busch seht mer en latt Hasch.** One sees a lot of deer out in the woods. LRT

drausam, *adj* - trustworthy. = **gedraut.** KYG2070

Drauweg(e)rischt, *n* - grape arbor. **Unser ~ is voll gerankt.** Our grape arbor is full of vines. LRT

Dreck, *m* - dirt. Proverb: **Was grewwer is wie ~, geht vun selwert weck.** That which is coarser than dirt, goes away by itself. (You say this to your children, when you are sweeping the floor in their presence.) LRT,4/21/2000

dreckich, *adj* - muddy, unclean. **Wie kummt's as der Kichebodde so ~ is?** How's come the kitchen floor is so muddy? **Der Bodde is ~.** This floor is dirty. LRT

Dreckkeffer, *m* - tumblebug. = **Kiehdreckroller.** KYG2073

Drecknescht, *n* - mud nest. **Die Scheierschwalme mache sich immer so en ~.** The barn swallows always make themselves such a mud nest. LRT

dreede, *pp* **gedreede** - to step. **Du hoscht uff mei Fuuss gedreede.** You stepped on my foot. LRT

dreehe - to threaten. = **drohe, droie.** KYG2004

dreehend, *adj* - threatening. = **droherisch.** KYG2004

dreeschde - to comfort. **Der himmlisch Vadder dutt uns ~.** The heavenly Father comforts us. LRT

dreffe, *pp* **gedroffe** - to hit, strike. **Er is immer so wieschderlich gfaare mit seine Kaer bis er mol ee Daag en Baam gedroffe hot.** He always drove his car so recklessly until one day he hit a tree. LRT

Drefts, *f*, *pl* **~e,** *pl* - tare. *cf* **Ungraut.** KYG1970

Dreh, *f* - **1** curve in the road. **Sie hot ihre Kaer umgschmisse datt an selle ~.** She overturned her car there on that curve. LRT. **2** turn. **die ~ mache** - to make the turn. KYG2076. **Er hot die ~ net gemacht un is zum Feld**

neigfaahre. He didn't make the turn and drove into the field. LRT

drehe - to turn. **en nei Blaat ~** - to turn over a new leaf. **fer besser ~** - to turn for the better. KYG2078. **Der Yunger kann der Fleeschfeimacher ~.** The young guy can turn the meat grinder. **es unnersewwerscht ~** - to turn upside down. LRT

Dreher, *m* - turner. KYG2078. **Kannscht du der ~ sei fer die Pannekuche, wann sie's breiche?** Can you be the pancake turner when they need it? LRT

Drehing, *f* - threat. KYG2004

Drehmiehl, *f* - turner mill. KYG2079

Drehscheib, *f* - turntable. KYG2080

Drehung, *f* - torsion. KYG2040

drei-ditzich, *adj* - three-teated. KYG2006. **So dann un wann gebt en ~i Kuh meh Millich as en vier-ditzichi.** Now and then a three-teated cow produces more milk than a four-teated one. LRT

drei-eckich, *adj* - **1** three-cornered. KYG2005. **Wann mer zwee ~i Schticker zammer dutt, grickt mer ee vier-eckiches.** If one puts two three-cornered pieces (triangles) together you get a four-cornered piece. LRT. **2** three-sided. = **drei-seidich.** KYG2005. **Die Deppichmacher gleiche ~i Schticker zammer schtickle.** The quilt makers like to piece together triangular pieces. LRT

Drei-eenichkeit, *f* - Trinity. = **Drei-in-eens.** KYG2062. **Gott in ~, segne uns.** God in three persons, bless us. LRT

Drei-fuuss, *m* - tripod. KYG2063. **En grosser Eisekessel un en ~ gehne zammer.** A large iron kettle and tripod go together. LRT

Drei-geils-wog, *f* - triple-tree. = **Dreiwog.** KYG2007. **Drei Schaffgeil sin net viel wert unni en ~.** Three draft horses are not of much value without a triple-tree. LRT

drei-plei, *adj* - *<Engl* three-ply. = **drei-doppelt, drei-drachdich.** KYG2005. **Fer selli satt Arewet sett mer ~ Gaarn yuuse.** For that kind of work, one should use three-ply yarn. LRT

drei-schteckich, *adj* - three-storey. KYG2005. **Sell is en schee ~ Haus.** That's a nice three-story house. LRT

drei-seedich, *adj* - three-stringed. KYG2005

drei-sitzich, *adj* - three-seated. KYG2005. **En ~er Wagge is yuscht was unser Familye brauch.** A three-seated wagon is just what our family needs. LRT

drei-yaehrich, *adj* - three-year-old. KYG2006. **Wann Kinner ~ sin, sell is en scheeni Elt.** When children are three-years-old, that's a nice age. LRT

dreibehnich, *adj* - three-legged. KYG2005. **Ich gleich ~i Millichschtielin.** I like three-legged milk stools. LRT

Dreibgaul, *m* - buggy horse. LRT/Leb

dreiblettrich, *adj* - three-leaved. KYG2005. **Der Glee is ~, awwer dann un wann findt mer'n vier-bletteriches.** Clover is three-leafed, but now and then one finds a four-leafed one. LRT

Dreibuschelsack, *m* - three-bushel sack. KYG2004. **En ~ voll Weeze is zu schwer fer mich.** A three-bushel sack full of wheat is too heavy for me. LRT

dreierlei, *adv* - of three sorts. KYG2004

dreifach, *adj* - threefold. KYG2005. **Ihre Singes is ~.** She sings the treble part (soprano). LRT

Dreigeilsfuhr, *f* - three-horse team. KYG2005. **En ~ brauch en Drei-Woog.** A three-horse team requires a triple-tree. LRT

dreihatzich, *adj* - true-hearted. KYG2068

Dreiheitsunndaag, *m* - Trinity Sunday. KYG2062

dreimol, *adv* - thrice, three times. *cf* **drittlich.** KYG2007. **Ich hab dir sell schund ~ gsaat un sell sett genunk sei.** I've already told you that three times and that should be enough. **Sie hen ihn ~ gfange fer faahre, wann er gsoffe waar.** They caught him three times for driving under the influence of alcohol (DUI). LRT

Dreimunetsoldaat, *m* - three-month soldier. KYG2005. [Civil War]

dreischtetckich, *adj* - three-storied. **Ihre Haus is ~.** Their house is three-storied. LRT

dreissich, *adj* - 30. KYG1999. **Sei Aldi hot ~ Pund verlore in zwee Munet.** His wife lost 30 pounds in two months. LRT

Dreissich-daag-uhr, *f* - 30-day clock. KYG1999. **Heidesdaags is en ~ nimmi gut genunk, as wie fer der Guck.** Now-a-days a 30-day clock isn't good enough, except for its appearance. LRT

dreissichscht, *adj* - 30th. **der ~ vum Munet** - the 30th of the month. KYG1999. **Der ~ Moi hen mir immer en Famillye Picknick.** The 30th of May (Memorial Day) we always have a family picnic. LRT

Dreivaddeldaaler, *m* - 75¢. **~ kaaft net viel heidesdaags.** Seventy-five cents doesn't buy much nowadays. LRT

Dreivaddels, *n* - three-quarters. = **Dreivaerdels.** KYG2005. **~ vum e Daag is ebmols lang genunk fer schaffe.** To work three-quarters of a day, sometimes, is enough. LRT

dreiyaehrich, *adj* - three-year-old. **Er is en ~er Buh.** He is a three-year-old boy. LRT,4/18/2000

Dreizehnder, *m* - the number 13. KYG1999. **Geb mir en unglicklicher ~.** Give me an unlucky number 13. LRT

dreizeht, *adj* - thirteenth. KYG1999. **Deel Leit gleiche net wann der ~ uff en Fridaag fallt.** Some people don't like

Friday the thirteenth. LRT

dreizinkich, *adj* - three-pronged. KYG2005. **~i Gawwele sin gut fer Weeze-garewe in die Dreschmaschien schmeisse.** Three-prong forks are good to throw wheat sheaves into the thrashing machine. LRT

Dreizollmeesel, *m* - three-inch chisel. KYG2005. **Was dutt mer mit'm ~?** What does one do with a three-inch chisel? LRT

Dreizollplenk, *f* - three-inch plank. KYG2005. = **Dreizollblank. Dreizollblanke sin zimmlich raar.** Three-inch planks are quite scarce. LRT

Dreppsle, *n* - a slight shower. **Bissel ~ is besser wie gaar ken Rege.** A little shower is better than no rain at all. LRT

Dresch(er)mann, *m* - thrasher. KYG2006. **En ~ hot verlenger als viel Bauer ihre Dresches geduh.** Years ago, a thrasherman did many farmer's thrashing. LRT

Dresch(er)zeit, *f* - thrashing time. KYG2007

Dreschdenn(t), *n* - thrashing floor. = **Dreschfloor, Scheierdenn.** *cf* **Newedenn.** KYG2006. **Ich hab mol gsehne wu en Dreschmachien der ~ Bodde nunnergebroche hot.** I once saw where a thrashing machine broke down the thrashing floor (planks). LRT

dresche, *pp* **gedrosche** - to thrash. **Des Yaahr hen sie ihre Weeze gedrosche mit re Maschien.** This year they thrashed their wheat with a

machine. LRT

Dresche(s), *n* - thrashing. KYG2006

Drescherei, *f* - thrashing operation. KYG2007. **Do kummt der Ed Scharick mit seine ~.** Here comes Ed Shirk with his thrashing rig (*Frick* thrashing machine and *Huber* tractor). LRT

Dresching, *f* - thrashing. KYG2003

Dreschmaschien, *f* - thrashing machine. *cf* **Dreschbax, Drescher, Rick.** KYG2006

Dreschrick, *m* - thrashing outfit. KYG2007. = **Drescherei.** Leb. Co./ LRT

Drickellumbe, *m* - tea towel. = **Scharrlumbe.** KYG1978. = **Schpiellumbe.** LRT

Dricker, *m* - trigger. *cf* **Schneller, Schnaepper, Schnepper, Zick.** KYG2061. **Yunger, zieg der ~.** Young man, pull the trigger. LRT

dridde, *refl* - **1** to happen three times. KYG2004. **Es zwett dritt sich.** Twice will turn to three. [Proverb]. **Die menscht Zeit dutt's zwett sich ewwe ~.** Most times, two times ends up with three times. LRT. **2** to triple. = **tripple. Es Zwett dritt sich.** That which doubles, triples. Leb. Co. LRT

Driddel, *n* - **1** third. **zwee ~ - ⅔. So en Deller voll is zu viel fer mich; geb mir yuscht en ~ devun.** Such a plate full is too much for me; just give me a third (of it). LRT. **2** widow's

third. KYG1998

drieb, *adj* - overcast. **Sis awwer ~, ich wunner eb's Rege gebt.** It's really overcast I wonder if its going to rain. LRT

Dries, *f, pl* **~e** - tonsil. KYG2034. = **Gland.** LRT

Drille, *n* - trill. KYG2061

Driller, *m* - turn button. **Sis ken rechder Weg fer en ~ drehe, so lang as mer'n iwwerzwarich losst, wann mer die Dier zuhawwe will.** There is no correct way to turn a turn button, so long as it is left crossways when one wants the door closed. LRT

drillere - to trill (of birds). **Die Veggel sin am ~.** The birds are chirping. LRT

Drilling, *f* - triplet. KYG2063. **Ich waar sei Lewe net bekannt mit re Familye as ~ ghat hot.** All my life, I've never known a family that had triplets. LRT. **2** ticking for a feather bed. KYG2013

Drinkschpruch, *m* - toast. KYG2028

dripple - to walk with short steps. KYG2159. **Allimol as ich selli Kuh melke will, will sie nix duh as wie ~.** Every time I want to milk that cow, all she wants to do is step around constantly. **Ich hass en Kuh as yuscht ~ will, wann ich sie melke will.** I hate a cow that just wants to move from side to side when I want to milk her. LRT

dritt, *adj* - third. **es ~ Mol** - the third time. **zum ~e** - in the third place. KYG1998. **Georg der ~ -** George the Third. KYG1999. **Yunger, sell waar's ~ Mol as du sell geduh hoscht; nau sell is verdaerbt sei es letscht Mol.** Young man, that is the third time that you did that; now darn it all, that is the last time. LRT

drittens, *adv* - in the third place. = **drittlich.** KYG1999

Dritter, *m* - the figure 3. KYG2004. **Witt du ~ sei?** Do you want to be a number three? LRT

drittletscht, *adj* - last but two. KYG2085. **Des is nau es ~ Mol as er die Arigel meh schpiele will.** This is the third last time that he wants to play the organ anymore. LRT

driwwergeh, *pp* **driwwergange** - "to go over," review. **leicht ~ -** to skim the surface. **Die Kaer hot Butzes gebreicht, mir sin schnell driwwergange.** The car needed cleaning, we went over it quickly. **Eb du sell Schtick zu de Zeiding gebscht, misse mir nochemol ~.** Before you give that article to the newspaper, we must review it once more. LRT

driwwerkumme, *pp* **is ~ -** to recover, get well again. **Er waar arig grank, awwer er is ~.** He was very sick but he recovered. LRT

driwwerlaafe - to walk over. = **riwwerlaafe.** *cf* **niwwerlaafe.** KYG2158. **Allimol as mir en frischer Gaarde mache, misse die Kieh ~.** Every time we make a fresh garden the cows have to walk over it. LRT

driwwerschlofe - to sleep on a

matter. **So en Preis fer en hunnert Acker, is schier net genunk; mir misse mol ~.** Such a price for a hundred acres is hardly enough, we'll have to sleep on it. LRT

drixe - to threaten without fulfilling (like threatening weather (rain)). **Es drixt der ganz Daag.** It's been threatening all day. KYG2004

Drixer, *m* - one shrewd in pressing a bargain. **Seller Mann is en ~, mer kann ihn yuscht net draue.** That man is a shrewd trickster; you just can't trust him. LRT

Drock, *m* -<*Engl* truck (vehicle). KYG2067. **Sei ~ is zu glee fer so viel Kieh laade.** His truck is too small to load that many cows. LRT

Drockraad, *n* - truck wheel. KYG2067. **Sell ~ fehlt die Naabkapp.** That truck wheel is missing the hubcap. LRT

Drockwese, *n* - trucking. KYG2067. **Des ~ is arig gewaxe in de letschde 50 Yaahr.** This trucking business has really grown in the last 50 years. LRT

Drockwoog, *f, pl* **~e** - truck scales. KYG2067. **In die letschde 50 Yaahr hen sie die ~e greeser mache misse.** In the last 50 years, they had to make the truck scales larger. LRT

drolle - 1 to go along at an easy trot. KYG2064. **2** to roll dough. LRT

drowwe, *adv* - **1** up. **~ in de Scheier** - up in the barn. **~ in de**

Welt - up in the world. *cf* **howwe, nuff, ruff, uff.** KYG2116. **Datt driwwe, datt ~, datt drunne, datt draus/ datt schteht der Tschann Kuck mit em Hemmerschwanz naus.** Over there, up there, down there, out there stands John Cook with his shirt tail hanging out. LRT. **2** on the top. KYG2037. **Datt ~ uff em Hiwwel schteht en U.S. Faahne.** Up there on the hill stands a U.S. flag. LRT

drowwedraus, *adv* - **1** away up. KYG2117. **~ in Nei Yarick mache sie en latt Wei.** Away up in New York (state) they make a lot of wine. LRT. **2** up at the top. KYG2037

drowwenaus, *adv* - up country. = **owwenaus, Land nuffzus.** KYG2116. **Datt ~ is es ewwe kelder as es do is.** You know up country it is colder that it is here. LRT

Druckfehler, *m, pl* **~** - misprint. **Die Zeidinge mache ewwe immer ~.** The newspapers will always make misprints. LRT

Druckne, *n* - a dry area (free from rainfall). **im ~** - under shelter. **Wann du weescht was gut is fer dich, bleibscht du im ~.** If you have any sense, you'll stay under shelter. LRT

druff saage - to top another's expression. KYG2037

druff-anne, *adv* - thereat, thereon. KYG1994. **Es kummt datt ~ aa.** It depends on that. LRT

druffhalde - to regard, take seriously. **Ich kann nie net viel**

~ uff was du mir saagscht. I can never take seriously what you tell me. LRT

druffhie, *adv* - on the strength of. **Wann's datt ~ geht, dann daede mir yuscht so gut fattmache.** On the strength of that, we'd just as well continue. LRT

drufflosgeh, *pp* **is drufflosgange - 1** to go about something without a plan. **Er is drufflosgange wie net gscheit.** He went about (that project) like a crazy fool. LRT. **2** to work furiously. KYG2245. **Er is drufflosgange, wie en Bull uff me Hoischtock.** He worked furiously like a bull on a hay stack. LRT,4/11/2000

drufflos'-schpringe, *pp* **drufflos-gschprunge** - to run wildly. **Er is drufflos-gschprunge as wann es sei Lewe gmehnt hot.** He ran wildly as though his life depended on it. LRT

druffschteh - 1 to stand on it. **2** to stand by one's word. **Ich saag dir, er schteht druff. Er is immer so gut as sei Watt.** I tell you, he stands by his word. He is always as good as his word. LRT,4/11/2000

druffwedder, *adv* - up against. KYG2116. = **druffundewedder. Er is ~ gange wie en Bull.** He went up against it like a bull. LRT

Drumbet', *f* - trumpet. KYG2068

Drummsaeg, *f* - two-man log saw. = **Gross-saeg.** KYG2086

Drump, *m, pl* **Drimp** - trump. KYG2068. **Hatz is ~.** Hearts is trump. LRT

drunne, *adv* - underneath. = **drunner.** KYG2097. **~ im Keller hen mir en latt Ess-sache.** Down under in the cellar we have a lot of food. LRT

drunnehewe - to suppress. **Kannscht du der Ewwer ~ so as ich ihn schneide kann?** Can you hold the boar down so that I can castrate him? LRT

Drupp, *f, pl* **Druppe** - school of fish, bevy, drove, herd, flock, group. LRT

Druwwel, *m* - trouble. **sich viel ~ aaduh** - to go to considerable trouble. **~ vannenaus** - trouble ahead. KYG2065. **Der ~ is er wees nix.** The trouble is he knows nothing. **Er hot sich Kopp iwwer Ohre in ~ grickt.** He got himself in trouble head over heels. LRT

druwwele, *refl* - to trouble. *cf* **sich bekimmere, bemiehe, bloge, schteere.** KYG2065. **Er dutt sich oft ~ iwwer nix.** Often he troubles (concerns) himself over nothing. LRT

Druwwelmacher, *m, pl* **~** - troublemaker. = **en rechder Zwaerich.** KYG2065. **So ~ breiche mir net.** We don't need troublemakers like that. LRT

druwwelsam, *adj* - troublesome. **Sell is en ~ Wese.** That's a troublesome affair. LRT

Druwwelszeit, *f* - time of trouble. KYG2065. **Sell waar ~ wie ihre Haus nunnergebrennt is.** That was the time of trouble,

when their house burnt down. LRT

druwwle, *pp* **gedruwwelt** - to trouble. **Des hot sie gedruwwelt bis zum Graab.** This troubled her to her grave (until she died). LRT

druwwlich, *adj* - troublesome. KYG2065. **Was is so ~ wehich sellem?** What is so troublesome about that? LRT

dufdich, *adj* - misty. **Sis ~ de Mariye.** It's misty this morning. LRT

duh - to do. **Ich will nix mit ihm zu ~ hawwe.** I don't want to have anything to do with him. LRT

Dullebaam, *m* - common tulip.(My) *Tulipa, spp.* = **Dollchaan, Dollebaan, Dolleblumm, Dullebaan, Dulleblumm, Dullebohn, Dullebuhn.** KYG2073

Dulleblummglut, *f* - tulip glow. KYG2073

dumbich, *adj* - tilted. KYG2017

dumm, *adj* - stupid. **wie ~ sei** - to be in a torpor. KYG2040. **Sell waar awwer ~.** But that was stupid. LRT

Dummheide, *pl* - mischievous acts, pranks. **Buwe, so ~ deift dir nimmi fattmache.** Boys, you may not continue making such mischief. **Fer ~ schpiele hen selli Buwe Welschkann uff unser Bortsch gschmisse.** To play a prank those boys threw corn on our porch. LRT

dummle - to make a subdued

noise. **Mer heert eppes am ~, ich wunner was es is.** One hears a subdued noise, I wonder what it is. LRT. **Yunger, du muscht dich dummle!** Young man, you have got to hurry! LRT

dunkelheidich, *adj* - dark-complected. **Ihre Kinner sin all bissel ~.** All their children are a bit dark-complected. LRT

Dunner, *m* - vituperative term for a person. = **Dunnerwedder.** *cf* **Luder, Dos, Rinnsvieh, Saddan, Schtinkluder.** KYG1987

Dunnerkeil, *m* - thunderbolt. = **Dunnerschlag, Gewidderschtreech.** KYG2011. **Dunnerkei(de)l** = gee whiz. Leb. Co. LRT

Dunnerschall, *m* - thunderclap. = **Dunnergrache, Gewiddergrach.** KYG2011

dunnerschtinkich, *adv* - terribly stinking. KYG1988

Dunnerwedder, *n* - thunder gust. KYG2012. [A curse word in Leb. Co. LRT]

Duschber - twilight. **Es waar ~ un mir hen noch ken Nachtesse ghat.** It was dusk and we had not had supper. LRT

dusslich, *adj* - uneasy. **Es is re ~.** She is uneasy. KYG2100

Duwack, *m* - tobacco. **~ uffschpiesse** - to put tobacco on laths. **~ tschaa-e** - to chew tobacco. **noch ~ schtinke** - to smell of tobacco. **~ schtrippe** - to strip tobacco. **der ~ abblaade** - to strip leaves off tobacco.

KYG2028. **Zu mir is ~ nix wie Gift.** To me, tobacco is nothing but poison. LRT

Duwack(s)brieh, *f* - tobacco juice. KYG2029

Duwackduch, *n* - tobacco cloth. KYG2028

Duwackgerischt, *n* - field scaffold for drying tobacco. KYG2028

Duwackkeefer, *m* - one who buys up tobacco, tobacco dealer. KYG2028

Duwackkessel, *m* - said of someone who chews tobacco in a repulsive manner. KYG2029

Duwackkutsch, *f* - tobacco clod frame. KYG2029

Duwacklettli, *n* - tobacco lath. KYG2029

Duwacksbrieder, *m* - tobacco brethren. KYG2028

Duwackscheer, *f* - tobacco shears. KYG2029

Duwackschtengel, *m* - tobacco plant. KYG2029

Duwackschtick, *n* - tobacco patch. KYG2029

Duwackschtock, *m* - tobacco plant. *cf* **Schtannblumm.** KYG2028

Duwackschtrick, *m* - tobacco rope. KYG2029

Duwackschtripper, *m, pl ~* - tobacco stripper. **Sie hen net genunk ~.** They don't have enough tobacco strippers. LRT

Duwacksieb, *f* - tobacco sieve. KYG2029

Duwackskaue, *n* - tobacco chewing. KYG2028

Duwacksrecher, *m* - marker used in planting tobacco. KYG2028

Duwackwarem, *m* - tobacco worm. *cf* **Holzwarem.** KYG2029

dwiddle - to twiddle. **die Daume ~** - to twiddle the thumbs. = **die Daume schwillere.** *cf* **die Daume schpiele** - to sit and twiddle the thumbs. KYG2082. **Guck mol, datt hockt seller glee Buh am Daume schpiele.** Look, there sits that little boy twiddling his thumbs. LRT

ebmols', *adv* - sometimes. **~ halde sie Gemee in de Scheier.** Sometimes they have church in the barn. LRT

ee-schtimmich, *adj* - unanimous. *cf* **allmenanner.** KYG2090

Eechebusch, *m* - wood lot of oak trees. **Wann mer ken Eechle finne kann in sellem ~, dann daed mer's besser vergesse.** If one can find no acorns in that wood lot of oak trees, one had better forget the matter. LRT,4/11/2000

Eechhaas, *m, pl ~e* - squirrel. **roder ~** - red squirrel. **Rodi ~e sin verfochtni Dinger, sie duhne die grohe Eechhaase weckyaage.** Red squirrels are fighters, they chase gray squirrels away. LRT

Eechhaasenescht, *n, pl* ~er - squirrel's nest. **~er baue misse en latt Arewet sei.** Building squirrel's nests must be a lot of work. LRT

eefachdich, *adj* - composed of a single strand. **Sei Gedanke sin immer ~.** His thoughts are always narrowminded. LRT

eefeldich, *adj* - **1** silly. **~ sei.** to be simple-minded. **Yunger, sei net so ~.** Young man don't be such a half-wit. *cf* **halwergscheit, lappich. 2** composed of a single strand. LRT

Eegeilshandtschicker - one-horse hand cultivator. Leb. Co./ LRT

Eegeilsreche, *m, pl* ~ - one-horse-drawn rake. **~ waare die beschde Satt.** One-horse-drawn rakes were the best kind. LRT

eegesinnich, *adj* - stubborn, self-willed. **Sei net so ~.** Don't be so self-willed. LRT

Eegip´de - ✪ Egypt, Africa. KYG2271

Eegleilslein, *f* - single line (in working horses). **Die ~ dutt mer feschtschnaeppe an der Zoppziegel.** The single line of working horses is snapped onto the check-rein. LRT

Eeheet, *f* - unity. = **Eenichkeit.** KYG2106

Eel-licht, *n* - torch. = **Fackel.** KYG2039

Eeli, *m* - Elias. **Mei Onkel hot en Schwoger, as ~ heest.** My uncle has a brother-in-law

named Elias. LRT,4/21/2000

eelich, *adj* - slick. **Die Schtrooss waar ~ un sell hot sie glatt gemacht.** The road was oily and that made it slick. *cf* **glatt.** LRT

Eeling, *f* - "oiling." **letschdi ~** - extreme unction. KYG2095

Eemaus - ✪ Emmaus, Lehigh Co., PA. = **Eemaas**

eenich, *adj* - single. **en ~ Land** - a united land. KYG2106. **Ya, ich bin ~ mit sellem.** Yes, I agree with that. LRT

Eenichkeit - unity. **En Karich brauch immer ~.** A church always needs unity. LRT

eens - one. **fer ~** - for one thing. KYG1997. **Well, mol fer ~ (ee Ding), mir hen genunk zu esse.** Well, for one thing we have enough to eat. LRT

eenschichscht, *superl adj* - the only one. **Sie sin die ~e as wisse, was sie am duh sin.** They are the only ones who know what they are doing. LRT

Eeschderreich, *n* - Austria, central European country. KYG2268

eeyaehrich, *adj* - one year of age. **Die Zwilling sin nau ~.** The twins are now one year of age. LRT,4/18/2000

eeyesinnich, *adj* - untoward, stubborn, self-willed. KYG2114. **Er is en ~er Glotzkopp.** He is a self-willed, stubborn blockhead. LRT

eezich, *adj* - unique. *cf* **keiyos.**

KYG2105

Effi, *f* - *dim* of **Eefaa.** Eva. LRT,4/21/2000

Effredaa - (Biblical) ✪ Ephrata, Lanc. Co., PA. **~ is baut zwansich Meil (der Weg wie die Grapp fliegt) weck vun wu ich uffgwaxe bin.** Ephrata is about 20 miles (the way the crow flies) away from where I grew up. LRT,4/21/2000. **~ is aa die Schtadt wu Bischli-Gnippli uffgwaxe is.** CRB,1/28/2002

ehnder, *adv* - rather, sooner. **Er daed ~ sell duh.** He'd rather do that. LRT

Ehrlichkeit, *f* - honesty. **Ich duh sei ~ hoch eschdimiere.** I have great appreciation for his honesty. = **Redlichkeit.** LRT

ei-riwwle - to crumble something into soup. **Duh paar Schticker Brot in die Supp ~.** Crumble a few pieces of bread in the soup. LRT

eib(l)icke - to turn in (the edges in hemming). KYG2077. **Ya, mer bickt's en Vaddel Zoll ei, no naeht mer's.** Yes, one turns it in a quarter inch and one sews it. LRT

eibalsemiere, *pp* **eigebalsamiert** - to embalm. KYG2098. **Sie hen sei Kareber eigebalsemiert.** They embalmed his body. LRT

Eibalsemierer, *m* - the embalmer. LRT

eibiege - **1** to turn in. = **eidrehe, neidrehe, neiwenne.** KYG2077. **2** to turn (the hem) under. KYG2078

eibilde, *refl* - to imagine. **sich eppes ~** - to take pride in doing (or being) something. KYG1890. **Ich kann mir ~ wie froh as sie waar fer deheem sei.** I can imagine how happy she was to be at home. **Ich kann mir gaar net ~, wie sell gucke sett.** I can't imagine how that should look. LRT

eibindle, *refl* - to dress up warmly. KYG2165. **Sis kalt heit, wann du nausgeh witt, muscht dich gut ~.** It is cold today, if you want to go outside you will have to dress up warmly. LRT

eiblaudre, *pp* **eigeblaudert** - to make someone believe, talk someone into. **Sie hen nanner eigeblaudert.** They convinced each other. **Vielleicht kannscht du ihn ~.** Perhaps you can talk him into it. LRT. **= eischwetze.** KYG1964

eibringe, *pp* **eigebrocht** - to bring in (income). **Die paar Schtund meh gschafft, hen aa meh Geld eigebrocht.** These few more hours of work brought in more money too. **Sei Bissniss bringt net viel Geld ei.** His business doesn't bring in much money. LRT,4/21/2000

eibrockle - to break crackers (bread) into soup. **Die Supp is bissel wasserich, du kannscht paar Graeckers ~.** The soup is a bit watery, you can break a few crackers into it. LRT

eidenke, *pp* **eigedenkt** - to be mindful of, think of. **Der Paep hot's eigedenkt; no waare mir all zufridde.** Dad thought of it; then we were all satisfied. LRT

eidrehe - to turn in (a seam). KYG2077. **Fer uffsaame dreht mer's ei, biggelt's nunner, un naeht's fescht.** To hem, one turns (the fabric) in, irons it down, and sews it fast. LRT

Eifaahrt, *f* - approach to the thrashing floor. **= Scheierbrick.** KYG2006. **Selli Scheier hot en haddi ~.** That bank barn has a steep approach to the thrashing floor. LRT

Eifall, *m* - sudden thought.

eifalle, *pp* **is eigfalle** - to occur to. **Des is mir yuscht mol so unverhofft eigfalle.** This just popped into my head unexpectedly. LRT

eifeddle[1] - to string tobacco on laths. KYG2028

eifeedle[2] - to thread a needle. **die Nodel ~** - to thread a needle. KYG2003. **Fer Nodle ~ muss mer gudi Aage hawwe.** In order to thread needles one must have good eyes (eyesight). **Do ich will dir weise wie mir die Naehmaschien-nodel ~.** Here I want to show you how we thread the sewing machine needle. LRT

Eifer, *m* - fervor. **Sei ~ gebt uns all bissel Hitz.** His fervor gives all of us a bit of ardor. LRT

eifiehre, *pp* **eigfiehrt** - to introduce. **Sie hen der Gaul eigfiehrt datt in der Venduring fer ihn abweise.** They lead the horse into the sale ring to show him off. LRT

eifrich, *adj* - enthusiastic. **Er is en ~er Mensch.** He's an enthusiastic person. LRT

Eifrichkeit, *f* - zeal. **Sellem Yunge sei ~ muss em gewiss verwunnere.** That young man's zeal is truly amazing. LRT,4/21/2000

eifriere, *pp* **eigfrore** - to place in a deep freeze (for later use). **Mir hen unser Seifleesch all eigfrore.** We froze all our pork (for later use). LRT

eigawwle - to pitch straw (in). **Guck yuscht mol seller Buh, wie er sei Ess-sach eigawwelt.** Just look at that boy, how ravenously he eats. LRT

eigewwe, *pp* **~** - to give in. KYG,2263. **Ya, er hot ~, as mir recht waare.** He admitted (agreed) that we were correct. LRT,4/21/2000. **Ich hab's net duh welle awwer endlich hab ich ~.** I didn't want to do it, but finally I gave in. LRT

eigfeddelt, *adj* - threaded. KYG2004. **Du hoscht schund en latt Nodle ~; du muscht gudi Aage hawwe.** You've threaded a lot of needles (already); you must have good eyes. LRT

eigreife - to take part. **= mitmache.** KYG1961

eigschneet, *adj* - snow-bound. **Fer zwee Daag waare mir ~.** For two days we were snow-bound. LRT

eihacke, *pp* **eighackt** - to chop into. **Die Katz hot ihre Glooe wieschderlich in sellem gleene Buh sei Beh eighackt.** The cat chopped her claws real nastily into that little boy's leg. LRT

eihauche - to inhale. **Duh sell**

net ~! Don't inhale that. LRT

eikaafe, *pp* **eikaaft** - to shop. **Ich hab mir genunk eigekaaft fer mich en ganz Yaahr halde.** I bought enough to last me a whole year. LRT

Eikaafes, *n* - shopping. **Ihre ~ is genunk fer sie mol ee Daag dropse mache.** Her shopping is enough to make her drop someday. LRT

eikehre - to stop at an inn. = **uffschtelle.** KYG1889

Eikummes, *n* - receipts. LRT

eilege, *refl* - to stock up. **sich ~ mit (Schlidde)** - to stock up on (sleds). KYG1883. **Mir hen genunk Fuder eigelegt fer's Vieh den Winder.** We have enough feed stocked up for the cattle this winter. LRT

eimauere, *pp* **eigemauert** - to wall in. KYG2160. **Unser Bressent is nau ganz eigemauert.** Our jail is now totally immured. LRT

einemme, *pp* **eignumme - 1** to make a garment smaller. **Seller Gaund is zu gross, du muscht ihn ~.** That dress is too large, you'll have to take it in. **Mei Fraa is hendich mit em Naehes, sie kann dir dei Gaund ~.** My wife is a skilled seamstress, she can take in your dress. **Sie hot ihre Gaund eigenumme.** She made her dress smaller. LRT. *cf* **eigriege, neinemme, reinemme.** KYG1962. **2** to take in (money). **Seller Pareed hot en latt Leit zammergebrocht un die Schtadt hot en latt Geld eignumme.** That parade brought

a lot of people together and the city took in a lot of money. LRT. **3** to include. **Des nemmt selli ei, wu ken Geld hen.** This includes those who have no money. LRT

Einemmes, *n* - income. **Selli Picknick hot gut ~ gebrocht.** That picnic brought in much in the way of proceeds. LRT

Eireschpiggel, *m* - Till Eulenspiegel, mythological character in German folklore. = **der Eisehannes.** KYG2017

eirisch, *adj* - Irish. **Yunger, schick dich net so ~ aa!** Young man, don't be such a comedian! LRT,4/21/2000

Eirisch, *m* - Irishman. **Ich wunner, wu der Naame ~er Demodi beikummt?** I wonder where the term Irish Timothy (Quack Grass) comes from. LRT,4/21/2000. Leb. Co.

eiropee´isch, *adj* - European. KYG2271

eisalze, *pp* **eigsalze** - to salt down. **Mir hen die Schunke eigsalze.** We salted down the hams. LRT

eischarefe - to give strict instructions. **Wann selli Kumpani in die Bissniss bleiwe will, dann misse ihre Leit ihre Wege ~.** If that company wants to remain in business, then their people (employees) need to sharpen (be more injunctive) about their actions. LRT

eischaufle, *pp* **eigschaufelt** - to shovel in (food). **Er hot's eigschaufelt, as wann er nix ghat hot fer esse fer en Yaahr.**

He shoveled (food) into his mouth as though he had nothing to eat for a year. LRT

eischidde - to pour medicine down an animal's throat. KYG2008

eischlagge, *pp* **eigschlagge** - to strike (of lightning). **Ya, es hot eigschlagge dattdrowwe in die Scheier. Mir kenne froh sei as es ken Feier gewwe hot.** Yes, the lightening struck up there in the barn. We can be glad there was no fire. LRT

eischlitze - to tear. *cf* **retze, reisse, verreisse, zarre.** KYG1976

eischlummere, *pp* **is eigschlummert** - to fall into slumber. **Du muscht mir vergewwe, ich waar eigschlummert gwest un ich hab net gheert was du gsaat hoscht.** You must forgive me, I dozed off and I didn't hear what you said. LRT

eischnalle, *pp* **eigschnallt** - to tighten. **Mir hen die Gscharre eigschnallt.** We tightened (buckled in) the harnesses. LRT

eischpritze - to sprinkle wash before ironing. **Heit duhne mir die Wesch ~ un mariye duhne mir sie biggle.** Today we sprinkle the wash and tomorrow we iron it. LRT

eischteh - 1 to stand in. **Kannscht du ~ fer dei Bruder?** Can you stand in for your brother? LRT. **2** to be responsible for. **Geh yuscht fatt fer en Woch, ich kann ~ fer dich.** Just leave for a week; I'll be responsible for you. LRT

eischtricke - to narrow the toes (in knitting stockings). KYG2030

eischwappe, *pp* **eigschwappt** - to swap. **Ich seh dir hett en neier Wagge; hett dir der alt eigschwappt?** I see you have a new wagon; did you trade in the old one? LRT

eischweere, *pp* **eigschwore** - to swear in. **Ya, der 20scht Yenner is er eigeschwore warre.** Yes, he was sworn in on January 20th. LRT

Eisefens, *f, pl* ~ - wrought iron fence. **Sis ball Zeit, as sie selli ~ schwatz aaschtreiche.** It's about time they paint that wrought iron fence black. LRT,4/18/2000

Eisegraut, *n* - stone crop. *Sedum, spp.* KYG1887

eisegroh, *adj* - iron-gray. **Selli Fareb is ~.** That color is gun metal (iron gray). LRT

eisehne - to see the point. **Er hot's yuscht net ~ kenne.** He just could not get the point. LRT

Eisehnes, *n* - insight, understanding. **Seller Mann hot ~ wie niemand schunscht hot.** That man has insight such as no one else has. LRT. **ken ~ hawwe** - to have no understanding. KYG2098. **Sei ~ is schwach.** His insight is weak. LRT

Eisemeesel, *m* - iron chisel. LRT

Eisemein(t), *f* - iron mine. LRT

eisetze - to set in. **Kannscht du**

sell Band gschwischich die zwee Saame ~? Can you set in that band between the two seams? LRT

eisich, *adj* - iron. LRT

Eisichgreiz, *n* - iron cross. LRT

Eislendisch, *n* - Icelandic (the language). LRT,4/21/2000

Eisnifall, *f, pl* ~**e** - iron trap. **Heit hab ich mir paar ~e gekaaft.** Today I bought two iron traps. LRT

Eitracht, *f* - union. *cf* **Gemeeschaft, Vereenichung.** KYG2105

eiweeche, *pp* **eigeweecht** - to soak, soften. **Yunger, du grickscht dei Hinnerdeel eigeweecht.** Young man [to a naughty boy], you are going to get your behind paddled. LRT

eiwetze, *refl* - to bedraggle one's trousers with mud. KYG2065

eiwickle, *pp* **eigewickelt** - to wrap up. **Am Schtor hen sie die Sache, was mir gekaaft hen, schee eigewickelt.** At the store, they nicely wrapped the items that we bought. LRT,4/18/2000

Eiwicklern, *f* - female wrapper. **Sie is die ~ fer gschenkti Sache, as die Leit kaafe datt am Schtor.** She is the wrapper of the gift items that the people buy there at the store. LRT,4/18/2000

eiwindre - to have winter set in. **Mir hen noch en latt Arewet eb's eiwindert.** We still have lots of work before winter sets in. LRT

Eiwuhner, *m, pl* ~ - resident. **Die ~ sin die Yacht leedich.** The residents are tired of this noise. LRT

eizwinge, *pp* **eigzwingt** - to force to swallow. **Sie hen's Kind eigezwingt fer sei Medizin schlucke.** They forced the child to swallow its medicine. LRT

Elbedritsche, *n* - Yelpin-stretcher (provincialism in the Shenandoah Valley, VA.) KYG,2262

Eldeschderbenk, *pl* - pews occupied by the church consistory (elders). LRT

Elend, *n* - misery. **Er hot sei ~ iwwermacht.** He has overcome his misery (and has died). LRT

elendich, *adj* - miserable. **Sell Bussli is en ~ glee Ding.** That kitten is a poor, miserable little thing. LRT. **Sell Biebli is awwer ~, es kann schier net laafe.** That chick is in misery, it can hardly walk. LRT,4/18/2000

Elendsgrippel, *m* - stunted or underdeveloped person or thing. **Er is en ~.** He is a poor stunted (crippled) person. LRT

Elendszaah, *m* - tooth of trouble. KYG2065

Ellboge, *m, pl* ~ - turning joint (in a pipe). KYG2079. **Wann die Ablaafpeif zu viel ~ hot, dutt sie glei verschtoppe.** If the drain pipe has too many elbows, it will soon become clogged. LRT

Ellsdaun - ✪ Allentown, PA. KYG2267

Ellsdauner, *m* - inhabitant of Allentown, PA. KYG2267

End, *n* - end. **ken ~ hawwe** - to be unlimited. KYG2107. **Es is ke ~ zu unserem Gott, Er is ewich.** There is no end to our God, He is eternal. LRT. **Hoffning hot ken ~.** Hope has no end. LRT

Endmauer, *f, pl* ~ - stone barn end. = **Giwwelend, Schtallblatt, Schtannend.** KYG1886. **Ich gleich die Kunschtarewet sehne was sie in die ~ an die alte Scheiere geduh hen.** I like to see the art work that was put in the stone end walls of the old barns. LRT

engbrischdich, *adj* - tight-chested. KYG2016

Englischer, *m, pl* **Englische** - Englishman. KYG2271

Englischi Walniss, *f, pl* ~ - English walnut. **~ hen helli Schaale.** English walnuts have light (colored) shells. LRT. = **Englischwalniss**

Englischwalniss, *f* - English walnut. *Juglans regia L.* = **Englischi Nuss, Englischi Walniss, Deitschi Nuss, Deitschi Walniss.** KYG2161

Engschde, *pl* - terror, fear, fright. *cf* **Faricht, Schrecke.** KYG1989. **Die ~ hen selli Leit immer gedruwwelt.** The terror (fear) always troubled those people. LRT

engschderlich, *adj* - filled with fear, terror, on tenterhooks. **Wie der Yung selli Flint gsehne hot, is er ~ warre.** When the young man saw that gun, he

became fearful. **Wu is eier Glaawe, dir seid immer so ~.** Where is your faith, you are always so fearful. LRT. *cf* **dottlich.** KYG1986.

eenichi Zeit, *adv* - any time. **Hoscht du ~ sellem Mann Geld gewwe?** Did you give that man money at any time? LRT. = **eenichmol**

eenichmol, *adv* - any time. = **eenichi Zeit.** KYG2018

Ennwill - ✪ Annville, Lebanon Co., PA. KYG2268

entgehelaafe - to walk to meet. KYG2158. = **gegenanner laafe.** LRT

epper-schunscht, *pron* - someone else. **Ich will's net, geb's zu ~.** I don't want it, give it to someone else. LRT

eppes, *pron* - something. **uff zu ~ sei** - to be up to something. KYG2117. **Sis ~ los do, awwer's macht ken Yacht.** There is something loose (wrong) here, but it makes no noise. LRT. **Es is ~ schunscht.** That is something else. KYG1994. **Ya, sell is ~ schunscht.** Yes, that is something else. LRT

erbaar´me, *refl* - to have mercy (on someone). **Wann mer sich ~ will, muss mer's erscht im Hatz hawwe.** To have mercy on someone, one must first have it in his heart. LRT

erbaa´remlich, *adv* - terribly. **Sis Gott ~ hees heit.** God, it's terribly hot today. LRT

erlaa´we, *pp* **erlaabt** - to permit.

Sie hen darich mei Hof faahre welle, awwer ich hab's net erlaabt. They wanted to drive through my yard, but I did not permit it. LRT

erlei´de - to undergo. = **unnergeh.** KYG2096

eschdemiere, *pp* **eschdemiert** - to regard. **Der Buh dutt sei Paep hoch ~.** The son has high regards for his Dad. LRT

Eschepuddel, *f* - last person out of bed on Shrove Tuesday. **Der ~ in ihrem Haus grickt ken Fettkuche bis schpot oweds.** The last person out of bed in their house on Shrove Tuesday doesn't get a donut until late at night. LRT

Eselschtreech, *pl* - pranks. **Sell is nix Neies, er macht immer so ~.** That is nothing new, he always pulls such pranks. LRT

Ess-zeit, *f* - time to eat. = **Iemszeit.** KYG2018. **Well, Buwe, sis ~.** Well boys, its time to eat. LRT

Essgranket, *f* - eating sickness. **~ hawwe** - to be afflicted with tapeworm. KYG1970

Esskareb, *m* - lunch basket. **Mach schur un bring dei ~ an die Picknick.** Make sure to bring your lunch basket to the picnic. LRT

eweck´reisse, *pp* **eweckgerisse** - to tear away. KYG1976. = **weckreisse**

eweck´schmeisse - to throw away. = **weckschmeisse, verwarefe.** *cf* **zottle.** KYG2009

eweck'bleiwe - to stay away. **Bleib eweck vun sellem Hund.** Stay away from that dog. LRT

eweck'laafe, *pp* eweckgeloffe - to walk away. *cf* **ablaafe, abschpringe, ausglaare, darichbrenne, darichgeh, fattschpringe, schinne, weckschpringe. Sie hen gemehnt, er daed en guder Scheffer mache, awwer er is yuscht eweckgeloffe.** They thought he would make a good worker, but he just walked away. LRT

Ewichkeit, *f* - eternity. **Er is in die ~ gange.** He went into eternity. LRT

ewwerscht, *adj* - top. *cf* **heegscht, owwerscht.** KYG2037. **Langi Yaahre zerick hen deel Leit als Fleesch gschmokt uff ihrem ~e Schpeicher.** Many long years ago some people smoked meat in their attics. LRT

Ewwerschtdeel, *n* - upper part. LRT

Ez, *m* - Ezra. KYG4/21/2000. **Der Onkel ~ gleicht deheem zu bleiwe.** Uncle Ezra likes to stay at home. LRT,4/21/2000

Faahne, *f, pl* ~ - tassels. **Es Welschkann hot die ~.** The corn has tassels. LRT

Faahrdeck, *f* - driving surface. **Die ~ uff sellre Brick is noch bedeckt mit Holzblanke.** The driving surface of that bridge is still covered with wooden planks. LRT,4/11/2000

faahre - to drive. **En Rees ~ (schpringe)** - to run a race. **Des**

Rees ~ is mir zu gfaehrlich. This race driving is too dangerous for me. LRT

Faahrgeeschel, *f* - teamster's whip. = **Fuhrgeeschel.** KYG1976

Faahrweg, *m* - driveway. **Sie hen scheeni Baem an ihrem ~ noochgeblanzt.** They planted nice trees along their driveway. LRT

faawle - to talk twaddle, speak incoherently. = **dumm schwetze.** KYG2081

Fachdischdel, *f* - torch thistle. KYG2039

Fackel-licht, *n* - torchlight. KYG2039

fackelfische - to fish by torchlight. KYG2039

faddich, *adv* - finished. ~ **mache** - to put on finishing touches. = **abfaddiche.** KYG2041. **Hoscht du dei Arewet ~ gemacht?** Did you finish your work? LRT/ Leb.Co. **Fer alles ~ mache, misse mir noch meh Hilf hawwe.** To finish everything, we need more help. LRT

falde - to tuck. *cf* **gut eiwickle.** KYG2072

Falschheet, *f* - untruth. = **Lieg, Unwaahrheet, Unwaahret.** KYG2114. = **Falschheit. Selli Lieg waar greesser wie der Barig.** That untruth was bigger than the mountain. LRT

Falze, *pl* - tucker (part of garment). KYG2072

Falzhowwel, *f* - tongue and groove plane. = **Fedderhowwel.** KYG2034

fange, *pp* gfange - to catch. **eppes in Zeit ~** - to catch something in time. KYG2019. **Sie hen all die Radde gfange, eb sie en latt Welschkann fresse hen kenne.** They caught all the rats before they could eat a lot of corn. LRT

Fangnaggel, *m* - hard toe nail of the elderly. KYG2030

Fangzaah, *m, pl* -zaeh - 1 canine tooth (in animal). KYG2035. **2** tusk. **Elefande hen grossi -zaeh.** Elephants have big tusks. LRT

farichde, *refl* - to be afraid. **sich marickunwaerdich ~ vor** - to be terribly afraid of. KYG1988. = **fariche. Sie fariche sich iwwer die Leewe.** They fear the lions. LRT

farichderlich, *adv* - terribly. KYG1988. **Er is ~ schtarick gfaahre.** He drove terribly fast. LRT

Faricht, *f* - audacity. KYG1981

farichtbaar, *adj* - truculent. KYG2067

farichtbutzich, *adj* - timorous. = **farichtsam.** KYG2021. **Er is ~ in alle Wege.** He is timorous in all circumstances. LRT

Farichtbutzli, *m* - *dim of* **Farichbutz** - timorous person. **Sell Buwwli is en ~.** That little boy is full of fear. LRT

faschtnemme - to take hold of. KYG1961. = **feschtnemme**

Fassing, *f* - ticking (of bed). = **Fedderfassing.** KYG2013. **Die ~ vun selle Fedderdeck is verrisse.** The ticking of that feather tick is torn. LRT

fattblaudre, *pp* **fattgeblaudert** - to continue talking. KYG1965. **Er hot fattgeblaudert, bis niemand meh in die Schtubb waar.** He continued talking until there was no one else in the room. LRT

fattdappe, *pp* **fattgedappt** - to walk away. **Er is fattgedappt.** He walked away. LRT

fattgehwelle, *pp* **~** - to want to go away. KYG2163. **Die Kinner hen ~.** The children wanted to go away. LRT

fattlaafe, *pp* **is fattgloffe** - to walk away. KYG2158. **In d'Mitt vun d'Nacht is der Yung fattgeloffe.** In the middle of the night, the young man walked away. LRT

fattlese - to continue to read. **Les yuscht fatt, sell is en gudi Gschicht.** Just read on, that's a good story. LRT

fattmache, *refl* - to depart. **sich gschwind ~** - to scuttle away. **Mach dich fatt!** Get going (depart)! LRT

fattreggere - to continue to rain. **Es reggert als fatt.** It continues to rain. LRT

fattschaffe, *pp* **fattgschafft** - to continue to work. **Er hot fattgschafft bis er zwee un achtzich Yaahr alt waar.** He continued to work until he was 82 years old. LRT,4/11/2000

fattschicke - to send away. **Ver lenger hot mer ~ kenne fer yuscht baut eenich eppes kaafe vun Sears Roebuck.** Years ago one could send away to purchase just about anything from Sears Roebuck. LRT

fattschlofe, *pp* **fattgschlofe** - to continue to sleep. **Er hot der ganz Mariye fattgschlofe.** He continued to sleep all morning. LRT

fattschnarixe, *pp* **fattgschnarixt** - **Die ganz Nacht hot er fattgschnarixt.** He continued to snore all night. LRT

fattschreiwe, *pp* **fattgschriwwe** - to continue to write. **Er hot fattgschriwwe bis er ken Babier meh ghat hot.** He continued to write until he had no more paper. LRT,4/18/2000

fattwaddle - to waddle. **yuscht so ~** - to toddle. KYG2030. **Er is alt, gross, un fett, awwer er kann noch ~.** He is old, big, and fat, but he can still waddle (along). LRT

fattweile - to tarry. *cf* **uffhalde, verweile, verziehe, waarde, weile.** KYG1971

fattyohle, *pp* **fattgyohlt** - to continue to yell. **Er hot fattgyohlt (aaghalde yohle) bis er rauh-helsich waar.** He continued to yell until he was hoarse. LRT,4/18/2000

fattzottle - **1** to scatter forth. **2** to continue to scatter. **Ya, zoddel yuscht so fatt, endlich hoscht du nix meh zu zottle!** Yes, just keep on scattering, ultimately you will have nothing

more to scatter! LRT

faul, *adj* - lazy. **Yunger, sei net so ~!** Young man, don't be so lazy! LRT,4/18/2000

faule - to rot, putrefy. **Die Grummbiere sin am ~, mer kann sie rieche.** The potatoes are rotting (putrefying), one can smell them. *cf* **verfaule.** LRT

Faulfleesch, *n* - foul tissue. KYG2026. **~ - schur die Haschkuh is schund en Woch dod.** Rotten meat---surely, the (deer) doe has been dead for a week. LRT

Faulheit, *f* - sloth, laziness. **Sei ~ dutt ihm ken gut.** His slothfulness doesn't do him any good. **So ~ bringt em ken Gsundheit.** Such laziness does not bring one healthiness. LRT. *cf* **Vielfrass**

Faulhuf, *m* - thrush (on horse's hoof). = **Wehfuuss.** KYG2010

Fauscht, *f* - fist. **en ~ mache** - to threaten with clenched fists. KYG2004. **Yunger, du machscht ken ~ an mich!** Young man, don't you threaten me with a fist! **Wann du net achtgebscht, grickscht die ~ graad uff dei Naas.** If you are not careful, you'll get this fist right on your nose. LRT

Faxe, *pl* - tomfoolery. = **Hanswaschtschtreech, Narreschtreech, Schwoweschtreech.** KYG2033

Fechderei, *f* - quarrels. **Die ~ bin ich leedich.** I am tired of these quarrels. LRT

Fechteck, *n* - quarreling

locality. **Wann dir eich so aaschicke wett, dann geht in eier ~.** If you want to act like that, then go into your fighting corner. LRT

Fechthaahne, *m* - bully, a young man prone to pick fights. **Yunger, du bischt yuscht zehe Yaahr alt, awwer du bischt schund en rechder ~.** Boy, you are only 10 years old, but already you are a real bully. LRT

Fedderkissi, *n* - pillow stuffed with feathers. LRT

feedmich, *adj* - stringy. **Die Buhne sin ~.** These beans are stringy. LRT

fehle - to be lacking, missing. **Sie hen gsaat, es fehlt eppes, awwer sie hen net saage welle, was es waar.** They said something was missing, but they didn't want to say what it was. LRT, 4/18/2000

Fehler, *m* - mistake. **Ich hab ewwe en ~ gemacht.** Of course I made a mistake. LRT

Fehlschlag, *m* - an unsuccessful attempt. KYG2113

fehlschlagge - to turn out unsuccessfully. KYG2113

Fehlyaahr, *n* - year of bad crops. **Zidder as mir uff daere Bauerei sin, des is unser erscht ~.** Since we have been on this farm, this is our first bad crop year. LRT,4/18/2000

Feier, *n* - fire. **~ schlagge** - to give forth sparks, throw fat into the fire, stir up anger. **Nau geb acht, selli Leckdricklein hot ~**

gschlagge. Now be careful, that electric cord emitted sparks. **Was geht aa datt, selli Leckdrick Cord hot ~ gschlagge?** What's going on there, that electric cord gave off some sparks? LRT. **Sell hot awwer ~ gschlagge!** That stirred things up, *i.e.* that stirred them to anger. KYG1882. **es ~ fixe** - to stoke a fire. KYG1884. *cf ~* **gewwe.** KYG2009.

Feierflamm, *f* - torch lily. *Kniphofia, spp.* KYG2039

feierlich, *adv* - seriously. **~, sell macht mich awwer bees.** Seriously, that makes me angry. LRT

Feierlichkeit, *f* - solemnity. **So ~ seht mer net oft.** One doesn't often see such solemnity. LRT

feierrot, *adj* - red-hot. **Sell Eise is ~.** That iron is red-hot. LRT

Feierschteeschteddel, *n* - ✪ Flintville, Lebanon Co., PA. KYG2271

feignochich, *adj* - small-boned. **Selli Bendihinkel sin ~.** Those bantam chickens are fine-boned. **= gleegnochich.** LRT

feimache, *pp* **feigemacht** - to break into small pieces, chop finely. **Es Fleesch muss feigemacht sei fer Wascht mache.** The meat has to be ground finely to make sausage. **Mir hen die Hickerniss feigemacht fer uns eirischde fer die Grischtdaagskichlin backe.** We chopped the hickory nuts in preparation to bake the Christmas cookies. **Wann mer Wascht mache will, dann muss mer aa es Fleesch feigemcht**

hawwe. It one wants to make sausage, then one also needs to have the meat finely chopped. LRT

Feimacher, *m* - "In Lebanon County we used to call the hand-turned meat grinder a ~." LRT

fein, *adj* - fine. **Mir misse den Meerreddich ~er maahle.** We must grind this horseradish finer. LRT

feireisse - to tear into pieces. **= verreisse.** KYG1976. **Wann du die Zeidinge ~ daedscht, no kennt niemand sie lese.** If you would tear newspapers into small pieces, then no one could read them. LRT

Feldi, *m* - *dim* of Valentin(e). **= Wall, Walli.** KYG2287

Feldkarebs, *f, pl* **~e** - pumpkin grown in cornfield. **Wann mer ~e un Welschkann zammerblanzt, sell is wie zwee Veggel dodmache mit eem Schtee.** When one plants pumpkins and corn together, that is like killing two birds with one stone. LRT

Feldschtee, *m* - field stone. KYG1886. **~ lese is net die schennscht satt Arewet.** Picking up field stones is not the nicest kind of work. LRT

felsich, *adj* - rocky. *cf* **schteenich, wackich. Ihre Felder sin oh so ~.** Their fields are mighty rocky. LRT

Fens, *f* - <*Engl* fence. **iwwer die ~ tschumpe** - to be unfaithful (of a husband). KYG2102

Fenschderkitt, *m* - putty. **Mer dutt ~ uff die Fenschdere mit me Kittmesser.** One puts putty on windows with a putty knife. LRT

Fenschderscheib, *f, pl* -**scheiwe** - window pane. **Ich gleiche selli alde -scheiwe mit die Luftlecher drin zu sehne.** I like to see those old windowpanes with the air bubbles in them. LRT

Fensetschumper, *m* - fence jumpers. **~ sin die wu unzufridde sin in ihre Gemee un losse sich aanemme an re annere Gemee.** "Fence jumpers" are those who become unsatisfied in their congregation and become members in another congregation. LRT

fescht, *adj* - fast. **die Dier ~ mache** - to secure the door. **Mach selli Dier gut ~, so as sie en Weil halt.** Fasten that door well so that it lasts a while. LRT

feschtbappe - to stick together. **Loss net alles ~.** Don't let everything stick fast. LRT

feschtbrode, *pp* **feschtgebrode** - to stick to the pan in frying. LRT

feschtgebappt, *adj* - stuck fast. **Sell Schtick Babier is uff der Bodde ~.** That piece of paper is stuck fast to the floor. LRT

feschthalde, *pp* **feschtghalde** - to keep hold of. **Ich hab feschtghalde bis ich nimmi hab kenne.** I held on until I couldn't any more. LRT

feschtnaggle - to nail on. LRT

feschtnemme - to take hold of. **Nemm mol do fescht, mir welle mol sehne, eb mir den Wagge ziehe kenne.** Take a hold here; we want to see if we can pull this wagon. LRT. = **faschtnemme**

feschtschtecke, *pp* **is ~** - to stick fast. **Sei Grubbax is ~ gebliwwe.** His pick got stuck fast. LRT

Fett-schtenner, *m* - lard can. **Seller ~ hebt fuffzich Pund.** That lard can holds fifty pounds. LRT

Fickmiehl, *f* - tic-tac-toe. KYG2014

fiehlbaar, *adj* - tangible. KYG1967

fiehle - to feel. **~ fer** - to be sorry for. **Mer muss gewiss ~ fer ihn.** One must really feel sorry for him. LRT. **Was macht dich schlecht ~?** What makes you feel bad? LRT

fiessle - to walk rapidly taking small steps. **Ya, fiessel yuscht, sell grickt dich nariyets hie.** Take all the little steps you want, (but) that will get you nowhere. **Du kannscht do rum ~, awwer recht laafe geht besser.** You can trample about here, but walking properly works better. **Schtarick laafe mit gleeni Schrittlin (~), sell is der Tschonni.** Rapid walking with small steps, that's Johnny. **Sie is 80 Yaahe alt, awwer sie fiesselt wie en Kind.** She is 80 years old but she walks rapidly (taking small steps) like a child. LRT

Fiessle, *n* - taking short steps.

Kind, ich gleich sell ~ net sehne. Child, I don't like to see those short little steps. LRT

Fiewer, *n* - fever. **Sei ~ waar schier 106°.** His fever was almost 106°. LRT

Fimftraad, *n* - turntable (for front part of a farm wagon). KYG2080.

fimfyaehrich, *adj* - five-year-old. **Ich hab en Kinskind, as en ~er Buh is.** I have a grandchild that is a five-year-old boy. LRT

Finger, *m, pl* **~** - finger. **En Hand hot vier Finger un en Daume.** A hand has four fingers and a thumb. LRT

Fingerhut, *m* - thimble. *cf* **Daumling.** KYG1997. **Du brauscht en neier ~, deiner hot en Loch.** You need a new thimble, yours has a hole. LRT

Fingerhutgneller, *m* - punishing tap with a thimble. KYG1969. **Sie is immer am naehe un hot nixnutzichi gleeni Buwe, sell macht sie en ~.** She is always sewing and has naughty little boys, that makes her a thimble tap punisher (to their heads). LRT

Fingerhutvoll, *m* - thimbleful. KYG1997. **En ~, wieviel is dann sell?** A thimbleful, how much is that? LRT

fingersdick, *adj* - thick as a finger. KYG1996

Fingersdicking, *f* - thickness of a finger. KYG1996

Fink, *n* - gen. of all warblers. *cf* **Schpetzliche, Singvoggel, die**

59

glenne Schpetzlicher, die glenne Veggel. KYG2163

finnif-un-zwanzich - 25. KYG2082. **Er is ~ Yaahr alt.** He is 25 years old. LRT

fiole - to torment. = **bloge, driwweliere, grageele, gwaele, deiwle, peiniche, aergere, buckere.** KYG2039

Fisch[1], *m, pl* ~ - fish. **~ drohle** - to troll fish. KYG2063. **Er gleicht d'~ nooch geh.** He likes to go after fish (fishing). LRT.

Fisch[2], *m, pl* ~ tenderloin. KYG1984. **En ~ aus me Seirick is es bescht Seifleesch in d'Welt.** A tenderloin out of a hog's back is the best pork in the world. LRT. = **Fischli**

Fischer, *m* - ulcer. = **Fissel, Fistel, Frissel, Gschwaer, Gschwier, Schwaer.** KYG2088

Fischlicht, *n* - tin flare. KYG2022. *cf* **Fischladann, Fischlutzer.** LRT

Fischoier, *pl* - roe. **Ich gleich gebrodni ~.** I like fried roe. LRT

fix un faddich, *adj* - all ready. **Ya, ich bin ~!** Yes, I'm all ready! LRT

flach, *adv* - flat. **Er hot sich ausgschtreckt un hot sich ~ uff der Grund gelegt.** He stretched himself out and lay flat on the ground. LRT

Fladderwisch, *m* - turkey wing (used as a duster). KYG2076. **Yaahre zerick waare ~ en hendich Ding.** Years ago a feather duster was a handy thing (most were a bunch of feathers and not a wing!). LRT. = **Fledderwisch**

Flammgraas, *n* - tumble grass. *Panicum capillare L.* = **Flaumgraas, Kitzelgraas.** KYG2073

flaxkeppich, *adj* - towheaded. KYG2043

Flaxkopp, *m* - towhead. KYG2043

Fleck, *m, pl* ~e - spot. **Es is Zeit fer den Gaund wesche, er hot alle sadde ~e.** It's time to wash this dress, it has all kinds of spots on it. **Der glee Buh hot en schpassich guckicher ~ in seim Aag.** The little boy has a funny looking spot in his eye. **Yunger, du hoscht ~e datt im Kessel gelosst.** Young man, you left some spots there in the kettle. LRT

Fleesch, *n* - flesh. **Sei Gnoche sin grobb un sei ~ hot net viel Fett.** He is raw-boned and his flesh doesn't have much fat. LRT

Fleeschhaffe, *m* - pot for preserving meat. LRT

Fleeschpei, *m* - meat pie. **Sis nix besser as wie en guder ~.** There is nothing better than a good meat pie. LRT

Fleeschsupp, *f* - soup made of meat. **~ is die bescht Satt.** Soup made of meat is the best kind. LRT

Fleggel, *m* - unmannerly fellow. = **Rauhbelz, Rauhbiggel.** KYG2108

Fleggeldresche, *n* - thrashing with a flail. KYG2006. **~, sell is eppes as mer nimmi dutt.** Flail thrashing, that is something that isn't done anymore. LRT

Fleggeldrescher, *m* - person thrashing with a flail. KYG2006

fleggelhaft, *adj* - unmannerly. *cf* **rauhbehnich, rauhbelzich, rilpsich, unaardlich, ungebutzt, unmanierlich.** KYG2108

fleggelhefdich, *adv* - terribly (often with sense of "very"). *cf* **gaar wedderlich** [used in Leb. Co. LRT], **gott-im-himmels, greisslich** [used in Leb. Co. LRT], **hesselaanisch, hesselborich, hesseldannich, hesselronisch, hesslich** [used in Leb. Co. LRT], **madderleinisch, unerbaremlich.** KYG1988. = **gotterbaremlich.** LRT/ Leb. Co.

Flex[1], *f, pl* ~e - sinew. **Yuscht owwich die hinner Seifiess schneit mer sie uff un ziegt die ~e raus. Datt schiebt mer no es Heeseholz nei un hengt die Sau uff.** Just above the hog's rear feet you make a cut and pull out the sinew. There you insert the gambrel and hang up the hog. LRT

Flex[2], *f, pl* ~e tendon. KYG1985. **Fer en Heeseholz yuuse fer Sei uffhenge muss mer die ~e finne kenne in die hinnerschde Fiess.** In order to use a gambrel in hanging up hogs, one needs to find the tendons in the hind feet. LRT

flick, *adj* - pubescent. **Die Ende sin schee, ~ un sis hoch Zeit as**

mir sie schlachde. The ducks are nice and prime (pubescent), and it's high time that we slaughter them. LRT

flicke, *pp* **gflickt** - to mend. **Well, die Schtrimp sin gflickt, awwer fer wie lang?** Well, the stockings are mended, but for how long? LRT

Flieg, *f, pl* **~e** - artificial trout fly. KYG2066

Fliegzeit, *f* - **1** time when young birds can fly. **Wann die Veggel voll gfeddert sin, no is es ~.** When the birds are fully feathered, it's time to fly. LRT. **2** time when birds migrate. KYG2018

Fliggeldisch, *m, pl* **~** - table with extendable wings. **~ sin hendich fer schnell greeser mache.** Drop leaf tables are convenient to quickly extend. LRT

flissich, *adj* - liquid fluid from a sore or infection. **Sell Gschwaer waar ~ fer paar Woche.** That boil was shedding pus-like fluid for two weeks. LRT

flitsche - to skip stones on the water surface. **Buwe gleiche sehne wie oft as sie die Schtee ~ mache kenne.** Boys like to see how many times they can make stones skip (across the water). LRT

Fluch, *m* - curse. **Er is ken ~ in de Luft waert.** He is not worth a curse in the sky. LRT, 4/18/2000

foddere - to ask, demand. **Er foddert zwanzich Daaler's Schtick fer sei Laefersei.** He is asking $20.00 each for his

shoats. LRT

Forell', *f, pl* **~e** - trout. KYG2066. **Er hot geschder paar ~e gfange.** Yesterday he caught a few trout. LRT

Frankreich, *n* - France. = **Franzoseland.** KYG2272

franzee´sisch, *adj* - French. KYG2272

Franzos´, *m* - Frenchman. KYG2272

fratzich, *adj* - stylish. **Er is en ~er Mensch.** He's a foppish person. LRT

Frehlichkeit, *f* - mirth. LRT/Leb.Co.

Freidreppe, *pl* - outside stone stairs. KYG1888

freigeh, *pp* **is freigange** - to set free. **Er waar zehe Yaahr in de Bressent, awwer no hen sie ihn ~ glosst.** He was in prison for ten years, but then they let him go free. LRT

freigewwich, *adj* - generous. **Er is en ~er Mensch.** He is a munificent person. LRT. KYG2112. **Selli Karicheleit sin immer so ~.** Those church people are always so generous. LRT

Freiheitsgrieg, *m* - War of the Revolution. KYG2163. **~, awwer hees en was du witt, des waar en wieschdi Schlacht.** War of the Revolution, but call it what you will, it was an ugly battle. LRT

freilaafe - to roam freely (of cattle). **Sie losse ihr Kieh ~.**

They let their cattle roam freely. LRT

freilosse, *pp* **freiglosst** - to set free. = **loslosse. Seller Mann waar zwanzich Yaahr in de Bressent, eb sie ihn freiglosst hen.** He was in prison for twenty years before they let him free. LRT

Fresch, *m* - thaw. KYG1992

fresse - to devour (food). **Gediere duhne ~ un Leit duhne esse.** Animals devour food and people eat their food. LRT

Fridder, *m* - *dim* of **Fridderich.** KYG2264

Friede, *m* - peace. **Wann mer yuscht Bissel ~ hawwe kennde.** If only we could have a little peace and quiet! LRT

Friedensbarig, *m* - ✪ Oley, Berks Co., PA. **Ich waar im yaahr 1956 en Schtudent-Schulmeeschder in ~ gewest.** In 1956 I was a student teacher in Oley, Berks Co., PA. LRT,4/21/2000

Friedensgrieg, *m* - War for Independence. KYG2163. **Der ~ hot sei Gewinnesfescht der viert Yuli.** The War for Independence has its victory celebration each July 4th. LRT

Friedeweg, *m* - the way of peace. LRT

Friedezeit, *f* - time of peace. LRT

Friehgrummbiereschtick, *n* - early potato patch. **Sell unnerscht Paert vum Feld is**

en ~. That lower part of the field is an early potato patch. LRT

friehmariyets, *adv* - early in the morning. **~ mache mir uns immer aus em Bett.** Early in the morning we always rise from our beds. LRT

Friehyaahrszeit, *f* - springtime. **Wann mer der Winder leedich is, no winscht mer fer ~.** When one is tired of winter, then one wishes for springtime. LRT

friere, *refl* - to shiver. **Es is kalt, es friert mich.** It's cold, I'm shivering. LRT

frisch warre - to bear young (of cattle). **Sell Rind sett fer's erscht Mol ~ den Harebscht.** That heifer should freshen (bear a calf) for the first time this fall. LRT,4/21/2000

froge - to ask. **schnarrich ~** - to ask sharply. **Wann mer net frogt, wees mer nix.** If one doesn't ask, one doesn't know anything. LRT

frogeswaert, *adv* - worth asking for. **Ihre Hilf is net ~.** Their help is not worth asking for. LRT, 4/18/2000

froh, *adj* - glad, happy. **Ich bin schur ~ as dir kumme seid.** I'm surely glad you came. LRT

Froscht, *m* - sole of horse's hoof. **En ~ muss allegebott nunnergeraschbelt sei.** The sole of the horse's hoof has to be rasped down every now and then. LRT

fruchtbaar, *adj* - fruitful. **~ sei** - to be fruitful. KYG1978. **Des**

waar en ~ Yaahr. This was a fruitful year. LRT

Fruchtschnitz, *pl* - sections of dried fruit. **Zu mir sin alle Sadde ~ gut.** To me, all sorts of dried fruit sections are good. LRT

Fudergang, *m, pl* **-geng** - feeding entry. **In die -geng is wu mer die Fuderkischde findt.** In the feeding entries is where one finds the feed chests. LRT

Fuhremennischt, *m, pl* **~e** - Team Mennonite, Wenger Mennonite. KYG1976

Fuhrgeeschel, *f* - buggy whip. **Ferlenger zerick hot mer immer en nei-ie ~ hawwe misse wann mer en Bauere Vendu hawwe hot welle.** Years ago one always had to have a new buggy whip if one was having a farm sale. LRT

Fuhrgeil, *pl* - team of horses. **Die Hund duhne immer vor die ~ schpringe.** The dogs always run ahead of the team of horses. LRT

Fuhrmann, *m* - teamster. KYG1976. **Seller ~ kann die Fuhr im Gang halde.** That teamster keeps the team moving. LRT

Fuhrwagge, *m* - team wagon. KYG1976. **Ihre ~ hot gudi Schparre.** Their team wagon has good brakes. LRT

fui! - (*interj*) ugh! KYG2088. **Ich saag ~ uff sell.** I say ugh to that. LRT

Fui! - ugh! don't touch!

KYG2041. **~, sell schtinkt.** "Fui," that stinks. LRT

futsch geh, *pp* **is futsch gange** - to fail. **Sei Bissniss waar unbrofittlich un is futsch gange.** His business was unprofitable and it went belly-up. LRT

Fuuss, *m, pl* **Fiess** - foot. **unner ~** - under foot. = **unnich de Fiess.** KYG2096. **Sie hot en halb dutzend Kinner unnich de Fiess ghat, sie hot sich schier net verrege kenne.** She had a half-dozen children under foot, she could hardly move. LRT

Fuuss-sohl, *f* - sole of foot. **Sie hot en wehi ~.** The sole of her foot is sore. = **Fiess-sohl.** LRT

Fuussbord, *n* - twelve-inch board. KYG2082. **Die alde Bedder hen en Koppbord un en ~.** The old beds have a head board and a foot board. LRT

Fuussdappe, *pl* - footprints. **Wer waar do? Es sin ~ ganz iwwer der Kichebodde.** Who was here? There are footprints all over the kitchen floor. LRT

Fuussweg, *m* - pathway. LRT

Fuxgaul, *m, pl* **-geil, Leb. Co.=Fixgeil** - sorrel horse. **Sell is en scheeni paar ~geil.** That is a nice pair of sorrel horses. LRT

G(e)schaff, *n* - working. **Mer grickt ebmols zuviel vun dem ~.** Sometimes one gets overburdened with work. LRT,4/11/2000

G(e)schleef, *n* - long, drawn-out work. **Fer achtgewwe uff**

gleeni Kinner daagenacht, is so'n ordlich ~. Caring for small children day and night is quite a drawn-out job. LRT,4/11/2000

Gaab, *f, pl* **~e** - talent. **Sellem Maedel ihre ~e sin fer singe.** That girl's talents are to sing. LRT. *cf* **Nadurgaab.** KYG1964

Gaardebauer, *m* - trucker. KYG2067. **Ya, er is en ~.** Yes, he is a truck farmer. LRT

Gaardepeffer, *m* - sweet pepper. **Ich gleich ~, er mag rot, grie, oder gehl sei.** I like sweet peppers, be they red, green, or yellow. LRT

Gaarnschlupp, *m* - loop of yarn. LRT

Gaepper, *m* - "yawns," yawning spell. **Fraa, du hoscht der ~, hoscht net gut gschlofe?** Wife, you've got the "yawns." Didn't you sleep well? LRT,4/18/2000

Gaerret, *m* - <*Engl* garret, top story (in a building). KYG2038. **Geh net heit nuff uff der ~, sis zu hees.** Don't go up on the garret today, it's too hot. LRT. =**ewwerscht, schpeicher**

gaese - to argue. **Seller Mann un Fraa duhne ~ vun mariyets bis oweds.** That man and woman argue from morning until night. LRT

gaffe[1] - to stare. **Ich denk ich kann an sell schee Maedel ~, wann ich will.** I guess I can stare at that pretty girl if I want to. LRT

gaffe[2] - to tell tales. KYG1981. **Wann er aafangt ~ — wees mer as es net die Waahret is.**

When he begins telling tales, one knows it is not the truth. LRT

Gaffmaul, *n* - tell-tale. = **Ohrebleeser, Ohrebloser, Retschballe, Retschbeddi, Retsch, Retscher, Retschmaul.** KYG1981

Galleschtee, *m* - gall stone. LRT

Gammditz, *m, pl* **~** - rubber nipple. **Was hen sie geduh eb sie ~ ghat hen?** What did they do before they had rubber nipples? LRT

gammle - to gamble. **mit Schtack ~ -** to gamble in stocks. KYG1883

Gang, *m, pl* **Geng** - trip to the physician. KYG2062

garewe - 1 to tan (process leather). **Ich will unser Haschhaut ~ losse.** I want to have our deer skin tanned. LRT. 2 to flog. *cf* **der Buckel weeche, abschwaarde.** KYG1966

Garewer, *m, pl* **~** - tanner. KYG1968. **~ sin hatt zu finne.** Tanners are hard to find. LRT

Garewerei, *f* - tannery. KYG1968. **Englisch Zenter in Lykoming Kaudi, PA hot als Yaahre zerick en ~ ghat.** Years ago English Center in Lycoming County, PA had a tannery. LRT

Garewerloh, *m* - tanner's bark. KYG1968

Garewersauer - tannin. KYG1968

Garewersgrub, *f* - tanner's vat. = **Lohgrub.** KYG1968

Garewershund, *m* - tanner's bitch. KYG1968

Gargel, *f* - throat. **die ~ abschneide** - to cut one's throat. = **Garigel, Geigel, Hals.** *cf* **Schlucker, Schluckerli, Schlund.** KYG2007

Gawwelzinke, *pl* - tines. KYG2022. **Die ~ sin alles verboge.** These (fork) tines are all bent. LRT

Gax, *f* - tiresome talker. KYG1965. **Mer wunnert yuscht wie er so en ~ is warre.** One just wonders how he got to be such a tiresome talker. LRT

gaxe - to cackle. **Sie kann ~ wie en Hinkel.** She can cackle (talk tirelessly) like a hen. LRT

Gebam'bel, *n* - loitering, messing around. **So'n ~ wie selli Yunge geduh hen unnich sellem Baam, sett net erlaabt sei. Guck yuscht, sie hen der Schtrick runnergrisse.** Such fooling around by those young fellows beneath that tree, should not be permitted. Just look, they tore the rope down. LRT

gebau'ert, *adj* - cultivated. **net ~** - uncultivated. KYG2095

Gebeiss', *n* - (constant) itching. LRT

Gebet'li, *n* - *dim* of **Gebet.** short prayer. LRT/Leb.Co.

Gebiebs', *n* - peeping. **Selli Bieblin ihre ~ bin ich leedich.** I'm tired of those chicks' peeping. LRT

Gebiss', *n* - set of teeth. KYG1978. **Ich hab immer**

gwisst was en Geils ~ waar, awwer's hot mich bissel lache gemacht wann mei Grememm ihre falschi Zaeh ihre ~ gheese hot. I always knew what a horse-bit was, but it made me laugh a bit when my grandma called her false teeth a **Gebiss**. LRT

Geblau´der, *n* - (continuous) talk. KYG1964. **~, ~, ebmols will mer yuscht saage, "Sei ruhich!"** Talk, talk, sometimes one just wants to say, "Be quiet!" LRT

Gebol´ler, *n* - rumbling noise. **Kummt sell ~ yuscht vum Schteebruch?** Is that rumbling noise coming from the stone quarry? LRT

Gebott´, *n* - offer. **Sei ~ waar zwanzich Daaler.** His offer (bid) was twenty dollars. LRT

gebrannt´, *adj* - unslacked. **~er Kallick** - unslacked lime. KYG2112

Gebred´dich, *n* - long-winded talk. **So en ~ waert em leedich.** One tires of such long-winded talk. LRT

Gebrum´mel, *n* - rumor. **Es waar en ~ in der Schtadt as es Hochzich gewe daed.** There was a rumor in town that there would be a wedding. LRT

Gebrutz´, *n* - pouting. **So'n ~ waert mer leedich.** One tires of such pouting. LRT

gedan´kelos, *adj* - unthinking. KYG2113. **Sell Schulhausumreisse waar en ~ Wese.** Tearing that school house down was a thoughtless process.

LRT

gedaucht´, *adj* - stooped. **Er laaft awwer ~.** He really stoops over when he walks. LRT

Geddisbarig, *m* - ✪ Gettysburg, Adams Co., PA. **Ya, in ~ hen sie mol en gross Gfecht ghat.** Yes, in Gettysburg there once was a great battle, the Battle of Gettysburg in the Civil War. LRT, 4/21/2000

gedemft´, *adj* - stewed. **Sie saage ~i Grummbiere sin gut fer em.** They say stewed potatoes are good for one. LRT

gedicht´, *adv* - thoroughly. = **gedichdich, dichtlich, geheerich.** *cf* **kindlich, salwiers.** KYG2001. **Er hot gedichdich Schlaeg grickt.** He got a thorough beating. LRT

Gedie´reausschtopper, *m* - taxidermist. KYG1974

Gedim´mel, *n* - tumult. *cf* **Daerm, Uffruhr.** KYG2074

Gedob´, *m* - (continued) raging. **Sei ~ waar genunk fer ihn in's Graab duh.** His raging was enough to put him in the grave. LRT. **So en ~ schtende mir net do.** Such raging we will not tolerate here. LRT

Gedrenk´, *n* - **1** beverage. **2** drink. **3** liquor. LRT

Gedrick´, *n* - discomfort of any part of the body. LRT

Gedrip´pel, *n* - unrestful stamping around (by the cow). **So'n ~ hot mer net gern, wann mer die Kuh melke will.** Such unrestful stamping around (by

the cow) is not welcome when you want to milk the cow. LRT

Gedun´ner, *n* - thundering. KYG2012

Geglep´per, *n* - a rattling noise. **Die ganz Nacht hot mer'n ~ gheert.** All night one could hear a rattling noise. **Suzie, duh selli Kessel weck, ich bin des ~ leedich.** Suzie, put those kettles away, I'm tired of this rattling. LRT

geglich´e, *adj* - popular. **Er is en gross ~ner Mensch.** He is a much-liked person. LRT

Gegnootsch´, *n* - fondling. **Des ~ waert mer iwwereweil leedich.** After a while one tires of this massaging. LRT

Gegnuff´, *n* - pommeling. **Sei ~ schtoppt net un ich bin's leedich.** His pummeling doesn't let up and I'm tired of it. LRT

Gegratz´, *n* - constant scratching. **Schtopp sell ~, iwwer dem fangt's aa blude!** Stop that scratching, soon it will bleed! LRT

Gegrei´dertee, *m* - tea made from herbs. KYG1974

Gegreisch´, *n* - yelling. **Iwwereweil waert mer sell ~ leedich.** After awhile one tires of that yelling. LRT,4/18/2000

geguckt´, *adj* - looked. **net ~ devor** - unlooked for. KYG2108

Geguck´, *n* - continual staring. **Sell ~ muss schtoppe.** That continual staring must stop. LRT

Gegwa´cker, *n* - (continual)

quacking. **Die Ende ihre ~ macht em wacker.** The ducks' quacking makes one awake (at night). LRT

Gegwael′, *n* - tormenting. KYG2039. **Sell ~ is genunk fer em narrisch mache.** That tormenting is enough to drive one crazy. LRT. **= Gwaelerei**

gegwol′le, *adj* - swollen. **Is sell Holz nass warre? Es guckt ~ zu mir.** Did that wood get wet? It looks swollen to me. LRT

geh, *pp* **gange** - to go. **zu dritt ~** - to go three at a time. KYG2004. **Sie sin zu dritt der Karichegang nunner gange.** They went down the church aisle in threes. LRT

gehe, *prep* - toward. **Fer ~ die Sunn faahre uff me Windernamidaag is ken Schpass.** To drive towards the sun on a winter afternoon is not fun. LRT

gehe Nadde, *adv* - toward the north. **~ hen sie schund en Fuuss Schnee.** Towards the north of us they already have a foot of snow. LRT

geheem′, *adj* - underhanded. KYG2096

gehenanner, *adv* - toward each other, toward one another. KYG2043. **Sie sin ~ gschprunge bis sie nannerumgschlagge hen.** They ran toward each other until they knocked each other down. LRT

gehenannerlaafe, *pp* **gehenannergeloffe** - to walk towards. **Mir sin gehenannergeloffe bis mir**

nanner aagedroffe hen. We walked toward each other until we met. LRT

gehl, *adj* - yellow. **Mer seht ordlich viel ~i Amischi Wegglin im Grosse Daal.** One sees rather many yellow Amish buggies in the Big Valley (Kishacoquillas Valley), Mifflin Co., PA. LRT, 4/18/2000

gehlachdich, *adj* - yellowish. **Zidder as es so drucke is, is seller Schwamm ~ warre.** Since it's become so dry, that meadow has gotten yellowish. LRT,4/21/2000

gehlbrau, *adj* - yellowish brown, tan. KYG1966. **Im Harebscht duhne deel Baem ~ drehe.** In the fall of the year some trees turn yellowish brown. LRT,4/21/2000. **Die Sunn hot uns all ~ verbrennt ghat.** The sun had tanned all of us yellowish brown. LRT. **= gehlichbrau**

gehlichbrau, *adj* - tawny. **= gehlbrau.** KYG1973. **~ is net gehl un aa net braun, sis aeryets gschwische drin.** Tan is neither yellow or brow, it's somewhere in between. LRT

Gehlsucht, *f* - jaundice. **Er hot die ~.** He has yellow jaundice. LRT

Gehlvoggel, *m* - "yellow bird," Eastern yellow warbler. *Dendroica aestira a.* **der glee ~ = Zelaatschpetzel, Zelaatvoggel.** KYG2163

Gehlweschp, *f, pl* **~e** - yellow jacket. **~e kenne em gedichdich schteche.** Yellow jackets can give one a nasty sting.

LRT,4/21//2000

Gehlwoch, *f* - Yellow Week. **= Himmelfaahrtwoch.** KYG2262

Geilbschlagge, *n* - farrier work. **Mit seim ~ schafft er ewwe so rumher.** With his farrier work he works in various places. LRT,4/11/2000

Geilschtalldier, *f, pl* **~e** - horse stable door. **Mir sedde die ~ aaschtreiche.** We should paint the horse stable door. LRT

Geilsdokder, *m* - veterinarian [used in Lebanon County, PA]. LRT

Geilsgebiss, *n* - horse's bit. LRT

Geilspulwer, *n* - powder fed to stock for conditioning. LRT/Leb.Co.

Geilstschacki, *m, pl* **~** - horse jockey. **Verlenger hen die ~ ebmols net en arig guder Naame ghat.** Years ago the horse jockeys (horse dealers) did not always have a good reputation. LRT

Geilswatzel, *f* - stone root. *Collinsonia canadensis L.* **= Gschwaerewatzel, Peilswatzel, Schtee-watzel.** KYG1888

Geilszaeh, *pl* - very large teeth. KYG1978

Geiz, *m* - **1** stinginess. KYG1881. **2** stingy person. **Er is en ~.** He is a stingy person. [rare. LRT]. LRT

geize - to be stingy. **= genixe, gnixe.** KYG1881

Geizhals, *m* - tightwad.

geizich, *adj* - stingy. *cf* **gnapps.** KYG1881. **Er is en ~er Mensch.** He is a stingy person. LRT

Geizichkeit, *f* - miserliness. LRT

Gekehr´, *n* - sweeping. **Sie hot gsaat, "Des ~ macht mich mied."** She said, "This sweeping makes me tired." LRT

Gekid´der, *n* - giggling. **Was is sell ~?** What is all that giggling about? LRT

Gelaaf´, *n* - continual walking. KYG2159. **Er saagt er is des alli Daag ~ leedich.** He says he is tired of this daily walking. LRT

gelam´mediere, *pp* **gelammediert** - to complain. **Sie hot gelammediert bis sie leenich im Haus waar.** She carried on complaining [in an audible manner] until she was alone in the house. LRT

gelannt´, *adj* - scholarly. **Er is en ~er Mensch.** He is a scholarly person. LRT

geldhungerich, *adj* - money-hungry. **Ich hab nie net viel Zeit ghat fer ~e Leit.** I never had much time for money-hungry people. LRT

Gelen´der, *n* - railing. **Sell ~ an de Bortsch is en gut Ding fer hawwe.** That railing at the porch is a good thing to have. LRT

Geles´, *n* - (infernal) reading. **Wann is des ~ verbei?** When will this reading end? LRT

Gelieb´der, *m* - paramour

geliebt´, *adj* - beloved. **Er is en ~er Mensch.** He is a beloved person. LRT

Gelieg´, *n* - lying. **Schtopp dei ~! Sell is ken Verschtand!** Stop your lying! That is nonsense! LRT

gelschderich, *adj* - scared, terror-stricken. = **vergelschdert, verschteert. Der ganz Hinkelschtall waar ~.** The whole henhouse was terror-stricken. **Nochdem as die Fix im Hinkelhaus waare, waare die Hinkel arig ~.** After the foxes were in the chicken house the chickens were very terror-stricken. LRT

Geluscht´, *n* - desire. **Er hot zu viel ~.** He has too much desire. LRT

Gelzer, *m* - unskilled surgeon. = **Groddegelzer.** KYG2112

gemee´schefdich, *adj* - in union. **en ~i Karich** - a union church [Reformed and Lutheran]. KYG2105

Gemelk´, *n* - (everlasting) milking. **Des ewich ~ muss ewwe alli Daag geduh sei.** This eternal milking has to be done everyday. LRT. **Iwwer e Weil waert des ~ em leedich.** After a while one tires of this eternal milking. LRT

Gemies´, *n* - truck (vegetables). KYG2067. **Sie hen alle Sadde ~e in ihrem Gaarde.** They have all kinds of vegetables in their garden. LRT

gemmle, *pp* **gegemmelt** -

<Engl, to gamble. LRT

Gemun´kel, *n* - unintelligible grumbling. KYG2105. **Yunger, schtopp sell ~, es kann niemand dich verschteh.** Young man, stop that grumbling, no one can understand you. LRT

Genaeh´, *n* - **1** sewing. = **Naehe(s). 2** sewed articles. **Sie macht en ordlich guder Daagluh mit ihrem ~.** She makes a pretty good daily wage with her sewing. LRT

geneicht´, *adj* - apt to. KYG2027

Genischt´, *n* - tangle of brush, weeds, etc. KYG1967

Gensyoch, *n* - yoke put on geese. KYG2263

genzlich, *adj* - completely, totally. *cf* **ganz.** KYG1979. **Des is ~ zu viel Arewet.** This is entirely too much work. LRT

Gerap´pel, *n* - continual rattling. **Des ~ in seine Kaer schtoppt ewwe net.** The continual rattling in his car just won't quit. LRT

Gerech´dichkeit, *f* - righteousness. **Es is nix wie ~.** There is nothing like righteousness. LRT

gerech´derweis, *adv* - rightly. **Wann du eppes saagscht, wees mer as es ~ gsaat is.** When you say something, one knows it is rightly said. LRT

Gerenn´, *n* - running. *cf* **Schpringe. Kannscht net a bissel langsamer geh, des ~ is**

net fer mich. Can't you walk a bit more slowly, this running is not for me. LRT

gering′, *adj* - trifling. = **net viel waert.** KYG2061

Gerischt′, *n* - walking frame (of a sawmill). KYG2159

Geriss′, *n* - tearing. KYG1977

Geruch′, *m* - scent, smell. **Seller ~ macht em schier dod.** That scent almost kills you. **Ich gleich der Bisskatze ~ net.** I don't like the skunk odor. LRT. = **(G)schmack, (G)schpur.**

geschdrich, *adj* - of or pertaining to yesterday. KYG2262

Geschnud′del, *n* - drinking in a sloppy manner. **Tschecki, schtopp sell ~.** Jakey, stop that sloppy drinking. LRT

Geschnuf′fel, *n* - sniffles. **Yunger, do is en Schnuppduch, blos dei Naas. Des ~ bin ich leedich.** Young man, here is a handkerchief, blow your nose. I'm tired of this sniffling. LRT

Geschtol′per, *n* - (repeated) stumbling. **Du muscht Acht gewwe, des ~ verbrecht dir mol ee Daag dei Beh.** You must be careful, this continued stumbling will break your leg one day. LRT

Getick′, *n* - ticking of a clock. KYG2012

Gewa′reb, *n, pl* **Gewarewer** - node in stem of plant. **Wann mer Blummschteck nunnerschneide will, sett mer** die Nescht abschneide an die Gewarewer. When one wants to cut down flower plants, one should cut the branches at the nodes. LRT

gewarrt′, *adj* - tangled. **~ Schtroh** - tangled straw. *cf* **rankich** (vines), **ranklich** (vines), **verhuddelt, verkehrt, verwickelt, ghuddelt, verwarrt, in enanner drin.** KYG1967

gewa′xe, *adj* - grown. **Unser Kinner sin all ~.** Our children are all grown. LRT

Gewesch′, *n* - continual washing. KYG2168. **Des ~ muss alli Woch geduh sei.** This continual washing is a weekly chore (needs to be done weekly). LRT

Gewex′, *n* - tumor. = **Gschwaer, Gschwier, Gschwulscht.** *cf* **Schwelling.** KYG2074

gewid′dergschlagge, *adj* - thunderstruck. **Ich waar so ~, ich hab net gewisst was Kopp odder Schwanz waar.** I was so confused, I didn't know head from tail. LRT

Gewid′dermiehl, *f* - name given to an old mill, years ago in Lebanon County, PA. LRT

Gewid′derregge, *m* - thunder shower. KYG2012. **Mir hen Wasser iwweraal ghat vun sellem ~.** We had water everywhere from that thunder shower. LRT

Gewid′derschtarem - thunder and lightning storm. **Mir hen heit en ~ ghat.** We had a thunderstorm today. **Es guckt as** wann mir en ~ griege meechde.** It looks as though we may get a thunderstorm. LRT

Gewid′derwolk, *f, pl* **~e** - thundercloud. KYG2012. **Selli ~e bringe uns heit noch en Gewidderregge.** Those thunder clouds are going to bring us a thunder shower yet today. LRT

gewid′derich, *adj* - thundering. *cf* **gewidderschwer.** KYG2012. **Des waar awwer schund ~ die Woch.** We have had our share of thundering this week. LRT

Gewid′dersaeg, *f* - up and down saw. = **Ruffunrunnersaeg.** KYG2117

Gewiehl′, *n* - rooting. **Ich hab genunk vun der Sei ihre ~.** I have had enough of the hogs' rooting. LRT

Gewinn′, *f, pl* **~e** - thread of a screw. **ihre ~e schlippe** - to slip their threads. **Die ~e uff denne Schrauwe sin bissel verhunst.** The threads on these screws are a bit messed up. LRT

gewin′ne - to win, prevail. **Wann mer lang genunk aahalt, dutt mer endlich ~.** If one hangs in there (tries) long enough, he will finally prevail or win. LRT

Gewin′neschneider, *m* - thread cutter. KYG2004

gewis′selos, *adj* - unconscionable. KYG2094

Gewis′senszwang, *m* - twinge of conscience. KYG2083

gewiss′, *adv* - truly. = **waahrhafdich, waricklich,**

verhafdich, zwaar. So ~ as alles. As true as can be. KYG2068. So ~ as alles, sis denk en "Schock," awwer sie sin geschder do weckgezoge. True as can be, I think it comes as a shock, but they moved away from here yesterday. LRT

gewitt′re, *pp* gewittert - 1 to threaten a thunderstorm. KYG2004. 2 to thunder. Es is am ~. It is thundering. Harich mol, sis am g(e)wittre. Listen, it's thundering. LRT

gewittrich, *adj* - threatening a thunderstorm. KYG2004. Ich gleich des ~ Wedder net. I don't like this threatening weather. LRT

Gewun′ner, *n* - suspense. Des waar en grosser ~ bis mer mol gwisst hot was am aageh waar. This was quite a suspense until we finally knew what was going on. LRT

gewwe, *pp* ~ - to give. epper eens ~ - to sock someone. Yunger, wann du dich net bedraagscht, geb ich dir eens. Young man, if you don't behave yourself, I'll sock you one. Sie hot ihm eens ~ uff die Hannschaal. She gave him a rap on his skull. LRT

Geyae′mer, *n* - (constant) moaning. Sei ~ waert mer glei leedich. One soon tires of his constant moaning. LRT

Geyux′, *n* - horse-play. Der Onkel Yarick hot gsaat, "So'n ~ is niemand wert!" Uncle George said, "No one is worthy of such horse-play!"

gezackt′, *adj* - toothed

(indented). = zackich, zacklich. KYG2036

Gezack′er, *n* - 1 trudging. KYG2068. 2 tiresome driving about. KYG2026

Gezann′, *n* - wrath. Sell ~ fattmache is zu viel fer mich. That continued wrath is too much for me. LRT,4/18/2000

Gezarr′, *n* - (continual) teasing. KYG1977. So en ~ waart mer alsemols leddich. Sometimes, one tires of such (continual) teasing. LRT

Gezaw′wel, *n* - (constant) struggling, wriggling. Schlack die Sau nochemol uff der Kopp, ihre ~ geht noch aa. Strike the hog on the head again, her wriggling continues. Sell ~ schtoppt ewwe net. There's just no end to that continual wriggling. LRT,4/18/2000

Gezew′wel, *n* - commotion. yung ~ - young people. KYG2264

Gezing′el, *n* - (continual) tongue-wagging. KYG2034. Ich hab en ~ im linkse Ohr. I have a tingling sensation in my left ear. LRT

Gezwack′er, *n* - twinge. *cf* Schtich. KYG2083. Du saagscht du hoscht en ~ in deim linkse Aarem, gell? You say you have a twinge in your left arm, not so? LRT

gezwil′licht, *adj* - twilled. = zwillich. KYG2083

Gfaahr, *f* - risk. Em Bischli-Gnippli sei Waddebuch saagt: "Wer sich in die ~ begebt,

kummt drin um." Dick Beam's dictionary says: "He who places himself in danger is overcome by it." LRT

Gfiehl, *n* - 1 (sense of) touch. 2 (repeated) touching. KYG2041

gfiehllos, *adj* - torpid. KYG2039

gfillt, *adj* - filled. Ich gleich gfillder Seimaage. I like filled pig stomach. LRT

Gfrees, *n* - trash.

Gfress[1], *n* - (comical) face. Mach ken so en ~! Don't make such a face!

Gfress[2], *n* - ugly face. Mach net so en wiescht ~. Don't make such an ugly face. LRT

Gfrog, *n* - (constant) questioning. Sei ~ halt yuscht uff bis mer ganz ausgfrogt is. His constant questioning just continues until one has no more answers. LRT

Gfuker, *n* - to-do. KYG2030

Gfusser, *pl* - fuzz. Wu kummt sell ~ bei was du uff deim Wammes hoscht? Where does that fuzz come from that's on your jacket? LRT

Ghaschpel, *n* - thoughtless movements. KYG2002

gheere, *pp* gheert - to belong. Zu wem ~ sie? To whom do they belong? LRT

Ghuddelwese, *n* - tangled thread. KYG2003

Gichdere, *pl* - convulsions. Is

sie unmechdich odder hot sie die ~? Is she unconscious or does she have the convulsions? LRT

Gickerigie, *m* - cock-a-doodle-do. **"~," sell is wie der Haahne graeht.** "Gickerigie," that is how the rooster crows. LRT

Giesskann, *f, pl* ~e - sprinkling can. **~e sin hendich fer Blumme wessere.** Sprinkling cans are convenient to water flowers. LRT

Giesskannekopp, *m* - sprinkler (of sprinkling can). **Ich hab unser ~ verlore.** I lost our sprinkler from our sprinkling can. LRT

Gifdegretz, *m* - rash from poison ivy. LRT

Giftranke, *pl* - poison ivy vines. LRT

Giftschwamm, *m* - toadstool. = **Groddefress, Groddeschtul, Groddefuuss, Schwamm, Deiwelsbrod.** KYG2027

Gippel, *m* - top (in climbing). **Sie sin nuff uff der ~ vum Barig gegraddelt.** They climbed the summit of the mountain. LRT

Gipser, *m* - towheaded child that follows parents in field. KYG2943

gixe, *pp* **gegixt** - to sting. = **giexe, schteche.** KYG1880

Gixer, *m* - hiccough. LRT

Glaas, *n, pl* **Glesser** - 1 glass. **un glenne Glesser an sellem** - and small glasses at that.

KYG1992. **Ich daed gleiche en ~ Millich hawwe.** I'd like to have a glass of milk. LRT. **2** thermometer. KYG1995. = **Wedderglaas.** LRT

Glaas-schliffer, *m, f, pl* ~e, Leb.Co.=**glaasni-schliffere** - a sliver of glass. **Geb Acht datt sin ~e uff em Bodde.** Be careful there are slivers of glass on the floor. LRT

Glaasaag, *n* - glass (false) eye. **Mer kann sei ~ schier net sehne.** One can hardly notice his glass (false) eye. LRT

Glammhoke, *m* - crane hook. **Was gut is en Glamm unni Hoke?** What good is a crane without a hook? LRT

Glang, *m, pl* **Glenge** - tone. *cf* **Laut.** KYG2033

Glappbordfens, *f* - <*Engl* clapboard fence. **Selli ~ sett aagschtriche sei.** That pale fence needs (should be) painted. LRT

Glappbordschteddel, *n* - small group of houses surrounded with picket fences. **Yuscht nard vun Mt. Zion in Lebnen Kaundi hen mir en glee Schtettli as ~ heest.** Just north of Mt. Zion in Lebanon County, PA we have a hamlet called "Clapboardstown." LRT

glatt, *adj* - slippery. **Mir sin glicklich as mir do sin; es Eis waar arig ~ de mariye.** We are lucky that we are here; the ice was really slick this morning. LRT

glattschprauich, *adj* - smooth-chaffed. **Ich gleich ~er Weeze**

besser wie graanicher. I like awnless wheat better that the awned wheat. LRT

Glee, *m* - clover. **Ich gleich vier blettrich ~ zu finne.** I like to find four-leafed clover. LRT

Gleederkammer, *f* - (cabinet-like) wardrobe. *cf* **Gleederschank.** KYG2164

Gleederschank, *m* - wardrobe. **Seller ~ is zu glee fer all unser Gleeder.** That wardrobe is too small for all our clothes. LRT

Glees, *m, pl* ~er - rut (track). **Ich will nix zu duh hawwe mit me Weg as diefi ~er hot.** I don't want anything to do with a road that has deep ruts. LRT

glei, *adv* - soon. (Cbs, Dn, Nlr, SELn, Nd, NWSI, SESr, Un, SEYk, Mn, Ccr, Cn, Elh). = **eb lang** (NECr, Scl), **ball** (Cln, Nn, SESr, SEYk), **ballemol, iwwer e Weil, mit naegschdem, bei naegschdem. ~ widder** - soon again. KYG. **~ gehn ich heem.** Soon I'm going home. LRT

glei-dennooch, *adv* - shortly thereafter. **Sell waar ~.** That was soon afterwards. LRT

gleich, *adv* - similar. **Ich hoff net as mir ~ gucke.** I hope we don't look the same. LRT

Gleiches, *n* - something similar. **Es hot ken ~.** It is unrivaled. KYG2111. **Sei Fraa waar's naegscht sei ~.** His wife was most nearly like him. LRT

gleichgildich, *adj* - unconcerned. = **unbekimmerlich.** KYG2094

glenze - to shine, glitter. **Es is net alles Gold was glenzt.** It's not all gold that glitters. (Proverb) LRT

Glepperbohl, *f, pl* **~e** - mixing bowl. **Mer dutt's weiss vun die Oier gleppere in die ~e.** One beats the egg-whites in the mixing bowls. LRT

glepperich, *adj* - rattling. **~i Fenschdere gleich ich net.** Rattling windows I do not like. LRT

glessaagich, *adj* - wall-eyed. = **glaasaagich.** KYG2160

Glewwer in de Odre - thrombosis. KYG2008

glicke, *pp* **geglickt** - to succeed. **Es hot ihm geglickt.** He succeeded. **Ya, sei Schreiwes hot ihm geglickt.** Yes, his writing was a success. LRT

Glickschuss, *m* - unexpected success. KYG2101

Gliedergramp, *m* - muscular cramps. **Du hoscht widder ~, du gingscht besser zum Dokder.** You have muscular cramps again, you had better see a doctor. LRT

Glingerschteddel, *n* - ✪ Klingerstown, PA. KYG2274

glinglich, *adj* - tinkling. KYG2023. **Die Schliddebelle sin arig ~.** The sleigh bells are very tinkling. LRT

Glockemaul, *n* - iron mouth (of a church bell). LRT

Glopp, *m* - rap. **Harich mol! ~! ~! Sis epper an die Dier!**

Listen! Knock! Knock! There's someone at the door! LRT

gloppe, *pp* **gegloppt** - to palpitate, pound. **Sell hot awwer mei Hatz ~ gemacht.** Boy, that made my heart pound. **Ich denk sell hot awwer sei Hatz ~ gemacht wie sie ihm gsaat hen as er en Millyoon Daaler gwunne hot.** I guess that made his heart pound, when they told him he won a million dollars. LRT

Glopperei, *f* - pounding. **Ich bin froh, wann die Schreiner heemgehne; die ~ bin ich leedich.** I'll be glad when the carpenters go home; I'm tired of this pounding (hammering). LRT

Gloppiches, *n* - pounding. **eppes ~** - something to hammer with. **Ich hab eppes ~ im Kopp.** I have a pounding in my head. LRT

Glotz, *m, pl* **Gletz** - segment of a tree trunk. KYG2070. **Gletz muss mer Schier hawwe wann mer Hinkel keppe will.** Chopping blocks (segments of tree trunks) are almost a necessity if one wants to behead chickens (with an axe). LRT

Glowe, *m* - staple. **~ odder Schtiepel, hees sie was du witt, mer yuust sie fer Fensedroht feschtmache an die Poschde. ~** or **Schtiepel,** call them what you will, they are staples used to fasten fence wire to posts. LRT

gluschdich, *adj* - desirous. **Sell macht em awwer ~.** Indeed that makes one desirous. LRT

Gnaadehidde - ✪ Gnadenhutten (in PA and in

OH) <*StG* **Gnadenhütten.** KYG2272

gnacke, *pp* **gegnackt** - to tick. = **gnecke, ticke.** KYG2013. **Die Uhr is am ~.** The clock is ticking. LRT

gnackere, *pp* **gegnackert** - to be unsteady. = **wankle.** KYG2113

gnackerich, *adj* - tottering. KYG2040

Gnackmaschien, *f* - telegraph transmitter. KYG1979

gnackrich, *adj* - unstable. *cf* **schnepperich.** KYG2113. **Im Winder is der Disch un die Schtiel arig ~.** In the winter this table and the chairs are very creaky. LRT

gnaersche, *pp* **gegnaerscht** - to gnash the teeth. KYG2036. **Sell laut wiescht, wann er sei Zaeh gnaerscht.** That sounds ugly when he grinds his teeth. LRT

Gnall, *m* - a loud report. **Was waar sell? Sell waar awwer en lauder ~.** What was that? That was a really loud sound. LRT

Gnalleise, *n* - *facet.* worthless gun. **Er hot gsaat, "Dunner un's ~!" Was hot er gmehnt?** He said, "Thunderation!" What did he mean? LRT,4/18/2000

gnapps, *adv* - scantily. **Sell Esssach waar ~ genunk fer en gleener Hund fiedere.** That food was hardly enough to feed a little dog. **Zehe Pfund Fleesch is ~ genunk fer zwansich Leit fiedere.** Ten pounds of meat is hardly enough to feed twenty people. **Er is ~.** He skimps. **Sell Esse fer all selli Leit waar ~**

genunk. That food for all those people was scarcely enough. LRT. *cf* **kaum**

gnappse, *pp* **gegnappst** - to stint. *cf* **gnarre.** KYG1881

Gnappser, *m* - stingy fellow. KYG1881

gnarre, *pp* **gegnarrt** - to snarl. **Der Hund hot an uns gegnarrt.** The dog snarled at us. LRT

Gnarwel, *m* - poorly healed wound. **Er hot en wieschder ~ uff yedem Fuuss.** He has bad-looking scar tissue on each foot. LRT,4/18/2000

gnarwlich, *adj* - **1** rough. **Dei Haut is ~. Sin sell Waarze?** Your skin has some roughness. Are those warts? LRT. **2** stumpy (speaking of an old tree). **Ya, sell Beintholz is ~.** Yes that pinewood is full of knots. LRT

Gnarze, *m* - **1** blemish on fruit caused by sting. KYG1880. [Not confined strictly to stings.] **Die Eppel sin voll ~; seller Schlosseschtarem hot n' Schaade geduh.** The apples are full of blemishes; that hail storm did its damage. **Die Eppel hen en latt ~.** The apples have lots of deformities LRT. **2** stumpy old tree. LRT

gnatzich, *adj* - **1** scrubby (of corn). **Em Tscheck sei Welschkann is ~ des Yaahr.** Jake's corn is scrubby this year. **2** deformed, imperfect. **Die Eppel sin awwer ~.** The apples are deformed. LRT

Gnechthaus, *n* - tenant house. KYG1984. = **Lehnshaus.** LRT/

Leb. Co.

Gnechtschaft, *f* - thralldom. KYG2003

gnetschich, *adj* - soggy. **Schmeiss sell ~ Brot weck.** Throw that soggy bread away. LRT

Gnewwel, *m* - bolt at the end of a chain. LRT

gnewwle, *pp* **gegnewwelt** - to twist tight. KYG2084

gniedief, *adv* - up to the knees. KYG2117. **Zu mir is ~ im Schnee laafe net viel Schpass.** To me walking in the snow up to my knees, is not much fun. LRT

Gniekehl, *f* - posterior part of knee joint. **Ich hass nix ariger as wie kalt Wasser in die ~ gschpritzt griege.** I hate nothing more than to have cold water sprayed on the back of my knees. LRT

Gnieriehm, *m* - stirrup. = **Schtei-biggel, Schteifbiggel, Schteigbiggel.** KYG1882

Gniewand, *f* - part of wall between roof and garret floor. KYG2160. **Die Dachschtiel hewe die ~ am Blatz.** The wooden roof supports hold the walls between the roof and garret floors in place. [The supports actually serve as the studs for the **Gniewand.** LRT.]

Gnipp, *m* - knot. **hadder ~** - tight knot. KYG2016. **Sell is en hadder ~.** That is a tight knot. LRT

gnippe, *pp* **gegnippt** - to tie in a knot. KYG2015. **Er kann gut ~.**

He knots well. LRT

Gnippel, *m* - truncheon. = **schwerer Hewel.** KYG2069

Gnochefleesch, *n* - meat closest to the bone. **Es ~ schmackt's bescht.** The meat next to the bones tastes the best. LRT

Gnocheflex, *f* - tendon. *cf* **Schparroder.** KYG1985

Gnoddelarewet, *f* - tedious job. KYG1978

Gnoddelwoll, *f* - wool full of sheep manure. KYG2242. **Es nemmt Geduld fer ~ uffbutze.** It takes patience to clean up wool that is messed up with manure. LRT,4/11/2000. *cf* **Gnoddelwoller**

Gnoll, *m, pl* **~e** - tuber. = **Gnolle.** KYG2072

gnollich, *adj* - tuberous. KYG2072

gnootsche, *pp* **gegnootscht** - to fondle. **Kaeti, ich will dir eppes saage, bleib weck vun sellem Yunge, er gleicht die Maed ~.** Katy, I want to tell you, stay away from that young man, he likes to fondle the girls. LRT,4/11/2000. **Er gleicht sell Maedel bissel ~.** He likes to fondle that girl a bit. LRT. = **rumgnootsche.** KYG2019

Gnopp, *m, pl* **Gnepp** - button. **Gnepp im Kopp** - tricks, shrewdness. **Du hoscht en ~ verlore an deim Hemm.** You lost a button on your shirt. LRT

Gnowwlichwascht, *f* - garlic-flavored sausage. **Wann sell Rinsfleesch vun Gnowwlich**

schmackt, nemme mer's zerick un froge fer unser Geld. If beef got tainted from wild garlic—which the cattle got in their pasture—my parents would return the beef for a refund. LRT

goldegehl, *adj* - golden yellow. KYG2261. **Selli ~e Blumme sin wunnerbaar schee.** Those golden yellow flowers are exceptionally beautiful. LRT,4/21/2000

gotterbaremlich, *adv* - terribly. **Es waar ~ hees heit.** It was terribly hot today. LRT

Gottesdinscht, *m* - worship service. **Mir hen en ~ alli Sunndaag Mariye am zwanzich Minudde bis elf Uhr.** We have a church service every Sunday morning at twenty minutes of eleven o'clock. LRT,4/18/2000

Gotteswatt, *n* - the Word of God. **Gott sei Watt is gut; er gebt uns was mir froge devor odder eppes Bessers.** God's word is good. He always gives us what we ask or something better. LRT,4/11/2000

Gotteswelt, *f* - God's world. **Was in der ~ geht dann do aa?** What in (all God's) the world is going on here? LRT,4/11/2000

Gottlieb, *m* - Theophilus. KYG2286. **In Lebnen Kaundi hen mir mol en ~ Heffelfinger ghat.** In Lebanon County, we had a Gottlieb Heffelfinger. LRT,4/21/2000

gottlos, *adj* - ungodly. KYG2103. **Selli Yunge hen sich ~ aagschickt.** Those young men acted in an ungodly

manner. LRT

Graab, *n, pl* **Graewer** - grave. **Mei Paep hot en mannich ~ gegraawe am Karichhof an die Zoar Ludderisch Karich an Mt. Zion, Leb. Co., PA.** My dad dug many a grave at the cemetery at Zoar Lutheran Church at Mt. Zion, Leb. Co., PA. LRT

Graabeise, *n* - <*Engl* digging iron [iron bar used for digging (postholes, graves, etc.)]. LRT

Graabgreiz, *n, pl* **~er** - cross on a grave. **Deel vun selle Griegsgraabhef hen hunnerts von ~er.** Some of those military cemeteries have hundreds of grave crosses on them. LRT,4/11/2000

Graabschrift, *f* - tombstone inscription. KYG2033

Graabsschteehacker, *m, pl* **~** - tombstone cutter. **Wie mir an die Zoar Karich in Mt. Zion, PA gewuhnt hen, hab ich ordlich oft ~ gsehne uff em Karichhof.** When we lived at the Zoar Church in Mt. Zion, PA, I saw tombstone cutters pretty often at the cemetery. **Die ~ duhne scheeni Arewet heidesdaages.** The tombstone cutters do nice work now-a-days. LRT. = **Graabsschteemacher**

graad, *adj* - straight. **Daer Schaffblatz brauch yuscht Leit as Sache ~ halde kenne.** This place of employment only needs people who can keep things straight LRT

graadaus, *adv* - in plain terms. KYG1987. **Ich will dir ~ saage, was ich mehn.** I want to tell you

in plain terms (right out) what I mean. LRT

graadeswegs, *adv* - right away. **Kumm ~!** Come right away! **Duh's ~!** Do it now! LRT. = **graadewecks**

graad-eweck, *adv* - thereupon. **Die Schul hot ausgelosst un ~ is sie widder an die Arewet gange!** School was out and immediately there upon she went to work again. LRT. = **dattdruff**

graadfatt, *adv* - straight on. **Faahr ~.** Drive straight on out that way. LRT

graadnunner, *adv* - straight down. **Guck ~, no sehscht du ihn.** Look straight down and you will see him. LRT

Graahne, *m* - stop-cock. KYG1889

grabsche, *pp* **gegrabscht** - to snatch. **Er hot alles gegrabscht as er finne hot kenne.** He snatched everything that he could find. LRT

Graft, *f* - strength. **Sei ~ is meh as die menschde Leit hen.** His strength is greater than what most people have. LRT

Grageel'er, *m* - quarreler, an insistently troublesome person. KYG2065. **Du witt dich vun ihm weckhalde; er is en ~.** You want to stay away from him, he is a constant argumentative complainer and is insistently troublesome. **Grageele un ~ sin net willkumm in meim Haus.** Violent quarreling and quarrelers are not welcome in my house. LRT

Graman'zelwese, *n* - fancy trimmings. KYG2062

Granket, *f, pl* ~e - illness. **Selle Kinner duhne alli Sadde ~e fange.** Those children catch all kinds of diseases. LRT

Gratz, *m* - scratch. = **Gritz, Gritzer, Marick. Ich seh dei Kaer hot en gleener Gritzer.** I see your car has a little scratch. LRT

Gratz, *m* - ✪ Gratz, PA. KYG2272

Gratzes, *n* - tickling sensation. = **Kitzles.** KYG2014

gratzich, *adj* - **1** partly fermented. **Der Seider schmackt bissel ~.** The cider tastes a bit scratchy, *i.e.* partly fermented. **2** tickling. KYG2014. **Mei Hals is ~.** My throat is tickling. LRT

graunze - to speak indistinctly. = **schtruddle.** KYG1964

Graut, *n* - top of a plant. KYG2037. **Es ~ vun selle Zelaatesteck macht gut Esses.** The tops of those lettuce plants make good eating. LRT

Grautselaat, *m* - Cole slaw. LRT

grawwle - to crawl. **Die Warem sin am ~.** The worms are crawling. LRT

Grees, *f* - size, measurements. **Wann mir seller Buh recht gleede welle, misse mir sei ~ hawwe.** If we want to dress that boy properly, we need to have his measurements. LRT

Grefde, *pl* - stamina. **Seller alt Mann hot schier ken ~ meh.** That old man has almost no stamina anymore. LRT

grefdich, *adj* - stalwart. **Er is ~ fer sei Elt.** He is strong for his age. LRT

greische - to squeal (of pigs). **Mer kann die Sei heere ~, ich denk sie sin hungerich.** One can hear the pigs squealing, I guess they are hungry. LRT

Greischerei, *f* - confusion of shouts. **Gschwischich Mann un Fraa gebt's ebmols so en ordlichi ~.** Sometimes between man and wife there is quite a confusion of shouts. LRT

Greissel, *m* - nausea. **epper der ~ gewwe** - to turn the stomach. KYG1885

greissle, *refl* - to make one shudder, turn one's stomach. **Es greisselt mich.** It makes me shudder. LRT/Leb Co. **Es greisselt mir.** It turns my stomach. *cf* **Es is mir iwwel.** I'm sick at the stomach. KYG1885. **Bisskatze abziege, yuscht fer datt draa denke, greisselt mich.** To skin skunks, just to think of it, turns my stomach. LRT

greisslich, *adj* - terrible. **Selli dod Kuh voll Maade drunne im Schwamm waar en ~ Ding fer sehne.** That dead cow full of maggots down in the meadow was a horrible thing to see. LRT

Greiz, *n* - **1** the small of the back. **Du kannscht vielleicht sehne wie ich laaf as es mir weh dutt im ~.** Perhaps you can see from the way I'm walking

that I've got pain in the small of my back. LRT. **2** burden. **Sei Arewet waar ihm en ~.** His work was tiresome (a burden). KYG2026

Greizholz, *n* - scantling. **En guter Schreiner brauch en gut ~.** A good carpenter needs a good scantling. LRT

Greizweg, *m* - crossroad. KYG2270. **Die Schmidde Familye wuhnt graad datt am ~.** The Schmidt family lives right there by the crossroad. LRT,4/21/2000

Greizweh, *n* - backache. LRT

grempe - to catch in turning. KYG2079

grempisch, *adv* - walking with a stooped gait. KYG1889. **Er is yung fer so ~ laafe.** He is young to walk with such a stooped gait. LRT

grenke - to take sick. KYG1963

grenklich, *adj* - invalid, unhealthy. **Sie waar schund paar Yaahr arig ~ gewest.** For several years she has been very sickly. **Seller Mann waar sei ganz Lewe lang ~, mer hot schier net gedenkt as er so lang Lewe daed.** That man was so sickly his whole life, one hardly thought that he would live this long. LRT. = **unwohl.** KYG2104

grenzelos, *adj* - unbounded. KYG2092

greppe - <*Engl* to grab; to regret a loss. **Seller Hund verliere dutt mich awwer ~!** Losing that dog really "grabs"

73

me, really troubles me. LRT

Gret, *f* - Greta, Margaret. = **Gretschel.** KYG2284

Grickli, *n* - **1** small gravy pitcher. LRT. **2** little creek. CRB

griddelich, *adj* - sticklish, testy, trying. LRT. = **griddlich**

griddlich, *adj* - testy. KYG1990. **Selli Kinner sin immer so ~.** Those children are always so testy. LRT. = **griddelich.** *cf* **eegesinnich**

grie, *adj* - unripe. KYG2111. **Deel Leit gleiche** Bananas, **wann sie bissel ~ sin, awwer ich gleich sie viel besser wann sie bissel schwatz sin.** Some people like bananas when they are a bit green (unripe), but I like them much better when they are very ripe (a bit black). LRT. = **unzeidich, net zeidich**

Grieg(s)zeit, *f* - time of war. KYG2018. *cf* **Weltgrieg**

griege, *pp* **grickt** - **1** to get. **es vun epper ~ -** to get a scolding from someone. **Wann du net Acht gebscht, griegscht du en gudi Schelding.** If you are not careful, you will get a good scolding. LRT. **2** to become upset. **Es hot ihn wiescht grickt.** It really upset him. LRT

Grieger, *m* - warrior. = **Greigsmann, Soldaat.** KYG2166

Griegerei, *f* - making war. KYG2166. **Die ~ is ken Schpass.** The making of war is no fun. LRT

Griegs-schiff, *n, pl* ~**er** -

warship. KYG2166. **Mir hen schund en latt gudi ~er ghat.** We (the U.S.) have already had a lot of good warships. LRT

Griegsboppel, *n* - war baby. KYG2163. **Der Tschecki waar gewiss en ~. Er waar gebore nein Munet nochdem as der Grieg veriwwer waar.** Jakie was truly a war baby. He was born nine months after the war was over. LRT. = **Griegsboppli**

Griegsbulfer, *n* - war powder. = **Griegspulfer.** KYG2165

Griegsdunner, *n* - thunder of war. KYG2011. **Er hot gsaat ~, un ich hab gaar net gwisst was er gemehnt hot.** He said Griegsdunner, and I had no idea what he was talking about. LRT

Griegsgaul, *m, pl* -**geil** - war horse. KYG2164. -**geil basse net arig gut heidesdaags.** War horses are not very appropriate now-a-days. LRT

Griegsgraabhof, *m, pl* -**hef** - military cemetery. **Deel vun denne** -**hef hen hunnerts von Graabgreizer.** Some of those military cemeteries have hundreds of grave crosses on them. LRT, 4/11/2000

Griegskummeraad, *m* - war comrade. KYG2163. **Der H. Walter Schtump waar em Karl sei ~.** H. Walter Schtump was Karl's war comrade. LRT

Griegszeit, *f* - time of war. KYG2163. **Sis schier immer ~ ariyets in daere Welt.** It's almost always wartime somewhere in this world. LRT

Grimm, *f* - turn. KYG2076

grindich, *adj* - scabby. **Sei Haut is ~.** His skin is scabby. LRT

Grindkopp, *m* - battered head. **sich en ~ aaschwetze** - to get into trouble. KYG2065. **Er is en ~, alle Moler as er hot, hot er verdient.** He is a scabhead, he has earned every scab (and scar) that he has (being the trouble maker that he is). LRT

Grischtdaage, *pl* - Christmas. **frehlichi ~ -** Merry Christmas! **der zwett Grischtdaag** - the day after Christmas. LRT

Grischtdaagsbaem, *pl* - Christmas trees. **Sie hen sell ganz Weedschtick in ~ geblanzt.** They planted that whole pasture field in Christmas trees. LRT

grischtlich, *adj* - Christian. **Es waar yuscht des ~ Ding zu duh.** It was just the Christian thing to do. LRT

Grissel, *m, pl* ~ - **1** upset stomach. **der ~ gewwe** - to turn one's stomach. = **sei Maage rumdrehe.** KYG2077. **2** distasteful, cold shivers. **Sell is awwer en ~.** That is a cold shivering matter. LRT. **3** thrill. KYG2007

grissele, *refl* - to shudder. **Sell grisselt mer awwer!** That makes me shudder. LRT

grisslich, *adj* - thrilling. *cf* **greisslich.** KYG2007

Gritzel - scrawl. **Was fer en ~ de Fix is mer dann sell?** What kind of scrawl is that? LRT

Gritzel-fixel, *n* - fine tracery work. = **Gritz-fixel.** KYG2045. = **Gritzeldiefix.** LRT/Leb.

grodde-falsch, *adj* - mad as a toad. KYG2027

Groddefuuss, *m* - toad's foot. KYG2027

Groddegixer, *m* - toad bleeder. KYG2027

Groddeglumme, *pl* - turtle head. KYG2080

grollkeppich, *adj* - curly headed. **Er is ~.** He is a curly head. LRT

Grood, *m* - stitch. *cf* **Schteche.** KYG1882

groozich, *adj* - 1 musty. 2 moldy. **Die Schunke sin ~.** The hams are moldy. LRT

gross-gfressich, *adj* - big-mouthed. **en ~ Weibsmensch** - a shrew. KYG1988. = **gross-meilich.** LRT/Leb.

grossfiehlich, *adj* - <*Engl* big feeling. **Er schickt sich immer so ~ aa.** He always acts so pompous. LRT

Grosskopp, *m, pl* -**kepp** - big wig. **Die -kepp hen ewwe iwwergenumme.** The big wigs have just taken over. LRT

grossmechdich, *adj* - very tall. KYG1965. **Ya, er is en ~er Ding.** Yes, he is a very tall guy. LRT

Grub, *f, pl* **Gruwe** - underground container. KYG2096

Grummbiereausmacheszeit, *f* - potato digging time. LRT

Grummbierekeffer, *pl* - potato beetles. **Die ~ lege scheeni gehli Oier (Niss).** The potato beetles lay nice yellow eggs. LRT,4/11/2000

Grummbiereschaale, *pl* - potato peels. **"~" waar's erscht gross Watt, as mei gleener Bruder gsaat hot.** "Potato peels" was the first big word that my little brother said. LRT

Grummbiereschtock, *m* - potato stalk. LRT

grummle - to grumble. LRT

grummlich, *adj* - prone to grumble. **Sei net so ~!** Don't be so prone to grumble. LRT

Grund, *m* - ground, earth. **Yunger, du witt feschtschteh uff deim eegene ~.** Young fellow, you will want to stand firm on your own ground. LRT

Grundax, *f* - groundhog. **Wann ich ~ esse will, macht's mir nix aus, eb's en Kitz adder'n Kaader is.** If I want to eat groundhog, it makes no difference to me if it's a female or a male. LRT,4/11/2000

Grundfareb, *f* - tone. KYG2033

Grundnissbudder, *m* - peanut butter. **~ un Molassich uff Brot gschmiert macht awwer gut Esses.** Peanut butter and molasses spread on bread make especially good eating. LRT

Grundsau, *f* - groundhog. **Deel Leit saage die ~ un ihre**

Wedderbrofeedes is nix as wie Hombock. Some people say that the groundhog's weather prophesy is nothing but hombug. LRT,4/11/2000. = **Grundax**

Grundweschp, *f* - wingless wasp. KYG2169

gruschdich, *adj* - out of sorts. **Was is dann letz mit dir? Du schickscht dich awwer ~ aa.** What is wrong with you? You are really acting out of sorts. LRT

Grusselkopp, *m* - curly top. KYG2037. = **Grollkopp.** LRT

Grutzer, *m* - runt [a poor sickly one]. **Er is en scheener Buh, ich wees net fer was as sie ihn en ~ heese.** He's a nice boy, I don't know why they call him a runt. **Er is en gleener ~, awwer ich lieb ihn.** He's a poor little sickly one, but I love him. LRT

grutzich, *adj* - 1 runty, stunted. **Wann's so drucke bleibt, dann griege mir blendi ~ Welschkann.** If it stays this dry, we can expect plenty of stunted corn. LRT. **Es Welschkann is ~ des Yaahr, weil's so drucke waar.** The corn is small this year because it was so dry (limited rainfall). LRT. **2** damaged by sting of insect. KYG1880

Gsang, *n* - singing. **Ihre ~ hot schee glaut.** Their singing sounded good. = **Gsing, Singerei, Singes.** LRT

Gscharr[1], *n* - scraping, scratching. **Die Hinkel ihre ~ is hatt uffs Graas im Hinkelhof.** The chickens' scratching is hard on the grass in the chicken yard.

LRT.

Gscharr², *n* - dishes, ware. **~ wesche (schpiele, uffschpiele)** - to wash dishes. **KYG2176. Sie hen's ~ all gewesche.** They washed all the dishes. LRT.

Gscharrkischt, *f, pl* **~e** - toolbox. = **Tscharrkischt.** KYG2035. **Gudi ~e sin net wolfel.** Good tool boxes are not cheap. LRT

Gscharrlumbe, *m* - washrag. *cf* **Waschlumbe, Weschlumbe, Schpiellumbe.** KYG2168

Gscharrschank, *m* - tool closet. KYG2035

gscheid, *adj* - intelligent. **Ya, er is en ~er Buh.** Yes, he is an intelligent boy. LRT

Gscheides, *n* - sensible. **Eppes ~ is mir immer liewer as wie eppes Dummes.** Something sensible always appeals to me more than something stupid. LRT

Gschicht, *f* - state of affairs. **Ei du Yammer, nochemol, wann sell awwer net en ~ waar.** Oh, my sakes, if that was not an affair. LRT

Gschick, *m* - knack. **Er kann sich ken rechter ~ gewwe.** He hasn't quite got the knack. **Er kann sich yuscht ken ~ gewwe fer Riggel mache.** He just doesn't seem to have the knack to make rails. LRT

gschicklich, *adv* - convenient. **Sis yuscht net arig ~.** It is just not very convenient. LRT

Gschicklichkeit, *f* - skillfulness.

Seller Schreiner hot en wunnerbaari ~. That carpenter has wonderful skillfulness. LRT

gschickt, *adj* - skillful, handy. **net ~** - unqualified. KYG2110

Gschiddel, *n* - continual shaking. = **Gewackel. So en ~ verschreckt mich.** Such a (continual) shaking frightens me. LRT

Gschiess, *n* - (continual) shooting. **Des ewwich ~ waert em leedich.** One tires of this constant shooting. LRT

Gschiss un Wese - a fuss over something. **Sie hot immer en ~ gmacht wann em Tschanni sei Haar bissel lang sin warre.** She always made a big fuss when Jonny's hair got a bit long. LRT

Gschlawwer, *n* - **1** foolish, obscene talk. KYG1964. **2** slobbering. LRT

Gschleck, *n, pl* **~e** - tasting of dainties. KYG1972. **Selli ~e sehne mache mei Maul wessere.** Seeing those goodies makes my mouth water. LRT

Gschleef, *n* - a drawn-out undertaking. KYG2098. **Mer wunnert wuher as so en ~ recht sei kann.** One wonders from whence there can be such a drawn out undertaking. LRT

Gschlof, *n* - continual or unusual sleeping. **Epper as so en ~ hot, muss grank sei.** Someone who sleeps so continually must be sick. **Sei ~, Daag un Nacht, is ungwehnlich.** His sleeping, day and night, is abnormal (unusual). LRT

Gschmack, *m* - (sense of) taste. = **Schleck, Versuch.** KYG1972. **An seine Elt is sei ~ nimmi arig gut.** At his age his sense of taste is not very good anymore. LRT

Gschmees, *n* - botflies. **~ sin selle wieschde Micke, was selle gehle Niss uff die dode Gediere lege.** Botflies are those ugly flies that lay those yellow nits (eggs) on dead animals. LRT

Gschmeiss, *n* - throwing. = **Schmeisse.** KYG2010

Gschmok, *n* - continual smoking. **Sei ~ is genunk fer ihn dodmache.** His smoking is enough to kill him. LRT

gschmolze, *adj* - melted. **Wann mer die Fenschdere net nuffschiewe kann, dann sett mer sie allegebott schmiere mit gschmolzner Wax.** When one can't push open the windows, then one should rub melted wax on them from time to time. LRT

Gschnarix, *n* - snoring. **Sei ~ kann mer heere im Keller, wann er uff em Schpeicher is.** His snoring can be heard in the cellar when he is upstairs. LRT

gschnidden, *adj* - wrought. **Gschnittni Neggel sin altguckich.** Wrought iron nails look old-fashioned. LRT,4/18/2000

gschnitzt, *adj* - sliced. **Die Eppel sin ~; mariye owed hen mir Lattwarick.** The apples are sliced; tomorrow evening we will have apple butter. LRT

Gschnuffel, *n* - 1 sniffling. **Guck mol em Hund sei ~, vielleicht is en Haas um der Weg.** Look at that dog's sniffing, maybe there's a rabbit around here. LRT. **2** secret rummaging. **Was fer en ~ duscht du immer?** What kind of a secret rummaging are you always doing? LRT

Gschockel, *n* - rocking. **Der Gremmpaep gleicht sei ~.** Grandpa likes his rocking. LRT

gschore, *adj* - shorn. **~ni Schof** - shorn sheep. **Schofscheerdaage sin verbei, die Schof sin ~.** Sheep shearing season is past, the sheep are shorn. LRT

gschosse, *adj* - gone to seed (of plants). **Die Zwiwwle sin ~.** The onions have gone to seed. LRT

Gschpann, *n* - team. = **Fuhr.** KYG1975

Gschpott, *n* - (continual) mocking. **So'n ~ is yuscht net arig grischtlich.** Such mockery is just not very Christian. LRT

Gschpraech, *n* - talk. **Ihre ~ hot net lang ghalde.** Their talk(ing) didn't last long. LRT. = **Gschwetz.** KYG1964

Gschpritz, *n* - (continual) spurting. **Vun so'm ~ hot mer wisse kenne as eppes am rinne waar.** From such continual spurting one could know that something was leaking. LRT

Gschpuchde, *pl* - pranks. LRT

Gschpur, *f* - trace. KYG2045. **Sell sin Haaseschpure.** Those are rabbit tracks. LRT. =

Schpur

Gschreib, *adj* - writing. **Sie hen gsaat, sie kenne em Venduschreiwer sei ~ net lese.** They said they can't read the sale clerk's writing. LRT,4/18/2000

Gschtamp, *n* - (continual) stamping. **Yunger, sell ~ muscht du schtoppe.** Young man, you must stop that stamping. LRT

Gschtank, *m* - stink, stench. = **Gschtink, Schtink.** KYG1881. **Seller ~ hot mich schier grank gemacht.** That stench almost made me sick. LRT

gschtoppt, *adj* - stuffed. **Der Sack waar ~ voll mit Hinkelfeddre.** The bag was stuffed full with chicken feathers. LRT

Gschtodder, *n* - (constant) stuttering. **Sei ~ is so schlimm mer kann ihn schier net verschteh.** His stuttering is so bad, one can hardly understand him. LRT

Gschwaer, *n* - boil. LRT

Gschwenzel, *n* - tail-wagging. KYG1960. **Binn selle Kuh ihre Schwanz fescht, ich bin ihre ~ leedich.** Tie that cow's tail fast, I'm tired of her tail-wagging. LRT

gschwewwelt, *adj* - three sheets to the wind (intoxicated). KYG2004

gschwind-bsunne, *adj* - sharp-witted. **Er is en ~ner Mensch.** He is a sharp-witted person. LRT

Gschwindichkeit, *f* - speed. **in re ~ -** in less than no time. KYG2018. **D'Feierleit ihre ~ hot d'Nochbere ihre Haus gschpaart.** The speed of the fire people saved the neighbor's house. LRT

Gschwitz, *n* - (continual) sweating. **Des ~ macht em sei Gleeder glei Wesch nass.** This sweating soon makes one's clothes soaking wet. LRT

Gschwulscht - swelling. **Selli Kuh hot ~ in ihrem Eider.** That cow has swelling in her udder. LRT

Gsicht, *n* - face. **Ya, Yunger, ich bin am schwetze vun dir; ich will hoffe, du kannscht en graad ~ halde.** Yes, young man, I'm talking about you; I hope you can keep a straight face. **Yunger, du machscht awwer'n wiescht ~!** Young man, you are really making an ugly face. LRT,4/18/2000

Gsichtfareb, *f* - complexion. **Sei ~ guckt net gut.** His complexion doesn't look good. LRT

gsoffe, *adj* - drunk. **Er waar ~.** He was drunk. LRT

Gsuch, *n* - (continual) searching. **Des ~, was immer aageht, is genunk fer em der Leede gewwe.** This constant searching is enough to tire one out. LRT

Gsuddel, *n* - (wet) dirty work. **Tobi, schtopp du sell ~ odder du grickscht dich gut gebritscht.** Toby, stop playing in those puddles or you will get a good paddling. LRT. =

Gsuddelarewet, Gsuddelwese

Gsuddelarewet, *f* - (wet) dirty work. **Der Bodde uffbutze in e Schlachthaus is en ~.** Cleaning up the floor in a butcher shop is (wet) dirty work LRT

gsuddle - to play in water puddles (of children). LRT

gsund, *adj* - healthy. **Bischt du widder ~ un munder?** Are you in good health and spirits again? LRT

Guckbax, *f* - **1** television set. **2** monitor. **Heitesdaags hen die Waddefresser aa en ~.** Nowadays the computers have a monitor. LRT. [This word is what I always heard on WEEU Reading. LRT]

gucke, *refl* - to look. **sich net meh gleich ~** - to not look like the same person. **Er guckt sich nimmi gleich.** He no longer looks like himself. LRT

gucke - to look. **Wann du ken Aage hettscht, kennscht net ~.** If you had no eyes, you couldn't look and see. **Sie hen geguckt un geguckt, awwer sie hen's net finne kenne.** They looked and looked, but they couldn't find it. LRT

Guckmaschien, *f* - television set. = **Guckbax.** KYG1980

Guller, *m* - turkey gobbler. = **Gullerei, Welschhaahne.** KYG2076

gullere - to gobble. **Selli Welschhaahne ~ der ganz Daag, sis en Wunner as sie net en weher Hals griege.** Those turkey gobblers gobble the whole day long, it's a wonder they don't get a sore throat. LRT

Gumme, *pl* - palate [roof of mouth]. **Sie hot en weher ~.** The roof of her mouth is sore. **Die falsche Zaeh mache ebmols mei ~ weh.** Sometimes the false teeth make my palate sore. LRT

Gunn, *f* - honor, favor, good wishes. **Ich duh ihm der ~ net aa.** I can't wish him well. LRT

gunne, *pp* **gegunnt** - to wish. **Ich hab ihm sell gegunnt.** I wished him that. LRT

gut, *adv* - well. **~ gerode** - to turn out well. KYG2077. **en ~ gerodner Soh** - a son that turned out well. KYG2078. **Es waar ihne ~ gerode.** Things turned out well for them. **Sell Geschwulscht in die Kuh ihre Eider guckt net ~.** That swelling in the cow's udder doesn't look good. LRT. **Seller Kaes schmackt ~.** That cheese tastes good. NMM

gutgschmackich, *adj* - sweet-scented. NMM

Guthatzichkeit, *f* - kindheartedness. LRT

gutmache, *pp* **gutgemacht** - to make restitutions. **Sei Kieh hen diefi Lecher in der Karichhof gedrede, awwer er hot's gutgemacht.** His cows made deep holes in the cemetery, but he made restitutions. LRT

Gwaaleise, *n* - tormenting child. KYG2039

gwaartweis, *adv* - by the quart. **Mer kaaft Inscheineel ~.** One buys motor oil by the quart. LRT

Gwaelaarsch, *m* - **1** troublesome person. KYG2039. **2** trying child. = **Gwaelholz.** KYG2071

gwaelich, *adj* - tormenting. KYG2039. **Yunges, sei net so ~ zu deim Bruder.** Child, don't be so tormenting to your brother. LRT

Gwiddebaem, *pl* - quince tree. **Mer seht nimmi viel ~.** One doesn't see many quince trees anymore. LRT

gwilde - to quilt. **Im Grosse Daal** [Mifflin Co., PA] **duhne die Weibsleit noch en Latt ~.** In the Kishacoquillas Valley the women still do a lot of quilting. LRT

Gwiltnodle, *pl* - quilting needles. **Ich daed gleiche wann dir all die ~ ausfeddle daede.** I'd like if you would unthread all the quilting needles. LRT

gwiss´, *adv* - surely. **~ as ich leb, hen sie mir en hunnert Daaler gewwe.** As sure as I'm alive, they gave me a hundred dollars. LRT

Gwitt, *f, pl* **~e** - a single quince. LRT

gwollere - to make a gurgling sound. **Was geht dann aa? Die Wasserpeif is am ~.** What is happening? The water pipe is gurgling. LRT

Haahnebottboi, *m, f* - rooster potpie. **Haahne as draus in die Felder rumschpringe un fresse, mache guder ~.** Roosters that run and feed in the

78

fields make a good rooster pot pie. LRT

haapt, *adj* - main. **Sell waar's ~ Ding.** That was the main thing. LRT

Haaptding, *n* - main point. **Es ~ is, wer waert bezaahlt?** The main point is, who gets paid? LRT

Haaptsach, *f* - the main thing. KYG1997. **Heit waar die ~ fer der Schnee gscheppt griege.** Today the important thing was to shovel the snow. LRT

Haaptsumm, *f* - total. *cf* **es ganz Ding.** KYG2040. **Die ~ was mir eigenumme hen, waar genunk fer all die Schulde bezaahle.** The total amount that we took in was enough to pay all the debts. LRT

Haarschwanz, *m* - braided pig tail (style of hairdo). [Only so-called when they were braided, **gflochde.** LRT]

Haarschwowwel - tuft of hair on crown of head. KYG2072. = **Schwowwel.** Dot Fry

Haarwarewel, *m* - hair twirl. **Er hot en ~ graad vanne am Kopp.** He has a hair twirl right at the front of his head. LRT

Haas, *m, pl* **~e** - rabbit. **~e yaage** - to hunt rabbits. LRT

Haasefett, *n* - rabbit grease. **Tschie, ~, nochemol!** Gee, "rabbit fat" once again. [An idle saying.] LRT

Haasefleesch, *n* - rabbit meat. **~ macht gut Esses.** Rabbit meat makes good eating. LRT

Haasefuussglee, *m* - stone clover. *Trifolium arvense L.* = **Haaseglee, Ketzli, Ketzliglee, Schtee-glee.** KYG1887

Haasehund, *m, pl* **~** - rabbit dog. **~ as gwisst hen wie die Haase rumzubringe waare mir die liebschde.** Rabbit dogs that knew how to bring the rabbits around were my favorites. LRT

Haasemaul, *n* - harelip. **Ich dauer die Leit wu gebore sin mit me ~.** I pity those people who are born with a harelip. LRT

Haasenescht, *n, pl* **~er** - rabbit's nest. **Mei Paep hot gudi Aage ghat; er hot oft die Haase sehne kenne in de ~er hocke, un aa no sie datt schiese.** My dad had good eyes; he could often see rabbits sitting in their nests, and then could shoot them there. LRT

Haaseschiesserei, *f* - rabbit shooting. **~ waar mir en latt Blessier, wie ich en Yunger waar.** Shooting rabbits was a lot of pleasure for me when I was a youngster. LRT

Haaseschpur, *f, pl* **~e** - rabbit track. **Ich gleich die ~e sehne im Schnee.** I like to see the rabbit tracks in the snow. LRT

Haaseschtall, *m, pl* **-schtell** - rabbit pen. **Ich wees was ~schtell ausbutze is.** I know what cleaning out rabbit pens is (like). LRT

Haaseschwanz, *m, pl* **-schwenz** - rabbit tail. **Ich hab als gegliche die ~schwenz rumherhenke im Haus.** I used to like to hang the rabbit tails

here and there in the house.

Haaseyaage, *n* - rabbit hunting. **Mir waare ~ gange gwest.** We had gone rabbit hunting. LRT

Haasli, *n* - *dim* of **Haas.** bunny. LRT/Leb.

haerchle - to rattle in the throat. KYG2008. = **ghaerichle.** [Leb Co.]. **Sei Hals is am ghaerichle.** His throat is rattling. LRT

Haerding, *f* - temper (of metal). KYG1981. **En schtaalich Messer muss ~ hawwe fer eppes wert sei.** A steel knife must have temper to be worth anything. LRT

Haffe, *m* - (chamber) pot. **uff der ~ misse** - to have to use the indoor chamber pot or the outdoor toilet. KYG2031. **Ich muss uff der ~ (geh), wu hett dir'n hie geduh?** I've got to go on the pot, where did you put it? Proverb: **Sis ken ~ so schepp, as ken Deckel druff fitt.** There is no person so undesirable that he/she cannot be matched with a mate. LRT

halbdunkel, *adj* - half-dark, shadowy. = **schaddich. Mir hen en ~er Hof.** We have a shady yard. LRT

halbleinisch, *adj* - being linsey-woolsey. **Yunger, sei net so ~.** Young man, don't be such an incongruous kid. LRT

Halbschtrang, *m* - chain forming end of trace. KYG2045

halbwegs, *adv* - in the middle of the way, *i.e.* halfway there. **Mir waare ~ datt.** We were halfway there. LRT

halbyaehrich, *adj* - six months old. **Er is en ~er Buh.** He's a six-month-old boy. LRT

halde, *pp* **ghalde** - to hold. **Sache zu sich selwer ~** - to be secretive. **Hald sell zu dir selwert!** You keep quiet about that! **Mir hen ihn hatt ghalde.** We were quite demanding of him. LRT. **sei Eegnes ~** - to be able to take one's part. KYG1963. **Naegscht Woch duhne mir Vendu ~.** Next week we will hold an auction sale. LRT

Hallunk´, *m* - thief. = **Schtehler.** *cf* **Schpitzbuh.** = **Dieb.** LRT/Leb.

Hals, *m* - 1 throat. **heeser ~** - hoarse throat. **en weher ~** - sore throat. = **Halsweh, Wehhals.** KYG2007. **Er hot en grosser Garickel an seim ~.** He has a big Adams apple at his throat. LRT. **2** neck. **Duh net mei ~ so hatt dricke!** Don't squeeze my neck so hard! LRT

Halsauszehring, *f* - throat consumption. KYG2008

Halsduch, *n* - scarf, small shawl. **En ~ is en gross Schnuppduch as mer um der Hals binnt.** A scarf is a large handkerchief which one ties around the neck. LRT

halse - to take around the neck. = **dricke.** KYG1962

Halsfrissel, *n* - sore on the throat. KYG2007

Halskarebse, *pl* - necked pumpkin. LRT

Halsweh, *n* - sore throat. **Mer**

kann's heere an deine Schtimm as du ~ hoscht. One can hear from your voice that you have a sore throat. **Winder is die Zeit fer ~ hawwe.** Winter is the time to have a sore throat. LRT

haltbaar, *adj* - tenable. KYG1983

haltnemme - to take hold. KYG1889. **Wann mir eppes draage welle, misse mir ~.** If we want to carry something, we have got to take hold. LRT

halwergscheit, *adj* - dim-witted. **Er is yuscht ~.** He's a real dimwit. LRT

Hambaryer Schnellposcht, *f* - *facet* tattle-tale (name given a newspaper). KYG1973

Hammerzehe, *m* - toe with an enlarged joint, bunions, etc. KYG2030

Hammlifleesch, *n* - veal. LRT

Hand, *f* - hand. **uff ~ griege** - to stock up. KYG1883. **Seller Schtor hot en latt Schtofft uff ~.** That store has a lot of stuff on hand. LRT. **~ draa mache** - to take hold (of a job). KYG1961. **epper in ~ nemme** - to take someone in hand. KYG1962. **Kannscht du epper en ~ gewwe?** Can you give someone a hand? LRT

Handduch, *n* - hand towel. **Wann ich mei Hend wesch, gleich ich wann en ~ hendich is.** When I wash my hands, I like when there is a towel handy (conveniently located). LRT

handesdick, *adj* - thick as a

hand. KYG1996

Handkarich, *f* - push cart. **En ~ is en hendich Ding.** A push cart is a handy thing. LRT

Handlanger, *m* - tender, assistant. KYG1984. **Wann en Backeschteeleger gut Zeit mache will, muss er en guder ~ hawwer.** If a brick layer wants to make good time, he needs a good (mortar) assistant. LRT

Handlumbe, *m* - handy towel. **Kannscht mir der ~ lange, ich muss mei Hend abbutze; sie sin nass.** Can you hand me the handy towel? I need to wipe my hands; they are wet. LRT

Handlumbeschtofft, *n* - toweling. KYG2043. **Mei Paep hot als ~ gyuust fer Handlumbe mache fer hees Eise rumhewe wie er an die Bethlehem Schtaahl gschafft.** My dad used to use hand rag material (canvas fabric) to make hot pads to lift hot iron when he worked at the Bethlehem Steel plant in Lebanon, PA. LRT

Handwarick, *n* - craft, skill. **Leit as ken ~ hen, kenne ken Arewet an selle Kumpanie griege.** People without skills can't get a job with that company. LRT,4/11/2000

Handwaricker, *m, pl* **~** - skilled workman. **Die ~ sin immer willkumm do.** Skilled workmen are always welcome here. LRT,4/11/2000

Handwaricksgscharr, *n* - tools. **~ mache em sei Arewet so viel leichder.** Tools make one work so much easier. LRT. = **Schaffgscharr.** KYG2035

Hank, *m* - suspended shelf in cellar. **Mei Memm hot als ihre Boi uff die Hank in der Keller geduh.** My mother used to place her pies on the suspended shelf in the cellar. LRT

Hannefbrech, *f* - wedge for cutting stone. KYG1886

Hannes, *m* - Jack. = **Hans, Yockel, Yockli.** KYG2284

hannhudderisch, *adj* - *lit.* Moravian, unintelligible. KYG2105. *cf* **Hannhudder**

Hannickel, *m* - John Nicholas. KYG2285

Hannli, *n* - *dim* of **Hann.** small horn. **Saag em Buwli er soll sei ~ recht laut blose.** Tell the little boy he shall blow his little horn real loud. LRT

Hannschaal, *f* - skull. **Seller Felse is ihm uff die ~ gfalle un er waar graad dod.** That rock fell on his skull and he was killed instantly. = **Hannschaedel.** *cf* **~ un Greitzgnoche** - skull and crossbones. LRT

Hanswascht, *f* - silly fellow. **~ bin ich net, wann sie mich doch so heese.** A silly fellow I am not, even though they call me that. LRT

Hansyarick, *m* - John George. KYG2285

Harbarig, *m* - stopping off place. KYG1889

Harebschtgewebwarem - fall web worm. **Selli ~ gleiche die Schwatzwalnissbaem.** Those fall web worms like the black walnut trees. LRT

Harrisbarig, *m* - ✪ Harrisburg. KYG2272

Hasch-schtall, *m, pl* **-schtell** (*facet*) - thicket. KYG1996

Haschbel, *m* - **1** turnstile. KYG2080. **2** reel. **Die Binnmaschiene hen en ~.** The binders have a reel. LRT. **2** the big winding wheel on the binder. LRT

Haschi - ✪ Hershey, PA. **En latt Leit heese ~ "Schocklaadschteddel."** Many people call Hershey "Chocolate Town." LRT,4/21/2000

haschblich, *adj* - unsteady. *cf* **schranklich, schwankich, wanklich.** KYG2113

hatt, *adj* - **1** tortuous. **Der Weg waar ~.** The road was tortuous. KYG2040. **2** hard, tough. **Er is hattschaffich.** He is hard working. LRT

hatt, *adv* - earnestly. **Er waar schund ~ draa demariye.** He was already hard at his work this morning. LRT,4/11/2000

hattglaawich, *adj* - skeptical. **Mer kann ihm schier nix saage; er is so ~.** One can hardly tell him anything; he's so skeptical. LRT

hatthatzich, *adj* - unmerciful. **Er is en ~er Glotzkopp; er sett in d'Bressent sei.** He is merciless blockhead; he should be in jail. LRT

hattmeilich, *adj* - tough-mouthed. KYG2042. **Selli Geil sin ~.** Those horses are tough

mouthed. LRT

hattmelkich, *adj* - not yielding milk readily. **Die ~e Kieh hen zu gleeni Lecher in ihre Ditz.** The cows that do not yield their milk readily have too small holes in their teats. LRT,4/21/2000

hattniggisch, *adj* - **1** unfeeling. = **kalthatzich.** KYG2102. **2** stubborn. = **hattgnickich. Er is en hattgnickicher Glotzkopp.** He is a stiff-necked (stubborn) blockhead. LRT

hattschaffich, *adj* - hard-working, industrious. **Er is en ~er Mensch.** He is a hard-working (industrious) person. LRT

Hatz, *n* - heart. **zu ~ nemme** - to take seriously. KYG1963. **Ich denk, sei ~ dutt weh.** I guess he's really saddened. LRT

Hatzgloppe, *n* - throbbing of the heart. KYG2008. **Sie hot's ~.** Her heart is throbbing. LRT

hatzhafdich, *adj/adv* - stout-hearted(ly). **Er is ~ druff losgange.** He went about it in a stout-hearted way. LRT

Hatzwatzel, *f* - taproot. **En Baam as en gudi ~ hot, blost net gern um.** A tree that has a good tap root does not blow over easily. LRT. = **Harrwatzel.** KYG1970

haudich, *adj* - tough (of a steak). KYG2042

haus, *adv* - out of doors. **Er losst sei Kaer immer ~** He always leaves his car outside. LRT

Haus, *n* - house. **en ~ uff epper baue** - to trust someone completely. KYG2070. **Er dutt en ~ uff sei Bruder baue.** He puts complete trust in his brother. LRT. **nuff an's ~** - up to the house. KYG2116. **Sie sin nuff an's ~ gfaahre so as sie net weit zu laafe ghat hen.** They drove up to the house so they didn't have far to walk. LRT

hausbleiwe - to remain outside. *cf* **hausschteh. Yunger, du muscht ~.** Young man, you must stay outside. LRT

Hausdier, *f* - outside door. **Mer sett em sei ~ immer gschlosse halde.** One should always leave his outside door locked. LRT

hausschteh - to remain (stand) outside. **Der Bauer losst sei Hoireche immer ~.** The farmer always leaves his hayrake outside. LRT

Hautgranket, *f* - skin disease. **Er hot en ~ as em net bekannt is.** He has a rare skin disease. LRT

hawwe, *pp* **ghat** - to have. **Do hoscht des!** Take it! KYG1963. **Mir hen yuscht vun dir ghat.** We were just talking about you. KYG1965. **Ich will nix mit sellem zu duh ~.** I don't want any part of that. LRT

Hawwer, *m* - oats. **Er schpiert sei ~.** He thinks too much of himself. KYG1998. **~mehl fer Mariye-esse soll arig gut sei fer em.** Oatmeal for breakfast is supposed to be very good for one (us). LRT

Hawwerkeffer, *m, pl* **~** - thryps.

KYG2010

Hawwerleis, *pl* - oats lice. **Die ~ sin nimmi naegscht so schlimm as wie sie als waare.** The oats lice are not nearly as bad as they used to be. LRT

Hawwerschtacker, *m* - thumb. (*facet.*) = **Daume.** KYG2010

hawweswaert, *adj* - worth having. **En gudi Heemet is ~.** A good home is worth having. LRT, 4/18/2000

hechle - to give a tongue-lashing. = **abbalsemiere.** KYG2034

Hecht, *m* - pike (fish). LRT

Heck, *f* - briar bush. **Selli ~ waar mir im Weg gewest un ich hab mei Beh vergratzt.** That briar bush was in my way, and I scratched my leg. = **Heckeschtock.** LRT

Hecke, *pl* - bushes. KYG2241. **Sie wuhne ganz draus in de ~, awwer sin gut zufridde datt.** They live way out in the woods, but they are very happy there. LRT,4/11/2000

Heckeax, *f* - ax to chop off underbrush. KYG2095

Heckebascht, *f, pl* **~** - brush made of twigs. KYG2082. **Die ~e sin gut fer der Dreck vun die Schof baschde.** A brush made of twigs is good to brush the mud from sheep. LRT

Heckeschtraeme, *m* - fence row. LRT/ Leb.

Heckli, *n* - *dim* of **Hack.** - small hoe. LRT

Heebgaarn, *n* - two-handed net. KYG2085. **En ~ is gut fer Fischlin fange.** A two-handed net is good to catch (net) minnows. LRT

heechscht, *superl adj* - top-most. **~ Paert** - top-most part. = **owwerscht, heegscht.** KYG2038. **Sell is der ~ Baam in d'Nochberschaft.** That is the highest tree in the neighborhood. LRT

Heedelbarig, *m* - ✪ Heidelberg, PA. KYG,2273. = **Heidelbarig.**

Heekli, *n* - *dim* of **Hoke. 1** little hook. **2** small crochet hook. LRT

Heelmiddel, *n* - remedy. **Unser ~ waar immer, "Heele, heele, Hinkeldreck!"** Our remedy was always, "Heal, heal, chicken droppings!" LRT

heem - home. **weck vun ~** - away from home. LRT

heembringe - to bring home. **Bring blendi Geld heem, no sin mir all zufridde.** Just bring plenty of money home, then we will all be satisfied. LRT

heemdickisch, *adj* - underhanded. *cf* **heemlich, unnerhendich, verschtohle.** KYG2096

Heemetschteddel, *n* - hometown. **Schaefferstown waar mol Weil unser ~ nochdem as mir gheiert waare.** Schaefferstown was once our hometown after we were married. LRT,4/21/2000

heemgemacht, *adj* - homemade. **Selli Fraa kann schur gudi ~i Gleeder mache.** That woman

82

can sure make good homemade clothes. LRT

heemlicherweis, *adv* - secretly. = **hinnerum. Alles was er dutt is hinnerum.** Everything he does is in secret. LRT

heemnemme - to take something home. KYG1962. **Do nemm die Helft vun dem Kuche mit heem.** Here, take half of this cake home with you. LRT

heemschicke, *pp* **heemgschickt** - to send home. **Wie ich in de College waar, hab ich ebmols dreckichi Wesch heemgschickt fer die Mamm sie wesche.** When I was in college, I used to send dirty wash home for mom to wash. LRT

heemschleiche, *refl, pp* **is heemgeschliche** - to return home stealthily. **Seller Buh hot in de Schul sei selle, awwer er is heemgeschliche.** That boy should have been in school, but he sneaked home. LRT

heemschnieke, *pp* **heemgschnieckt** - to sneak home. **Es waar schier dunkel un die Buwe sin heemgschniekt.** It was almost dark and the boys sneaked home. LRT

heemzus, *adv* - homeward. **Sie sin ~ gange.** They went homeward. LRT

heereswaert, *adj* - worth hearing. **Die Biewelsgschichde sin ~.** Bible stories are worth hearing. LRT,4/18/2000

heese - **1** to report. **2** to indicate. **es heest...** - it is

reported. **Des Wedder denowed heest, "Daheem bleiwe!"** The weather this evening indicates, "Stay at home!" LRT

Heese, *pl* - feet. **Seller Mann hot grossi ~.** That man has big feet. LRT

Heesli, *n, pl* **~n** - *dim* of **Haas.** bunny. LRT/Leb,4/21/2000. = **Heesche**

hefdich, *adj* - strong. **Sell waar en ~er Schtarem.** That was a violent storm. LRT

Heffe, *pl* - table crockery. **Sie hen fimf ~ Lewwerwaschtfilsel gekocht.** They cooked five crocks full of pudding meat. LRT

Heffli, *n* - *dim* of **Haffe.** small pot. LRT

heglich, *adj* - **1** ready to strike (as a cat). **2** prone to claw (as a cat). **Duh selli Katz naus, sie is zu ~!.** Put that cat out, she's too prone to claw everything! LRT

Heh, *f* - height. **in die ~ faahre** - to explode with anger. **Sie hot ihn gfrogt fer ruhich sei un er is in die ~ gfaahre, ich hab gemehnt er fresst sie lewendich.** She asked him to shut-up and he exploded; I thought he would eat her alive. LRT

Hehler, *m* - receiver of stolen goods. KYG1884

hehlhalde, *pp* **hehlghalde** - to keep a secret. **Seller Mann hot en Latt schlechdi Sache geduh, awwer er hot alles hehlghalde.** That man did lots of bad things, but he kept quiet about

everything. LRT

heidich, *adv* - of today. = **heitzedaagich.** KYG2030

Heidli, *n* - *dim* of **Haut.** film on boiled milk. LRT. = **Heidel**

heile - to weep. **Er hot net ~ kenne.** He was tearless. = **Es Aagewasser is net kumme.** KYG1977. **Sie waar so verzwatzelt, sie hot net ~ kenne.** She was so lost in amazement, she couldn't shed any tears. LRT

Heile, *n* - sobbing. **Ferwas bischt du am ~?** Why are you crying? LRT

Heilichkeit, *f* - holiness. LRT

Heilkunscht, *f* - therapeutics. KYG1994

heimlicherweis, *adv* - secretly. **Alles was er dutt is ~.** Everything he does is in secret. LRT

Heiraatsgedanke, *m* - thoughts of marriage. *cf* **Heiraschpelgedanke** (*facet*). KYG2002

heit, *adv* - today. **~ iwwer acht Daag** - today a week. KYG2029. **vun ~ aa** - from today. **~ iwwer 14 Daag** - two weeks from today. KYG2030. **Well, Yunges, vun ~ aa weck bischt du alt genunk fer in die Schul geh.** Well, little one, from today on you are old enough to go to school. LRT

heitowed, *adv* - this evening. KYG2034. = **denowed.** LRT

Hell, *f* - hell. **ihm die ~ waarm**

mache - to put the screws to someone. **Die ~ is hees!** Hell is hot! LRT

Hell-lewe, *n* - *lit.* life in hell. disagreeable, unpleasant living. KYG2109

Hellerschteddel, *n* - ✪ Perrysburg, PA. KYG2278

Hellhauns, *m* - *lit.* hell hound. an unscrupulous person. KYG2112

hellisch, *adj* - hellish. **en ~ Lewe.** LRT

Helm, *m* - handle of a tool. KYG2035. **Der ~ uff sellem Schleggel is verbroche gange wie sie driwwer gfaahre sin mit d'Geil un em Wagge.** The handle on that sledge (hammer) was broken when they drove over it with the horses and wagon. LRT

Hemmbiereschtock, *m, pl* - **schteck** - raspberry stalk. **Die eensichscht Zeit, as ich - schteck gleich, is wann die Hemmbiere zeidich sin.** The only time I like raspberry plants is when the raspberries are ripe. LRT

Hemmeraremel, *m, pl* -**aeremel** - shirt-sleeve. **Dei -aeremel sin zu lang.** Your shirt-sleeves are too long. LRT

Hemmerschtofft, *n* - material to make a shirt. **~ macht aa gudi Debbichblacke.** Shirt material also makes good quilt patches. LRT

Hemmerschwanz, *m* - shirt-tail. **Tschannie, dei ~ is haus.** Johnnie, your shirt-tail is out.

LRT

Hend, *pl* - hands. **Yunger, wesch dei ~, sie sin dreckich.** Young man, wash your hands; they are dirty. LRT

Hengel, *m* - string of fish. **Sei ~ Fisch hot schier zehe Pund gewoge.** His string of fish almost weighed ten pounds. LRT

Hengscht, *m* - stallion. **Wann mer yungi Geil hawwe will, nemmt's aa en ~.** If one wants colts, it also takes a stallion. LRT

Henner, *m* - nickname Henry. **Der ~ hot en grossi Familye.** Henry has a large family. LRT,4/21/2000

herdappe, *pp* **hergedappt** - to approach with heavy steps. **Wie kummt's as du so do hergedappt bischt?** How is it that you came here with those heavy steps? [This would be a very specific and unusual case.] LRT

herdappele - to trip along. = **hinnedrei schtolpere.** KYG2062. **Mer hot ihn gheert do herzudapple kumme.** One could hear him trudging here with his heavy steps. LRT

herdrehe, *refl* - to turn this way. KYG2000. **Der Zaahdokder saagt, "Kannscht du dich ~?"** The dentist says, "Can you turn this way?" LRT

hergeh, *pp* **is hergange** - 1 to occur. **Do is es awwer hergange.** There were some high doings. **Die Graabschtee sin umgschmisse; was is dann hergange do?** The tombstones are upset, what happened here? LRT. 2 to take place. **net arig glatt ~** - to keep the house in a slovenly manner. **Die Versammling is net arig glatt hergange.** The meeting didn't run very smoothly. LRT

hergewwe, *pp* **~** - 1 to contribute. **Die Gemeesleit hen Blendi ~ heit.** The church members contributed well today. 2 to surrender. **Er hot gaar nix ~ welle.** He didn't want to surrender anything. LRT

herlaafe, *pp* **is hergloffe** - to walk this way. KYG2159. **Bischt du der ganz Weg do hergloffe?** Did you walk here the whole way? LRT

herlange - to pass something (to a person at the table). **Ich brauch sell Messer, lang mer's mol gern her!** I need that knife, will you please hand it to me? LRT

herreide, *pp* **is hergeridde** - to ride here on a horse. **Er is uff seim Gaul do hergeridde kumme.** He came here riding on his horse. LRT

herrolle - to roll this way. **Roll sie her zu mir.** Roll (those balls) here to me. LRT

herschicke, *pp* **hergschickt** - to send hither. **Wann du selli Gaunch net gleichscht, dann schick sie her zu mir.** If you don't like that swing, then send it here to me. LRT

herschtelle, *refl* - to represent oneself. **Schtell dich do her in mei Blatz, ich muss heemgeh.** Stand here in my place, I must go home. LRT

hesslich, *adj* - ugly. **Sell hoch Wasser waar en ~ Wese ganz iwwer die Gegend.** That high water (flood) was an ugly thing throughout the region. LRT

Hesslichkeet, *f* - ugliness. = **Unscheeheet.** KYG2088. **Die ~ vun selle dode Gediere hot mer gegrisselt.** The ugliness of those dead animals made me shudder. LRT

hewe, *pp* **ghowe** - to hold. **Die Buwe hen der Tschecki ghowe.** The boys overpowered Jakie. LRT

hewwle, *pp* **ghewwelt** - to kick (of cow). **Die Kuh hot ghewwelt wie der Deifel.** The cow kicked like the devil. LRT

Hexemeeschder, *f* - magician. LRT

hibsch-guckich, *adj* - trim-looking. *cf* **nett, schee.** KYG2061. **Er is en ~er Mensch.** He is a trim-looking person. LRT

hie un do, *adv* - here and there. KYG1994. **~ hot's bissel gschneet.** Here and there it snowed a bit. LRT

hie un her, *adv* - to and fro. KYG2027. **Der Baermedickel vun d'Uhr gaunscht ~.** The pendulum of the clock swings to and fro. LRT

Hie-un-haa-blug, *m* - tumbler plow. KYG2073

hie-un-herschwinge - to swing back and forth. **Der Baermedickel schwingt yuscht**

so hie un her. The pendulum just swings back and forth. LRT

hieblanze, *refl, pp* **hiegeblanzt** - to plant oneself. **Ich hab mich graad datt in die Mitt vun all selle Leit hiegeblanzt, un ich bin der ganz Daag datt gebliwwe.** I planted myself right there in the middle of all those people, and I stayed there all day. **Ya, blanz dich yuscht datthie; ich hab nix dagehe.** Yes, you just settle down right there; I'm not opposed to it. LRT

hiedappe - to step somewhere. **Geb acht wu du hiedappscht.** Be careful where you step. LRT

hiedraage, *pp* **hiegedraage** - to carry thither. KYG2000. **Die Leit hen en latt Sache datt hiegedraage ghat fer die Aernkarich.** The people had carried a lot of things forward for the Harvest Home service. LRT

hiedrehe - to turn towards. KYG2078

hiedrolle - to trot along. KYG2064

hiegritzle, *pp* **hiegegritzelt** - to scribble down. **Sei Naame is ganz glee do unne hiegegritzelt.** His name is scribbled down really small here at the bottom (of the paper). LRT

hiehewe - to hold to a place. **Heb's hie, bis ich's fescht genaggelt hab.** Hold it in place until I've nailed it fast. LRT

hiehocke - to sit in a place. **Yunger, hock dich do hie, un bleib bis ich saag, du kannscht**

geh. Young man, sit right there and stay until I say you can go. LRT

Hiehocke, *n* - sitting down. **Des ~ is besser wie schteh.** Sitting down is better than standing. LRT

hielaafe, *pp* **is hiegloffe** - to walk to a place. KYG2159. **Er is datt hiegeloffe un hot's Fenschder uffgemacht.** He walked over there and opened the window. LRT

hienemme, *pp* **hiegenumme** - to take to a place. **Er hot bissel Ess-sach mit datt hiegenumme ghat.** He had taken a bit of food along with him to that place. LRT. = **hiebringe.** KYG1962

hiereide - to ride there. KYG1994. **Mir waare baut en Schtund datt wie er hie-zu-reide kumme is uff seim Gaul.** We were there about an hour when he came riding there on his horse. LRT

hieschaffe, *refl* - to get to a place. **Mir misse seller Offe graad datt uff seller Blatz ~.** We must get the stove exactly on that very spot. LRT

hiescheine - to shine thence (of the moon). **Ich hab net gedenkt, as die Sunn so weit ~ daed.** I would not have thought the sun would shine that distance (into the house). LRT

hieschicke - to send to a place. **ammenents ~** - to send some place. **Schick es yuscht ammenents hie, es macht nix aus wu.** Just send it somewhere, it doesn't matter where. **Wu kann mer ~ fer so Sache**

ausfinne? Where can one send (to whom can one write) to find such things out? LRT

hieschiewe - to push towards. **Du kannscht der Schank datt ~.** You can push the cupboard towards and against the wall. LRT

hieschlagge - to strike at something. **Fer den Bull dodschlagge, dann duscht du graad do ~.** To kill this bull, you will want to strike him right here. LRT

hieschnelle - to toss to. KYG2040

hieschteh - to stand idle. **Schteh net yuscht datt hie, mer hen en latt Arewet.** Don't just stand there idly, we have a lot of work to do. LRT

hieschtelle - to set down. **Schtell die Rooschtpann datthie uff der Disch.** Set the roasting pan down there on the table. **Schtell yuscht der Kiwwel datthie.** Just set the bucket down there. LRT

hieschtelle, *refl, pp* **hiegschtellt** - to take one's place on a stand. **Der Peliesmann hot sich datt hiegschtellt, un's hot niemand sich verregt.** The policeman took his place on the stand and no one moved. LRT

hieschwimme - to swim to a place. **Es Wasser is dief genunk, du kannscht datt ~.** The water is deep enough, you can swim there. LRT

hiesehne - to see as far as. **Mer kann net datt ~, es is zu weit weck.** One cannot see there, it is too far away. LRT

hiesetze - to set down. **Du kannscht der Kiwwel graad datt ~.** You can set the bucket right there. LRT

hiessich, *adj* - of this country. KYG2000

hieweise - to show the way there. **Kannscht du ihm weise, wu er hiegeh sett?** Can you show him where he should go? LRT

hiewenne, *refl* - to turn to. KYG2078

hiewinsche, *refl* - to wish oneself there. KYG1994. **Ich hab mich datt ~ welle.** I was wishing that I had been there. LRT

hilzich, *adj* - **1** wooden. **Ich mach meine Fraa ihre ~i Heekelhoke.** I make my wife's wooden crochet hooks. **Die ~e Beseschtiel sin mir die liebschde.** I prefer the wooden broom handles. LRT,4/11/2000. **2** hollow (of a radish). **Die Reddich sin ~.** The radishes are hollow. LRT

Himmel, *m* - sky. **Der ~ is drieb.** The sky is threatening. KYG2004. **Weit dattdriwwe kann mer Wedderleechschtraahle sehne im ~.** Far over there in the sky, one can see bolts of lightning. LRT

Himmelsbaam, *m* - stinkwood. **= Paradiesbaam, Schumackbaam.** KYG1881

Himmelswelt, *f* - the world of heaven. KYG2247. **Yunger, du schtehscht do. Was in de ~ hettscht du gern?** Young man, you're standing here. What, for Heaven's sake, do you want? LRT,4/11/2000

Hinkeldreck, *m* - trifling matter. KYG2061. **"Heele, Heele ~ bis Marieye frieh is alles weck. " So hat die Mom als gsaat wann mer die Haut bissel verschunne hot."**Heal, heal, chicken dirt, by tomorrow morning all will be well." That's what Mom used to say if we scuffed our skin a bit. LRT

Hinkelschenkel, *m, pl* **~** - chicken leg. **Es is nix besseres fer esse as wie ~.** There's nothing better to eat than "drumsticks." LRT

hinne, *adv* - in the rear. **~ am Haus schteht en grosser Baam.** To the rear of the house stands a big tree. LRT

hinnebei, *adv* - approaching from the rear. **Ich hab net gwisst, wu er waar, bis er ~ kumme is.** I didn't know where he was until he came in from the rear. LRT

hinnedraa, *adv* - behind the rest, on behind. **Es macht nix aus, was er dutt, er is immer ~.** It doesn't matter what he does, he is always behind the rest. **Laaf do ~ nooch so as du sehne kannscht, wann eppes letz geht.** You walk on behind here so that you can see if anything goes wrong. **Bleib datt ~ un heb fescht am Wagge.** Stay behind there and hold fast to the wagon. LRT. *cf* **hinnehand.** KYG2019

hinnedrin, *adv* - in the rear part.

~ in die Kaer is en voller Kareb. In the back of the car is a full basket. LRT

hinnedrowwe, *adv* - the way back up. KYG2117. **Sie wuhne do ~ uff em Barig.** They live way back up here on the mountain. LRT

hinnedruff, *adv* - on the rear part of. **Duh der Kiwwel ~ schtelle.** Set the bucket on the back. LRT

hinneher, *adv* - following in the rear. **Der Hund kummt immer ~.** The dog always brings up the rear. LRT

hinne-nanner, *adv* - tandem. = **hinnernanner, nooch en nanner.** KYG1967

hinnenannernooch, *adv* - in tandem. **Mir waare ~ gfaahre gewest.** We had driven in tandem. LRT

hinnenei-schiesse, *pp* **hinnenei-geschosse** - to shoot into (the back of). **Sei Schmatze sin ihm hinne in der Hals neigeschosse.** His pain shot into the back of his neck. LRT =**hinnenei-faahre**

hinneneischnieke, *pp* **hinneneigschniekt** - to sneak in the back way. **Er is hinne zu de Dier neizuschnieke kumme.** He came sneaking in the back door. LRT

hinnenooch, *adv* - in pursuit. LRT

hinnenuff, *adv* - up by the back way. KYG2117. **Nemm seller Weg datt ~, no bischt glei datt.** Take that road up the back way, then you'll soon be there. LRT

Hinnerdeel, *n* - posterior. LRT/Leb.Co.

Hinnerdreppe, *pl* - steps in the rear of the house. **Unser Haus hot ken ~.** Our house has no rear steps. LRT

hinnere - to hinder. **Es hinnert ihn alles.** He is very touchy [everything bothers him]. KYG2041. **Mer kann duh was mer will, so lang as es nix hinnert.** One can do what one wants so long as it doesn't hinder anything. LRT

hinnerhendich, *adv* - behind times. = **hinner Zeit.** KYG2020

hinnerlich, *adv* - poorly. **Es geht ihm ~.** He is in poor circumstances. LRT

Hinnerraad, *n* - rear wheel. **Der Teier waar flaett gange uff seim ~.** The tire went flat on his rear wheel. LRT

hinnerschichgeh - to go backwards. **Du alder Geesbock, witt immer ~, awwer ich will hawwe as du vaschichgehscht.** You old goat (buck), you always want to go backwards, but I want you to go forward. LRT

hinnerschichschprenge - to reverse. *cf* **en anner Weg browiere. Wie dutt mer en Dreschmachien ~? Ei, mer schwenkt der Dreibrieme.** How do you reverse the thrashing machine? Why, you give the drive belt one twist. LRT

Hinnerschtedreppe, *pl* - steps at rear of house. LRT

hinnerum, *adv* - **1** behind. **2** around the back.

hinnewedder, *adv* - against the rear. **Schieb ~ der Wagge, bis er aafangt rolle.** Push against the back of the wagon until it starts to roll. **Seller Gees is ~ die Kaer gschprunge.** That goat ran against the back of the car. **~ sei** - to be in a tight fix. KYG2016. **Er waar heftich ~ gewest.** He was really in terrible straits. LRT

hinnich, *prep* - behind. **~ de Zeit** - behind the time. KYG2019. **Sie hen der Gees ~ d'Scheier gfunne.** They found the goat behind the barn. LRT

Hitz, *f* - temperature. **die ~ nuffschprenge** - to raise the temperature. KYG1982. **Sei ~ waar 105.** His temperature was 105. LRT

Hiwwel, *m* - hill. **en scharefer ~ nuff** - a sharp grade uphill. KYG2118. **Die Kinner gleiche seller Scharef ~ fer schliddefaahre.** The children like that steep hill for sledding. LRT

hochmiedich, *adj* - supercilious. **~i Grischtkindlin mehne nix zu mir.** Haughty contemptious Christmas gifts mean nothing to me. LRT

Hochzichblumm, *f* - **1** tiger flower. *Tigridus, sp.* KYG2016. **2** tawny day lily. KYG1973

Hochzichgleeder, *pl* - trousseau. KYG2066. **~ sin oft mols funkelnei.** Wedding clothes are oft times brand new. LRT

hocke, *refl* - to take a seat. **Hock dich, du guckscht mied.** Take a seat, you look tired. LRT

Hofdaerli, *n* - gate in the yard fence. **Es ~ bleibt net zu.** The yard gate won't stay closed. LRT, 4/18/2000

Hoffens, *f* - yard fence. **Die ~ sett geweisselt sei.** The yard fence should be whitewashed. LRT, 4/18/2000

Hoffning, *f* - hope. **Mir lewe uff ~.** We live on hope. LRT

Hofvoll, *m* - yardful. KYG2258. **Die Kinner hen en ~ Schpielsache.** The children have a yardful of playthings (toys). LRT,4/18/2000

Hoi-wenner, *m* - tedder. = **Kicker.** KYG1978. **unser ~ is verhunst.** Our hay tedder is ruined. LRT

Hokezaah, *m* - tusk of a boar. KYG2081

hokle, *pp* **ghokelt** - to hook. **Er hot's fescht ghokelt.** He hooked it firmly. LRT

holberich, *adj* - rough. **Sell is en ~er Weg.** That is a rough (bumpy) road. LRT

Hollener, *m* - Hollander. KYG2273

holperich, *adj* - very rough. **Sell waar awwer en ~er Weg.** That was a very bumpy road. LRT

holz-, *adj* - wooden. **Ya, sell is en scheeni holzni Schissel.** Yes, that is a nice wooden bowl. LRT,4/11/2000

Holzappel, *m, pl* **-eppel** - crab apple. **Ich gleich mei -eppel gezuckert mit Simmet un Neggli.** I like my crab apples sugared with cinnamon and cloves. LRT,4/11/2000

Holzarewet, *f* - woodwork. KYG2239. **Er gleicht die fei ~ innewennich in de Heiser duh.** He likes to do the (fine) trim woodwork in the inside of houses. LRT,4/11/2000

Holzax, *f* - wood ax. **Sei ~ is am schtump warre.** His woodax is getting dull. LRT,4/11/2000

Holzblank, *f, pl* **~e** - wooden plank. **Die Faahrdeck uff sellre Brick is noch bedeckt mit ~e.** The driving surface of that bridge is still covered with wooden planks. LRT,4/11/2000

Holzblatz, *m* - wood place. **Der ~ waar der Blatz, wu mir Holz gsaegt, ghackt un gschpalde hen.** The wood place was the place where we sawed, chopped and split wood. LRT,4/11/2000

Holzblock, *n* - wood block, chopping block. **Noch ee Ding fer der Holzblatz waar fer Hinkel keppe, un fer sell duh hot mer'n ~ gebreicht.** Still another use of the wood place was to behead chickens (with an ax), and that required a wood block. LRT,4/11/2000. *cf* **Holzblatz**

Holzbock, *m* - **1** walking stick (insect). KYG2159. **2** saw buck. **Wann mer Feierholz zu Leng saege will, kummt en ~ hendich rei.** If one wants to saw firewood to lengths, a sawbuck comes in handy. LRT

Holzdraages, *n* - carrying wood. **~ macht em mied.** Carrying wood makes one tired. LRT, 4/11/2000

Holzdrehbank, *f* - wood lathe. **Net alli Mensche hot die Gaabe fer Holz drehe uff re ~.** Not everybody is gifted to lathe (shape) wood on a wood lathe. LRT,4/11/2000

Holzesch, *f* - wood ashes. **~ uff die Grummbiereschteck/ halt Deel vum Ungeziffer weck.** Wood ashes on the potato plants will keep some of the insects away. LRT,4/11/2000

Holzfeier, *n* - wood fire. **~ in de Feierhaerd is awwer gewiss gemietlich.** A wood fire in a fire-place is truly pleasant. LRT,4/11/2000

Holzfeil, *f* - wood file. **Zu mir is en ~ en Raschbel.** To me a wood file is a rasp. LRT,4/11/2000

Holzglamm, *f* - wood clamp. **Yunger, du witt net dei Finger in die ~ gepetzt griege.** Young man, you don't want to get your finger pinched in that wood clamp. LRT,4/11/2000

Holzglotz, *m, pl* **Holzgletz** - segment of a tree trunk. **En ~ is en hendich Ding fer die Hinkel ihre Kepp abhacke.** A wood block is a handy thing to chop off chicken's heads. LRT

Holzhacker, *m* - wood chopper. **Ya, er waar ewwe en ~ vun Yungem uff.** Yes, he was a wood chopper from his youth. LRT,4/11/2000

Holzhaendel, *m* - wooden handle. **Ich gleich die**

Schtempel, as meh hen wie yuscht en ~; sie sin ganz vun Holz gemacht. I like the stampers that have more than just a wooden handle; they are entirely made of wood. LRT,4/11/2000

Holzhaufe, *m* - wood pile. **Der ~ is zu glee; er halt uns net waarem der ganze Winder.** The wood pile is too small; it won't keep us warm the entire winter. LRT,4/11/2000

Holzhaus, *n* - wood house. **En ~ is notwennich, so as mier unser Holz drucke halde kenne.** A wood (storage) house is needed so that we can keep our wood dry. LRT,4/11/2000

Holzheisli, *n, dim* of **Holzhaus.** little wood house. **Yunger, saag net ~ zu mir; ich mehn unsers is gross genunk as mir's en Holzhaus heese kenne.** Young man, don't say (little) wood shed to me; I think ours is large enough to be called a wood house [said in jest]. LRT,4/11/2000

Holzkareb, *m* - wood basket. **Wann ich seller ~ zu voll mach, no is er zu schwer un ich kann en net draage.** If I make that wood basket too full, it's too heavy and I can't carry it. LRT, 4/11/2000

Holzkiche-offe, *m* - kitchen wood stove. **Ya, sell is en ~, awwer wann du bissel meh Hitz brauchscht, kannscht paar Welschkanngrutze neischmeisse.** Yes, that's a kitchen wood stove, but if you need a little more heat, you can throw in a few corn cobs. LRT,4/11/2000

Holzkischt, *f* - wood chest to hold firewood and to sit on. **Wie ich glee waar, hab ich ebmols uff die ~ gschlofe.** Sometimes when I was little, I slept on the wood chest. LRT,4/11/2000

Holzland, *n* - wooded country. **Ennicher Weg as mer guckt, des is ewwe ~.** Any way one looks, this is indeed wooded country. LRT,4/11/2000

Holzmeesel, *m* - wood chisel. **En ~ sett mer gut scharef halde.** A wood chisel should be kept good and sharp. LRT,4/11/2000

Holzoffe, *m* - wood-burning stove. **Unser ~ im Keller macht blendi Hitz.** Our wood-burning stove in the cellar provides plenty of heat. LRT,4/11/2000

Holzschraub, *f, pl* **-schrauwe** - wood screw. **Ich brauch en Dutzend -schrauwe.** I need a dozen (steel) wood screws. LRT,4/11/2000

Holzschraubschtock, *m* - wood vise. KYG2242. **Die alt Satt ~schteck waare alles Holz: die Schraub, der Schtiel un's Gebiss.** The wooden vices were totally made of wood: the screw, the handle, and the bit. LRT,4/11/2000

Holzwand, *f* - wooden wall. **Die ~ gschwischich die Geilsschtell is gut gemacht.** The wooden wall between the horse stalls is well-made. LRT,4/11/2000

Holzwarem, *m, pl* **-waerem** - woodworm. **~ sin die Ursach fer selli Lecher in selle Bord.** Woodworms are the reason for those holes in those boards.

LRT,4/11/2000

Holzweg, *m* - road through the bush for logging. **Die Geil hen selli Bleck der ~ runnergezoge.** The horses pulled those logs down the logging road. LRT,4/11/2000

Holzwegtee, *m* - common tansy. *Tanacetum vulgare L.* = **Kiehbidders, Reefaare, Reefart, Reeform, Reeblumm, Reifaare, Reifart, Reifaa, Reifaade, Yungweiwertee, Reifaahre, Reinfart.** KYG1968

Holzzappe, *m* - wooden peg. **Seller ~ hebt der Essich im Fass.** That wooden peg holds the vinegar in the barrel. LRT,4/11/2000

hopple - to tie, hobble. KYG2015

Hossebeh, *n* - trousers leg. KYG2066. **Sei ~ is darichgwore datt am Gnie.** His trouser leg is worn through at the knee. LRT

Hossebreis, *n, pl* **~er** - trousers cuff. KYG2066

Hossegaellese, *pl* - trousers galluses. KYG2066. **Sei ~ sin abgemarickt wie en Zollschtaab.** His trouser suspenders are marked off (printed) like a foot rule. LRT

Hossegnie, *n* - trousers knee. KYG2066. **Sei ~ hot en Loch.** His trouser knee has a hole. LRT

Hossegnopp, *m, pl* **-gnepp** - trousers button. KYG2066. **Sei -gnepp sin am losreisse.** His trouser buttons are tearing loose. LRT

Hosselatz, *m* - trousers fly. = **Schlitz.** *cf* **Scheierdor** (*facet.*) KYG2066. **Yunger, dei ~ is uff.** Young man, your fly is open. LRT

Hossesack, *m, pl* **-seck** - pants pocket. **Loss dei Hend aus deine ~seck, fer sell hot mer Hendsching.** Keep your hands out of your pants pockets ~ for that you have gloves [to keep your hands warm]. **~seck griege nimmi so gern Lecher wie sie verlenger zerick hen.** Trouser pockets are not as prone to get holes as they were long ago. LRT

Hossesackwedder, *n* - pants pocket weather. **~, sell is mei Zeit vum Yaahr.** ~, that is my time of the year. LRT

Hosseschlitz, *m* - fly (on pants). **Yunger, dei ~ is uff.** Young man, your fly is open. LRT

Hosseschnall, *f* - trousers buckle. KYG2066. **Die menschde Hosse hen ken Schnalle.** Most trousers don't have buckles. LRT

Hossesitz, *m, pl* **~e** - trousers seat. = **Hosse-aarsch.** KYG2066. **Sei ~ is verschmiert.** His trouser seat is soiled. LRT

Howwelschpaa, *m, pl* **-schpae** - shavings from a plane. **-schpae mache gut Schtrae-es fer Haaseschtell.** Shavings make good bedding for rabbit hutches. LRT

Huddel, *m* - tangle in hair. KYG1967. **Du hoscht awwer en ~ in deine Haar.** My, but you have a tangle in your hair.

LRT

Huddelschtroh, *n* - tangled straw from thrasher. KYG1967. **~ dutt ebmols der Bloser verschtoppe an die Dreschmaschien.** A straw tangle sometimes blocks the blower on the thrashing machine. LRT

Huddelwese, *n* - tangled affairs. = **Ghuddelwese.** *cf* **Ketzerei.** KYG1967. *cf* **Huddlerei.** LRT

Huddelwisch, *m* - hasty, unreliable horse (or person). KYG2110

Huddlerei, *f* - confusion, mixed-up affair, working in haste. **So en ~ hab ich noch nie net gesehne ghat.** I had never seen such confusion. LRT. **Mit so en're ~ will ich nix zu duh hawwe.** I will have nothing to do with such a mixed-up affair. **So en ~ macht em schier daremlich.** Working in such an overhasty fashion almost makes one dizzy. LRT, 4/11/2000. *cf* **Huddelwese, Ghuddelwese**

huddlich, *adv* - in a hurry. **Ferwas bischt so ~?** Why are you so hurried? CRB

Hufnaggel, *m, pl* **-neggel** - shoeing nail. **Mer kann Fingerring vun ~neggel mache.** One can make finger rings from shoeing nails. LRT

hulpere, *pp* **gehulpert** - to move in an uneven manner. KYG2101. **Sie sin datt iwwer seller schteenich Weg recht schrecklich nunner gehulpert.** They went down over that stony road in a terribly rough manner. LRT

Hummler, *m* - bumblebee. **Er waar so verhuddelt, er hett net gwisst eb en ~ ihn gschtoche hett odder net.** He was so confused he wouldn't have known if a bumblebee had stung him or not. LRT

Hundli, *n* - *dim* of **Hund.** doggie. = **Hundel**

Hunds-schtann, *f, pl* **~e** - Sirius, dog star. **Die ~ gebt uns die Hundsdaage.** The dog star (Sirius) gives us the Dog Days (of summer). LRT

Hundsfleh, *pl* - dog's fleas. **Ich hett liewer Schippe uff meim Kopp as wie ~.** I would rather have dandruff on my head than dog's fleas. LRT

Hundsfotz - dog's vagina. LRT

Hundspiffel, *n* - **1** insignificant matter. **Sell is ken ~ waert.** That isn't worth a hoot. **2 Oh, ~!** - an idle saying. LRT

Hundsschtrumpel, *f* - a hoot, a trifle. **Ich geb ken ~ drum.** I don't give a hoot. LRT

hunnert - 100. **so amme ~ rum** - about 100. KYG1994. **Ich hab dir's en ~ mol gsaat un du weescht's alsnoch net.** I told you a hundred times and you still don't remember. LRT

Hunnichdau, *m* - sticky moisture (covering vegetation in late summer). KYG1879

Hunnichgraut, *n* - toad flax. *Linaria vulgaris Mill.* = **Hundsgraut, Hundsblumm, Hanngraut, Hunds-seech, Rosmarei, wildi Rosmarei.** KYG2027

Hunnichkichli, *n* - cookie made with honey. LRT

Hunsdroll, *m* - even-gaited trot. KYG2064

Hunslewe, *n* - *lit.* dog's life; unsatisfactory life. KYG2111. **Well, sie hot endlich ihre Elend iwwermacht; sie hot en recht ~ ghat.** Well, she finally died; she was living in misery. LRT

Hunszecke, *f* - tick burrowing in dog's hide. KYG2013

Huppsgrott, *f* - toad. **Ich hab verlenger gleeni ~e gyuust fer "bait" fer fische fer "Bass."** Years ago I used small toads for bait to fish for bass. LRT. *cf* **Seechgrott.** KYG2027

hupse, *pp* **ghupst** - to jump. **Wie en Haas is er iwwer sell Fessli ghupst.** He jumped over that little barrel like a rabbit. LRT

Hut, *m* - hat. **weecher ~** - soft felt man's hat. **Was mehnt sell, er hot en weisser ~ aa?** What does that mean, he's wearing w white hat? LRT

hutzich, *adv* - desperate. **Es guckt ~ aus.** Things look desperate. KYG1998

huuschtle - to cough slightly. **Wie kummt's as er so fei huuschdelt?** How come he's coughing so weakly? LRT

Iedrich, *m* - cud. **der ~ verliere** - to be unable to chew the cud (of cattle). KYG2089. **Oftmols wann en Kuh grank is, verliert sie der ~.** Frequently when a cow is sick, she loses her ability

to chew cud. LRT

Iemeschwaarm, *m* - swarm of bees. **Mir hen en ~ uff em Garret ghat.** We had a swarm of bees on the attic. LRT

ihne - (to) them. **Was fehlt dann ~?** What is their problem? LRT

ihrer, *m,* **ihres,** *n,* **ihre,** *f, poss pron* - theirs. **Ihres is es bescht.** Theirs is the best. KYG1993. **Ihres (Koches) is immer es bescht.** Their (cooking) is always the best. LRT

immer, *adv* - always. **Selli zwee sin ~ un ewich am grageele.** Those two are constantly in verbal torment. LRT,4/11/2000

innerlich, *adv* - internally. **Dutt's dir ~ weh im Bauch?** Are you having pain (discomfort) inside your belly? LRT

Insche Grick, *f* - ✪ Indian Creek, Harleysville, Mont. Co., PA.

Inschingfraa, *f* - squaw. **Ich hab sei Lewe ken ~ aagedroffe.** I never met a squaw. LRT

Inschingzelt, *n* - tepee. = **Inschezelt.** KYG1987

Inschlich(t)-lichtli, *n, pl* ~n - tallow candle. KYG1966. **~n, gebt's kenni meh.** Tallow candles aren't made anymore. LRT

Inschlichlichtmacher, *m, pl* ~ - tallow chandler. **~, gebt's kenni meh.** Tallow chandlers no longer exist. LRT. =

Lichdermacher. KYG1966

iwwel - ~ nemme - to take offense. KYG1961

iwwelab, *adv* - in dire straits. **Mir waere ~, wann mir ken Geld hedde.** We'd be in dire straits if we had no money. LRT

iwwer, *prep* - over. **Die Kuh is ~ die Fens getschumpt.** The cow jumped over the fence. LRT, 4/21/2000

iwwer un iwwer, *adv* - repeatedly. **Der Groier hot ~ gfrogt fer en heecher Gebott.** The auctioneer asked repeatedly for a higher bid. LRT

iwwer epper hergeh, *pp* **is iwwer epper hergange** - to pitch into someone verbally. **Er is iwwer sie hergange bis sie ganz zitterich waar.** He pitched into her until she was all shaky. LRT

iwwer(e)nanner, *adv* - one on top of another. KYG2037. **Sie hen die Fenseriggel ~ gelegt.** They laid the fence rails one on top of the other. LRT

iwwerall, *adv* - everyhere. KYG2088. **Mir hen ~ Arewet gfunne.** We found work everywhere. LRT

iwwerbaue, *pp* **iwwergebaut** - to rebuild. **Die Amische sin zammegange un hen em Yonie un d'Katie ihre nunnergebrenndi Scheier iwwergebaut.** The Amish (neighbors) went together and rebuilt Jonie and Katie's burnt-down barn. LRT

iwwerbiede, *pp* **iwwergebodde**

- to outbid. **Ich hab nix heem zu nemme; uff alles hen sie mich iwwergebodde.** I have nothing to take home; they outbid me on everything. LRT

iwwerbinne, *pp* **iwwergebunne** - to tie again. KYG2015. **Deel vun den Weezegarwe misse iwwergebunne sei.** Some of these wheat sheaves need to be tied again. LRT

Iwwerbleiwes, *n* - remainder. *cf* **es Iwwerich, Iwwerrescht, die Sache was iwwerich waare** - the things that remained (or were left over). LRT

iwwerbren′ne, *pp* **iwwergebrennt** - to burn over. KYG2095. **Sell Feld waar nix wie Umgraut, no hen sie's iwwergebrennt.** That field was all weeds, then they burned it off. LRT

iwwerdecke, *pp* **iwwergedeckt** - to put on roof. **Sie hen die alde Schindle iwwergedeckt.** They covered the old shingles. LRT

iwwerdem′, *adv* - pretty soon. KYG1993. **~ misse mir verlosse.** Pretty soon we must leave. LRT

iwwerdrehe, *pp* **iwwergedreht** - to turn over. **eppes** (*acc.*) (**es Geld**) **zu epper ~** - to turn something (money) over to someone. KYG2078. **Wie sie achtzich Yaahr alt waare, hen sie alles iwwergedreht zu die Kinner.** When they were 80 years old, they turned everything over to the children. LRT

iwwerdresche - to thrash out (a matter). KYG2006

iwwerduh, *pp* **iwwergeduh**- to put on the stove. **Ich hab die Grummbiere iwwergeduh fer's Nachtesse.** I put the potatoes on the stove for supper. **Die Fraa hot's Nachtesse iwwergeduh.** My wife put the supper (things) on the stove. **Mir hen die Grummbiere iwwergeduh. Mir kenne esse in baut zwanzich Minude.** We put the potatoes on the stove. We can eat in about twenty minutes. LRT

Iwwereiling, *f* - mistake made through overhaste. LRT

iwwerflissich, *adj* - superfluous. **Alles was sie duhne is ~.** Everything they do is overdone (more than necessary). LRT

Iwwerfluss, *m* - superabundance. **Die Obschtaern waar en ~ des Yaahr.** The fruit harvest was a superabundance this year. LRT

iwwerfresse, *pp* **iwwergfresse** - to eat too much. KYG2034. **Ebmols duhne Kieh ~.** Sometimes cows eat too much. LRT

iwwergeh, *pp* **iwwergange** - to review. **Mer sin iwwer all die Babiere gange un hen ken Fehler gfunne.** We went over all the papers and found no mistakes. LRT

Iwwergewicht, *n* - overweight. **Seller Mann is ganz ~!** That man is extremely overweight. LRT

iwwergraabsche - to retain an undue portion. KYG2100

iwwergrabschich, *adj* - overly

greedy. **Es hot ewwe immer Leit as ~ sin.** There are always people who are overly greedy. LRT

iwwergscheit, *adj* - smart-alecky. **Yunger, sei net so ~!** Young man, don't be such a smart aleck! LRT

iwwergucke - to overlook. LRT

Iwwerhand′ nemme - to take control. **Wann mer Iwwerhand nemmt, no wees mer was aageht.** If one takes control, then one knows what is going on. LRT

iwwerhe′we - **1** to hold over. **Heb's iwwer bis mir widder Gemee hen.** Hold it over until we have church again. LRT. **2** to hold in reserve. **Heb's iwwer bis Mariye.** Hold it until tomorrow. LRT

iwwerhe′we, *refl* - to injure oneself by lifting too much. KYG2034. **Mer kann sich weh duh, wann mer sich iwwerhebt.** One can become injured by lifting too heavily. LRT

iwwerhole - to catch up with. KYG2117

Iwwerhosse, *pl* - overalls. **Sei ~ waare alles mit Mischt verschmiert.** His overalls were soiled with manure. LRT

Iwwerlaad, *f* - covering placed over coffin at time of burial to protect the coffin from decay, roughbox. KYG2266. Also **Rauhlaad** = roughbox, vault

iwwer(ge)laade, *adj* - overloaded. **Gebt Acht un faart**

langsam, seller Wagge is ganz ~. Be careful and drive slowly, that wagon is way overloaded. LRT

iwwerlese, *pp* **iwwergelese** - to read over. **Wann du die Sache iwwergelese hettscht, dann daedscht du wisse, was am aageh is.** If you had read over these things, you'd know what's going on. LRT

iwwerletzich, *adv* - here and there. KYG1994

iwwerlewe - to live over again. **Alle Daag dutt sie seller Unglick ~.** Everyday, she relives that accident. LRT

iwwermache - to revamp. **Kannscht du den Kaschde ~? Er is zu glee.** Can you redesign this box? It's too small. LRT

iwwermarye, *adv* - day after tomorrow. KYG2033. **~ kummt mei Nochber heem.** Day after tomorrow my neighbor will come home. LRT

iwwernacht, *adv* - overnight. **Sie sin ~ gebliwwe.** They stayed overnight. LRT

iwwernemme, *pp* **iwwergenumme** - **1** to take advantage of. **2** to take charge of. KYG1960. **3** to take upon oneself. KYG1962. **4** to take over. **McDonalds hot Boston Market iwwergenumme.** McDonald's took over Boston Market. **Der Tschunyer hot nau die ganz Bauerei iwwergnumme.** Junior has now taken over the whole farm. LRT

Iwwerrock, *m* - topcoat. KYG2037. **Wann die Kelt**

nunnergeht zu null, daed mer besser en ~ aaduh. When the temperature (cold) goes to zero, one had better wear an overcoat. LRT

iwwerrumple - to take by surprise. KYG1962

iwwerschlucke - to get something in the wrong throat. KYG2008

iwwerschmeisse - to throw over. = **niwwerschmeisse.** KYG2009. **Er hot der Balle weit iwwer sellem Buh sei Kopp gschmisse.** He threw the ball way over that boy's head. LRT

iwwerschnappe, *refl* - to speak indiscreetly. KYG1964

iwwerschneppe - to overturn from top-heaviness. KYG2038. **Ebmols dutt ihre Gleederbaam ~ wann sie en iwwerlaade mit Gleeder.** Sometimes their clothes tree tips over, when they overload it with clothes. LRT

iwwerschreiwe - to rewrite. **Kannscht du die Gschicht ~, so as die Kinner sie besser verschteh kenne?** Can you rewrite the story so the children can better understand it? LRT

iwwerschridde, *refl, pp* **iwwergschritt** - to overstep. **Er hot sich bissel iwwergschritt.** He went a bit too far. LRT

iwwerschteh - **1** to survive. **2** to remain. **Well, sin mer reddi fer die Vendu, was schteht noch iwwer?** Well, are we ready for the sale, what remains to be done? LRT

iwwerschtolpere, *pp* **iwwergeschtolpert** - to come upon unexpectedly. KYG2101. **Sie is iwwer seller Schtee gschtolpert.** She stumbled over that stone. LRT

Iwwerschuss, *n* - surplus. **Sie kenne der ~ hawwe.** They can have the surplus. LRT

iwwerschwetze - to review, discuss, take over. **Eb mir sell Haus kaafe, misse mir noch deel vun denne Sache ~.** Before we buy that house, we still have to discuss a few of these things. **Ich brauch ken Antwatt heit, dir kennt's ~ un mich wisse losse.** I don't need an answer today, you can talk it over and let me know. LRT

iwwersehne, *pp* **iwwergesehne** - to supervise (a matter), oversee. **Er hot gsaat, er daed die Bissiness ~.** He said he would oversee the business. **Es Karicheraad hot's Karich aaschtreiche iwwergesehne.** The church counsel supervised the church painted project. LRT

iwwerwaxe, *pp* **~** - to outgrow. **Er hot sei Gleeder ~.** He outgrew his clothes. LRT

iwwerwinne, *pp* **iwwergewunne** - to win over. **Sie hen nix zu duh hawwe welle mit ihm, awwer er hot sie iwwergewunne.** They didn't want to have anything to do with him, but he won them over. LRT

iwwerzeidich, *adj* - overripe. **Arebele schmacke so gut wann sie bissel ~ sin.** Strawberries taste especially good when they are a bit overripe. LRT

iwwerziehe, *pp* **iwwergezoge** - to upholster. KYG2118. **Sie hen sei weecher Schtul mit grie Duchschtofft iwwergezoge.** They upholstered his easy chair with green fabric. LRT

Iwwerzug, *m* - tick (for a bed). = **Ziech.** KYG2013

iwwerzwarich, *adj* - turned around. KYG2078. **Alles waar ~ vum Weg as es sei hett selle.** Everything was contrary from the way it should have been. LRT

Kaader, *m* - **1** an unusual person. KYG2115. **2** tomcat. = **Tammkatz.** KYG2033. **Seller ~ macht ken Yungi meh; mir hen en schneide glosst.** That tomcat will sire no more young ones; we had him castrated. LRT

Kaaf, *m* - purchase. **Er hot en guder ~ gemacht.** He made a good purchase. LRT

kaafe, *pp* **gekaaft** - to buy. **uff Baricks ~ -** to buy on trust. KYG2070. **Er hot uff Bariye gekaaft.** He bought on credit. LRT

Kaardedischel - teaselwort. KYG1977

kaeferich, *adj* - inclined to purchase. LRT

Kaerde - teasel. KYG1977

kaese - to turn into cheese. KYG2078

kaesich, *adj* - cheesy. **Die Millich is am ~ waare.** The milk is getting cheesy. LRT

Kaet, *f* - Katie. **Die ~ macht**

---

guti Eppelboi. Katie makes good apple pie. LRT,4/21/2000

Kafde, *pl* - notches between teeth of a saw. KYG1978. **Selli Saeg hot schier meh ~ as mer zaehle kann.** That saw has almost more notches than one can count. LRT

Kallicksack, *n* - lime bag. **En ~ sett net meh wie fuffzich Pund wiege.** A bagful of lime should not weigh more than 50 pounds. LRT

Kallickschtee, *m* - limestone. LRT

Kann, *f, pl* ~e - can. **blechne ~ -** tin can. KYG2021. **Wann du am Schtor verbei gehscht, kannscht du mir paar ~e gebackni Buhne bringe.** When you go by the store, you can bring me a couple of cans of baked beans. LRT

Kanne, *pl* - kernels. **~ ausmache -** to remove kernels. **Mei Nochbere duhne immer en latt Walnisskanne ausmache.** My neighbors always shell lots of walnut kernels. LRT

Kanneschtoge, *f* - ✪ **1** Conestoga Creek alias River, which flows through Lanc. Co., PA. **2** Conestogo River, Waterloo Co., Ontario, Canada

kannich, *adj* - full of seeds. **Die Hemmbiere sin mir schier zu ~.** The raspberries are nearly too full of seeds for me. LRT

Kannschtock, *m* - rye stack [This is virtually non-existent nowadays.] LRT

Kansel, *f* - pulpit, chancel. LRT

Kapp, *f* - **1** cap. **en ~ druff duh -** to throw the trump card (in the game of **Haasenpeffer**). KYG2009. **2** toe of a shoe. **Schuhkapp.** KYG2030

Karebs, *pl* ~e - pumpkin. **~e koche—was schunscht dutt mer mit ~e?** Cooking pumpkins—what else does one do with pumpkins? LRT

Karebseblatt, *n, pl* **-bledder** - pumpkin leaf. **Die Keffer hen die -bledder alles verfresse.** The bugs have eaten (totally riddled) the pumpkin leaves. LRT

Karebsefleesch, *n* - pumpkin meat. **~ gekocht mit Grummbiere un bissel Budder macht aartlich gut Esses.** Pumpkin meat cooked with potatoes and a bit of butter makes pretty good eating. LRT

Karebseroller, *m* - "pumpkin roller," yokel. KYG2263

Karepetlumpe, *m, pl* ~ - carpet rag. **Ich hab schund Karepet gheekelt mit ~.** I've already crocheted carpets with carpet rags. LRT

Karich, *f* - church. **deitschi ~ -** service in German. **So vanne in die 1900 hen die Ludderische in Mt. Zion noch eemol der Munet deitschi ~ ghat.** In the early 1900's, the Lutherans in Mt. Zion still had German services once a month. LRT. *cf* **der Karich** = cart.

Karichearigel, *f* - church organ. LRT

Karichebank, *f, pl* **-benk** - pew. **De elder as mer waert, de hadder as die -benk warre.** The older one gets, the harder are the church pews. LRT

Kariche-schwell, *f* - threshold of a church. KYG2007. **Deel Leit duhne der Kopp nunner wann sie iwwer die ~ gehne.** Some people bow their heads when they cross the threshold at church. LRT.

Karichezeit, *f* - time for service to begin. KYG2018. **Zehe Uhr Sunndaags vormidaags is ~ fer uns.** Ten o'clock Sunday forenoon is the time for our church service to begin. LRT

Karichhofmauer, *f* - wall surrounding a cemetery. KYG2160. **Die ~ waar vun Kallickschtee gemacht.** The cemetery wall was made of limestone. LRT

Karitsch, *f, pl* **~e** - surries. **Yaahre zerick waare mol ~e as sie "Jenny Linds" gheese hen.** Years ago there were once surries that were called Jenny Linds. LRT

Kaschezeit, *f* - time when cherries are ripe. KYG2018. **Well, Tscheck, sis widder ~. Witt du unseri widder roppe fer die Helft?** Well, Jake, the cherries are ripe again. Do you want to pick ours again for the half? LRT. [An old PG practice was for someone to provide the labor to pick the cherries and receive half of the crop in pay. LRT]

katz, *adj* - short. **~ un dick** - thick-set. KYG1996. **Seller Schtrick is zu ~.** That rope is too short. LRT

Katzegegwael, *n* - cat-tormenting. **Sell ~ muss schtoppe!** That cat-tormenting must stop! LRT, 4/18/2000

Katzegreemer, *m* - a child who likes cats. LRT

katzlich, *adv* - recently. **Yuscht do ganz ~ hen mir zwee Leichde ghat in eem Daag.** Just recently we had two funerals in one day. LRT

katzrum, *adv* - with a sharp turn about. KYG2076. **Yuscht katz um die Dreh rum schteht sei Haus.** Just a short distance around the turn stands his house. LRT

Keddeschtreng, *pl* - the traces. **Wann du die ~ eighenkt hoscht, dann sin mir faddich eischpanne.** If you've hooked up the traces, we are finished hitching up. LRT

Keenichheisli, *n* - queen bee cell. LRT

Kehlband, *n* - **1** throat band. **2** throat latch (on bridle). KYG2008. **= Halsband. En Geilszaahme muss en ~ hawwe.** A horse's bridle needs a throat band. LRT

Kehr, *f, pl* **~e** - a turn in the road. KYG2076

Kehrich, *m* - sweepings. **Ich hett liewer ~ as wie Kiehdreck.** I'd rather have sweeping dirt than cowdirt. LRT

keiche, *pp* **gekeicht** - to pant. **Sell Kind hot die ganz Nacht gekeicht.** That child panted all night. LRT

Keidel, *m, pl* **~** - wedge. KYG2242. **Fer'n zwelf-Fuuss Block schpalde, nemmt's etliche eisni ~.** To split a twelve-foot log, several wedges are required. LRT, 4/11/2000

keime, *pp* **gekeimt** - to sprout. **Guck mol, der Weeze is am ~ uff de Schack.** Look, the wheat is sprouting on the shocks. LRT

Keschderiggel, *m, pl* **~** - chestnut rail. **~ reide** - to play seesaw. **Ich wott mir hedde noch gudi ~.** I wish we still had good chestnut rails. **~ waare immer die beschde.** Chestnut rails were always the best ones. LRT

Keschteecheschtiwwel, *m* - tanned boots (in oak tanning). **= Keschteecheschtiffel.** KYG1967

Kessel, *m* - lit. kettle; old auto. **So'n alder ~ will ich net.** I don't want such an old auto like that. LRT

Kesselien' - nickname for gasoline. LRT

kessle, *pp* **gekesselt** - to ram around. **Mir sin niwwer noch em Schteddel gekesselt mit em Tschimmi seiner Kaer.** We rammed over into town with Jimmy's car. LRT

Kessler, *m* - itinerant tinkerer who mended (or sold) tinware. **= Kesselgreemer.** KYG2023

Kett, *f, pl* **~e** - chain. **mit ~e binne** - to shackle. **Wann ~e verreisse, hot mer Druwwel.** When chains tear, one has

95

trouble. LRT

Ketzer, *m* - mischievous fellow. **Wann seller glee ~ so uffhalde dutt, dann grickt er sich noch in blendi Druwwel.** If that little mischievous guy keeps it up, he will get himself into plenty of trouble. LRT

Kicharewet, *f* - work in the kitchen. **Sie waar schier der ganz Daag an ihre ~.** She was doing work in the kitchen almost all day. LRT,4/11/2000

Kichedisch, *m* - kitchen table. **In unserem Haus is der Schreibdisch der ~.** In our house the writing table is the kitchen table. LRT,4/18/2000

kidde - to putty. **Die Aaschtreicher duhne die Fenschdere ~.** The painters putty the windows. LRT

Kiehbohre, *m* - straw mow. **Der ~ is der Bohre owwich em Kiehschtall.** The **Kiehbohre** is the straw or hay mow above the cow stable. LRT

Kiehdokder, *m* - veterinarian. **Unser ~ hot en glee Messerli darich die Ditz nuffgschowe fer die Lecher greeser mache un die Kieh leichder melkich mache.** Our veterinarian pushed a small knife up through the teats to make the (teat) canals larger and make the cows easier to milk. LRT. = **Geilsdokder** [Leb Co.]

kimmere, *refl* - to take interest in. **Er kimmert sich gaar nix iwwer sell.** He cares nothing about that. **Er dutt sich immer ~ iwwer mich.** He always takes an interest in me. LRT

Kinnerlehr, *f* - catechetical instruction. **in die ~ (Unnericht) geh** - to take catechetical instruction. **Die Ludderische duhne ihre Kinner in die ~ schicke.** Lutherans send their children to catechetical instruction. LRT. = **zum Parre geh.** KYG1961

Kinnersach, *f* - toy. = **Kinnerschpielsach, Schpielsach.** KYG2045

Kinnerschtreech, *pl* - childish pranks. LRT

Kinschtlerei, *f* - powwowing. LRT

kippe - to topple. *cf* **schtatze, nidderschtatze, umfalle.** KYG2038

kischdich, *adj* - slightly tipsy. KYG2025

Kisselwedder, *n* - sleety weather. **Des ~ bin ich leedich.** I'm tired of this sleeting weather. LRT

kittre - to giggle. **Selli Kinnner sin immer am ~.** Those kids are always giggling. LRT

kitzle - to fill with secret joy. **Ebmols Sache as Kinner duhne, duhne em wunnerbaar ~.** Sometimes, things that children do, really fill one with secret joy. LRT

Kitzlerei, *f* - tickling. KYG2014. **Wann selli Yunge mol ihre ~ aafange, kann mer sie schier net schtoppe.** Once those kids start their tickling, one can hardly stop them. LRT

kitzlich, *adj* - touchy. *cf*

needlich, nutzlich. KYG2041. **Maedli, we kummt's as du ~ bischt?** Little girl, how come you are so ticklish? **Mer wunnert yuscht fer was as deel Leit so ~ sin.** One wonders why some people are so ticklish. LRT. *cf* **grittlich.** KYG2014

kluch, *adj* - wise, clever. **die Drei Kluche Menner** - the Three Wise Men. KYG2004. **Er is en ~er Mensch.** He is a wise person. LRT

kochich, *adj* - boiling. **Sell Wasser is ~.** That water is boiling. LRT

Kochkarebs, *f* - sweet pumpkin. **~e mache gudi Boi.** Sweet pumpkins make good pies. LRT

Kochoffe, *m* - range, cook stove. **Sie hen en Majestic ~.** They have a Majestic [company] range. LRT

Kochpann, *f* - sauce pan. LRT

Kodo´rus, *f* - ✪ Codorus Creek, York Co., PA. KYG2270

Kohle-offe, *m, pl* -effe - coal-burning stove. **-effe sin so schee waarem.** Coal stoves are so nice and warm. LRT

kollere - to make a gurgling sound (in the throat). KYG2008. **Seller Kessel voll Wasser uff em Offe is am ~.** That kettle of water on the stove is giving a boiling gurgling sound. LRT

Kolwe, *pl* - **1** spikes of the timothy. KYG2021. **2** cob. **Ich gleich mei Siesswelschkann vun die ~ esse.** I like to eat my sweet corn from the cob. LRT

Kopp, *m* - **1** head. **Du kannscht dich yuscht uff der Kopp schtelle wehich mir.** You can just stand on your head on account of me. **ab im ~ sei** - to be simple minded. **Wann epper ab is im ~, muss mer achtgewwe.** If someone has gone wacko, one must be careful. **der ~ nucke** - to tilt the head back. KYG2017. **Er muss schlaeferich sei, guck mol wie er sei ~ nuckt.** He must be sleepy, look how he's tilting back his head. **2** a hill that is a peak and not a ridge. LRT

Koppduch, *n, pl* **-dicher** - head piece. **Net all die "Schaale" sin ~dicher.** Not all shawls are head pieces. LRT

Koppgratzes, *n* - much thought, "headscratching". *cf* **Kopprechnes.** KYG2002. **Sei ~ hot net viel gebatt.** His much thought (head scratching) didn't help much. LRT

Kordbendel, *m* - cord string. **Er hot en grosser Balle ~ uffghowe ghat.** He had saved a big ball of cord string. LRT

Koscht, *f* - board, fare, victuals. **Ich duh mei ~ verdiene.** I earn my room and board. LRT

koschtfrei, *adv* - free of cost (for boarding). LRT

kosslich, *adj* - untidy. *cf* **noochlessich, schlappich.** KYG2114

kotzerich, *adj* - nauseous. **Seller Gschtank is genunk fer em ~ mache.** That stench is enough to make one feel like vomiting. LRT

Kotzgrixel! - The deuce take it! = **Grick's der Schellem!** KYG1963

kotzrich, *adj* - nauseated. **Alli mol as ich sell ess, macht's mich ~.** Every time I eat that, I become nauseated. LRT

Kowwel - top curl (of child). KYG2037

Kramm, *m* - wares. *cf* **Schtorsach, Waar.** KYG2164

Kudderments, *pl* - things. **so ~** - such things. KYG1997

kumme - to come. **Wann er kummt, kummt sei Aldi aa.** If he comes, his wife will come as well. **Ya, sis eppes iwwer ihn ~.** Yes, something came over him. LRT,4/18/2000

Kuni, *m* - *dim* of **Kunraad.** Conrad. **Mei erschdi Schulmeeschdern hot en ~ gheiert.** My first school teacher married a Conrad. LRT,4/21/2000

kupple - to unite in marriage. KYG2106

Kutzel - untidy woman. = **Schlapp.** KYG2114

Kutzeschteddel, *n* - ✪ Kutztown, Berks Co., PA. KYG2275

Laabnescht, *n* - leafy squirrel's nest. **Wann die Eechhaase ken Nescht finne kenne im e hohle Baam, no misse sie sich ewwe en ~ baue.** If squirrels can't find a nest in a hollow tree, then they must build a leaf nest for themselves. LRT

Laabverreisser, *m* - forage shredder, a machine used on the farm. LRT

Laademacher, *m* - casket maker. LRT

Laademann, *m* - casket man. LRT

Laadschtecke, *m, pl* **~** - ramrod. **Gudi ~ verbreche net gern.** Good ramrods rarely break. LRT

laafe - to walk. **Langsam ~ uff 'me scheener Daag is so blessierlich.** To stroll on a nice day is so pleasurable. LRT

Laafes, *n* - walking. KYG2159. **Sei viel ~ halt ihn gsund.** His much walking keeps him healthy. LRT

laafich, *adj* - **1** running. **en ~i Naas** - a running nose. **2** rutty. **Die Kuh is ~, die annere wisse es.** The cow is in heat, the other ones (cows) know it. LRT

Laafkoldiweeder, *m* - walking cultivator. KYG2159

laagere - to speak irresponsibly. KYG1964

laermend, *adj* - tumultuous. KYG2075

Lammix, *m* - lummox [clumsy, stupid person]. **Seller Mann is en rechder ~.** That man is a real lummox. LRT

Landeegner, *m* - land owner. KYG2262. **Der ~ muss ewwe die Taxe bezaahle.** The land owner must indeed pay the taxes. LRT,4/21/2000

Landregge, *m* - **1** a steady rain.

Ich wett immer liewer en ~ hawwe as wie en Gwidder-rege. I'd always rather have a steady rain than a thunderstorm. **~ sin die, unni Wedderleech un Gwidder.** Steady rains are those without lightning and thunder. **2** extensive, incessant rain. **Wann's als recht drucke waert, no saage sie: "Was mir breiche, is en guder ~."** When there is a dry spell, they say: "What we need is a good soaking rain." LRT

Landschaft, *f* - section. **Do in unser ~ hen mir en latt Amische.** Here in our section, we have a lot of Amish people. LRT

Landschillgrott, *f, pl* **~e** - 1 terrapin. **2** tortoise. = **Schillgrott.** KYG2040. **Schillgrodde sin gewiss marickwaddichi Gediere.** Tortoises are indeed remarkable creations (creatures). LRT

lang, *adv* - long. **Es is noch ~ hie.** It is a long time yet. KYG2018

lang, *adj* - long. **Es nemmt en ~i Zeit fer sell geduh griege.** It takes a long time to get that done. LRT

lang hie, *adv* - long ago. **Es is noch ~.** It's been a long time. KYG2263

lang-schichdich, *adj* - long, drawn out. **Des waar en ~ Wese.** This was a long drawn-out affair. LRT

lange - to hand. **Kannscht du mir die Schaufel ~?** Can you hand the shovel to me? LRT

langsam, *adj* - slow. **~ is besser wie gaar net.** Slow is better than not at all. LRT

langwaerich, *adj* - tedious. = **langweilich, verdriesslich.** KYG1978. **Der Butcherdaag kann en ~er Daag sei.** Butcher day can be a tedious one. LRT

Langweile, *n* - tedium. KYG1978

langweilich, *adj* - tiresome. *cf* **leedich, miehseelich, verleed, verleedlich, verleedsam.** KYG2026. **Des Deppich mache is en ~ Wese.** This quilt making is a long and tedious process. LRT

lanneswaert, *adj* - worth learning. **Ya, ich denk des Waddefresserwese is ~.** Yes, I think this P.C. technology is worth learning. LRT,4/18/2000

Lanning, *f* - education. **ken ~ hawwe** - to be unlettered. KYG2107. **Er hot en hochi ~, awwer's weisst sich net.** He has a good education, but it doesn't show. LRT

Lapperei, *f* - twaddle. KYG2081

larebsich, *adv* - with indistinct pronunciation. **Er schwetzt so ~, es laut as wann er Mosch im Maul hett.** He speaks so indistinctly, it sounds as though he has mush in his mouth. LRT

Laschder, *n* - much stuff. **Du hoscht awwer en ~ Schtofft do geduh!** You did a gosh awful amount of things here! LRT

laude - to sound. **schee ~** - to sound well. **Ihre Musik dutt schee ~.** Their music sounds nice. **Sell laut wiescht.** That sounds bad. LRT

Laudermillich, *f* - milk. **"~ un gaar ken Raahm"** - all milk and no cream. [joke about family name of LRT's wife's great-grandparents] LRT

lautschmackich, *adj* - strong-smelling. **Meerreddich is immer so ~.** Horseradish is always so strong-smelling. LRT

Laxiering, *f* - physic. **Deel Leit griege en ~ vun Sauergraut.** Some people find sauerkraut to be a laxative. LRT

Lechaa, *f* - ✪ Lehigh River.

Lechaadaal, *n* - ✪ Lehigh Valley.

lechle - to titter. = **kittre** *cf* **ziddere.** KYG2027

leddere, *pp* **geleddert** - "to leather," beat. **Ya, die Buwe hen ihn geleddert.** Yes, the boys beat him (but good). LRT,4/18/2000

leddich, *adj* - unmarried. **~ Maedel** - single girl. KYG2108

leddicherweis, *adv* - single. **Sie hot ~ en latt Geld verdient.** As a single girl she earned a lot of money. **Sie hot sell Kind ~ ghat.** She had that child while being unmarried. LRT

leddichweis, *adj* - unfathered. **en ~ Kind** - a fatherless child. KYG2102

lee, *adj* - alone. = **leenich.** KYG2090

leed duh - to be sorry. **Es dutt mir Rei un Leed.** (said by repentant excommunicated plain sect member). **eem ~ duh** - to make someone sorry. **Es dutt eem ~ fer so eppes heere.** It makes one feel bad (sad) to hear something like that. LRT

Leede, *m* - sorrow, grief. **em ~ duh** - to make someone feel sorry. **Sell gebt mir der ~.** That is a turn-off for me. LRT. **der ~ draa hawwe** - to be tired of. **Ich hab der ~ draa.** I am tired of it. KYG2025. **Ich denk der glee Buh hot ihne der ~ gemacht davon.** I guess the little boy tired them of the matter. PB,7/13/25. **Deel vun dem Guckbax Schtofft gebt em der ~.** Some of this TV stuff gets to be a total boredom. LRT

Leederschprosse, *m, pl* **~** - rung of a ladder. **En schwerer Ding wie sell kennt die ~ nunnerbreche.** A heavy guy like that could break the ladder rungs down. LRT

Leederwagge, *m, pl* **-wegge** - farm wagon with racks. **-wegge kenne gfaehrlich sei; mer muss achtgewwe as mer net darich die Leedere nunnefallt.** Wagons with racks can be real dangerous; one must be careful not to fall down through the ladders (racks). LRT

leedich, *adj* - to be tired of something. **Die Hitz un Schmudichkeit do in Pennsilfaanie im Summer vum Yaahr 1999 waar ich arig ~ warre.** I really got tired of the heat and humidity that we had in PA in the summer of 1999. LRT

leenich, *adv* - single-handedly.

Es hot ken gotzicher Mensch mir gholfe, ich hab der Gaarde ~ mache misse. Not a single person helped me, I had to dig the garden single-handedly. LRT

leenich, *adj* - alone. **Ich waar ~ datt im Dunkle un hab gaar net gewisst wu ich waar.** I was alone there in the dark and had no idea where I was. LRT

lehne, *pp* **gelehnt** - to borrow. **Mir hen die Soot-Drill gelehnt vun die Nochbere.** We borrowed the grain drill from the neighbors. LRT

Lehnsbauer, *m, pl* **~** - tenant farmer. KYG1984. **Sei Grosseldre waare ihre ganz Lewelang ~ (-sleit).** His grandparents were tenant farmers (folks) all their lives. LRT

Lehnsblatz, *m* - rented place. **Meim Paep sei Eldre sin alle zwee gschtarewe uff'm ~ (Bauerei).** My father's parents both died on a rented place, *i.e.* a farm. LRT

Lehnshaus, *n* - tenant house. KYG1984. **Sell ~ sett aagschtriche sei.** That tenant house should be painted. LRT

Lehnsleit, *pl* - tenant family. KYG1984. **Dir hett wunnerbori gudi ~.** You have a mighty good tenant family. LRT

Lehnsmann, *m* - tenant. KYG1984. **Der ~ hot uns Feierholz gebrocht.** The tenant brought us firewood. LRT

Leichder, *m* - taper made of paper. KYG1969

Leichtbeschteller, *m* - funeral planner (preparer). LRT

Leichtmann, *m* - funeral man. LRT

leichtsinnich, *adj* - scatter-brained. *cf* **gedankelos. Er is net zu verdraue, er is zu ~.** He is not to be trusted, he is too scatter-brained. LRT

Leichtsinnichkeet, *f* - thoughtlessness. KYG2002. **= -keit.** [Leb. Co.] **Sei ~ hot gaar nix gebatt.** His thoughtlessness was no help at all. LRT

Leichtversariyer, *m* - one who cares for, provides for the funeral. LRT

leidlich, *adj* - comfortable. **Sell is mir net ~.** I don't feel comfortable with that. LRT

leie - to fall in wet weather (of wheat). **Der Weeze leit.** The wheat is lying down in the field (as a result of the wet weather). **= lege.** KYG2160. **Der Weeze leit um vun all dem Regge was mir ghat hen.** The wheat is lying down because of all the rain we had. LRT

Leingaul, *m* - single line leader. LRT

leitschei, *adj* - afraid of people. **En latt gleeni Kinner sin ~, abbaddich wann's fremmi Leit sin.** A lot of small children are afraid of people, especially if they are strangers. LRT

Lengeschder Kaundi - ✪ Lancaster County, PA. **Es sin en latt gudi Bauer in ~.** There are a lot of good farmers in Lancaster County.

LRT,4/21/2000

leppisch, *adj* - unsavory, tasteless, insipid. KYG2111. **Seller Seider schmacke ~.** That cider tastes flat. **Die Supp schmackt ~.** The soup tastes insipid. = **abgschtanne.** LRT

letscht, *adj* - last. **Es ~ sei is besser wie gaar net sei.** Being last is better than not being at all. LRT. **es ~ her** - toward the end. KYG2042. **Do's ~ her hen mir nix gheert.** Here recently we heard nothing. LRT

letschtyaehrich, *adj* - last year's. KYG2259. **Sell ~ PA Deitsch Fescht waar's bescht, as ich noch gsehne hab.** That PA German festival of last year was the best I've seen. LRT,4/18/2000

letz, *adv* - 1 wrong. **sei Lewe net ~** - unerring. KYG2101. **Er kann yuscht nix ~ duh.** He can just do nothing wrong. **2** inside out. **Tscheck du hoscht dei Hosse ~ aa.** Jake, you have your pants on inside out. LRT

letz, *adj* - wrong. **eppes ~** - something wrong. **Es is eppes ~.** There is something wrong. **Sell waar ~, was er gsaat hot.** What he said was incorrect. **Was is ~ mit ihm?** What's his problem? LRT

letz geh, *pp* **letz gange** - to go wrong. **Es es ihm letz gange ee Mol iwwer's anner.** He has been thwarted time and time again. KYG2012

Lewe, *n* - **1** life. **Sei ~ waar ihm immer die greescht Freed.** His life was always one of great joy. **2** quick (of fingernails). **Wann**

mer am Fingerneggel abschneide is, is es net hatt fer ins ~ schneide. When one is cutting fingernails, it is not difficult to cut into the quick. LRT

lewen'dich, *adj* - living, full of life. **~ voll** - teeming full. KYG1978. **Wann en Gedier zawwelt, wees mer as es ~ is.** If an animal kicks, struggles, or wiggles one knows it's alive. LRT

Lewesfaade, *m* - thread of life. KYG2003

Lewespaad, *m* - path of life. LRT

Lewisbarig, *m* - ✪ Lewisburg, PA. **Die Ludderische hen en Synod-Affis in ~.** The Lutherans have a synod (Upper Susquehanna Synod) office in Lewisburg, PA. LRT,4/21/2000

lichthell, *adj* - lit with lights. **Schpot die letscht Nacht hab ich niwwergeguckt an ihre Haus un's waar noch ~; ich wees net was am aageh waar.** Late last night I looked over at their house and the lights were still bright; I don't know what was going on. LRT

Lichtposchde, *m, pl* **~** - street lamp. **Die Schtadt vun Wellsboro, PA hot scheeni ~.** The town of Wellsboro, PA has beautiful lampposts. LRT

Lichtschtraal, *n* - streak of light. **Sis schtichdunkel, awwer alligebott seht mer en ~.** It is pitch dark but every now and then one sees a streak of light. LRT

lieb, *adj* - dear. **Es waer mir**

yuscht so ~, wann sie deheem bleiwe daede. I'd just as soon they stayed at home. LRT

lieblich, *adj* - precious. **Unser Kindskind is en ~er, gleener Ding.** Our grandchild is a precious little fellow. LRT

lieblichbidder, *adj* - descriptive of tansy tea. KYG1968

lieblos, *adj* - uncharitable. KYG2093

Liebschtick, *n* - favorite song. **Sell is mir awwer en ~.** That is a favorite song of mine. LRT

Liewesgruss, *m* - token of affection sent to a loved one. KYG2031

Liewesmaahldisch, *m* - sawbuck type table (set up at Love Feast). **Die Mannsleit un die Weibsleit hen ihre eegni ~.** The men and the women have their own (separate) Love Feast tables. LRT

lieweswaert, *adj* - worthy of love. KYG2251. **Sell Kind is gewiss ~.** That child is truly worthy of love. LRT,4/18/2000

Lillidramm, *m* - tincture for healing cuts, bruises, etc. KYG2022

Lilliye, *f* - lily. **scheckiche ~** - Turk's-cap lily. *Lilium superbum L.* KYG2076

Limbaryer, *adj* - Limburger. **Viel Leit gleiche der Geruch vun ~ Kaes net.** Many people don't like the odor of Limburger cheese. LRT,4/21/2000

Limpli, *n* - *dim* of **Lumpe.**

small rag. LRT/Leb.

Lissie, *f* - Lizzie, Elizabeth. **Meim Papp sei Gschwischdersoh hot die ~ Grummbeh [Grumbine] gheiert.** My dad's cousin married Lizzie Grumbine. LRT4/21/2000. = **Liss**

Loch, *n, pl* **Lecher** - hole. **Es sin alle sadde Lecher.** There are all kinds of holes. LRT. **in's ~ geh** - to be unable to win the number of tricks bid (in cards). KYG2090. *Proverb:* **Sie mache ee Loch zu, un's anner uff.** They rob Peter to pay Paul. LRT

lockere - to loosen by tapping. KYG1970

lodderich, *adj* - shaky. = **wabblich, wacklich, zidderich. Seller Wagge is ~, er muss alt sei.** That wagon is wobbly, it must be old. LRT

loddle - to walk slowly. *cf* **schleiche.** KYG2159

Loh, *m* - tanbark. = **Garewerloh, Garewerinn, Lohrinn.** KYG1967

Lohgrub, *f, pl* **-gruwe** - tan pit. KYG1968. **~, ich hab sei Lewe kenni gsehne.** Tan pit, never in my life have I seen one. LRT

Lohmiehl, *f* - tanning mill. KYG1968

lohrot, *adj* - color of tanbark. KYG1967

losschrauwe - to unscrew. **Wann du seller Deckel losschraubscht, kann ich vielleicht sehne was letz is.** If you unscrew that lid, perhaps I

can see (learn) what the problem is. LRT

los-schnalle - to unbuckle. **Duh sellem Hund sei Halsband ~.** Unbuckle that dog's neck band (collar). LRT

losdunnere - to thunder freely. KYG2011

losfaahre, *pp* **losgfaahre** - to depart. **Er is druff losgfaahre, as wann der Deifel aa los waar.** He drove pellmell as though the devil were loose, and after him as well. LRT

loshoke - to unclasp. = **uffhoke, uffmache.** KYG2093. = **abhenke.** LRT

loskopple - to uncouple. = **loslosse.** KYG2094

loskumme, *pp* **~** - to become untied. KYG2114. **Selli Henk am Eisekessel is ~; mir misse sie feschtschweese.** That handle on the iron kettle came off; we need to weld it (back on). LRT

loslosse[1] - to let loose. **Loss der Hund los!** Let the dog loose (run)! LRT

loslosse[2], *pp* **losgelosst** - **1** to go into a tirade. = **sich nauslosse.** KYG2025. **Wie sie ihm gsaat hen as er nix zu drinke hawwe daerf, hot er awwer losgelosst.** When they told him that he could have nothing to drink, he really went into a tirade. LRT. **2** to unhand, unleash. KYG2103. **Ya, mir hen die Kieh losgelosst.** Yes, we let loose (unchained) the cows. LRT

losmache - to unloose. KYG2108. **Selli Schraub is so**

hatt fescht gedreht, ich kann sie net ~. That screw is turned in so tight, I can't loosen it. LRT

losreisse, *pp* **losgerisse** - to tear loose. KYG1976. **Der Wind hot die Schindle losgerisse.** The wind tore loose the shingles. LRT

losschaffe, *refl, pp* **losgschafft** - to work something loose. **Der Gaul hot sich losgschafft un waar im Scheierhof am rumgschpringe.** The horse worked himself loose (freed himself) and was running around in the barnyard. LRT,4/11/2000

Lossement, *n* - kaboodle. **So'n ~ hett mir liewer net!** We'd rather not have such an uproar! LRT

loswarre, *pp* **~** - to become unfastened. KYG2102. **Ya, die Kelwer sin ~.** Yes, the calves became unfastened. LRT

loswickle - to unravel. *cf* **abwickle, auszoppe.** KYG2110. **Wickel mol seller Schtrick los, ich will sehne wie lang as er is.** Unravel that rope, I want to see how long it is. LRT

luddere - to use the truth carelessly. KYG2071

Luder, *n* - stinker. *cf* **Schinnoos, Schtinkluder.** KYG1881

Luderaadler, *m* - turkey buzzard. **Die ~ hen gudi Aage.** Turkey buzzards have good eyes. LRT

Ludermann, *m* - rendering man. **En Wedderleech schtraale hot selli Kuh dod**

gschlagge, ruf der ~. A bolt of lightning killed that cow, call the rendering man. LRT. *cf* **Schinnerhannes**

Luderwagge, *m* - scavenger's wagon. **Zwee dodi Kieh, es is Zeit fer der ~ rufe.** Two dead cows, it's time to call the scavenger's wagon. LRT

ludre - to smell rotten. **Seller dod Hund dutt farichderlich ~.** That dead dog stinks terribly. LRT

Ludre, *n* - stench. **Sell ~ kann ich schier net schtende.** I can hardly stand that stench. LRT

Luft, *f* - air. **en beissichi ~** - a zip in the air. KYG2266. **Des is en beissichi ~; ich glaab as mir Schnee griege.** There's a bite in the air; I believe it's going to snow. LRT,4/21/2000

Luft, *f* - air. **Er is ewwe mol widder am heesi ~ blose.** Once again he is blowing hot air. LRT, 4/11/2000

Luftrinn, *f, pl* ~**e** - bark of trunk. KYG2070

Luftrohr, *n* - trachea. KYG2045. **Sie hen gsaat sei ~ waar verschtoppt.** They said his trachea was closed up. LRT

Lumpesack, *m, pl* -**seck** - rag bag. **Fer lenger zerick waare die ~seck frieher Fuderseck gwest.** Years ago rag bags were originally feed bags. LRT

Lungefiewer, *n* - fever accompanying pulmonary tuberculosis. KYG2072. **Ebmols hen deel Leit ~ un sie wisse's net.** Sometimes some

people have pneumonia and they don't know it. LRT

Lungentzinding, *f* - pulmonary tuberculosis.= **Lungezucht.** KYG2072

luschdier′e, *refl* - to enjoy oneself. **Gsundheit im Kopp un im Kareber is der Weg fer sich ~.** Health in the head and body is the way to be joyful. LRT

Luschtlewe, *n* - riotous living. **Es is gut as es ~ net fer alle-epper is.** It is good that riotous living is not for everyone. LRT

Luttrischer, *m* - a Lutheran. LRT

Maage, *m* - stomach. **grank uff em ~** - nausea of the stomach (before vomiting). **en schlechder ~** - of stomach with digestive problem. **uff em ~ leie** - to lie on one's stomach. KYG1885. **Hoscht du ken Mariye-Esse ghat? Dei ~ is am rapple.** Didn't you have breakfast? Your stomach is rumbling. LRT

Maagebidders, *n* - stomach bitters. KYG1885

Maagebolleres, *n* - rumbling of the stomach. KYG1885

Maagedokder, *m* - stomach specialist. KYG1885

Maagedroppe, *pl* - medicine for the stomach. KYG1885

Maagedruwwel, *m* - stomach trouble. KYG.885. **In Lebnen Kaundi hen mir als Will-Kur Maagedroppe ghat. Wann mer ~ ghat hot, hot en

Teeleffel vun sellem (Will-Kur) em glei uffschtosse gemacht.** In Lebanon County we used to have Will-Kur "stomach drops." If the stomach was hurting, a teaspoon of that (Will-Kur) would soon make one burp. LRT

Maagefehler, *m* - stomach disorder. KYG1885. **Wer en latt ~ hot, sett geh en Dokder sehne.** One who has a lot of stomach disorder should see a doctor. LRT

Maagegramp, *m* - spasm of the stomach. KYG1885

Maagegrebs, *m* - stomach cancer. KYG1885

Maagepill, *f* - stomach pill. KYG1885. **Eeniche Pill as mer nemmt geht in der Maage, so was die Grenk is en ~?** Any pill that one takes goes into the stomach, so what the heck (duce) is a stomach pill? LRT

maager, *adj* - unproductive (of land). KYG2110. **Der Grund in sellem Feld is arig ~; sehscht wie gehl as es Welschkann guckt?** The soil in that field lacks fertility; do you see how yellow the corn looks? LRT

Maagezaah, *m, pl* **Maagezaeh** - stomach tooth. KYG1885. **Mer kann die Maggezaeh roppe, awwer sell hot nix zu duh mit Maagegramp aabringe odder wecknemme.** One can pull the stomach teeth, but that has nothing to do with causing or taking away stomach spasm. LRT

mache - to make, manufacture. **Deel Deitsche duhne Pissebettblummetschelli**

mache. Some Pennsylvania German folks make dandelion blossom jelly. LRT. **Wann mer Fehler macht, sett mer sie widder gut mache kenne.** If one errs, one should be willing to substantiate them. LRT

Machedunkie, *f* - ✪ Mahantongo, PA. **Die Mannsleit hen alli Yaahr ihre PA Deitsch Versammling im Friehyaahr an die Unner ~.** The men have their PA German gathering each year in the spring at the Lower Mahangongo, PA. LRT4/21/2000

Maedel, *n* - girl. **Sie is en elder ~ as wie sie guckt.** She is an older girl than she appears to be. LRT. **Er hot sich en schee guckiches ~ gfunne.** He found himself a nice-looking girl. LRT

Maedelfreind, *f* - girl friend. **Wie mei Fraa noch mei ~ waar, hab ich re mol heemgemachdi Brotwascht gewwe.** When my wife was still my girl friend, I once gave her some of our homemade sausage. LRT

maednarrish, *adj* - girl crazy. **Seller Buh is ~.** That boy is girl crazy. LRT

Maedschtofft, *n* - mischievous girls. **Latts vun dem ~, was mer heert devun, kann mer yuscht schier net glaawe.** A lot of this girls' mischief stuff that we hear about, one can just hardly believe. LRT

maerderan'nisch, *adv* - murderously. **Sie hot ~ gegrische.** She screamed murderously. LRT

maerderisch, *adv* - murderously. **~ greische -** to yell in an unearthly manner. KYG2100

maerderlich, *adv* - murderously. **Die Maed hen ~ gegrische.** The girls yelled (screamed) murderously. LRT,4/18/2000

Maerdi, *m* - Martin. **Mei Grossdaadi, der ~ Peiffer, waar Yaahre zerick Schtorkipper an Mt. Zion in Lebnen Kaundi, PA.** My grandfather, Martin Peiffer, was a storekeeper years ago at Mt. Zion, Lebanon Co., PA. LRT,4/21/2000

maessich, *adj* - temperate. = **nichdern.** KYG1982

Maessichkeit, *f* - temperance. KYG1982

Magazin´ - storage place for powder. KYG1890

Mangel, *m* - want, need. **~ leide -** to suffer from want. KYG2162. **Er hot ken ~.** He has no need. LRT

mangelhaft, *adj* - unsatisfactory. KYG2111

mangle - to want, need. *cf* **bedarefe, brauche, breiche, verlange, winsche.** KYG2163

Mannichfalt, *f* - third stomach of ruminants. KYG1884

Mannichfaltbauch, *m* - third stomach (of cow, bull). KYG1884

mannichmol, *adv* - many times, some times. KYG2020. **~**

kummt er heem nooch de Halbnacht. Many times he comes home after midnight. LRT. **~ im Winder hen sie die Kinner frieh heem gschickt vun de Schul.** Many times (frequently) in the winter they sent the children home early from school. LRT

Mannsarewet, *f* - heavy work. **Hot sie all selli Arewet geduh? Well, sell is awwer ~!** Did she do all that work? Well, that is heavy work (and should be a man's job). LRT,4/11/2000

mannsleitnarrisch, *adj* - crazy about men. **Sell yung Weibsmensch is ~.** That young woman is crazy about men. LRT

Mard(er)gschicht, *f, pl* -**gschichde** - murder stories. **Im Yaahr 1935 waar mei Paep uff re Tschuri fer'n ~.** In the year 1935 my dad was on the jury for a murder trial. LRT

Marick, *n* - target. *cf* **Scheib, Ziel.** KYG1970. **Sell waar graad uff em ~; sie hen gsaat selli alt Kaer daed $5000 hole (an die Vendu) un sie hot.** That was right on the mark; they said that old car would bring $5000 at the auction, and it did. LRT

Marickschiesse, *n* - target shooting. KYG1970. **Ich hett liewer as sie ~ daede as wie Dauwe schiesse.** I'd rather they did target shooting instead of pigeon shooting. LRT

marickwaerdich, *adv* -
1 terribly. **~ verschrocke -** terribly frightened. *cf* **scheech, verkollebiert.** KYG1988.   **2** remarkably. **Sell waar en ~i grossi Leicht.** That was a

103

remarkably large funeral. LRT. **Sei Breddich waar ~ gut.** His sermon was remarkably good. LRT

Mariye-rot, *n* - red morning sky. **~ bis Owed Dreck im Kot.** If in the morning sky is red, by the evening there will be mud on the ground (proverb). LRT

Mariyeseit, *f* - morning side. **die ~ vum Haus** - the east side of the house. LRT

Mariyezeiding, *f* - morning newspaper. **Mir griege immer en ~.** We always get a morning newspaper. LRT

Marrascht', *m* - 1 mud. 2 mess. **Sis net arig schee fer so en ~ hawwe.** It's not very nice to have such a mess. LRT

Marye, *m* - morning. **gehe ~ - 1** toward the east. 2 toward morning. KYG2042. **Mir sin gehe ~ gange un bis Owed waar die Sunn uff unserem Buckel.** We went east and by evening the sun was on our back. LRT

Maschtdarem, *m* - rectum. *cf* **Afder.** LRT

Maschtox, *m, pl* **~e** - fattening steer. **~e mehne es gebt ee Daag Rinsfleesch.** Fattening steers, mean one day there will be beef. LRT

Maschtsau, *f, pl* **-sei** - fattening pig. **Vun Laefersei waxe sie zu -sei.** From shoats they grow to fattening pigs. LRT

matt, *adj* - weak, faint. **Ich bin so mied un ~ ich kann schier gaar nimmi fatt.** I'm so tired

and weak I can hardly go anymore. [A Leb. Co. saying.] LRT

mauere - to lay up a wall. KYG2160. **Kannscht du uns en Mauer ~ (lege)?** Can you lay up a wall for us? LRT

Mauereck, *n* - angle of a wall. KYG2160

Mauerlatt, *f* - wall plate. KYG2161

Mauerwand, *f* - stone (foundation) wall. KYG1888. **Die ~ in unserem Haus rinnt (Wasser).** The foundation wall of our house leaks (water). LRT

Maul, *n* - mouth (of man or beast). **des ~ verschrauwe** - to screw up one's mouth. **Ich waer froh wann er yuscht sei ~ halde daed.** I'd be glad if he would just shut his mouth. **Ya, henk yuscht dei ~, was ich gsaat hab, waar die Waahret.** Yes, you just pout (be a pouting person), what I said was the truth. LRT. **es ~ zwinge** - to twist the mouth. KYG2084. *Proverb:* **Mer guckt em gschenkde Gaul net ins ~.** One should not look in a gift horse's mouth. LRT

Maulvoll, *n* - mouthful. **epper en ~ gewwe** - to tell someone a thing or two. KYG1981. **Du hoscht ihm en ~ gewwe.** You gave him a piece of your mind. LRT

Medaer´ing, *m* - puss. **Gschwaere sin die menscht Zeit voll ~.** Boils are usually full of puss. LRT

meddle - to tamper. = **middle.**

KYG1966

meeglicherweis, *adv* - possibly. LRT

Meeschderschtiffel, *m* - top boots. = **Meeschderschtiwwel.** = **hochi Schtiwwel.** KYG2037

Mehning, *f* - opinion. **Er hot ewwe net uffgewwe bis ich ihm die ~ gsaat hab.** He didn't give up until I gave him a piece of my mind. LRT

meilelang, *adv* - miles long. **Er is fer ~ rumgekesselt bis er sich Gesselien kaafe hot misse.** He drove around for many miles until he had to buy some gasoline. LRT

meileweit, *adv* - for miles. **Er is ~ gfaahre.** He drove for miles. LRT

meislischtill, *adj* - perfectly still, still as a mouse. **Was geht dann aa? Du hockscht datt un bischt ~?** What is going on? You're sitting there and you're still as a mouse. LRT. (Leb. Co. = **meiseschtill**), (= **maus-schtill, meiselschtill.** KYG1880)

Melkbenkli, *n, pl* **~n** - milk bench. **Unser ~n hen immer drei Beh ghat.** Our milk stools always had three legs. LRT

Melket, *f* - milking. **die erscht, zwett un dritt ~** - the first, second, and third milking. **Die sext ~ nochdem as die Kuh's Kalb hot, kennt dir die Millich uffhewe.** The sixth milking after the cow calves you can save the milk (for human consumption). LRT

menan´ner, *adv* - together.

hause ~ - to live together as man and wife. KYG2030. **Ich un die Fraa un die Kinner sin immer ~ in die Karich gange.** My wife and I and the children always went to church together. LRT

Menscheschinner, *m* - tyrant. = **Tirann.** KYG2087

Menscheverschtand, *m* - human understanding. **gsunder ~** - healthy, human understanding. KYG2098. **Er hot yuscht ken ~.** He just has no common sense. LRT

Messband, *n, pl* **-benner** - tape measure. KYG1969. **En 50 Fuuss ~ is hendich fer hawwe.** A 50-foot measuring tape is a convenient thing to have. LRT

Messerschpitze, *m, pl* **~** - knife point. **Geb Acht, selli ~ sin scharef.** Be careful, those knife points (tips) are sharp. LRT

Mexigaa´ner, *m* - Mexican. KYG2268

mexigaa´nisch, *adj* - Mexican. KYG2275

Mickebritsch, *f, pl* **~e** - fly swatter. **Mir breicher en neie Michebritsch.** We need a new fly swatter. LRT

Middaag¹, *m* - noon. **noch ~** - toward the south. KYG2042. **Mir sin gehe ~ zu gange.** We went toward the south. LRT.

Middaag², *m* - the noon meal. **~ mache** - to stop working for the noon hour (KYG1889), to make the noon meal (KYG1960). **Sis Zeit fer's ~ esse.** It's time for the noon meal. LRT.

Middaag³, *m* - noon time. **Well, sis ~ un Zeit fer esse.** Well, it's noon time and time to eat. LRT, 4/11/2000

midde(s)darich, *adv* - through the middle. KYG2008. **Die Feierinscheine sin graad ~ die Schtadt gange.** The fire engines went right through the middle of town. LRT. **Der Gaul is graad ~ der Gaarde gschprunge.** The horse ran right through the middle of the garden. LRT

mied, *adj/adv* - tired. **sich ~ laafe** - to tire oneself walking. KYG2159. **Mir hen uns ~ geloffe.** We tired ourselves from walking. LRT. **Ich bin so ~ un so matt / ich kann schier gaar nimmi fatt.** I'm so tired and weak, I can hardly move (go). LRT

Miedichkeit, *f* - tiredness. KYG2026

Mieh, *f* - trouble, bother. **der ~ waert sei** - to be worth the trouble. **sich viel ~ aaduh** - to go to great trouble. **~ suche** - to seek trouble. **~ mache** - to make trouble. KYG2065

Miehl, *f* - mill. **Der Daed hot zehe Seck Welschkann an die ~ genumme fer gschrode griege.** Dad took ten sacks of corn to the mill to have it ground. LRT

Miehlbach, *m* - ✪ Miehlbach, Lebanon Co., PA. KYG2276. **Mir waare mol Gemeesleit mit Leit vun ~.** We once were (fellow) church members with people from Miehlbach, PA. LRT, 4/21/2000

miehseelich, *adj* - toilsome.

KYG2031

Millerschtadt, *f* - ✪ Millersville, Lanc. Co., Pa., home of *Es Bischli-Gnippli,* nom de plume of C. Richard Beam, who wrote *Es Pennsilfaanisch Deitsch Eck* for the Sugarcreek *Budget, Die Botschaft* of Lancaster, PA., the Ephrata *Shopping News*, and others, 1975*ff.*

Millerschteddel, *n* - ✪ **1** Bethel, Berks Co., PA. KYG2269. **~ is naegscht an de Lebnen/ Baricks Kaundi Lein.** Bethel (the village) is near the Lebanon-Berks Co. Line. LRT, 4/21/2000. **2** ✪ Macungie, PA. KYG2275.

Millichgeld, *n* - money earned from the sale of milk. **Die Bauer nemme ihre ~ un duhne was sie welle mit.** The farmers take their money from the sale of milk and do what they want with it. LRT

Millichgrautsume, *pl* - milkweed seeds. **~ sin arig wertvoll fer Reddetschaeckets mache.** Milkweed seeds are very valuable to make life jackets. LRT

Millichriwwelsupp, *f* - milk soup made with flour and lard. **Ich gleich ~.** I like milk rivvel soup. LRT

Millichseili, *n* - suckling pig. = **Wutzli.** LRT

millichwaarm, *adj* - warm as milk. KYG2164

Millifitz, *f* - **die ganz ~** - the whole thing. KYG1997

Minsboi, *m, f, pl* ~ - mince pie. **~ sin am beschde wann sie bissel Dramm drin hen.** Mince pies are at their best when they contain a little whiskey. LRT

Mischmasch, *m* - gobble-di-gook. **Was fer ~ is mer dann sell?** What kind of gobble-di-gook is that? LRT

Mischtschlidde, *m* - manure sled. LRT/Leb,4/11/2000

misseraa'wel, *adj* - miserable. **der ~ Daag** - that miserable day. KYG1991

missfellich, *adj* - unacceptable. KYG2090

misslich, *adj* - uncertain. = **unbeschtimmt, ungewiss, unsicher, net fer schur.** KYG2093

mitaus, *conj* - unless. *cf* **unne, wann...net.** KYG2107

mitdem as, *conj* - since. **~ as er sell geduh hot, muss er noch en dausend Daaler meh bezaahle.** Since he did that, he'll have to pay an additional thousand dollars. = **zidder as (wie).** LRT

mitenanner, *adv* - with each other, together. **Sie hen's ~ (menanner).** They have an understanding. KYG2098. **Sie sin ~ in die Karich gange.** They went to church with each other. LRT

mitfaahre - to ride along with. **Du darfscht mit uns faahre.** You may ride with us. LRT

Mithelfer, *m* - helper. **Er is em Dokder sei ~.** He is the doctor's

assistant. LRT,4/11/2000

Mithelfern, *f* - female assistant. **Sie hot sich nuffgschafft bis sie em Bressident sei ~ waar.** She worked her way up until she was the president's assistant. LRT,4/11/2000

mitkoche, *pp* **mitgekocht** - to cook several things together. KYG2030. **Mir hen Grummbiere mit de griene Buhne gekocht.** We cooked potatoes with the green beans. LRT

mitleide - to sympathize. **Sie hen schur schund en latt Druwwel ghat; es bescht as mir duh kenne is ~.** They surely have had a lot of trouble already; the best we can do is to sympathize. LRT

mitlese - to read at the same time. **Yunger, ich les die Gschicht fer dich, du kannscht ~.** Young man, I'll read this story for you, you can read along. LRT. **Ich gleich Bicher lese as die Kinner ~ kenne.** I like to read books that the children can read along with me. LRT

mitmache - to take part. **Ya, du kannscht yuscht mit dem Greische ~.** Yes, you can just participate in this screaming. LRT

mitsamde, *adv* - together with. = **mitsamden, samt, samde, zamde.** KYG2030. **Mir hen Welschkann un Weeze, ~ Grummbiereschaale de Hinkel neigschmisse.** We threw corn and wheat along with the potato shells into the chickens. LRT

mitschicke - to send along.

Wann er ihre en Brief schickt, sett er aa bissel Geld ~. If he sends her a letter, he should also send along a little money. LRT

Moierschteddel, *n* - ✪ Myerstown, PA. **Wie ich dreizeh Yaahr alt waar, is unser Famillye noch ~ gezoge un mir hen zwee Yaahr datt gewuhnt.** When I was 13 years old, our family moved to Myerstown, PA and we lived there for two years. LRT,4/21/2000

Mol, *n* - time. **es letscht ~** - the last time. KYG1992. **Es letscht ~ as mir Bsuch ghat hen, hen die Buwe en Fenschder verbroche.** The last time we had visitors the boys broke a window. LRT

Mol, *n* - time. **yedes ~** - each time, every time. = **alle ~, alle Buff.** *cf* **allimol rum** - every time around. **ee ~** - one time. = **ee Zeit. uff ee ~** - at one time. KYG2018. **es zwett ~** - the second time. KYG2019. **paar ~** - a few times. KYG2020. **Er waar mol ee ~ gange Hasch yaage un er hot gsaat, "Ee ~ Hasch yaage is genunk fer mich."** He once went deer hunting and he said, "Hunting deer one time is enough for me." LRT

Moos, *n* - limit. **Wieviel is sei ~?** How much can he tolerate? LRT

mucke, *refl* - to stir. *cf* **sich vermucke, sich verrege.** KYG1882. **Er hot sich net vermuckt.** He didn't stir. LRT

Muddergraut, *f* - Oswego tea. KYG1974

muldere - to take miller's toll. KYG1962

Mulderei, *f* - taking miller's toll. KYG2031

Mundschtick, *n* - mouthpiece. **en gut ~ hawwe** - to be a ready talker. KYG1965

munetweis, *adv* - by the month. **Mer kaaft em sei Leckdrick ~.** One purchases the use of electricity by the month. LRT. **~ griege mir unser Leckdrickrechning.** We get our electric bill monthly. LRT

Muschderbuch, *n* - pattern book. LRT

Mutmosing, *f* - presumption. **Was fer'n ~ waar dann sell?** What kind of a presumption was that? LRT

Naas, *f* - nose. **Ya, runzel yuscht dei ~!** Yes, just turn up your nose! LRT

Naasegschwetz, *n* - twang. KYG2081

Naasepetzer, *m* - nose-lead used on cattle. **Wann seller Bull ken Ring in de Naas hot, dann misse mir en ~ yuuse.** If that bull doesn't have a ring in his nose, we will have to use a nose-lead. LRT

naasich, *adj* - nosey. **Yunger, sei net so ~!** Young fellow, don't be so nosey! LRT

Naazrett - ✪ Nazareth, Lehigh Co., PA. KYG2276

Nacht, *f* - night. **die ~** - tonight. KYG2034. **Mir kennde die ~ Schnee griege.** We could (possibly) get snow tonight. LRT

Nachtesse, *n* - supper. **Dir bliebt fer's ~, gell?** You are staying for supper, is that right? LRT

nachthell, *adj* - moonlit. **Sis ~.** It's a moonlit night. = **mondhell.** LRT

Nachtmaahlszeit, *f* - time for the Holy Communion service. KYG2018. **Der erscht Sunndaag, alli Munet is ~.** The first Sunday of each month is the time for Holy Communion. LRT

Nachtmohl, *n* - Holy Communion. **~ ausdeele** - to serve Holy Communion. **Mer kann ewwe yuscht net oft genunk ~ hawwe.** One can just not have Holy Communion too often. LRT

Nachtmol, *n* - Holy Communion. **es ~ nemme** - to partake of Holy Communion. KYG1960. **Yaahre zerick hen mir als Samschdaag oweds die Vorbereiding ghat un no's ~ Sunndaag mariyets.** Years ago we had the preparatory service Saturday evenings and then the Holy Communion Sunday mornings. LRT

Nachtwechder, *m* - night watchman. **Er is en ~.** He is a night watchman. LRT

nackich, *adj* - naked. **Sell Kind waar bloss ~ gebore.** That child was born bare naked. LRT

naddlich, *adv* - toward the north. = **naerdlich, gehe Nadde.** KYG2043

Naehbax, *f* - sewing box. **Sie hot en scheeni ~.** She has a nice sewing box. LRT

Naehkareb, *m, pl* **~e** - sewing basket. **En Fraa as en Latt naeht, muss en ~ hawwe.** A woman who sews a lot must have a sewing basket. LRT. **Geb acht, datt schteht de Mamm ihre ~!** Be careful, here sets Mom's sewing basket! LRT,4/11/2000. *cf* **Naehkaerwel**

Naehmaschien, *f, pl* **~e** - sewing machine. **Leckdrick ~e sin Meeschder.** Electric sewing machines have taken over. LRT

naehmlich, *adj* - same. **Du hoscht der ~ Letschtnaame as mir hen.** You have the same last name as we do. LRT

Naggelpetzer, *m* - nail clipper. LRT. = **Naggelzang.**

Narregschwetz, *n* - foolish talk. = **narrisch Gschwetz.** KYG1964. **Sell narrisch Gschwetz gleich ich net.** I don't like that crazy (foolish) talk. LRT

Narreschtreech, *m* - tomfoolery. **~ wie sell kumme yuscht vun nix nutzichi Buwwe wir dir.** Tomfoolery like that come only from mischievous boys like you. LRT

Narrheet, *f* - mental derangement. **Was fer ~ heest mer dann sell?** What kind of craziness is that? LRT

nass, *adj* - wet. **Sis ~ draus.** It's wet out there (it's raining or has rained). LRT

Naumannschteddel, *n -* ☻ Newmanstown, Leb. Co., PA. **Der Dr. Robert Kline wuhnt naegscht an ~.** Dr. Robert Kline, President of the PA. German Society, lives near Newmanstown, PA. LRT,4/21/2000

naus-schmeisse - to throw out. = **raus-schmeisse.** KYG2009. **Schmeiss die Grummbiere-Schaale naus zu de Hinkel.** Throw the potato shells out to the chickens. LRT

naus-schridde - to step out. **Wann du der Schpank hoscht, dann schritt yuscht naus.** If you have the daring, then just step on out. LRT

naus-schtatze - to tumble out. = **rausbatzle.** KYG2073 . **Er is zum Fenschder nausgschtatzt.** He tumbled out through the window. LRT

naus-schteh - to protrude. **Was hot er in seine Hosseseck, sie schtehne hiwwe un driwwe naus?** What does he have in his pants pockets, they are protruding on both sides? LRT

nausduh - to put out. **Duh der Hund naus in der Hof, er muss scheisse.** Put the dog out in the yard, it needs to have a bowel movement. LRT

nausgeh - 1 to go out. **2** to go to the outdoor toilet. KYG2031. **Wann du's net gleichscht do hin, dann kannscht ~.** If you don't like it in here, you can go outside. LRT

nausgreische - to cry out. **hell ~** - to cry out at the top of one's voice. KYG2037. **Du waarscht an de Vendu; Du hoscht** gebodde un sie hen dich net gsehne un net gheert. Du hettscht nausgreische selle. You were at the sale; you bid and they didn't see or hear you. You should have cried out. LRT

nauslaafe, *pp* **is nausgeloffe -** to walk out. **Sie sin nausgeloffe.** They staged a walk-out. **Die Mannsleit sin naus ins Weedfeld geloffe.** The men walked out into the pasture field. LRT. = **rauslaafe.** KYG2158

nausmache, *pp* **nausgemacht - 1** to backbite. **~ iwwer epper -** to talk about someone in a bad way. KYG1964. **2** to sow (grain). **Mir hen der Hawwer nausgemacht.** We sowed the oats. LRT

nausmisse - to have to go to the outdoor toilet. *cf* **uff der Haffe misse.** KYG2031. **Ebmols im Winder, wann mer naus geh hot misse, waar's net arig leidlich.** Sometimes in the winter, and one had to go out to the outdoor toilet, it wasn't very agreeable (pleasant). LRT

nausreide, *pp* **is nausgeridde -** to ride out. **Loss uns ~ ins Land.** Let us ride out into the country. LRT

nausrenne - to thrust out. = **naus-schtosse.** KYG2010. **Die Buwe hen selli Schtang zum Fenschder nausgerennt.** The boys thrust that rod out through the window. LRT

nausschicke, *pp* **nausgschickt -** to send out. **Mir hen's Buch naus noch California gschickt.** We sent the book out to California. LRT

nausschidde - to pour out. **Schitt die Supp naus, sie is verdarewe.** Pour the soup out, it is spoiled. LRT

nausschiewe[1] - to postpone. = **abschiewe.** LRT

nausschiewe[2] - to push out. **Wann'd die Katz net dohin hawwe witt, dann schieb sie naus!** If you don't want the cat in here, then shove it out! LRT

nausschpanne, *pp* **nausgschpannt -** to stretch (a rope). **Die Mamm hot die Weschlein nausgschpannt.** Mother put up the washline. LRT

nausweise - to show out. **Kannscht du ihm ~?** Can you show him out? LRT

Nawwelband, *n, pl* **-benner -** umbilical band. = **Nawwelbinn.** KYG2088

Nawwelbruch, *m, pl* **-brich -** umbilical hernia. KYG2089. **Wann ich en Bruch hawwe misst, dann wett ich liewer en ~ hawwe as wie en Seckelbruch.** If I were to have a hernia, I'd rather have an umbilical hernia than a scrotal hernia. LRT

Nawwelschnur, *f* - umbilical cord. = **Schniwwlingband.** KYG2089. **Die ~ is was es Kind lewendich halt eb's gebore is.** The umbilical cord is what keeps the child (fetus) alive before it is born. LRT

Neezfaade, *m* - thread. **Sei Lewe henkt yuscht amme ~.** His life hangs only by a thread. KYG2003

Neezschpule, *m* - thread spool. KYG2004. **Aldi hilzni ~ sin ebmols Geld wert.** Sometimes old wooden (thread) spools are worth some money. LRT

Nei England, *n* - ⚙ New England. KYG2276

Nei Yarick - ⚙ New York. **Im Yaahr 1947 is unser Hochschulglass noch ~ gange.** In 1947 our highschool class went on a trip to New York, NY. LRT,4/21/2000

neibatzle, *pp* **neigbatzelt** - to stumble in. **Der Hund is zum Fass neigebatzelt.** The dog tumbled into the barrel. LRT

neiblanze, *refl* - to install (plant) oneself. **Blanz dich do gschwische nei!** Plant yourself in between here (on a crowded bench). LRT

neiblicke, *pp* **neigeblickt** - to peep into. **Er hot darich's Schlisselloch neigeblickt, bis er eppes gsehne hot, as er net sehne hett selle.** He peeped in through the keyhole until he saw something he should not have seen. LRT

neidappe, *pp* **neigedappt** - to walk or step into carelessly. KYG2158. **Die Kinner sin in seller Kiehdreck neigedappt.** The kids carelessly walked into those cow droppings. LRT. **Er is neizudappe kumme un's hot niemand gewisst wu er beikumme is.** He stepped on in there and no one knew where he came from. LRT. **Er is graad zu sellem Kiehdreck neigedappt.** He stepped right into that cow manure. LRT

neidrede, *pp* **neigedredde** - to step into. **Er is graad datt in sell Grundsauloch neigedrede.** He stepped right into that groundhog hole. LRT

Neies, *n* - new. **eppes ~** - something new. **Sell waar eppes ganz ~.** That was something totally new. LRT

neifiedre - to feed a thrashing machine. KYG2007. **Wann mer dresche will muss epper die Garwe zu de Machien ~.** If there is to be thrashing, some one has to feed the sheaves into the machine. LRT

neiflechde, *pp* **neigeflochde** - to twine in. KYG2083. **Sie hen scheeni Farewe in seller Karebet neigflochde.** They braided lovely colors into that carpet. LRT

neigeh, *pp* **is neigange** - to go into. **Geh nei!** Go in! KYG2158. **Er is neigange un hot rumgeguckt un er hot nix gfunne.** He went in and looked around and found nothing. LRT. **Es sin en latt Leit dattdrin. Witt du ~?** There are a lot of people in there. Do you want to go in? LRT

neigraawe, *refl, pp* **neigegraawe** - to dig oneself in. **Datt uff sellem Dreckweg, hot er die Kaerredder gschprengt bis er sich dief neigegraawe ghat hot.** There on that dirt road he ran his car wheels until he had himself deeply entrenched. LRT

neigratze - to scrape in. **Gratz alles zum Kessel nei.** Scratch everything into the kettle.

neigreische - to yell into. KYG2261. **Greisch in selli Peif nei un yaag die Haase raus, so as ich sie schiesse kann.** Yell into that pipe and chase out the rabbits, so that I can shoot them. LRT, 4/18/2000

neigriege, *refl, pp* **neigrickt** - 1 to incriminate onself. **Er hot sich neigrickt.** He incriminated himself. LRT. **2** to be liable for. **Er grickt sich nei fer zehe Daaler.** He's liable for $10. LRT

Neigschwetz, *n* - talking in (interfering). KYG1965. **Yunger, des ~ is uns net aagenehmt.** Young man, this talking (interfering) is not appreciated by us. LRT

neihaschple - to enter unexpectedly. KYG2101

neilaafe, *pp* **neigeloffe** - 1 to run in (of water). **Es hot so hatt geregert, es is Wasser in der Keller neigloffe.** It rained so hard, water ran into the cellar. LRT. **2** to walk in. = **reilaafe.** *cf* **beidappe.** KYG2158. **Er is neigloffe in's Wasser bis an die Gnie.** He walked into the water up to his knees. LRT

Neiland, *n, pl* **-lenner** - patch of woods (where timber was cut down and young timber is growing). **Die -lenner mache gut Haase-Yaages.** The wood patches (freshly timbered) make for good rabbit hunting. LRT/Leb,4/11/2000. = **Holzschlack**

neilese - to pick up and place in a container. **Tschannie, duh all selli gleene Schteenlin in der Kiwwel ~!** Johnnie, pick up all those little stones and put them into the bucket. LRT

neiraase - to enter tumultuously. KYG2074

neirechle - to include in the bill. **Wann du mir saagscht, was des Aaschtreiche koschde soll, hoff ich du duscht alles ~.** When you tell me what this paint job will cost, I hope you figure in everything. LRT

neireide, *pp* **is neigeridde** - to ride in. *cf* **reireide. Loss uns nei ins Schteddel reide.** Let us ride into town. LRT

neireisse, *pp* **neigerisse** - to tear a hole (slit) in. KYG1976. **Sehscht seller Fuddersack, die Hund hen en Loch neigerisse.** See that feed sack, the dogs tore a hole into it. LRT

neireiwe - to rub into. **Ich schpier schlecht genunk, du brauchscht's net ~.** I feel bad enough, you don't have to rub it in. LRT

neirenne - to thrust in. *cf* **neischiewe, neischtosse, reirenne.** KYG2010. **Ya, renn's yusht nei, wann's aa weh dutt.** Yes, just thrust it in, even if it hurts. LRT

neisaege - to saw into. **Geb acht, saeg net dattnei, schunscht rinnt's Fass.** Be careful that you don't saw in there or the barrel will leak. LRT

neischaffe, *refl, pp* **neigschafft** - to work one's way into a place. **Er hot sich neigschafft an de Schtaalkumpanie, nau hot er sex Daag die Woch Arewet.** He worked himself into a job with

the steel company, now he has work six days a week. LRT,4/11/2000

neischidde - to pour in. **Wann mer nix ~ dutt, dann is es ewwe leer.** If nothing is poured in, then of course it's empty. LRT

neischmeisse - to throw in. KYG2009. **Ya, schmeiss es de Sei nei.** Yes, thrown it into the pigs. LRT

neischparre - to pen in. **Wann'd die Hund net haus hawwe witt, dann schparr sie nei in seller Kewwich!** If you don't want the dogs out (running around), then pen them in that cage! LRT

neischtatze, *pp* **neigschtatzt** - to accidentally fall or tumble in. **Er is koppvedderscht zum Wasser neigschtatzt.** He fell headfirst into the water. LRT

neischtecke - to stick into a place, tuck in. KYG2072. **Du kannscht seller Brief graad datt gschwischich die Diere ~.** You can stick that letter right there between the doors. LRT

neischtelle - to set in a place. **Wann der Wind zu hatt blost, dann sett sie ihre Blummeschteck vun de Bortsch nemme un sie nei in's Haus schtelle.** If the wind blows too hard, then she should take her flower plants from the porch and set them in the house. LRT

neischtocke - to enter stiffly with a cane. KYG1879

neischtoppe - to stop in at. KYG1889. **Wann mir in deim Schteddel sin, welle mir ~.**

When we are in your town, we want to stop in (to see you). LRT

neischwetze, *pp* **neigschwetzt** - to talk into. **Sie hen mich neigschwetzt.** They talked me into it. LRT

neisehne - **1** to see into (something). **In so Sache kann ich gaar net ~.** I just cannot see into (grasp) such things. **2** to understand. **Sell is eppes as ich net ~ kann.** That is something I do not understand. LRT

neiwickle - to wrap into. KYG2252. **In's Hinkel witt du es Hatz, es Lewwer un der Hals ~.** Within the chicken you'll want to wrap the heart, the liver and the neck. LRT,4/18/2000

neiziehe - to pull in. **Wann mer fische geht un mer fangt en Fisch, no muss mer'n ~.** If one goes fishing and catches a fish, then it has to be pulled in. LRT

nemme - to take. **en Sitz ~** - to take a seat. **Yunger, nemm dei Sitz.** Young man, take your seat. LRT. = **sich hocke.** KYG1961

nenneswaert, *adj* - worth mentioning. **Was ~ is, is aa die menscht Zeit Gelt waert.** What is worth talking about is usually worth some money too. LRT. **Eppes wie sell is net ~.** Something like that is not worth mentioning. LRT,4/18/2000.

Nepsel - game of tipcat. **~ schpiele** - to play tipcat. KYG2024

neschde - to make a nest. **Guck mol, die Veggel sin am ~.**

Look, the birds are making a nest. LRT

Neschtgweckerli, *n* - term of endearment (for infant). *cf* **Schnutz.** KYG1987. **Sie is en gaar liewes ~.** She is a very dear little child. LRT = **Neschtgwackerli**

Neschtli, *n, pl* **~n** - *dim* of **Nascht.** twig. = **Witt, Wipp, Wippli, Zweig.** KYG2082. **Wann der Wind recht hatt blost, seht mer immer en latt gleeni ~n unnich sellem Baam.** When the wind blows real hard, one always sees a lot of small twigs under that tree. LRT

net fer schur, *adv* - uncertain. **Ich wees ~ was sell is.** I am uncertain as to what that is. LRT

Newebortsch, *f* - side porch. **Es is schee schaddich uff die ~.** It's nice and shady on the side porch. LRT

newedraus, *adv* - on the back road. **Mir waare ~ gewest uff sellem enge Weg.** We were out back on that narrow road. LRT

neweherlaafe, *pp* **is newehergeloffe** - to walk by the side of. **Wie mir am Hoi mache waare, is seller glee Buh newe am Wagge hergeloffe.** As we were making hay, that little boy walked beside the wagon. LRT

newehie, *adv* - on the side (in hitching a horse). **Fiehr der Newegaul riwwer un schtell ihn ~. Der Handgaul kann des net leenich ziehe.** Lead the side horse over here and stand him here to the side. The lead horse can't pull this by himself. LRT

newewedder, *adv* - against the side. **Schieb die Leeder datt ~, so as sie schtehe bleibt.** Push the ladder against the side (of the garage) so it will remain standing. LRT

newich, *prep* - by the side of. **Sie hen mei Backebuch ~ em Weg gfunne.** They found my wallet by the side of the road. = **newe,** *cf* **denewe.** LRT

newichnanner, *adv* - alongside each other, side by side. **~ kumme** - to have a squabble. **Sie waare ~ kumme gewest, awwer's hot niemand en bludichi Naas grickt.** They had a squabble, but no one got a bloody nose. LRT. **Kennt dir ~ bleiwe?** Can you remain side by side? LRT. =**newenanner**

newichnannerhocke, *refl* - to sit side beside each other. **Mir hocke uns newichnanner.** We will sit beside each other. = **beisammehocke, newenannerhocke.** LRT

newichnannerleie, *pp* **-gelege** - to lie beside each other. **Hoscht du sie net gsehne? Ei, sie hen graad newichnannergelege.** Didn't you see them? Why, they were lying right beside each other. LRT

newichnannerschtelle - to place alongside each other. LRT

Nexerei, *f* - teasing. = **Genex.** KYG1977

nexich, *adj* - tantalizing. KYG1969

nidder, *adj* - shallow. **Es Wasser is ~.** The water is shallow. **Wann's net reggert,** waert's Wasser ~. If it doesn't rain, the water gets shallow. LRT

nidderschiesse, *pp* **niddergschosse** - to shoot low. **Er hot der Marick verfehlt, sehscht, er hot niddergschosse.** He missed the mark, you see, he shot low. *cf* **nunnerschiesse.** LRT

Niedrichkeet, *f* - trimness. KYG2062

niesse - to sneeze. **Niess yuscht, sell macht vielleicht dei Naas uff.** Just you sneeze, that might open up your nose. LRT. **Hoscht en Babierdichli? Ich muss ~.** Do you have a tissue? I have to sneeze. LRT

nischdle, *pp* **genischdelt** - to nestle. **Er hot sich uff die Kautsch genischdelt.** He nestled on the couch. LRT

niwwerdrehe, *pp* **niwwergedreht** - to turn over. *cf* **riwwerdrehe, umdrehe, umkehre, umschtilpe, rumdampe.** KYG2077. **Die Sunndaagschul hot all sell Geld niwwergedreht zu de Karich.** The Sunday School turned over all that money to the church. LRT

niwwergheere - to belong on the other side. **Seller Bese gheert niwwer in die Karich.** That broom belongs over in the church. LRT

niwwerhocke, *refl* - to sit on the other side. **Yunger, hock dich niwwer uff die anner Seit zu de Mannsleit.** Young man, sit on the other side with the men. LRT

111

niwwerlaafe - to walk over (to a place). KYG2159. **Dir kennt datt ~ un rumgucke.** You can walk over there and look around. LRT

niwwerloddle - to trudge lazily over to. KYG2068

niwwerreeche - to reach across. **Kannscht du so weit datt ~?** Can you reach over there that far? LRT

niwwerreide, *pp* **is niwwergeridde -** to ride across. **Wann die Brick net datt waert, dann kennde mir net datt ~.** If the bridge were not there, then we couldn't ride over there. LRT

niwwerschicke - to send over. **Schick seller Brief niwwer noch Deitschland.** Send that letter over to Germany. LRT

niwwerschidde - to pour over (to). **Schitt seller Kiwwel voll Schlapp niwwer zu de Sei.** Pour that bucket full of slop over to the hogs. LRT

niwwerschiewe - to push over (from here to there). LRT

niwwerschridde - to step over. **Schritt dattniwwer wu ken Kiehdreck is.** Step over there where there is no cow manure. LRT

niwweryaage - to chase to the other side. **Es is Zeit fer die Kieh datt ~, so as mir sie melke kenne driwwe in die anner Scheier.** It's time to chase the cows over there so that we can milk them in the other barn. LRT

niwwwerzus, *adv* - across over yonder. KYG2263. **Datt ~ gehe Lewisbarig hen sie en latt Rege ghat.** Over in the direction of Lewisburg they had a lot of rain. LRT,4/21/2000

Nixnutz, *m* - **1** mischief. **~ nooch sei -** up to mischief. KYG2117. **Sell is alles fer ~.** That's all for naught(iness). LRT. **2** worthless one. **Sie saage, er is en ~, awwer sell is net ganz recht.** They say he is a worthless fellow, but that is not totally correct. LRT,4/18/2000

Nixnutzichkeit, *f* - naughtiness. **Denne Yunge ihre ~ macht mich schier narrisch.** These kids' naughtiness almost drives me crazy. LRT. **Sellem Yunge sei ~ schafft ebmols uff seinere Memm ihre Narefe.** That boy's naughtiness sometimes works on his mother's nerves. LRT,4/18/2000

nixwaert, *adj* - worthless. **Seller Haufe Gfrees waar yuscht ~.** That pile of trash was just (simply) worthless. LRT,4/18/2000

noch, *adv* - still, yet. **Er is ~ eifrich.** He is still eager. KYG1880. **Er is ~ gsund un munter.** He is still healthy and hale. LRT

Nochbersbuh, *m* - neighbor boy. **Unser ~ is umkumme im Zwedde Weltgrieg.** Our neighbor boy was killed in World War II. LRT,4/11/2000

nochdem, *adv* - after that. **~ as mir in de Karich waare, hen mir en guder Essblatz gfunne.** After we were in church, we found a good eating spot

(restaurant). LRT

Nochricht, *f* - tidings. = **Botschaft.** KYG2014

Nodis, *f* - <*Engl*. notice. **Des is die letscht ~ as mir griege.** This is the last notice we will receive. LRT

Nodle, *pl* - needles. **uff ~ geh -** to walk on pins and needles. KYG2159. **Sie waar uff ~ gange bis ihre Buh heemkumme is vum Grieg.** She was living on pins and needles until her son came home from the war. LRT

Nohi, *m* - Noah. **Ya, der ~ Glein lebt nimmi.** Yes, Noah Kline is no longer living. LRT, 4/21/2000

noochaarde - 1 to resemble. = **gleich gucke. Sell Maedli dutt ihre Memm ~.** That little girl resembles her mother. LRT. **2** to take after. KYG1962. **Seller Buh dutt seim Paep ~.** That boy takes after his dad. LRT

noochbasse - to trudge after. KYG2067

noochbede - to repeat the words of another in prayer. **Tschann, kannscht du mir des Gebet ~?** Johnnie, can you repeat this prayer after me? LRT,4/11/2000

noochbinne - to tie sheaves after cradler. KYG2015

noochblanze - to replant. **Ebmols wann mer des Welschkaann zu frieh blanzt, muss mer es ~.** Sometimes if one plants the corn too early, one must replant it. LRT. **Deel Yaahre dutt's Welschkann**

schlecht ruffkumme---no muss mer's ewwe ~. Some years corn germinates poorly---then one must replant it. LRT

noochdappele, *pp* **noochgedappelt** - to follow in a stiff manner. KYG1879. **Selli alt Fraa is ihne noochgedappelt.** That old lady followed them stiffly. LRT

noochdrodde - to toddle after. KYG2030

noochdrolle - to trot after. = **noochdradde.** KYG2064

noochfolge - to follow. **Was noochfolgt, wees mer net.** What is to follow, one doesn't know. NMM

noochfolgend, *adj* - subsequent.

noochgewwe, *pp* ~ - 1 to sink, sag, give way. **Der Bodde datt in de Kich is am ~.** The floor in the kitchen is sagging. **Die Mauer unnich dem Haus is am ~.** The foundation wall under this house is receding (giving way). LRT. **2** to give in, collapse. **Die schteenich Mauer hot ~.** The stone wall collapsed. LRT,4/21/2000

noochgucke - **1** to see to. **2** to take care of. **Kannscht du die Kelwer ~ mariye frieh?** Can you take care of the calves tomorrow morning? LRT

noochhalde - to keep up with. = **sich noochschaffe.** KYG2117. **Er geht so schtarick, mer kann ihm schier net ~.** He goes so fast, one can hardly keep up with him. LRT

noochkumme, *pp* ~ - to

succeed, follow. **Der Clinton is hinnich em Busch ~.** Clinton followed after Bush (as president). LRT

noochlosse - to slack off. **Der Rege is am ~.** The rain is slowing down. LRT

noochnaame, *pp* **noochgenaamt** - to name after. **Er is nooch seim Gremmpaep genaamt.** He is named after his grandfather. LRT.

noochreide, *pp* **is noochgeridde** - to ride after. **Er is nooch em Wagge geridde.** He rode after the wagon. LRT

noochretsche - to tell lies behind someone's back. KYG1981

noochsaage - to repeat. **Harich, no kannscht du mir's ~.** Listen, then you can repeat it after me. LRT

noochschicke - to send after. **Wann mer net wees wu er is, wie kann mer es ihm ~?** If one doesn't know where he is, how can we send it after him? LRT

noochschiesse, *pp* **noochgschosse** - to shoot after. **Er hot nooch zwee Haase gschosse, awwer er hot sie alle zwee verfehlt.** He shot at the two rabbits, but he missed each of them. LRT

noochschleefe - to drag after. **die Fiess yuscht ~** - to trudge along. KYG2067. **Wann du seller Block ~ witt, dann brauchscht du en Schleefkett.** If you want to drag that log after (you), you need a drag chain. LRT

noochschmeisse - to throw after. KYG2009. **Du kannscht's ihm ~, awwer er is shund zu weit vannenaus gange fer ihn dreffe.** You can throw it after him, but he has already gone too far ahead. LRT

noochschpringe - to pursue, run after. **Deel Maed duhne die Buwe ~ wie net gscheit.** Some girls run after the boys like crazy. LRT

Not, *f* - need. **mit aller ~** - by the skin of one's teeth. KYG1978. **Was is dei ~?** What is your need? LRT. **Die Famillye waar in grossi Not.** The family was in great need. LRT. **~ leide** - to be in want. KYG2162. **Ich kumm net in ~.** I shall not want. KYG2163. **Wann mer reich is wie er is, hot mer ken grossi ~.** When one is rich like he is, one has no great needs. LRT

Notgleech, *m, pl* **~er** - mending link. **~er sin en hendich Ding fer hawwe.** Mending links are a handy thing to have. LRT

Notschtall, *m* - rack for shoeing fractious horses. **Ich waar mol alles vergelschdert beim e Blaeckschmidt un en hessedronischer Gaul was er im e ~ ghat hot.** I was once terrified by a blacksmith and a terribly fractious horse that he had in a rack. LRT

nuff, *adv* - up to the top. KYG2037

nuffdrehe - to turn up. **sei Naas ~ an Leit** - to snub people. **Ya, dreh yuscht dei Naas nuff, ich geb nix drum.** Yes, you can just turn up your nose, I don't care.

113

LRT. **Duh die Hemmergraage ~.** Turn up your shirt collar. **Duh dei Hemmaermel ~.** Turn up your shirt sleeves. LRT. **die Zehe ~** - to turn up one's toes. KYG2078. **Vergess net der Faahne ~ an de Poschtbax.** Don't forget to turn up the flag on the mail box. LRT. **Sis kalt dohin, mir misse die Hitz ~.** It's cold, we'll have to turn up the heat. LRT

nuffgeh - **1** to rise (of prices). **Wann die Sache raar warre, no gehne die Preise nuff.** When things get scarce, the prices go up. LRT. **2** to go up. **Wann ich dir saag, du sollscht ~, mehn ich du sollscht so hoch geh as du kannscht.** When I say go up, I mean you are to go as high as you can. LRT

nuffglempe - to turn up (the edges of tin, zinc). KYG2078

nuffgraddle - **1** to crawl up. **Es is ordlich hoch, kannscht du datt ~?** It's quite high, can you crawl up there? **2** to climb up. **widder uff der Gaul ~** - to remount the horse. **Bischt du zu alt fer selli hoch Leeder ~?** Are you too old to climb up that tall ladder? LRT

nuffhewe - to lift up. **Ich heb dir's nuff.** I'll lift it up for you. LRT

nuffreide, *pp* **is nuffgeridde** - to ride up. = **ruffreide, uffreide. Er is der Hiwwel nuffgeridde.** He rode up the hill. LRT

nuffreisse, *pp* **is nuffgerisse** - to tear up. KYG2258. **Dir Mannsleit, kennt dir sell Darrbabier ~?** You men, can you tear up that tar paper (from the roof)? LRT,4/18/2000. **Wie sell Schtick Eise in die Heh gfloge is, hot's en Schtick Haut an seim Beh nuffgerisse.** When that piece of iron flew up, it tore up a piece of skin on his leg. LRT

nuffrenne, *pp* **nuffgerennt** - to ram up through. **Ich hab die Gawwel nuff darich's Dach gerennt!** I rammed the fork up through the roof! LRT

nuffringle - to wrinkle up. **die Naas ~ (dewehe)** - to turn up one's nose (at something). KYG2078

nuffrunzle, *pp* **nuffgerunzelt** - to wrinkle up. **Er hot sei Naas nuffgerunzelt wie sie ihm Meerreddich uff sei Fleesch duh hen welle.** He turned up his nose when they wanted to put horseradish on his meat. LRT

nuffschaffe, *refl, pp* **nuffgschafft** - to work one's way up. **Sie hot sich nuffgschafft bis sie em Bressident sei Mithelfern waar.** She worked her way up until she was the president's assistant. LRT,4/11/2000

nuffschiewe - to push up. **Kannscht du sell Fenschder ~?** Can you push that window up? LRT

nuffschlagge - to turn up (a collar). KYG2078

nuffschprenge, *pp* **nuffgschprengt** - to chase (up a hill). KYG2117. **Der Hund hot die Katz die Schteeg nuffgschprengt.** The dog chased the cat up the stairs. LRT

Nuffunrunnermiehl, *f* - up and down mill. KYG2117

nuffweise - to show the way up. **Weis ihm der Weg nuff.** Show him the way up(stairs). LRT

nuffwenne - to turn up (sleeves). KYG2078

nuffzus, *adv* - on the way up. KYG2117. **Sie sin datt ~ gange.** They went up that way. LRT

Nuffzug, *m* - updraft. **Der ~ in sellem Schannschtee is gut.** The updraft in that chimney is good. LRT

Null, *f* - zero. **Bissel kalt demariye, der Thermomeder leest ~.** A bit cold this morning, the thermometer reads zero (said in jest). LRT,4/21/2000. = **Nix, Seifer, gaar nix**

nunnerbatzle, *pp* **nunnergebatzelt** - to tumble down. KYG2073. **Sell Kind is die Schteeg nunner in der Keller gebatzelt.** That child tumbled down the stairs into the cellar. LRT

nunnerbinne - to tie down. KYG2015. **Wann mer der Ox nunnerbinnt, no is es hendich fer ihn schiesse.** If one ties the steer down, then it is convenient to shoot him. LRT

nunnerdinne - to thin down. KYG1997

nunnerdrehe, *pp* **nunnergedreht** - to turn down, reject. **Die Baenk hot den neie Direkder hawwe welle, awwer die Glieder hen ihn nunnergedreht.** The bank

114

wanted the new bank director, but the stockholders turned him down. LRT. **Dreh dei Hemmaermel nunner.** Turn your shirt sleeves down. LRT

nunnerfaule, *pp* **nunnergfault** - to rot down. **Selli alt Scheier is alles zamme nunnergfault.** That old barn is completely rotted down. LRT

nunnergeh - 1 to recede (of water). **Sis recht drucke un's Wasser geht als weider un weider nunner.** It's really dry and the water (level) is going further and further down. **2** to settle (of a grave). **Der Grund uff em Graab geht nunner, wann der Kareber un die Laad verfaule.** The ground on the grave settles down as the casket and the body decay. LRT. **3** to set. **Yuscht so langsam ~.** To set slowly (of the sun or moon). KYG2162. **Sie hen ihn yuscht langsam in seine Laad ~ glosst.** They just let his casket go down slowly. LRT

nunnergelumpt, *adj* - ramshackle. **Ihre Haus is awwer gewiss ~.** Their house has truly become a ramshackled one. LRT

nunnerglempe - to turn down (the edges). KYG2077

nunnerlaafe - to walk down. **Wann's Wedder schee is, duhne mir nunner an die Karich laafe.** If the weather is nice, we walk down to the church. LRT

nunnernemme, *pp* **nunnergenumme** - to take down. **Sell Zelt hen sie heit nunnergenumme.** They took

that tent down. LRT

nunnerrolle - to roll down. = **runnerrolle. Duh dei Schtrimp ~.** Roll down your stockings. LRT

nunnerscheere, *pp* **nunnergscheert** - to trim back. **Die Baemlin vanne am Haus hen mir ordlich hatt nunnergscheert.** We trimmed back the small trees in front of the house pretty drastically. LRT

nunnerschicke - to send down. **Der Deiwel schickt ihm es nunner.** The devil will send it down to him. LRT

nunnerschlucke, *pp* **nunnergschluckt** - to swallow down. **Er hot selli Schnitz ordlich schnell nunnergschluckt ghat.** He had swallowed those snitz pretty quickly. LRT

nunnerschnarre, *pp* **nunnergschnarrt** - to jerk down. **Ich hab seller Deckel nunnergschnarrt.** I jerked down that lid. LRT

nunnerschreiwe, *pp* **nunnergschriwwe** - to record, jot down. **Du daedscht sell besser ~, no vergesscht du's net.** You had better jot that down, then you won't forget it. LRT

nunnerschtamble, *pp* **nunnergschtambelt** - to stamp. **Der Grund um seller Poschde muss nunnergschtambelt sei.** The ground around that post must be stamped down. LRT

nunnerschtoppe - to shut down. **Schtopp die Inschein nunner.**

Shut down the engine. LRT

nunnersehne - to see down. **Wann mer owwe uff em Seilo is, kann mer schier net nunner uff der Bodde sehne.** When one is on top of the silo, one can hardly see down to the bottom. LRT

nunnersetze - to set down. **in Wadde ~ -** to set down in words. **Wann du weescht wie mer des dutt, dann settscht's ~ so as anneri es aa lanne kenne.** If you know how to do this, then you should write it down so that others can learn it too. LRT

nunnerweise - to show the way down. **Weis ihm der Weg nunner.** Show him the way down(stairs). LRT

nunnerwesche, *pp* **nunnergwesche** - to wash down. **der Kellerschteeg ~ -** to wash down the cellar steps. KYG2167. **Sie hot die Kellerschteeg nunnergwesche.** She washed down the cellar steps. LRT

nunnerzaahme - to tame down. KYG1966

Obschtyaahr, *n* - a year rich in fruit. KYG2259. **Die Reife waare frieh verbei des Yaahr, un fer sell is es en gut ~.** The frosts were over early this year, and that is why the fruit is plentiful. LRT. **Des is awwer gewiss en gut ~!** (But) this is surely a good fruit year. LRT,4/18/2000

Ochdem, *m* - breath. **~ ziehe -** to take a breath. KYG1960. = **Odem**

Offe-eise, *n* - stove lid lifter. **En ~ macht's meeglich fer en Deckel vum Offe hewe.** A stove lid lifter makes it possible to lift a lid from the stove. LRT

Offebank, *f* - bench behind stove. **Wann du hees sei witt, dann hock dich weil uff die ~.** If you want to be hot, then sit on the bench behind the stove for a while. LRT

Offebeh, *n* - stove leg. **Wann's ~ abbrecht, kann mer en Backeschtee unnich der Offe schtelle wu's Beh waar.** If the stove leg breaks, one can put a brick under the stove where the leg was. LRT

Offeblaeck - stove black. **~ macht en Offe schee gucke.** Stove black makes a stove look nice. LRT

Offedeckel, *m, pl* ~ - stove lid. **Die ~ sin alles versaut, sis Zeit fer sie butze un blaecke.** The stove lids are all messed up, its time to clean and blacken them. LRT

Offedier, *f* - stove door. **Wann mer die ~ uffmacht un die Eschedier zumacht, no brennt's Feier net so schtarick.** If one opens the stove door and closes the ash door, the fire slows down. LRT

Offefaundri, *f, pl* ~s - stove foundry. **Wann mer kenn ~s hedde, hedde mir ken Effe.** If we had no stove foundries, we'd have no stoves. LRT

Offeholz, *n* - stove wood. **~ is all recht, awwer Kohle sin besser.** Stove (fire) wood is OK but coals are better. LRT

Offeleng, *f* - stove length. **Wann mer saagt ~, mehnt mer wieviel Blatz as en Offe nemmt in 're Schtubb.** When we refer to stove length, we mean how much space the stove takes in a room. LRT

Offepoker, *m, pl* ~s - stove poker. **~s sin en notwennich Ding, wann mer Holz odder Kohle brenne will.** Stove pokers are a necessary thing if one wants to burn wood or coal. LRT

Offerohr, *n* - stove pipe. **Paar mol's Yaahr hot mer ewwe als es ~ butze misse.** A few times each year we had to clean the stove pipe. LRT. **Sell ~ is darichgeroscht, der Schmok kummt raus.** That stove pipe is rusted through (and has a hole), the smoke is coming out. LRT

Offerohrloch, *n* - stove pipe hole. **Fer'n Offe uffschtelle, nemmt's en ~.** In order to set up a stove, there needs to be a stove pipe hole (in the ceiling). NMM

Offescheifli, *n* - soot scraper. **Sell is ken ~ wert.** That isn't worth a soot scraper (hoot). LRT

Offeschelf, *n* - stove shelf. **Sell ~ sett abgebutzt sei.** That stove shelf should be cleaned off. LRT

oftmols, *adv* - often. KYG2020. **~ wees mer net weller Weg as mer geh sett.** Often one doesn't know which direction to go. LRT

Ohr, *n, pl* ~e - ear. **die ~e schpitze** - to perk up the ears. LRT

Oiergeld, *n* - money earned

from the sale of eggs. **Uff denne gleene Bauereie grickt die Fraa die menscht Zeit's ~.** On these small farms the wife usually (most times) gets the proceeds from the sale of the eggs. LRT

Ombrella-flicker, *m* - umbrella mender. KYG2089. **Im Yaahr 2002 wees ich net as mir meh ~ hen in dem Land, USA.** In the year 2002, I don't know that we have umbrella-menders in the country, USA anymore. LRT

Ombrella-schtock, *m, pl* - schteck - umbrella handle. KYG2089. **-schteck gucke schier wie Laafschteck.** Umbrella handles look almost like walking canes. LRT

Onkel, *m* - uncle. **~ Semm** - Uncle Sam. KYG2093. **Der ~ Semm dutt en latt Leit ernaehre.** Uncle Sam supports a lot of people. LRT

Oschderoiersuche, *n* - Easter egg hunt. **Die Kinner duhne immer sell ~ gleiche.** The children always enjoy that Easter egg hunt. LRT

Owed, *m* - evening. **Bis ~ waare sie all mied gewest.** By evening they were all tired. LRT. **am ~ rum** - sometime in the evening. **Sie sin so am ~ rum heemkumme.** They came home sometime in the evening. LRT. **gehe ~** - toward evening. = **uff der ~**. KYG2043. **Sie sin gehe ~ gange un hen die Sunn in ihrem Gsicht ghat un no glei waar's dunkel.** They went west and had the sun in their face and then soon it was dark. LRT

Owedrot, *n* - sunset glow. **Well,**

es gebt ken Rege mariye, guck mol wie schee ~ as es is. There will be no rain tomorrow, look how pretty the sunset glow is. LRT

owwe, *adv* - above. **vun ~ runner** - from top to bottom. = **vun ~ bis unne.** KYG2037. **Alles is ~, unne odder ariyets in die Mitt.** Everything is above, below or somewhere in between. LRT

owwedraa, *adv* - at the top of it. KYG2037. **Seller Yunge is ganz ~ mit seine Schularewet.** That young guy is way at the top in his school work. LRT

owwedraus, *adv* - **1** up country somewhere. KYG2116. **Sie wuhne datt ~ in de Bariye drin ammenents.** They live somewhere up there in the mountains. LRT. **Sie wuhne datt ~ naegscht an Troy ammenents.** They live up country somewhere near Troy. LRT. **2** up at the top, out up somewhere. KYG2117. **glei ~ sei** - to lose one's temper easily.

owwedrin, *adv* - up in above. = **owwenei.** KYG2116. **Die Dauwe verschteckle sich ariyets datt ~.** The pigeons hide themselves somewhere up above there. LRT

owwedriwwer, *adv* - **1** superficially. **Die Karich hen sie net recht gut gebutzt, sie sin yuscht Bissel ~ gange.** They didn't clean the church real well, they just went over it really superficially. LRT. **2** over the top. KYG2037. **Sie hen iwweraal ~ geguckt un hen nix finne kenne.** They looked everywhere over the top and

could find nothing. LRT

owwedruff, *adv* - on top. KYG2037. **Duh der Deckel vum Kessel ~.** Put the lid of the kettle on top. LRT. **Ya, du kannscht selli Eppel ~ lege.** Yes, you can lay those apples up on top. LRT

owweher, *adv* - along the top. = **owwehie.** KYG2037. **~ an de Mauer hen sie en schwatzer Schtreefe gemacht.** Along the top of the (masonry) wall they placed a black stripe. LRT

owwehie, *adv* - along up above. KYG2117. **Leg sell Messer ariyets datt ~.** Lay that knife somewhere up there. LRT

Owwerdenn, *n* - loft over the thrashing floor, overden. **Mei Paep is mol darich die losse Bord uff em ~ nunner uff der Hoiwagge gfalle.** My dad once fell down through the loose boards from the loft over the threshing floor onto the hay wagon below. LRT

owwerei, *adv* - from up country. KYG2117. **Die Ieme kumme ariyets do ~.** The bees are coming in somewhere up here. LRT

owwewedder, *adv* - against the top. KYG2037. **~'s Dach hen sie en Fahneposchde feschtgemacht.** Up against the roof they fastened a flag pole. LRT

Oxefuhr, *f* - team of oxen. KYG1975. **En ~ mehnt nix unni en Yoch.** A team of oxen is of no account without a yoke. LRT

oxich, *adv* - stubborn. **Schick dich net so ~ aa!** Don't act so stubborn! LRT

Paapscht, *m* - Pope, Bishop of Rome. **Wann en Mann mol ~ is, is er ~ so lange as er lebt.** Once a man is the pope, he will be pope as long as he lives. LRT

paare, *refl, pp* **gepaart** - to pair. **Guck mol, selli Dauwe, sie hen sich gepaart.** Just look, those pigeons have paired themselves. LRT

paarweis, *adv* - by twos. KYG2085. = **zwee uff emol.** LRT

packe, *pp* **gepackt** - to take a hold of. **Es hot ihn hatt gepackt.** He took it badly. KYG1963

Paert - < *Engl* part. **Ich bin froh as er sei ~ nemmt.** I'm glad he takes his part. LRT

Paettipaenn, *f* - pie pan. LRT/Leb.Co.

Pallemschteddel, *n* - ✪ Palmyra, Lebanon Co., PA. **Mei Fraa kummt vun ~.** My wife's hometown was Palmyra. LRT,4/21/2000

Palz, *f* - ✪ Palatinate, StG **die Pfalz,** province in SW Germany - in 2002 part of Rheinland-Pfalz. **Viele vun unser Pennsilfaanische Deitsche Voreldre sin vun de ~ kumme.** Many of our PA German ancestors came from the Palatinate in Germany. LRT,4/21/2000

Pannhaas, *m* - scrapple. **~ abhewe** - to lift the cooked scrapple in the kettle from over the fire. **Wer hot die bescht Reseet fer ~ mache?** Who has the best recipe to make scrapple? LRT

Paschingbaam, *m* - peach tree. LRT

Pattwascht, *f* - pot pudding. LRT

Pauli, *m* - *dim* of **Paul.** little Paul. **Ya, der ~ Rittle lebt ewwe aa nimmi.** Yes, of course, Paul Rittle is no longer living. LRT,4/21/2000

pauschbackich, *adj* - pouch-cheeked. **Sis ken Wunner, as er ~ is, er hot immer en Tschaa Duwack im Maul.** It is no wonder that he is pouch-cheeked; he always has a chew of tobacco in his mouth. LRT

Peckli, *n* - *dim* of **Pock.** pimple. LRT

peeke - to engage in sexual intercourse. LRT

peffere, *pp* **gepeffert** - to put a high price on something. **Der Weg wie sie die Schuh gepeffert hen, kenne sie sie yuscht bhalde, un wann ich baarfiessich geh muss.** The high price they are asking for these shoes, they can just keep them, even if I have to go barefooted. LRT

Peffergraut, *n* - pepper cabbage with green, red, or yellow pepper in it. LRT

Peideller, *m* - pie plate. LRT/Leb.Co.

Peif, *f* - steam factory whistle.

LRT

Peifarigel, *f, pl* ~e - pipe organ. **Es sin aa anneri Sadde Arigele as net ~e sin.** There are other kinds of organs which are not pipe organs. LRT

peife - to tweet. **Die Veggel ~.** The birds tweet. KYG2081. Idiom: **Ya, ich peif der druff.** I don't give a hoot for it. LRT

Peik, *m, f* - <*Engl* pike, piked road, turnpike. KYG2079. **Seller nei ~ macht schee Faahres.** That new pike makes for nice driving. LRT. **Sie sin der ~ nuffgfaahre.** They drove up the pike. LRT

peine, *pp* **gepeint** - to torment. **Die Schmatze hen ihn schrecklich gepeint.** The pains really tormented him. LRT

Pelzer, *m* - native to **die Pfalz** in Germany. KYG2278

pelzisch, *adj* - Palatine. KYG2278

Pennsbarig, *m* - ✪ Pennsburg, PA. KYG2278

Pennsgrick, *f* - ✪ Penns Creek, PA. KYG2278

Pennsilfaanie - ✪ Pennsylvania. **Ich bin zufridde fer in ~ sei, bis der Harr mich heemnemmt.** I'm satisfied to be in PA until the Lord takes me home. LRT,4/21/2000

pennsilfaanisch, *adj* - Pennsylvania. KYG2278

pennsilfaanisch-deitsch, *adj* - PA German, PA Dutch. **~ is mir arig lieb.** PA Dutch is very dear

to me. LRT,4/21/2000

peppeldaesche, *pp* **gepeppeldaescht** - to stucco. **Sie hen ihre Haus gepeppeldaescht grickt.** They had their house stuccoed. LRT

Peschtli, *n* - *dim* of **Poschde.** little post. LRT/Leb.Co.

petze - to pinch. **eens ~** - to take a strong drink (of liquor). **Ich hab mol en Schulmeeschder ghat, as gegliche hot unser Backe ~, net aus Zann, awwer aus Lieb, awwer's hot doch wehgeduh.** I once had a teacher who liked to pinch our cheeks, not out of anger, but out of love, but it hurt anyway. LRT. **= eens schnuddle.** KYG1961

pflege - to tend, take care of. **= tende.** KYG1984

Pflicht, *f* - duty. **Die Sei fiedere, sell is dei ~.** Feed the hogs, that is your duty. LRT

Picknick, *f* <*Engl.* - picnic. **an dere ~** - at the picnic. KYG1991. **Eemols Yaahr hen mir en Kariche ~.** Once a year we have a church picnic. LRT

pienzich, *adj* - sickly and complaining about it. **Er is en ~er Mensch.** He's a delicate person. LRT

Pilgers Ruh, *f* - ✪ "Pilgrim's Rest," on Route 501 between Pine Grove and Bethel. KYG2279

Pitt, *m* - Peter. **~ Boyer is en bekannder Naame in Mt. Zion, Leb. Kaundi, PA.** Peter Boyer is a familiar name in Mt. Zion, Leb. Co., PA.

LRT,4/21/2000. = **Pidder, Piet**

Pittsbarig, *m* - ✪ Pittsburgh, PA. **Allimol wann ich noch ~ faahr, schteht selli Schtadt mir immer aa.** Each time I go to Pittsburgh, that city appeals to me. LRT,4/21/2000

Plattzang, *f* - flat tong. KYG2033

pockich, *adj* - pockmarked, *i.e.* suffering from acne, pimple-faced. **Mer wunnert yuscht fer was as deel Buwe so ~ sin im Gsicht.** One wonders why some boys are so pockmarked in their faces. LRT

Posaun', *f*, *pl* ~e - trombone. KYG2068

Posaunekor, *m* - trombone choir. KYG2069

Poschdeschtamber, *m*, *pl* ~ - tamping tool. KYG1966. **~, deel sin vun Holz, un deel sin vun Staahl gemacht.** Tamping tools, some of them are made of wood and some are made of steel. LRT

Psch! Sch! - be still! KYG1880

puddle, *refl* - to puddle (of chickens, geese and ducks). **Guck mol dattdraus, wie die Ende un die Gens sich ~ im Wasser.** Just look out there how the ducks and the geese are puddling in the water. **Die Hinkel ~ sich im lose Grund odder in die Holz- odder Kohle-esch.** The chickens are puddling in the loose earth or in the wood or coal ashes. LRT/Leb. Co.

puh dausich! - pew! **Ei, selli**

Grummbiere sin awwer faul, sie schtinke, ~, nochemol! Oh my, but those potatoes are rotten, they stink, pew! LRT

Pulschder - hassock, bolster or cushion. LRT

pulwere - to powder. LRT/Leb. Co.

Pundappel, *m* - pound apple. LRT

Pusch, *m* - **1** clump of shrubbery, KYG2072. **Seller ~ grickt alle Summer scheeni Blumme.** That bush has nice flowers every summer. LRT. **2** tuft. **Iwweraal datt im Schwamm wu Kiehdreck waar, waar en ~ Graas.** Everywhere there in the meadow where there was a cow dropping, there was a clump of grass. LRT. = **Wischel, Wischli**

Puschdur', *f* - posture. **Wie ich en yunger Schuler waar, hot unser Schulmeeschdern uns glannt fer en gudi ~ hawwe.** When I was a young pupil, our teacher taught us to have good posture. LRT

puttre, *refl* - to take a dust bath (of fowls). KYG1961. **Guck mol, wie die Hinkel sich ~ datt draus uff em Eschehaufe.** See how the hens are dusting themselves out there on the ash pile. LRT

Raadbieger, *m* - (blacksmith's) tire bender. KYG2025

Raade, *f* - tansy. = **Schnellgraut.** KYG1968

raawe, *pp* geraawe - to rob. **Sie hen ihm alles geraawe, as er**

ghat hot. They robbed him of everything he had. LRT

Raawerei, *f* - theft. **Die ~ macht ewwe als fatt.** The thievery just continues. LRT

Rachebrecher, *m* - a tough one. = **Rachebutzer.** KYG2042

Raddefall, *f* - rat trap. **Schtell mol dei ~ un seh mol was du fangscht.** Set your rat trap and see what you can catch. LRT

Raddegift, *n* - rat poison. **~ macht de Radde ihre Blut dinn, bis sie sich dod blude.** Rat poison thins the rats' blood until they bleed to death. LRT

Raddeloch, *n* - rathole. **Im ~ is en Raddenescht un aa fer schur en Raddeschwanz.** In the rathole is a rat's nest and certainly a rat's tail. LRT

Raddenescht, *n* - place of undesirables. KYG2099. **Sell Wattshaus is en recht ~.** That hotel is a place of undesirable people (a real "rats' nest"). LRT. **Oi, waar sell awwer net en ~ war!** Oh my, was that ever a rat's nest! LRT

Ragu'ne, *pl* - raccoons. **Mei Onkel un sei Buh hen en latt ~ un Muschgrodde gfange.** My uncle, Miles T., and his son, Roy T., caught a lot of raccoons and muskrats. **~ yaage** - to hunt raccoons. LRT

Rank, *f* - **1** tendril. *cf* **Finger, Schpinner.** KYG1985. **2** vine. **Selli Drauwe ~e sedde ausgschnidde sei.** Those grape vines should be trimmed. LRT

ranke - to put forth vines. **Des**

nass Wedder macht awwer die **Drauwe ~.** This wet weather is really making the grapes put forth vines. LRT

Ranke, *pl* vines. **Heidesdaags gebt's Karebse as recht katzi ~ hen.** Now-a-days there are pumpkins that have real short vines. LRT

Rann, *f <Engl.* run - small stream. **Ich hab Sunnefisch gfange an die ~.** I used to enjoy catching sunfish at the run (small stream, called the run). LRT

Ranze, *m* - belly. **Er hot's ganz Wese in sei ~ geduh.** He put the whole thing in his belly. LRT

Rappelkaschde, *m* - rattletrap. **So'n ~ will ich net.** Such a rattletrap I do not want. LRT

rappelkeppich, *adj* - of a person with twisted ideas. KYG2084. **Mer wees nie net, was er am denke is, er is ewwe bissel ~.** One never knows what he is thinking, he is simply a bit twisted. LRT

Rappelkeschtli, *n* - *dim* of **Rappelkaschde.** a little rattletrap. LRT

Rappli, *n* - child's rattle. LRT

Raschpel, *f* - rasp. **Wann mer en Gaul bschlagge will, muss mer aa en ~ hawwe.** If one wants to shoe a horse, one also needs a rasp. LRT

Rasselschlang, *f, pl* ~e - rattlesnake. **Ich farich mich vun ~e.** I'm afraid of rattlesnakes. LRT

Rasselschlangefett, *n* - rattlesnake grease. **~, was gut is sell?** Rattlesnake grease, what good is it? LRT

Ratt, *f* - rat. **Er hot die ~ geroche.** He smelled the rat, *i.e.* he was forewarned. KYG2165. **Ya, er hot die ~ gfange.** Yes, he caught the rat. LRT

Raudebidders, *n* - tincture of rue. KYG2022

rauh, *adj* - rough. **Selli Rinn is ~, mer kennt sich gut verschinne, wann mer der Baam graddle daed.** That bark is rough; one could really abrade one's skin if one climbed the tree. LRT

rauhbaschdich, *adj* - rough, rude, ungentlemanly. KYG2103. **Wie kummt's as selli Yunge so ~ sin?** Why is it that those youngsters are so robust, rude, and rough? LRT

Rauhbelz, *m* - tough person. = **Rauhbiegel.** KYG2042

Rauhlaad, *f* - a plank or concrete rough box into which the coffin is placed in the grave. LRT. = **Iwwerlaad**

rauhschaalich, a*dj* - rough-shelled. **Deel Biere sin arig ~.** Some pears are very rough shelled. LRT

rauhschteenich, *adj* - rough-stoned. **~e Scheier** - barn built of rough stones. KYG1886. **Sie hen en schee ~ Haus.** They have a nice rough-stoned house. LRT

raus mit! - out with it. **Die Biewel saagt du muscht ehrlich sei, so ~ die Waahret.** The Bible says that you must be truthful, so come out with the truth. LRT

raus-schaffe, *refl, pp* **rausgschafft** - to work one's way out of a situation. **Sie waare zugedeckt im Hoibohre, awwer sie hen sich rausgschafft.** They were buried in the hay mow, but they worked their way out. LRT

raus-schnappe - to utter unguardedly. KYG2103

raus-schneppe - to tilt out. KYG2017

raus-schteeniche, *pp* **rausgschteenicht** - to chase out by throwing stones. KYG2010. **Mir hen die Haase vun de Hecke rausgschteenicht.** We chased the rabbits out of the bushes by throwing stones. LRT

raus-schwareme, *pp* **rausgschwaremt** - to swarm out. **Die Ieme sin zu sellem Loch rausgschwaremt.** The bees swarmed out of that hole. LRT

rausbeisse - to bite out. **Eb du seller Appel esscht, muscht selli faule Blacke ~.** Before you eat that apple, you will need to bite out those rotten spots. LRT

rausblaudre, *pp* **rausgeblaudert** - to cause one to change one's mind. **Er hot's duh welle, awwer sie hen ihn rausgeblaudert.** He wanted to do it, but they talked him out of it. LRT

Rauschbeidel, *m* - uncouth fellow. = **Schtoffelgluck.**

rausche - to roar (of the wind). **Der Wind dutt awwer ~!** The wind is really roaring! LRT

rausdappe - to walk out heavily. KYG2158. **Der Haahne is vum Kewwich rauszudappe kumme.** The rooster came trampling out of the cage. LRT

rausdrehe - to turn out, *pp* **rausgedreht. net genunk ~** - to underproduce. KYG2097. **Sie drehe net genunk Lattwarick raus fer alli-epper zufridde mache.** They don't produce enough apple butter to satisfy everyone. LRT. **Es waare net viel Leit rausgedreht fer die Pennsilfaanisch Deitsch Versammling.** Not many people turned out for the PG gathering. LRT

rausdricke - to squeeze out. **der Butze ~** - to squeeze out the core of a boil. LRT

rausdunnere, *pp* **rausgedunnert** - to come out tumultuously. KYG2074. **Sie hen rausgedunnert, "Nee, mir duhne sell net."** They screamed tumultuously, "No, we will not do that." LRT

rausfaule, *pp* **rausgfault** - to rot out. **Seller Block is vun innewennich rausgfault.** That log rotted from the inside out. LRT

rausfoddre - to tempt. *cf* **verdraage, versuche.** KYG1983

rausgraawe - to unearth. KYG2100. **Die Mannsleit hen**

em Semm gholfe sei Kaer ~ vun de Schneebank. The men helped Sam dig his car out of the snow bank. LRT

rausheele - to heal perfectly. **Gschwaere misse heele vun innewennich raus.** Boils have to heal from the inside out. LRT

Rauskumm, *m* - result, outcome. **Der ~ waar nix Neies.** The result was nothing new. LRT

rauskumme, *pp* **~** - to turn out. KYG2077. **Selli nei Zeiding is ~ die Woch.** That new newspaper came out this week. LRT

rauslosse - to let out a seam. **Seller Gaund is zu katz, awwer du hoscht genunk Schtofft fer en ~.** That dress is too short, but you have enough fabric to let out the seam (and lengthen it). LRT

rausmache, *pp* **rausgemacht** - to remove (potatoes). KYG1962. **Die Schteck sin dod; es is Zeit fer die Grummbiere ~.** The stalks are dead; it's time to dig the potatoes. LRT. = **rausnemme**

rausnemme, *pp* **rausgenumme** - 1 to take out. **Der Dokder hot en grosser Schliwwer vun meine Hand rausgenumme.** The doctor took a large splinter out of my hand. LRT. = **rausmache. 2** to take in trade. KYG1962

rausroppe - to pull out by the roots. **Des Umgraut misse mir ~.** We've got to pull these weeds out. LRT

rausschaffe, *refl* - to make one's way out. **Der Voggel hot sich vun seim Kewwich rausgschafft.** The bird worked his way out of his cage. LRT

rausscheine - to shine out. **Die Lichder scheine vun die Fenschdere raus.** The lights are shining out through the windows. LRT

rausschreiwe, *pp* **rausgschriwwe** - to write out. **Hoscht du mir en Rechling rausgschriwwe?** Have you written out my bill? LRT

rausschteche, *pp* **rausgschtecht** - to remove from a kettle (with a fork). **Schtech mir en Deller-voll vun selle Lewwerschticker raus.** Fill my plate with those liver pieces (with your fork). LRT

rausschtecke, *pp* **rausgschteckt** - to project, stick out. **Er hot sei Kopp vum Fenschder rausgschteckt.** He projected his head out the window. LRT

rausschteh - to project, stand out. **Uff die unnerscht Seit vum Dach schtehne en latt Neggel raus.** On the underside of the roof there are a lot of nails projecting out. LRT

rausschtritze - to spurt out. **Seller Kiwwel hot en Loch es dutt Wasser ~.** That bucket has a hole; water is spurting out. LRT

rausschwimme - to swim out. **Wie kann mer ~, wu ken Wasser is?** How can you swim out where there is no water? LRT

rausseihe - to strain out. **Mir duhne der Sume und die Schaale vun die Drauwebrieh ~.** We strain out the seeds and the shells from the grape juice. LRT

rauswickle, *refl* - to unwind oneself. KYG2116

rauswiehle, *pp* **rausgewiehlt** - to root out. **Die Sei hen alles as waxt rausgewiehlt.** The hogs rooted out everything that grows. LRT

Recheschtiel, *m, pl* **~** - rake handle. **Reche un ~ mehne Arewet.** Rakes and rake handles mean work. LRT

Rechezaah, *m* - rake tooth. **En ~ is rausgebroche.** A rake tooth broke out. LRT

recht, *adv* - right, proper. **~ mache** - to remedy. **Wann du sell net gleichscht, des kenne mir dir ~ mache.** If you don't like that, we can make it right for you. LRT

recht, *adj* - 1 real, genuine. **Er is en ~er Deitscher.** He's a real Dutchman. LRT. = **schicklich.** 2 right, proper. **Wer net kummt zu rechder Zeit, muss esse was iwwerich bleibt.** *Proverb*: He who doesn't come (to eat) at the right time, must eat what is left over. LRT

Recht, *n* - right. **vun ~s wehe** - by rights. **Es waar em Schulmeeschder sei ~ fer de Schuler ihre Schularewet blaane.** It was the teacher's right to plan the students' schoolwork. LRT. **en ~ dezu** - title to something. KYG2026. **Er hot's ~ fer sei Buh heem-**

nemme. He has the (legal) right to take his son home. LRT

Rechtlewe, *n* - right living. **~ macht em gsund.** Right living makes one healthy. LRT

rechtzeidich, *adv* - at the right time. KYG2019

Reddin - ✪ Reading, PA. **Wann epper ~ saagt, kummt PA Deitsch mir in der Kopp.** When someone says Reading, PA German comes to my mind. LRT,4/21/2000

reede - to stir the fire. KYG1882

reedle - to shake. **die Esch ~** - to shake ashes through a sieve. = **riddle. Duh der Offe ~ un duh die Esch naus uff der Haufe leere.** Riddle the stove and pour the ashes out on the pile. LRT

Reefaar(t)bidders, *n* - tansy bitters. KYG1968

Reefaartee, *m* - tansy tea. KYG1968

Reefschrenker, *m* - tire shrinker. KYG2026

Rees, *f* - trip. **Sie hen en Rees genumme noch Deitschland.** They took a trip to Germany. LRT. = **Reis**

Reff, *n* - set of false teeth. KYG2035

regelmaessich, *adv* - according to the rule. **~, sell mehnt as Sache recht geduh warre, wie sie sei sedde.** Done with regularity, according to the rule, that means that things are done the way they should be. LRT

Reggeboge, *m* - rainbow. **Sis nix schenner as wie en ~.** There is nothing more lovely than a rainbow. LRT

Reggedaag, *m* - rainy day. **Wann mir mol en ~ griege, no kenne mir die Hinkel schlachde.** Once we get a rainy day, we can kill (and dress) the chickens. LRT

Reggeluft, *f* - rain-bearing wind. **Es schpiert wie en ~.** It feels like a rain air. LRT

reggerich, *adj* - rainy. **Alli Abrill watt's ~ do in dem Land.** Every April it gets rainy in this area. LRT

Reggeschaerm, *m* - umbrella. = **Amberell, Omberell.** KYG2089

Reggeschpritzer, *m, pl* **~** - light rain. **Die Wedderbrofeeder hen gsaat, es soll ~ gewwe.** The meteorologists said we are to have a light rain. LRT

Reggeschtarem, *m* - rain storm. **~, ich hett liewer Regge unni Schtarem.** Rain storm, I'd rather have a rain without the storm. LRT

Reggewasser, *n* - rain water. **~ schteht iwweraal.** Rain water stands everywhere. LRT

Reggewedder, *n* - rainy weather. **Wann's Wasser nidder watt, no dutt mer bede fer ~.** When the water gets low, then one prays for rainy weather. LRT

Rehr, *n, pl* **~e** - tube. **Sie hen gsaat, all die ~e in seine Lunge waare zugschtoppt, wie er**

gschtarewe is. They said that all the tubes in his lungs were blocked when he died. LRT. = **Peif.** KYG2071

Rehrerschteddel, *n* - ☺ Rehrersburg, Berks Co., PA. **~ is ewwe aa naegscht an de Lebnen/ Baricks Lein.** Of course, Rehrersburg is near the Lebanon-Berks County Line. LRT,4/21/2000

Reibbascht, *f, pl* **~e** - scrub brush. **~e sin net deier.** Scrub brushes are not expensive. LRT

reidappe - to step in. **Ferwas dappscht du dorei mit so dreckichi Schtiffel?** Why do you step in here with such dirty boots? LRT

reide - to engage in sexual intercourse. LRT

Reider, *m* - next to top rail. KYG2038

Reides, *n* - riding. **Sei ~, was er immer dutt, is genunk fer der Gaul dodmache.** His extensive riding is enough to kill the horse. LRT

reie, *refl* - to regret. **Es reit mich as ich sell geduh hab.** I regret that I did that. LRT. *cf* **Es dutt mir Rei un Leed.** I repent. [said by a repentant excommunicated plain-sect member.] KYG

reikumme - to come in. **Kumm rei!** KYG2158. **Wann du kummscht uns bsuche, brauchscht net an die Dier gloppe, kumm yuscht rei.** When you visit us, there is no need to knock at the door, just come on in. LRT

reime, *refl* - to tally. *cf* **glappe, verlese, iwwer eens rauskumme.** KYG1966

Reimewese, *n* - rhyming business. **Deel Leit hen so en ~, alles was sie schwetze, muss reime.** Some people have such a rhyming business, everything they say must rhyme. LRT

reiregere, *pp* **reigeregert** - to rain in. **Es hot zum Fenschder reigeregert.** It rained in the window. LRT

reireisse - to tear in. KYG1976. **Er is do reizureisse kumme mit seine Kaer, ich hab gemehnt er drefft eppes.** He came tearing in here with his car; I thought he would hit something. LRT

reirutsche - to slide in. **Er is do dazu reizurutsche kumme.** He came sliding on in here. LRT

Reis, *f* - trip. = **Rees.** KYG2042

Reis-supp, *f* - rice soup. **~ soll gut sei fer em.** Rice soup is supposed to be healthy for one. LRT

reischnieke - to sneak in. **Ich hab ihn net gheert ~.** I didn't hear him sneak in. LRT

reischtareme - to rush in. **Sie sin do reizuschtareme kumme, un sie hen mich verschrocke.** They came rushing in here and they scared me. LRT

reisse - to tear. **Reiss mir en Schtick Babier aus sellem Schreibbichli.** Tear a piece of paper out of that note pad for me. LRT

Reisses, *n* - pain. **Ich hab scharef ~ im Kopp de Mariye.** I have a sharp pain in my head this morning. LRT

Reitgaul, *m* - riding horse. **Wann du seller ~ verkaafe witt, dann loss mich wisse.** If you want to sell that riding horse, then let me know. LRT

Reitzaahm, *m* - riding bridle. **Es Gebiss is es Haaptding vum me ~.** The bit is the main thing of a riding bridle. LRT

reiwe - to rub. **eem eppes unnich die Naas ~** - to cast up to someone. KYG2036. **Wann dei Hals schteif is, dann sett epper'n gut ~.** If your neck is stiff, then someone should rub it well. LRT

Reiwerband, *f* - band of thieves. = **Raawerband.** KYG1996

Reiwerbruder, *m* - fellow robber. KYG1997

reizoppe, *pp* **reigezoppt** - to pull in by jerks. **Ich hab seller gross Fisch langsam reigezoppt.** I pulled that big fish in slowly by jerks. LRT

Renn, *m* - thrust. = **Schtoss.** KYG2010. **Der Bull hot de Kuh en ~ gewwe.** The bull gave the cow a thrust. LRT

Reseet', *f* - receipt. **Fer alle Sent as ich dir geb, muss ich en ~ hawwe.** For every cent I give you, I must have (need) a receipt. LRT

Resei'neboi, *m,f, pl* **~** - raisin pie. **~ sin mir recht lieb.** Raisin pie is of my liking. LRT

Retsch, *m* - gossip. **Seller Mann is en ~.** That man is a gossip. LRT

Retschbelli, *f* - tattle-tale. KYG1973. = **Retschbewwi.**

retsche, *pp* gretscht - to bear tales, tattle, gossip. **Wann epper net gretscht hett, hedde mir gaar nix gwisst dewehe.** If no one had tattled, we wouldn't have known a thing about it. LRT. **Du kannscht ihm yuscht net draue; er dutt immer ~.** You just can't trust him; he is always telling tales LRT. = **eppes riddle.** KYG1963

Retz(er), *m* - tease. KYG1977. **Geb ihm kenn Acht, er is yuscht en ~.** Pay no attention to him, he is just a tease. LRT. = **Zarrer; Ballickskitzler, Seckelschmeechler**

Rewwer, *m* - river. **der ~ nuff -** up the river. KYG2117. **Seller ~ is voll Hecht.** That river has lots of pike (fish). LRT. **Der Juniata ~ hot Oole as lenger sin wie drei Fiess.** The Juniata River contains eels that are longer than three feet. LRT

richde - to guide. **Seller Buh kann sei Schlidde gut ~.** That boy guides his sled well. LRT

Richder, *m* - **1** steersman. **Sell Schiff hot en guder ~.** That ship has a good steersman. LRT. **2** truer (tool). KYG2068

Richtscheit, *n* - ten-foot pole. KYG1985

Richtschnur, *f* - straight line. **Die Backeschteeleger breiche immer en ~.** The bricklayers always need a straight line. LRT

Rickmeesel, *m* - pork backbone (not loin), a cut of meat containing part of the backbone. LRT

Rickschtick, *n* - top sirloin. KYG2038. **En ~ is en gut Schtick Rinsfleesch.** A top sirloin is a good piece of beef. LRT

rieche - to smell. **Oi! Du riechscht awwer noch Gnowwlich!** Oh! Do you ever smell of garlic! LRT

Riecher, *m, facet.* - smeller. **Ich hab's Kalt, mei ~ schafft net.** I have a cold, my smeller is not working. LRT

riehrend, *adj* - touching. KYG2041

Riehrer, *m* - stirrer, implement used in stirring. **Fer eppes riehre, muss mer en ~, en Schtarrer odder en Riehrschtecke hawwe, sie sin all gleich, yuscht annerschderi Naame.** To stir something one must have a stirrer or a stirring stick—they are all the same, they just have different names. LRT. = **Schtarrer, Riehrschtecke.** KYG1882

Riehrleffel, *m, pl* ~ - mixing ladle (for kitchen). **Die ~ sin oftmols vun Holz gemacht.** Mixing ladles are often made of wood. LRT

Riehrschtecke, *m* - stirring rod. KYG1882. **Fer eppes riehre, muss mer en Riehrer, en Schtarrer odder en ~ hawwe, sie sin all gleich, yuscht annerschteri Naame.** To stir something one must have a stirrer or a stirring stick—they

are all the same, they just have different names. LRT. = **Riehrer, Schtarrer**

Rieme, *m* - thong of flail. KYG2000. [I'm more familiar with **Schwanzrieme** = crupper. LRT]

Ries, *m* - tall person. KYG1965

Rieselhoke, *m* - snout hook. **Do is der ~, du kannscht der Seikopp uffhenge.** Here's the snout hook, you can hang up the pig's head. LRT

Riewekeller, *m* - turnip cellar. KYG2079. **Fer so viel Riewesume saehe un no aa ausmache, nemmt's en ~ un en Rieweschtick. No kann mer en latt Rieweselaat un Riewesupp mache.** To sow that much turnip seed and then harvest (dig) them, takes a turnip cellar and a turnip patch. Then one can make a lot of turnip salad and turnip soup. LRT

Riewesaame, *m, pl* ~ - turnip seed. KYG2079. = **Riewesume**

Rieweschtick, *n* - turnip patch. KYG2079. **Fer so viel Riewesume saehe un no aa ausmache, nemmt's en Riewekeller un en ~. No kann mer en latt Rieweselaat un Riewesupp mache.** To sow that much turnip seed and then harvest (dig) them, takes a turnip cellar and a turnip patch. Then one can make a lot of turnip salad and turnip soup. LRT

Rieweselaat, *m* - turnip salad. KYG2078. **Fer so viel Riewesume saehe un no aa ausmache, nemmt's en Riewekeller un en**

Rieweschtick. No kann mer en latt ~ un Riewesupp mache. To sow that much turnip seed and then harvest (dig) them, takes a turnip cellar and a turnip patch. Then one can make a lot of turnip salad and turnip soup. LRT

Riewesume, *m* - turnip seed. **Fer so viel ~ saehe un no aa ausmache, nemmt's en Riewekeller un en Rieweschtick. No kann mer en latt Rieweselaat un Riewesupp mache.** To sow that much turnip seed and then harvest (dig) them, takes a turnip cellar and a turnip patch. Then one can make a lot of turnip salad and turnip soup. LRT

Riewesupp, *f* - turnip soup. KYG2079. **Fer so viel Riewesume saehe un no aa ausmache, nemmt's en Riewekeller un en Rieweschtick. No kann mer en latt Rieweselaat un ~ mache.** To sow that much turnip seed and then harvest (dig) them, takes a turnip cellar and a turnip patch. Then one can make a lot of turnip salad and turnip soup. LRT

Riggelfensegfaecher, *pl* - rail fence sections. **Die ~ sin zwelf Fuuss lang.** The rail-fence sections are 12 feet long. LRT

Riggelschloss, *n, pl* -**schlesser** - stock lock. KYG1884

Rilps, *m* - rough, unpolished fellow. KYG2109. **Er hot en gudi Lanning, awwer is en rechder ~.** He has a good education, but he is a real rough fellow. LRT

Ring, *m, pl* ~ - ring. **Mir hen de**

zwanzich Sei ~ in die Naes geduh. We put rings in the noses of the 20 pigs. LRT

ringe, *pp* **gringt** - to put a ring in an animal's nose. **Sis Zeit fer die Sei naus uff der Grund duh, awwer's erscht misse sie gringt sei.** It's time to put the hogs out on the ground, but first they must have rings put in their snouts. LRT. **Sie hen seller Bull geringt.** They put a ring in that bull's nose. LRT,4/18/2000

Rinnescheeler, *m* - tan spud. KYG1968

Rinnszung, *f* - beef tongue. **Ich gleich gschmokdi ~.** I like smoked beef tongue. LRT

Rippebuffer, *m* - thump in the ribs. KYG2011

Rippefleesch, *n* - ribs with meat. **~ is gut Esses. Sie saage immer, "Es Fleesch schmackt es bescht naegscht an die Gnoche."** Ribs make good eating. They always say, "The meat tastes the best close to the bone." LRT

Rippeschtick, *n, pl* ~**er** - rib roast. **Zu mir sin die ~er en latt wert.** To me the rib roasts are valuable. LRT

rippich, *adj* - showing the ribs (of a lean horse). **Seller Gaul guckt zu ~ zu mir.** That horse looks too lean to me. LRT

Rischderei, *f* - preparation. **Ich bin froh, as mir yuscht eemol's Yaahr darich so'n ~ geh breiche.** I'm glad that we only need to go through such preparation once each year. LRT

Riss, *m* - 1 tear. = **Schlitz.** KYG1976. **2** crack. **Sis en ~ im Bodde.** There's a crack in the floor. LRT

riwwernemme - to take across. KYG1962

roh, *adj* - unpasteurized, raw. **die ~ Millich** - unpasteurized milk. KYG2109. **Ich mehn, mer sett ken ~ Fleesch esse.** I don't think one should eat raw meat. LRT

Roi, *f, pl* ~**e** - **1** row. **Ich hab zwee ~e Grummbiere geblanzt.** I planted two rows of potatoes. LRT. **Wann die ~e net graad sin, no is eppes los.** If the rows are not straight, then there is a problem. LRT. **Datt am End vum Feld sin selli katze ~e.** There at the end of field are those short rows. LRT. **2** turn (in line). **Du kummscht aa an die ~.** Your turn will come. KYG2076. **Bleib yuscht in de ~, dei Zeit kummt glei.** Just stay in line, your turn will come soon. LRT

roiyeweis, *adv* - in rows. **Mir duhne die Buhne roppe so ~.** We pick the beans by the row (a row at a time). LRT

rolle - **1** to roll. **Die Golfballe ~ immer datt der Hiwwel nunner.** The golf balls always roll down the hill there. LRT. **2** to wallow. **Die Sei ~ im Dreck.** The hogs are wallowing in the dirt. KYG2160. **Deitsch ~** - to speak P.G. fluently. KYG1964

rolle, *refl* - to roll oneself. **Die Sei ~ sich im Dreck.** The hogs are wallowing in the mud. LRT

rollich, *adj* - in heat. **Selli Loos**

is ~. That sow is in heat. LRT

roppe, *pp* **geroppt** - to pull. **Heit warre die Haar geroppt.** Today you'll be taken over the coals. KYG1963. **Heit grickscht du dei Haar geroppt.** Today you will be put in your place. LRT

Ros, *f, pl* **~e** - rose. **Zu mir sin die rode ~e die schennschde.** To me, the red roses are the prettiest. LRT,4/11/2000

roschdich, *adj* - rusty. **Die Schliddelaefer waare ~, fer sell hen mer sie glitzere misse.** The sled runners were rusty, for that reason we had to polish them. LRT

Roschtblacke, *pl* - rust spots. **Sell Messer hot ~, kannscht sie abfege?** That knife has rust spots; can you scour them off? LRT

Rosebledderli, *n, dim* of **Roseblatt.** little rose leaf. LRT/Leb

Roseschtock, *m* - rose bush. LRT

Rosewasser, *n* - rose water. LRT

rosich, *adj* - porous. **Seller Kuche guckt awwer ~.** That cake looks very coarse (porous). LRT

rot, *adj* - red. **Sie hot's wennich ~ gemacht.** She tinged it with red. KYG2022. **~ is mei liebschdi Fareb.** Red is my preferred color. LRT

rotaagich, *adj* - blood-shot. **Wie kummt's, as du so ~ bischt?**

How come your eyes are so blood-shot? LRT

rotblummich, *adj* - red-flowered. **Sie hen en schee ~er Gaarde.** They have a lovely red-flowered garden. LRT

rotfligglich, *adj* - red-winged. **Ich gleich die ~e Schwatzveggel zu sehne.** I like to see the red-winged blackbirds. LRT

rothaarich, *adj* - red-haired. **Wie kummt's as die ~e Leit so summerfleckich sin?** Why is it that the red-haired folks are so covered with freckles? LRT

Rotlaafe, *n* - **1** stiffening of limbs. KYG1879. **2** red infectious streaks of limbs. **Mit ~ wie sell, muscht du en Dokder sehne.** With red infectious streaks like that (on your leg) you need to see a doctor. LRT

rotlaafich, *adj* - with red streaks in the inflamed tissue. **Guck yuscht mol wie ~ as dei Aarem is.** Just look how red streaked and inflamed your arm is. LRT

rotlich, *adj* - reddish. **Sei Haar sin arig dunkel, awwer bissel ~.** His hair is quite dark, but a bit reddish. LRT

Rotlicht, *n* - red-light. **Nau is er in Druwwel, er is darich's ~ gfaahre.** Now he's in trouble; he drove through the red-light. LRT

rotscheckich, *adj* - red-speckled. **Datt draus is en ~er Voggel.** Out there is a red-speckled bird. LRT

rotschtenglich, *adj* - red-stemmed. **Ich will ~er Balsem kaafe.** I want to buy red-stemmed balsam. LRT

rotzich, *adj* - snotty. **~i Kinner** - sniveling children. **Ich bin froh, wann des ~ Wese verbei is.** I'll be glad when this sniveling season is past. LRT

Rotzleffel, *m* - term of contempt (for callow youth). KYG1987

Rotznaas, *f, pl* **-nees** - small fry, "snot nose." **Selli glee ~ daed besser glei heemkumme, es is schier Zeit fer esse.** That small fry had better come home soon; it's almost time to eat. LRT

Royet, *f* - turn. KYG2076

royetweis, *adv* - row by row. KYG2076. **~ hen sie ihre Grummbiere ausgemacht.** They dug their potatoes, a row at a time. LRT

Ruder, *n* - rudder. **an's ~ losse** - to permit someone to take the wheel. KYG1963

Rudi, *m* - nickname for Rudolph. **Ich ken niemand mit em Vornaame ~.** I know no one with the nickname for Rudolph. LRT,4/21/2000

ruff, *adv* - up to a place. = **nuff.** KYG2117. **Wann kummscht du mol do ~? Mir hen dich schund lang net gsehne.** When are you coming up here? We haven't seen you for a long time. LRT

ruffkumme - to come up. **der Weg ~** - to come up the road. KYG2117. **Er is der hinnerscht Weg ~.** He came up the back road. LRT

ruffschaffe, *refl* - to work itself up (or out)(as a nail in a floor board). KYG2245. **Die Neggel datt im Bodde schaffe sich ruff, ich denk, mir misse Schrauwe neiduh.** The nails there in the floor are working themselves up, I guess we'll have to put screws in. LRT,4/11/2000

ruffschmeisse - to throw up. **Allemol as sell Kind Fisch esst, muss es ~.** Every time that that child eats fish, it has to vomit. LRT

Rugerei, *n* - (confounded) resting. **So en ~ Fescht alle Nummidaag is gaar net notwennich.** Such a resting party every afternoon is not at all necessary. LRT

Ruh, *f* - rest. = **Ruuk, Ruhblatt. Er muss sei ~ hawwe.** He needs his rest. LRT. *cf* **Ruhzeit**

ruhe, *refl* - to rest. **Nau hoscht du mol Zeit fer dich gut zu ~.** Now you finally have time to rest properly. LRT. = **ausruhe**

ruhich, *adv* - quiet, still. **Halt dich ~!** Keep quiet! LRT. **~ mache** - to still. KYG1880. **Yunger, mach dich ~!** Young man, you be quiet! LRT

ruhich schteh - to stand still. **Mir gehne nariyets hie, alles is am ~.** We are going nowhere, everything is at a stand still. LRT

Ruhzeit, *f* - time of rest. KYG2018. **Ya, well, Buwe, ~ is do!** Yes, well, boys, it's time to

rest. LRT. [Leb. Co. = **Ruuhzeit**]

Rukkissi, *n* - rest pillow. **Ich kann besser ruhe unni ~.** I can rest better without a rest pillow. LRT

Rukschtee, *m* - (roundish) stone put on top of fence post. KYG1886

rumbasse - to boss. **Dutt er dich immer so ~?** Does he always boss you around like that? LRT

rumbatzle, *pp* is **rumgebatzelt** - to roll or tumble over and over. KYG2073. **Er is rumgebatzelt, mer hett schier denke kenne, er waer en Balle.** He rolled over and over, one could almost think he was a ball. **Die Wutzlin sin hinne uff em Drock rumgebatzelt wie mir seller blotzich Weg nunnergfaahre sin.** The piglets tumbled around in the back of the truck when we went down that bumpy road. LRT

rumbinne, *pp* **rumgebunne** - to tie in another place. KYG2015. **Selli Kelwer misse rumgebunne sei.** Those calves must be tied in another place. LRT. = **weckbinne**

rumblarre - to talk boisterously. KYG1964. **Der Weg wie er rumblarrt, daed er yuscht so gut fluche.** With his boisterous talking, he might just as well be cursing. LRT

rumbringe - to bring another around to one's way of thinking. KYG1998. **Mir hen sie yuscht net ~ kenne fer'n Bariye mache mit uns.** We just could

not bring them around to reach an agreement (bargain) with us. LRT

rumdappe - to ramble about. **Er dappt yuscht rum un wees net was er am duh is.** He just rambles around and doesn't know what he is doing. LRT

rumdaregle - to stagger around. **Es guckt, as wann er zu viel zu drinke ghat hett, der Weg wie er am ~ is.** It looks as though he had too much to drink, the way he is staggering around. LRT

rumdokdere - to try all sorts of doctors. KYG2071. **Sie is des ~ leedich waare, nau nemmt sie gaar ken Medizin meh.** She got tired of trying all sorts of doctors, now she takes no medicine at all. LRT

rumdratsche - to trudge around. KYG2068

rumdrehe, *refl* - **1** to turn onself around. **Dreh dich rum so as mir dei Gritzer sehne kenne.** Turn around so that we can see your little scratch. LRT. **2** to turn oneself over in bed. KYG2077

rumdrehe - **1** to make a square turn. KYG2076. **2** to turn inside out. **Wann mer die Schtrimp rumdreht, eb mer sie wescht, is no's Gfusser innewennich, wann mer sie drickelt un dreht sie widder rum.** If one turns stockings inside out before one washes them, the fuzz (lint) remains on the inside when one dries them and turns them right side out again. LRT. = **letz mache.** KYG2077

rumdripple, *pp* **rumgedrippelt** - 1 to putter around. **Deel Kieh welle ~, wann mer sie melke will.** Some cows don't want to stand still, when one wishes to milk them. 2 to trample around. **Mir sin do rumgedrippelt bis unser Beh mied waare.** We trampled around here until our legs became tired. LRT. = **trippe, umfalle.** KYG2062.

rumdrollere - to trot around. KYG2064

rumfixe, *pp* **rumgefixt** - to renovate. **Die Nochbere hen ihre Haus rumgefixt.** The neighbors renovated their house. LRT

rumfroge, *pp* **rumgfrogt** - to ask around (in the neighborhood). **Mir hen in de Nochberschaft rumgfrogt, awwer's hot niemand eppes gwisst.** We asked around in the neighborhood, but no one knew anything. LRT

rumgeige - to be restive (of horses), *lit.* to fiddle around. **Selli paar Geil duhne nix wie ~.** That pair of horses does nothing but shift around. LRT

Rumgerutsch, *n* - squirming. **Gleener, du sollscht dei ~ schtoppe.** Little one, you are to stop your squirming. LRT

Rumgeschnarr, *n* - jerking around. **Des ~ bin ich leedich!** I'm tired of this jerking around. LRT

Rumgeschnuffel, *n* - snooping around. **Dei ~ bin ich leedich.** I am tired of your snooping around. LRT

rumgraawe - to dig up and turn over. KYG2078. **Friehyaahr is glei do, sis Zeit fer der Gaarde ~.** Spring will soon be here, it's time to dig the garden. LRT

rumher´schmeisse, *pp* **rumhergschmisse** - to throw about. KYG2009. **Die Leit hen alle sadde Gfraes rumhergschmisse ghat.** The people had thrown all kinds of trash (here and there). LRT

Rumher´-renne, *n* - rushing from place to place. **Wisst dir was? Des ~ koscht Geld.** Do you know what? This rushing around costs money. LRT

rumher´nemme, *pp* **rumhergenumme** - to take from place to place. KYG1962. **Sie hen uns rumhergenumme fer uns die Landschaft weise.** They took us from place to place to show us the landscape. LRT

rumher´schtolpere, *pp* **-gschtolpert** - to stumble around. **Er is in die ganze Nochberschaft -gschtolpert, bis sie ihn gfange hen.** He stumbled all around the neighborhood until they caught him. LRT

rumleie - to lie about. **Er hot ken Geld ~ glosst.** He left no money lying around. LRT

rummache, *pp* **rumgemacht** - to spade (the garden). **Hoscht du dei Gaarde rumgemacht?** Did you spade your garden? LRT

Rummedis-watzel, *f* - twin leaf. *Jeffersonia diphylla* (L.) *Pers.* KYG2083

rumnemme - to take around. **es Esse ~** - to take dinner around. KYG1963. **Die Meals-on-Wheels-Leit duhne die Esse ~ Dinschdaags un Dunnerschdaags.** The meals-on-wheels people take the meals around Tuesdays and Thursdays. LRT

rumpere - to make a big to-do. KYG2030

rumreide, *pp* **is rumgeridde** - to ride around. **~, des kannscht du duh wehe mir.** Ride around, you can do it as far as I'm concerned. LRT. **Er is uff ne rumgeridde.** He rode around on them. = He tyrannized them. KYG2087. **Sie sin uff de Reidgeil rumgeridde.** They rode around on the riding horses. LRT

rumreisse - to tear around. **Dir reisst rum bis dir mol umschmeisst!** You tear around (with your car) until you will eventually upset. LRT

rumrolle, *refl* - to roll oneself around on the ground. **Du kannscht dich yuscht uff em Grund ~, ich geb nix drum.** You can just roll yourself around on the ground, I don't care. LRT

rumrutsche - to slide about. **Mer wees nie net wu er is, er is immer am ~.** One never knows where he is, he is always running around. LRT

Rumrutscherei, *f* - squirming around. **Selli ~ batt dich nix.** That squirming around does you no good. LRT

rumsaage, *pp* **rumgsaat** - to

spread by telling. KYG1981. **Sis rumgsaat warre bis alliepper´s gwisst hot.** It was talked around until everybody knew it. LRT

rumschaffe, *pp* **rumgschafft -** 1 to rearrange (ideas). **Mir hen der ganz Kicheblaan rumgschafft.** We rearranged the whole kitchen plan. LRT. **2** to bring about a change of time. KYG2019. **Mir hen die Zeit rumgschafft so as meh Leit kumme kenne.** We changed the time so that more people can come. LRT. **3** to work over (earth). KYG2245. **Es Welschkannland is nau rumgschafft, mir kenne der Weeze saehe.** The corn ground is worked over, we can now sow the wheat. **4** to revise. **Sie hen der Blaan vun ihrem neie Haus bissel rumgschafft.** They revised the plan of their new house a bit. LRT,4/11/2000. **5** to work in different places. **Mit seim Geilbschlagge schafft er ewwe so rumher.** With his farrier work he works in various places. LRT,4/11/2000

rumschicke, *pp* **rumgschickt -** to send around. **Sie hen ihn um die Scheier rumgschickt.** They sent him around the barn. LRT

rumschiddle, *pp* **rumgschiddelt -** to shake around. **Faahr net so schtarick, selli Ess-sache sedde net so rumgschiddelt sei.** Don't drive so fast, that food should not be shaken around like that. LRT

rumschlappe - 1 to go around in shabby attire. **Es is Zeit fer dei Gleeder wesche, du seddscht net so ~.** It's time to wash your clothes, you should

not go around looking like that. **2** to slop around. **Du muscht dei Schtiffel aaduh, wann du so ~ witt.** You've got to put your boots on if you want to slop around like that. LRT

rumschleiche - to sneak around. KYG2159. **Er dutt immer so langsam ~.** He always sneaks around slowly. **Er schleicht immer rum wie en Fux.** He always sneaks around like a fox. LRT

rumschmeisse, *pp* **rumgschmisse -** to toss, strew. **sei Kopp ~ -** to toss one's head. KYG2040. **An de Schtross noch is immer en latt Gfress rumgschmisse.** Along the road there is always a lot of trash thrown around. LRT

rumschmeisse, *refl* - to toss in bed. KYG2040. **Er schloft nie net gut; er schmeisst sich die ganz Nacht im Bett rum; sis sei Narefe.** He never sleeps well; he tosses around in bed all night; it's his nerves. LRT

rumschpucke - to go about at uncanny times. KYG2020. **Wann die Yunge en ganzi Nacht ~, wees mer gaar net was zu denke.** When the young men wonder around all night, one doesn't know what to think. **Selle Buwe sin immer am ~ as wann sie am Schpeckmeis am suche waere.** Those boys are always spooking around as though they were hunting bats. LRT

rumschtarre, *pp* **rumgschtarrt - 1** to wander around. = **rumschtiere, rumwandle, rumwandere.** KYG2162. **2** to stir around in. **Sie hen in sellem**

Eschehaufe rumgschtarrt, awwer sie hen nix as eppes waert waar finne kenne. They stirred around in that ash pile but they couldn't find anything of value. LRT

rumschtelle, *pp* **rumgschtellt -** to rearrange (things). **Sie hot ihre Blummeschteck ganz annerscht rumgschtellt.** She rearranged the placement of her flower plants. LRT

rumschtichle - to hint around. **Mer wees nie net was er im Sinn hot; er is immer am ~ wehe eppes.** One never knows what is on his mind; he is always hinting around about something. LRT

rumschtimme - to vote the ticket of the opposite party. KYG2103

rumschtraehe, *pp* **rumgschtraeht -** to scatter about or around. = **rumzottle. Mir hen gedrickelder Schofmischt um selli Blummeschteck rumgschtraeht.** We spread dried sheep manure around those flower plants. LRT

rumschtrawwle, *pp* **rumgschtrawwelt -** to straggle around. **Der Hund hot rumgschtrawwelt bis er all die Radde gfange ghat hot.** The dog struggled around until he had caught all the rats. LRT

rumschtrotze, *pp* **rumgeschtrotzt -** to strut around. **Er is rumgschtrotzt wie en Keenich.** He strutted around like a king. LRT

rumschwimme - to swim

around. **Die Fisch duhne immer ~.** The fish always swim around. LRT

rumweise - to show around. **Mir gleiche unser Bsuch do in unserem Daal ~.** We like to show our visitors (company) around in our valley. LRT

Rumwelze, *n* - wallowing around. KYG2160

rumwenne - to turn the furrows. KYG2077. **Des is guder leichder Bodde, er dutt sich schee ~.** This is good light soil, the furrows turn nicely. LRT

rumwiehle, *pp* **rumgewiehlt** - to turn over by rooting. KYG2078. **Die Sei hen den Grund alles rumgewiehlt.** The pigs completely uprooted the ground. LRT

rumzarre - to tantalize. *cf* **bloge, gwaele, necke.** KYG1968. **Er dutt nix as wie ~; er versprecht eppes un no dutt er's net.** He does nothing but tantalize; he makes promises and the he doesn't fulfill them. LRT

rumziehe - to change residence (often). **Selli Leit sin immer am ~.** Those people are always moving (from one place to another). LRT

rumzottle, *pp* **rumgezoddelt** - to scatter unintentionally. **Sehscht net, du hoscht die Buhne rumgezoddelt, weil dei Kareb en Loch hot.** Don't you see, you have scattered (unintentionally) beans because your basket has a hole. LRT

rundaxlich, *adj* - <*Engl* round-

shouldered. **Yunge Buwe as ~ sin mache mich umleitlich.** Young round-shouldered boys make me uncomfortable. LRT

runnerbatzle - to tumble down. KYG2073. **Er is vum Dach runnergebatzelt.** He tumbled down off of the roof. LRT

runnerbiede - to underbid. KYG2095. = **unnerbiede, wennicher biede**

runnerhupse - to hop away. **Wann du den Wagge net gleichscht, dann hups yuscht runner.** If you don't like this wagon, then just jump off. LRT

runnerlese - to unload piece by piece. KYG2107. **Kannscht du mir selli Briggel vum Wagge ~?** Can you unload for me those tree limbs from the wagon? LRT

runnermache, *pp* **runnergemacht** - **1** to pour (rain). **Ya, es hot letscht Nacht runnergemacht; es waar noch nass de Mariye.** Yes, it poured last night; it was still wet this morning. **Mammi, sehscht du wie's runnermacht?** Mother, do you see how it's raining? LRT. **2** to throw down. **Hoi, Schtroh ~** - to throw hay (straw) down for stock. KYG2009. **Ich daed gleiche, wann du Hoi ~ daedscht heit.** I'd like if you would throw hay down today. LRT

runnerreisse, *pp* **runnergerisse** - to tear the tablecloth from the table. KYG1976. **2** to tear down (a barn). **Ya, sie hen die Scheier runnergerisse.** Yes, they tore the barn down. LRT

runnerschaawe, *pp*

runnergschaabt - to scrape off. **Seller Dreck uff unser Kaer hot wiescht geguckt, no hen mir en runnergschaabt.** That dirt on our car looked ugly, so we scraped it off. LRT

runnerschridde - to step down. **Geb acht, ich helf dir do runnerschridde.** Be careful, I'll help you step down here. LRT

runnerschtosse - to thrust down. KYG2010

Runzel, *f, pl* **~e** - wrinkle. **Sell Hemm is iwwerall voll ~e.** That shirt is full of wrinkles. LRT, 4/18/2000

runzle, *refl* - to wrinkle up. **Sie runzelt sich die Schtann.** She's wrinkling her brow. LRT

runzlich, *adj* - full of wrinkles. KYG2254. **Er hot immer ~i Gleeder aa.** He always wears wrinkled clothes. LRT,4/18/2000

Russ, *m, pl* **~e** - a Russian male. **Wie ich yung waar, hen mir ken ~e in unser Nochberschaft ghat.** When I was a youngster, we had no one in our neighborhood with a Russian ancestry. LRT,4/21/2000

russisch, *adj* - Russian. KYG2279

Russland, *n* - ✪ Russia. KYG2279

Russlenner, *m* - Russian male. KYG2279

Rutsch, *f* - child that wriggles on its mother's lap. KYG,2254. **Yunges, du bischt awwer'n ~. Kannscht du dich net schtill**

halde? Youngster, you are such a ~. Can't you remain still? LRT,4/18/2000

rutschich, *adj* - **1** squirming. **Sei Yunges is arig ~.** His child is very squirmy. LRT. **2** wiggly. KYG2084. **Oh Kind, sei net so ~.** Oh child don't be so wriggly. LRT

ruuschde - to roost. **Die Hinkel sin am ~.** The chickens are roosting. LRT

ruussich, *adj* - sooty. **Die ganz Kich waar ~.** The whole kitchen was sooty. LRT

saage, *pp* **gsaat** - to say. **Es geht unni gsaat.** It goes without saying. KYG2110. **sich nix ~ losse** - to be unwilling to take advice. KYG2115. **Sie kenne ihm gaar nix saage, er haricht yuscht net.** They can't tell him a thing, he just won't listen. LRT. **in's Gsicht ~** - to say to one's face. KYG1981. **Ich saag dir was, du bischt en guder Mensch.** I tell you what, you are a good person. LRT. **Ich will ee meh Ding ~.** I want to say one more thing. KYG2163. **Ich will dir noch ee Ding ~.** I want to tell you one thing more. LRT

saame - to seam. **Der Gaund is faddich bis uff der Schtock ~.** The dress is finished except for hemming the skirt. LRT

Sach, *f, pl* **~e** - thing, matter. **eppes an der ~ sei** - to be some truth in the matter. KYG2070. **Es muss eppes an de ~ sei, schunscht hedde mir meh gheert.** There must be some truth in the matter or we would have heard more. LRT. **en latt ~** - a lot of things. **karyose ~ -**

strange things. KYG1997

Sackbendel, *m* - string to tie a bag. **Do is en ~ fer der Sack zubinne.** Here is a string to tie the bag shut. LRT. **Yeder Sack hot en ~ fescht.** Each bag has a tie string attached. LRT

Saddelgaul, *m* - saddle horse. **Mei Grossdochder hot en ~.** My granddaughter has a saddle horse. LRT

saddle - to saddle. **der Gaul ~** - to saddle a horse. **Es nemmt net lang fer en Gaul ~.** It doesn't take long to saddle a horse. LRT

Saddler, *m* - saddle maker. **Eens vun meine Vorvedder waar en ~ un en Gschaerrmacher.** One of my forefathers was a saddle- and harness maker. LRT

Saegbock, *m* - sawhorse. LRT,4/11/2000

saege - to cut with a saw. LRT/Leb. Co.

Saege-setz, *m* - tooth set. KYG2037

Saegloch, *n* - ✪ Saegloch Creek, which flows through **Yammerdaal,** *qv.* in northern Lanc. Co., PA.

saehe - to seed. **Mir sin am Weeze ~.** We are sowing wheat. LRT

safdich, *adv* - quietly, softly. **Sie schwetze ~.** They are speaking quietly. LRT

Safferich, *m* - saffron. *Carthamus tinctorius L.* =

Saffran. **Die Lebnen Kaundi Leit gleiche ihre ~.** The Lebanon County people like their saffron (as a flavoring and coloring in their cookery). LRT

Salweiblaat, *n* - sage leaf. *Salvia officinalis L.* **Ebmols wann ich en weher Blacke im Maul hab, duhn ich en ~ druff-neilege.** Sometimes when I have a sore spot in my mouth, I lay a sage leaf in upon it. LRT. = **Salwei**

Salz, *n* - salt. **Er is net sei ~ in de Supp waert!** He isn't worth the salt in his soup. LRT

Salzbexli, *n, dim* of **Salzbax.** little salt box. LRT/Leb

salzich, *adj* - expensive, *lit.* salty. **Sis ~!** It's expensive. LRT

Sammschdaag, *m* - Saturday. **Am ~ iwwer acht Daag gehne mir noch Nei Yarick.** A week from Saturday we will be going to New York. LRT

Sandboddem, *m* - sandy soil. **Wann mir eppes aerne welle vun em ~, nemmt's en latt Wasser.** If we want to harvest something from sandy soil, it takes a lot of water. LRT

Sapperlott! - *interj.* - zounds! KYG2267. **~ nochemol!** Ye Gods! LRT,4/21/2000

Sariye, *pl* - troubles. KYG2065

Satzbier, *n* - liquid yeast. **Der Satzhaffe is voll ~.** The yeast pot is full of liquid yeast. LRT, 4/18/2000

Satzfettkuche, *pl* - yeast doughnuts. **Ich gleich ~.** I like yeast doughnuts. LRT,4/18/2000

Satzhaffe, *m* - yeast pot. **Der ~ is voll Satzbier.** The yeast pot is full of liquid yeast. LRT, 4/18/2000

satzich, *adj* - yeasty. KYG2261. **Des Brot schmackt awwer ~.** This bread tastes yeasty. LRT,4/18/2000

Sauders - ✪ Souderton, Mont. Co., PA. KYG2280

Sauerappel, *m, pl* **Sauereppel** - sour apple. KYG1971. **Sauereppel Schnitz mache gudi Boi.** Sour apple snitz make good pies. LRT

Sauerdeeg, *m* - leaven scrapings (of the kneading trough). **Der ~ schmeisse mir naus.** We will throw the ~ out. LRT,4/18/2000

saufe - to tipple. = **tipple.** *cf* **draa rumschnaufe.** KYG2024. **Zu viel ~ is em nix wert.** Too much drinking does one no good. LRT

Saufschtubb, *f* - tap room. KYG1970

Schaad! - too bad. KYG2034. **Sis arig ~ wie viel Leit as AIDS hen heidesdaags.** It's too bad, how many people have AIDS now-a-days. LRT

schaalich, *adj* - shelly. **Die Grebskuche sin ~.** The crab cakes are shelly. LRT

Schaar, *f* - throng. = **Drupp.** KYG2008

Schaarbock, *m* - tarter on lower teeth. KYG1971

Schaawer, *m* - tanner's hide-shaving tool. KYG1968

schadde - to do harm. **Batt's nix, so schatt's nix.** There is no harm in trying. KYG2071. **Mir sedde sell Blaschder browiere uff seim wehe Gnie; wann's nix batt dann schatt's aa nix.** We should try that salve on his sore knee; there is no harm in trying. LRT

Schaddebaam, *m* - shade tree. **En grosser ~ is mir immer willkumm, wann's hees is.** A big shade tree is always welcome to me when it's hot. LRT

Schaddeseit, *f* - shady side. **Er waar uff die ~ vum Haus.** He was on the shady side of the house. LRT

schaddich, *adj* - shady. = **voll Schadde. Zidder as die Bledder gfalle sin, hen mir nimmi viel ~i Bletz im Hof.** Since the leaves have fallen, we don't have many shady places in our yard anymore. **Unser Hof is ~.** Our yard is shady. LRT

Schaefferschteddel, *n* - ✪ Schaefferstown, Leb. Co., PA. **~ waar mol Weil unser Heemet-schteddel nochdem as mir gheiert waar.** Schaefferstown was once our home when we were first married. LRT,4/21/2000

schaele, *pp* **gschaelt** - to shave (pare a surface). **Hoscht du die Grummbiere gschaelt?** Have you peeled the potatoes? LRT

Schaeler, *m* - **1** peeler. **2** sheller. LRT

Schaelmesser, *n* - peeling knife. LRT

Schaffbank, *f* - carpenter's bench. **Mer kann viel Sadde Sache schaffe uff re ~.** One can do many kinds of work on a workbench. LRT,4/11/2000. = **Howwelbank**

Schaffdaag, *m* - workday. **Buwe, vergess net, des is en ~.** Boys, don't forget this is a workday. LRT,4/11/2000. = **Waerdaag, Warrdaag**

schaffe, *pp* **gschafft** - **1** to work. **aus em Weg ~** - to put out of the way. **Sell Hoi sedde mir aus em Weg ~; ei schur, mir duhne's fiedere.** We should put that hay out of the way; why sure, we'll feed it. LRT. **Des schafft net.** That won't do. KYG1992. **Schmeiss sell weck, sell schafft net.** Throw that away, that won't work (or do). LRT. **2** to set out. **Er hot sich uff der Weg gschafft.** He got on his way (or went on his way). LRT,4/11/2000

Schaff-fraa, *f* - working woman. **Ya, sie is en ~.** Yes, she is a (hard) working woman. LRT, 4/11/2000

Schaffgaul, *m* - work or draft horse. LRT/Leb

Schaffgleeder, *pl* - work clothes. **Was geht aa do, sis Sunndaag un er hot sei ~ aa?** What's going on here, it's Sunday and he has his work clothes on? LRT,4/11/2000

schaffich, *adj* - thrifty. = **schpaarsam.** *cf* **waxich, wexich.** KYG2007

Schaffiem, *f, pl* ~e - worker bee. **Die ~e mache der Hunnich.** The worker bees make the honey. LRT,4/11/2000

Schaffmann, *m, pl* -leit - working man. **Mir hen die -leit frieh heemgschickt heit.** We sent the workforce home early today. LRT,4/11/2000

Schaffox, *m, pl* ~e - ox broken to work. **Do im Yaahr 2000 sin die ~e nimmi zu blendi.** Here in the year 2000 the work-broken oxen are not too plentiful. LRT,4/11/20000

Schaffschtubb, *f* - workroom. **Der Schtor hot aa en ~.** The store also has a workroom. LRT, 4/11/2000

Schaft, *m* - stock of a gun. = **Scheft.** KYG1883

Schall, *m* - sound, echo. **Seller ~ hot mer ganz iwwer's Daal gheert.** That sound (echo) could be heard all over the valley. LRT

schalle, *pp* gschallt - 1 to sound, ring, echo. **Des hot awwer gschallt.** There was quite a sound (an echo). LRT. **2** to reverberate. **Des Gloppe vun die Scheier baue hot iwwerall dorum gschallt.** The hammering from building the barn reverberated all around here. LRT

Schannschtee, *m* - chimney. **Schreib's in der ~ so as du's net vergesscht.** Write it in the chimney so that you don't forget it. LRT

scharef, *adj* - sharp. **en ~ Aag** - a sharp eye. **Er hot ~i Aage.** He has sharp eyesight. LRT

scharefaagich, *adj* - sharp-eyed. **Er is en ~er Mensch.** He is a sharp-eyed person. LRT

scharefsichdich, *adj* - hawk-eyed, sharp-eyed. LRT

schauderlich, *adj* - shuddering, dreadful. **Des is en ~ Wese.** This is a shuddering experience. **Sell is en ~ Wese.** That's a dreadful thing. LRT

Schaufelaag, *n, pl* ~e - "eye" of shovel handle. **Die ~e sin en hendich Ding.** The hand-hold on the end of a shovel handle are very handy. LRT

Schaufeleeg, *f* - cultivator. LRT

schaumich, *adj* - sudsy (of soap). **Wann ich mich baad, gleich ich wann die Seef ~ is.** When I take a bath, I like when the soap is sudsy. LRT

scheech, *adj* - terrified. *cf* **verkollebiert, verscheecht.** KYG1988

Scheedwasser, *n* - nitric acid. LRT

scheele, *pp* gscheelt - to strip (bark). **Sie hen der Eecheblock gscheelt.** They stripped the oak log. LRT

Scheffer, *m* - worker. **Sie waare die beschde ~,** as mir sei Lewe ghat hen. They were the best workers we ever had. LRT,4/11/2000

scheisse - to shit. **Ich scheiss der druff.** I don't give a hang for what you say. LRT

scheissich, *adv* - insignificant, *lit.* "shitty." **Es waar yuscht so**

en ~ glee Ding. It was just an insignificant little thing. LRT

Scheissloch, *n* - toilet hole. KYG2031. **Sis net der Waert as mer zum ~ nunner guckt, sis nix zu sehne.** It's not worthwhile that one looks down the toilet hole (in the outdoor toilet), there is nothing worth seeing. LRT

Schelf, *n, pl* ~er - *<Engl* shelf. **ewwerscht ~ -** top shelf. KYG2038. **Die ~er in sellem Schank sin zu voll.** The shelves in that cupboard are too full. LRT

Schellem, *m* - rogue. **Grick's der ~!** The devil take it! = **Hol's der Deiwel! Hol's der Granket!** KYG1963

schemme, *refl* - to be ashamed. **Du seddscht dich ~.** You should be ashamed of yourself. LRT

Schenandoah-Daal, *n* - ✪ Shenandoah Valley, VA. KYG2280

schenke - to give as a gift. **epper eppes ~ -** to give someone a gift. LRT

Schenkel, *m* - thigh. *cf* **Waade.** KYG1997. **Er hot sei ~ weh geduh.** He hurt his thigh. LRT

Schenkelgnoche, *m* - thighbone. KYG1997. **~ sin vun die letschde as verfaule im Graab.** Thighbones are among the last to decay in the grave. LRT

Scheppappel, *pl* -eppel - York Imperial apple, "crooked apples." **Mir PA Deitsche heese die** York Imperial **Eppel, -**

eppel." We PA Germans call York Imperial apples, "-ebbel." LRT

Scheppkiwwel, *m* - pail, wooden dipper. **Scheppkiwwel, sell is was mer brauch fer Wasser aus em Droog scheppe.** A pail, that's what one needs to dip water out of the trough. LRT. **Sie hen immer'n ~ im Schpringhaus.** They always have a dipper bucket in the spring house. LRT,4/11/2000

Scheppmaul, *n* - wry mouth. KYG2257. **Mach ken so en ~, du verschreckscht's Kind!** Don't make such a wry mouth (distort your face), you'll frighten the child! LRT,4/18/2000

scheppmeilich, *adj* - wry-mouthed. **Yunger Mann, du guckscht so ~! Was is letz?** Young man, you look so wry-mouthed? What is the problem? LRT,4/18/2000

Scheppmesser, *n* - drawing knife. LRT

schicke, *refl* - to develop a skill. **Er kann sich gaar net ~ fer scheeni Schunke ausdrenne.** He is unskilled when it comes to trimming out nice hams. LRT

schicklich, *adj* - suitable. **Is seller Schtuhl ~ fer newwich der Aldaar schtelle?** Is that chair suitable to set beside the altar? LRT

Schiddelgawwel, *f, pl* **-gawwele** - wooden fork (for shaking straw after thrashing). KYG2239. **Die yunge Bauersbuwe wisse heit net viel**

vun **-gawwele.** The young farm boys don't know much today about wooden shaking forks. LRT,4/11/2000

schiddle, *pp* **gschiddelt** - to shake. *cf* **wabble, wackle, zittre. Ich schiddel die Bledder vun sellem Baam.** I'll shake the leaves from that tree. **Allemol as er draadenkt, muss er sich ~.** Every time he thinks of it, he must shake himself. LRT

Schiebdier, *f, pl* **~e** - sliding door. **~e hen ken Benner.** Sliding doors have no hinges. LRT

Schier - *<Engl* share. **Er waar zufriede wie er sei ~ grickt hot.** He was satisfied when he got his share. LRT

schier gaar, *adj* - nearly. LRT

schiesse - to turn to seed. **Guck mol, die Zwiwwle sin am ~.** Look, the onions are turning to seed. LRT

Schiewer, *m, pl* **~** - **1** slide. **Wann mer der ~ uffmacht, no laaft's Welschkann runner aus em Kaschde.** If one opens the slide, then the corn runs down out of the bin. **2** sliding bolt. **Die ~ hewe die Diere zu.** The sliding bolts hold the doors shut. LRT

Schiffeegner, *m* - shipowner. **Bei die alde Pennsilfaanische Deitsche waare ganz wennich ~.** Among the old PA Germans there were very few shipowners. LRT

schifferich, *adj* - slate-colored. **Sell sin ~i Hinkel.** They are barred-rock chickens. LRT

Schikaa´go - ✿ Chicago, IL. KYG2271

Schillgroddedach, *n* - turtle roof. KYG2080

Schillgroddekallick, *m* - turtle-stone lime. KYG2080

schimmere - to twinkle. = **glitzere, zwitzere.** KYG2083. **Sis schier dunkel, awwer guck mol wie sell Dammwasser schimmert.** It's almost dark, but look how that dam water is twinkling. LRT

schimmerich, *adj* - shimmering. **Die Sunn macht sell Wasser awwer ~.** The sun really makes that water shimmer. LRT

Schindeldach, *n, pl* **Schindeldecher** - shingle roof. **(Holz) Schindeldecher sin raar heidesdaags.** (Wood) shingle roofs are scarce nowadays. LRT

Schinnbeh, *n* - shin bone. **Sie hot ihre ~ verbroche.** She broke her shin bone. LRT

Schinndreck, *m* - turd. = **Gnoddel, Schissdreck.** KYG2075

Schinner, *m* - deuce, heck. **Was der ~ geht aa do?** What the heck is going on here? LRT

Schinnerhannes, *m* - **1** term of opprobrium. KYG1987. **2** scavenger. **Der ~ hot die dod Kuh weckgfaahre.** The scavenger (truck) hauled away the dead cow. LRT

Schipp, *f* - shovel, spade. **net vun der ~ geh** - to be unable to express one's thoughts. KYG2002. **Der Schpitze vun**

de ~ is abgewore. The point of the spade is worn off. LRT

Schippach, *f* - ✪ Skippack Creek (region). KYG2280

schippe - to turn a suitor away. KYG2077

Schippli, *n, pl* ~**n** - pout. **en ~ mache** - to droop (or lower) the lip. **Es is so bedauerlich fer gleeni Kinner sehne wann sie ~n mache.** It is so pitiful to see little children pout. LRT

Schiss, *m* - trivial matter. KYG2063

Schisser, *m* - youngster. KYG2264

Schittler, *m* - shaker (**1** in mining. **2** on a thrasher.) **Die Dreschmaschien hot en ~ fer's Schtroh schittle.** The thrashing machine has a shaker for shaking the straw [free of the grain]. LRT

schkillpe - to throw something heavy off center. *cf* **umschmeisse, umschtatze.** KYG2009

Schkraephaufe, *m* - <*Engl* scrap heap. **Wann's net witt, schmeiss es uff der ~.** If you don't want it, throw it on the ~. LRT

schlaamse, *pp* **gschlaamst** - to slant. **Decher sin gschlaamst so as es Regewasser ablaaft.** Roofs are slanted so that the rain water will run off. LRT

schlaamse, *pp* **geschlaamst** - to slant. **Sell Dach sett hadder geschlaamst sei.** That roof should have more slope (slant).

LRT

Schlack, *m* - blow. **sanfder ~ -** tap. KYG1969

schlagge, *pp* **gschlagge** - to strike. **sanft ~ -** to tap lightly. KYG1969. **Es hot epper's vedderscht Glaas aus ihre Kaer gschlagge.** Someone struck the front glass (wind shield) out of their car. LRT

Schlaguhr, *f* - striking clock. **Hoscht du die ~ uffgezoge?** Did you wind the striking clock? LRT

Schlagwarick, *n* - striking works (of a clock). **Es ~ vun die Schlaguhr schafft net.** The striking works of the striking clock does not work.

Schlang, *f, pl* ~**e - 1** snake. **Seller glee Buh gleicht ~e.** That little boy likes snakes. **~, du hoscht mich verschreckt!** Oh, snake, you frightened me! LRT. **2** worm in a still. KYG1880

Schlange-oi, *n, pl* ~**er** - snake egg. **Ich hab sei Lewe ken ~er gsehne.** I have never seen any snake eggs. LRT

Schlangebuch, *n* - snake book. **Fer eppes lanne vun Schlange muss mer en ~ hawwe.** To learn about snakes one needs a snake book. LRT

Schlangehaut, *f* - snake skin. **En ~ hot aa Aage.** A snake skin has eyes too. LRT

Schlangeschteck, *m, pl* -**schteck** - snake plant. **Die Fraa hot paar Schlangeschteck.** My wife has several snake plants. LRT

Schlapp, *n* - **1** slob. **Sie is en ~ un en Schlump, du kannscht sie heese was du witt.** She is a slob and a slut, call her what you will. LRT. **2** untidy woman. **Sie is so schlappich mit ihre Arewet. Sie is en rechdi ~.** She is so untidy with her work. She is a real slob. LRT. **3** trollop. = **Schlump.** KYG2064

Schlappfass, *n* - slop barrel. **Uff em Harry Webbert sei Bauerei in Leb. Co. hen sie en Peif ghat as unnich der Bodde gange is vun me Drog im Hof bis nunner in der Seischtall. Datt hen sie als die Molke vum Butter mache un anner Schlapp in der Drog gschitt, no is es hiwwelnunner in's ~ in der Seischtall gloffe.** On the Harry Webbert farm in Leb. Co. they had a pipe that ran underground from a trough in the yard to the hog house. There they used to pour the whey from butter churning and other slop into the trough, then it would run downhill into the slop barrel in the hog house. LRT

schlappfiessich, *adj* - walking in a slovenly manner. KYG2159. **Sie hen gsehne wie ~ as er am laafe waar, un hen wisse welle was ihm fehlt.** They saw how slovenly he was walking and wanted to know what was wrong with him. LRT

Schlappfuuss, *m* - slovenly walker. KYG2159. **Was fehlt dann sellem ~?** What (on earth) is wrong with that slovenly walker? LRT

schlappich, *adj* - sloppy. **Yunger, sei net so ~!** Young man, don't be so careless! LRT

schlappseckich, *adj* - having a "beer belly". **Du bischt awwer ~.** My, but you have a "beer belly". LRT

schlarebse - to make a smacking noise (when eating, tasting). **Yungi, du seddscht net so ~ wann du esscht!** Young lady, you should not make such a smacking noise when you eat! LRT. **Wann du so ~ witt, dann geh naus in der Hof fer esse.** If you want to make such a smacking sound when you eat, then go and eat out in the yard. LRT

schlawwerich, *adj* - slobbering. **Wann er so ~ sei muss, muss er ewwe en Schlawwerduch hawwe.** If he is going to be that slobbery, he must have a bib. LRT

Schlawwermaul, *n* - person who speaks sputteringly. **Ich hab noch ken Kind gsehne as en ~ is wie ihn.** I never saw a child that was a slobbermouth like him. LRT

Schlechdichkeit, *f* - turpitude. KYG2080. **Sei ~ is glei vorkumme.** His depravity soon became evident. LRT

Schleckes, *n* - candy, sweets (which can be licked or sucked on). **Hoscht du mir ~ gebrocht?** Did you bring me sweets (candy)? LRT,4/11/2000

Schleffelwedder, *n* - thawing weather. KYG1992. **Ich bin froh as mir mol des ~ griege, der Schnee is nimmi schee-weiss.** I'm glad we have gotten this thawing weather, the snow isn't nice and white anymore. LRT

schleiche, *pp* **is gschliche** - to skulk. **Sie sin so ruhich darich's Haus gschliche, es hot niemand gwisst as sie datt waare.** They sneaked through the house so quietly, no one knew they were there. LRT

schleiche - to walk stealthily. **Er is datt zu die hinnerscht Dier rei zu ~ kumme.** He came sneaking in the back door there. LRT

Schleichfiewer, *n* - walking typhoid. KYG2087.

Schleng, *f* - sling (supporting bandage). **Er hot sei Aarem in en ~, weil er sei Aarem verbroche hot.** He has his arm in a sling because he broke it. LRT

Schlenk, *f* - thumb latch. KYG2011

schlenkerich, *adj* - swinging. **Seller Buh laaft immer so ~.** That boy always walks in such a swinging manner. LRT

schliddefaahre - to go sledding. **Die Buwe gleiche ~ geh.** The boys like to go sledding. LRT

Schliddelaefer, *m, pl* - runners on a sled. **Mir sedde bissel Schtaalwoll iwwer selli ~ reiwe fer sie glitzere mache.** We should rub a little steel wool over those sled runners to make them shine. LRT

Schlier, *m* - ulcerated abscess (boil or carbuncle). KYG2088

Schliffer, *m* - splinter. **Mamm, ich hab en ~ in meim Daume. Grick en Nodel un mach en raus.** Mother, I have a splinter

in my thumb. Get a needle and take it out. LRT

schlimm, *adj* - bad. **Seller aarem glee Buh is net ganz recht; sell is ~ genunk, awwer was noch ~er is, sis immer epper hinnich ihm.** That poor little boy is not quite normal; that is bad enough, but what is worse is that somebody is always tormenting him. LRT

schlimmer ab, *adj* - worse off. **Tscheck, bischt du ~ heit, as du geschder waarscht?** Jake, are you worse off today than you were yesterday? LRT,4/18/2000

schlimmscht, *superl adj* - worst. **Des is der ~ Schtarem, as mir ghat hen in de letschde fimf Yaahr.** This is the worst storm we've had in the last five years. LRT,4/18/2000

Schlipper, *m* - <*Engl* "sleeper," railroad tie. = **Riggelwegschlipper.** KYG2014

Schlittli, *n* - *dim* of **Schlidde.** little sled. **Sell glee ~ hen sie uns gewwe fer nix.** They gave us that little sled for nothing. LRT

Schlitz, *m* - rip. **Seller Sack hot en ~.** That bag has a rip in it. LRT

schlitzohricher, *adj* - slick (of person). **Sei Buh is en ~ Kall.** His son is a tricky fellow. LRT

schliwwerich, *adj* - rascally. **So'n ~er Mensch hett ich liewer net in die Freindschaft.** Such a rascally person I'd rather not have as a relative. LRT

schlixe - to cast stolen glances.

Schlodderfuuss, *m* - person walking with a shambling gait. KYG2159

Schlof, *m* - temple (in anatomy). KYG1983. **Mei Koppweh is graad in meim linkse ~.** My headache is right in my left temple. LRT

Schlofdreck, *m* - sleep matter (in the eyes). **Du hoscht ~ in deine Aage.** You have sleep matter in your eyes. LRT

Schlofkaer, *m, f, pl ~e* - <*Engl* sleeping car. **Selli ~e hen weechi Bedder.** Those sleeping cars have soft beds. LRT

Schlofkopp, *m* - sleepy head. **Seller ~ schloft ei an alli Versammling.** That sleepy head falls asleep at every meeting. LRT

Schluck, *m* - swallow. **Nemm en guder ~.** Take a good swallow. LRT

Schlucker, *m* - throat. **Sei ~ schafft net.** He is unable to swallow. LRT

schlummere - to slumber. **Er waar am ~.** He was slumbering. LRT

Schlump, *f* - prostitute. **Sie is en ~.** She is a prostitute. LRT

Schlupp, *m* - 1 ribbon. *cf* **Haarband. Sell Maedli hot en scheener ~ uff em Kopp.** That little girl has a pretty ribbon on her head. LRT. **2** bow. **Sell is en scheener ~ uff de Henk vun sellem Blummekareb.** That is a nice bow on the handle of that

flower basket. LRT

schmaalrannefdich, *adj* - narrow-brimmed. **Die Mannsleit in selle Gmee duhne ~i Hiet waere.** The men in that church wear narrow-brimmed hats. LRT

schmacke - to taste. = **schmecke, teesde, verschmacke, versuche.** KYG1972. **Wie schmackt die Wascht?** How does the sausage taste? LRT

schmackhaft, *adj* - toothsome. KYG2037

schmacklich, *adj* - tasteful. = **appedittlich.** KYG1972

Schmackwascht, *f* - person who tasted sausage meat for condiments. KYG1972

schmaertze - to smart. **Sell schmaerst awwer.** That really smarts. LRT

schmatze[1] - to cause pain. **Sell dutt em ~.** That pains one. LRT

schmatze[2] - to make a smacking sound (when eating). **Schmatz net so wieschderlich!** Don't make such a smacking sound! LRT. **Yunger, du settscht net so ~ wann du esscht.** Young man, you shouldn't make such a smacking sound when you eat. LRT

schmeisse, *pp* **gschmisse** - to throw, toss. **Schmeiss der Balle so hatt as du kannscht.** Throw the ball as hard as you can. LRT. **die Ringle ~** - to throw discus. **aus Zeit ~** - to throw out of time or rhythm. KYG2009. **Sie hen ihm nix in der Weg gschmisse.**

They didn't throw anything in his way (they did nothing to delay him). LRT. **vum Gaul ~** - to unhorse. KYG2104. **Er is vum Gaul gschmisse warre.** He was thrown from the horse. **Ich hab ihm gsaat, er soll sell net zu die Sei ~.** I told him he should not toss that to the hogs. LRT. *cf* **hieschnelle.** KYG2040

schmeisse, *refl* - to fall when tangled. KYG1967

schmelze - to melt. **Der Schnee is am ~.** The snow is melting. LRT

Schmidderei, *f* - the occupation of smithing. **~ is ken leichdi Arewet.** Smithing is not easy work. LRT

Schmidtkaschde, *m* - blacksmith's tool chest. KYG2035

schmiere, *pp* **gschmiert** - to smear. **Selli Gritzer uff deim Aarem, sedde gschmiert sei mit Blaschder.** Those scratches on your arms should be smeared with ointment. LRT

schmierich, *adj* - 1 messy. 2 greasy. LRT

Schmierseef, *f* - soft soap. **Mei Memm hot als ~ gyuust fer Gleeder wesche.** My mother used to use soft soap for washing clothes. LRT

Schmitteise, *n* - wrought iron. KYG2265. **Wann mer schmidde will, muss mer ~ hawwe.** If one wants to do forging, one needs wrought iron. LRT,4/18/2000

Schmittschapp, *m* - smithy. **Ich**

hab als unser Geil an der ~ genumme fer sie bschlagge griege. I used to take our horses to the blacksmith shop to get them shod. LRT

Schmokduwack, *m* - smoking tobacco. **~ sedde sie verbrenne eb die Yungen's griege.** Smoking tobacco should be burned before the youth get a hold of it. LRT

Schmoke(s), *n* - 1 smoking. **Die Mamm hot als gscholde iwwer em Daadi sei ~.** Mother used to scold about Dad's smoking. **2** the habit of smoking. LRT

Schmokhaus, *n* - smokehouse. **Unser ~ is zu glee.** Our smokehouse is too small. LRT

Schmokhausdach, *n* - smokehouse roof. **Unser ~ rinnt.** Our smokehouse roof leaks. LRT

Schmokhausdier, *f, pl* **~e** - smokehouse door. **Deel Leit duhne immer ihre ~e gschlosse halde.** Some people always keep their smokehouse doors locked. LRT

schmokich, *adj* - smoky. **Meim Grossdaadi sei Schtor waar als recht ~, wann die Mannsleit datt ghockt hen, am Karde schpiele, un am schmoke wie net gscheit.** My grandfather's store used to be really smoky when the men sat there playing cards and smoking like crazy. LRT

Schmokpeif, *f, pl* **~e** - smoke pipe. **Mer seht nimmi viel ~e.** One doesn't see many smoke pipes any more. LRT

schmunzle - to smile slyly. **Sei ~ macht em wunnere.** His smiling makes one wonder. **Yungi, schmunzel yuscht, es is mir so lieb.** Young lady, just smile, it is so dear to me. LRT

schmunzlich, *adv* - **1** simperingly. **Er hot mich so ~ aageguckt.** He looked at me simperingly. LRT. **2** smiling. **Sie hot mich so ~ aageguckt.** She looked at me with a smile. LRT

schmutzich, *adj* - sordid. **Selli Pann is noch ~, duh sie noch net weck.** That pan is still messy, don't put it away yet. LRT

schnackerich, *adj* - **1** tender. *cf* **zaart.** KYG1984. **2** slender, slim. LRT

schnaddere, *pp* **gschnaddert** - to shiver. **Sei Zaeh hen gschnaddert.** His teeth were chattering. LRT

Schnaeppersupp, *f* - <*Engl* "snapper" turtle soup. KYG2080. **~ macht gut Esses.** Snapping turtle soup makes good eating. LRT

schnarixe - to snore. **Epper as schnarixt wie sell, muss eppes letz hawwe mit de Naas.** Someone who snores like that must have something wrong with the nose. LRT

Schnarixer, *m* - snorer. **En ~ is ewwe aa en Mensch, vergess sell net.** A snorer is a human being, too, don't forget that. LRT

schnarrbehnich, *adj* - stiff (of horse with stiff joints). KYG1879

schnarre, *pp* **gschnarrt** - to jerk. **Die Geil hen mich vum Wagge gschnarrt.** The horses jerked me from the wagon. LRT

schnarrich, *adv* - jerky. **Faahr net so ~!** Don't drive so jerky! LRT

schnattre, *pp* **gschnattert** - to shake from the cold. **Er hot datt gschtanne un hot gschnattert; ich hab gemehnt sei Hut meecht vun seim Kopp falle.** He stood there and shook; I thought his hat would fall from his head. LRT

schnause[1] - to snoop. **Des is en Vendu, awwer seller Mann is yuscht am ~, er will nix kaafe.** This is a sale, but that man is only snooping, he doesn't want to buy anything. LRT

schnause[2], *pp* **gschnaust** - to secure edibles by stealth. **Er kann net hungerich sei, er hot sich an paar Bletz Ess-sache gschnaust.** He can't be hungry, he raided food at a few places. LRT

Schnawwelkeppli, *n* - a little cap with a visor. = **Schnawwelkapp.** LRT

Schneck, *f, pl* **~e** - snail. **Die ~e gleiche Bier saufe bis sie dod gehne.** The snails like to drink beer until they die. LRT

Schnee(g)schtiwwer, *m, pl* **~e** - squall (of snow). **Es gebt ~e.** There's going to be snow squalls. LRT

Schneeballe, *m* - snowball. **~ schmeisse is Kinnerschtreech as gfaehrlich sei kann.** Throwing snowballs is a childish prank that can be dangerous. LRT

Schneebank, *f, pl* **-benk -** snowdrift. **Yaahre zerick waare die Schneebenk en unhendich Ding.** Years ago, snowdrifts were an inconvenient thing. LRT

Schneeblug, *m, pl* **-bliek -** snow plow. **Do in Pennsilfaanie, was daede mir duh unni Schneebliek?** Here in Pennsylvania, what would we do without snow plows? LRT

Schneefens, *f, pl* **~e -** snow fence. **~e sin nimmi so blendi as sie als waare.** Snow fences are not as plentiful as they used to be. LRT

Schneeflock, *m, pl* **~e -** snow flake. **Es sin ken zwee ~e as gleiche-nanner sin.** There are no two snow flakes that are alike. LRT

Schneegans, *f, pl* **-gens -** snow goose. **Der Winder is am kumme, die Schneegens sin am fliege.** The winter is coming, the snow geese are flying. LRT

Schneegewidder, *n -* snow storm. **So en ~ seht mer net oft.** Such a snow storm one doesn't see often. LRT

Schneegruscht, *f -* snow crust. **Wann der Wind hatt blost, is mer froh wann der Schnee en gudi ~ hot.** When the wind blows hard, one is glad when the snow has a good snow crust (on top of it). LRT

schneegschtiwwerich, *adj -* of snow falling in squalls. **Die menscht Zeit wann's so ~ is,**

gebt's net en ganzi latt Schnee. Usually, snow squalls do not produce great amounts of snow. LRT

schneeich, *adj -* snowy. **Des ~ Wedder is gut fer's Land, awwer net so gut fer die Leit.** This snowy weather is good for the land (soil), but not so good for the people. LRT

Schneeluft, *f -* snow-laden air. **Denkt dir es gebt Schnee? Selli Luff schpiert wie en ~.** Do you think we'll have snow? That feels like a snow-laden air. LRT

Schneemann, *m -* snow man. **Guck mol, die Nochbere hen en grosser ~.** Look, the neighbors have a big snow man. LRT

Schneeschuh, *m -* snow shoe. **Unser ~ sin fer schee, mir hen sie uff die Wand ghengt.** Our snow shoes are for decoration, we hung them on the wall. LRT

Schneestarem, *m -* snow storm. **Sell waar en katzer ~.** That was a short snow storm. LRT

Schneevoggel, *m, pl* **-veggel -** snowbird, junco. **Es is schee fer sehne as die Schneeveggel net Sudd fliege.** It's nice to see that the snow birds don't fly south. LRT

Schneewasser, *n -* snow water. **~ is Wasser, ich denk es is ken Unnerschitt.** Snow water is water, I guess there is no difference. LRT

schneeweiss, *adj -* snow-white. **Ich gleich die Bariye sehne, wann sie ~ sin.** I like to see the mountains when they are white

with snow. LRT

Schneidbank, *m -* cutting bench. **Wie mei Paep en yunger Buh waar, hot er sei Daume schier abgschnidde uff der ~. Er hot yuscht ghunge an bissel Haut, awwer die Dokder hen en fescht genaeht un verhafdich er is fescht gheelt.** When my dad was young boy he almost cut his thumb off on a cutting bench. It was just hanging on by a little skin, but the doctors sewed it on and indeed it healed back. LRT

Schneider, *m -* tailor. **Heidesdaags sin net all die Leit was ~ heese Gleedermacher.** Now-a-days not all people whose name is "Schneider" are clothes makers. LRT

Schneider Kaundi - ✪ Snyder County, PA. **Eenich epper as in ~ wuhnt is waahrscheinlich deitsch.** Anybody who lives in Snyder Co. in probably of German background. LRT,4/21/2000

Schneiderschapp, *m, pl* **-schepp -** tailor's shop. KYG1960. **Schneiderschepp warre als wennicher.** Tailor shops are becoming fewer. LRT

Schneit, *f -* cutting edge of a tool. KYG2035. **Die ~ uff sellem Howwel is schtump.** The cutting edge of that plane is dull. LRT

Schneitgscharr, *n -* edged tool. KYG2035. **En Scheppmesser is en ~.** A draw knife is an edged tool. LRT

schnelle, *pp* **gschnellt -** to jerk,

crack. **Halt's yuscht aa, no grickscht dei Kopp gschnellt.** Just keep it up then, you'll get your head cracked sharply. LRT

schneppe - to tilt. *cf* **schtatze, umschtatze.** KYG2017

schneppere, *pp* **gschneppert** - to chatter. **Selli zwee hen der ganz Daag gschneppert.** Those two (persons) chattered all day. LRT,4/18/2000

schnepperich, *adj* - unstable (of boards). *cf* **wanke.** KYG2113

schneppisch, *adj* - unsteady (of mules). KYG2113

Schnickel, *m* - penis. LRT

Schniekdieb, *m* - sneak thief. KYG1996

schniekich, *adj* - persnickety. LRT. **Mei Kindsbuh is ~ mit seim Esse.** My grandson is persnickety with his eating. LRT

schnippse - to sob. **Guck mol, sell glee Buwli is am ~.** Look, that little boy is sobbing. (Leb Co) LRT

Schnitzboi, *m, f* - snitz pie. **Oui, es is nix bessers wie ~.** Oh, there is nothing better than snitz pie. LRT

schnitze - to tell a fib. = **Schnitz mache.** KYG1980

Schnitzelbank, *f* - shaving bench (to prepare shingles). **Die eensischt ~ as er hot is sei Singschtick.** The only shaving bench he has is the song called "**Schnitzelbank.**" LRT

Schnitzriwwelkuche, *m* - tart of

dried apples with sugar crumbs. KYG1871

schnock, *adj* - <*Engl* 1 snug. **Aldi, du hoscht awwer en ~er Gaund aa.** Wife, my, you have a snug dress on. LRT. **2** slender. **Ihre Gaund is ~.** Her dress is tight. *cf* **dinn.** LRT

schnuddle - to take strong drink. **Mer daed's net glaawe, awwer seller alt Mann is immer am Dramm ~.** One wouldn't believe it but that old man is always drinking whiskey. LRT

Schnuffler, *m* - spy. **Seller Hund is en guder ~, er kann eenicheppes finne.** That dog is a good hunter, he can find anything. LRT

Schnuppbax, *f, pl* **~e** - snuffbox. **~e kann mer ball immer sehne rausschtecke an de Mannsleit ihre Hosseseck.** Snuffboxes can usually be seen protruding from the pockets of men's pants pockets. LRT

Schnuppduwack, *m* - snuff tobacco. **~ is gifdich graad wie alle Duwack is.** Snuff is poisonous just as all tobacco is. LRT

schnuppe - to take snuff. KYG1961

Schnuppe, *m* - sniffles, runny nose. **Er hot der ~.** He has the sniffles. **Kind, mir sedde eppes duh, dei ~ is ordlich schlimm.** Child, we should do something, your running nose is pretty bad. LRT

Schnur, *f, pl* **Schnier** - twine, string, lace. KYG2083. **Der**

eensichscht Weg fer selli backeschteenich Mauer graad mache, is wann mer en feschdi ~ yuust.** The only way to make that brick wall straight, is to use a tight line. **En aagezogeni ~ is notwennich fer en Backeschteeleger.** A tight (drawn) cord is necessary for a brick layer. LRT

Schnutz[1], *m, pl* **Schnitz** - section of dried fruit. **Zu mir sin alle sadde Fruchtschnitz gut. Ich gleich ewwe Frucht.** To me all kinds of dried fruit sections are good. Indeed, I like fruit. LRT

Schnutz[2], *m* - term of endearment (for child). KYG1987. **Seller glee Buh is en siesser ~.** That little boy is a sweet child. LRT

Schockel-laefer, *m, pl* **~** - runner on a rocking chair. **Wann die ~ zu oft nass warre im Keller, duhne sie verfaule.** If the runners of the rocking chair get wet too often in the cellar, they will rot. LRT

Schoddebuhn, *f* - string bean. LRT/Leb

Schof-fens, *f* - sheep fence. **En ~ is ewwe en Fens.** A sheep fence is indeed a fence. LRT

Schofgleeder, *pl* - sheep's clothing. **Sie saage er is en Wolf in ~.** They say he is a wolf in sheep's clothing. LRT

Schofgnoddel, *m, pl* **-gnottle** - sheep excrement. **Schofgnottle sin gut fer der Hof.** Sheep manure is good for the yard. **Deel Leit hedde liewer -gnottle as wie Schofwoll.** Some people would rather have sheep manure than sheep wool. = **Schofmischt.** LRT

Schofhieder, *m* - shepherd. **Der Harr is mei ~.** The Lord is my shepherd. LRT

Schofhund, *m* - sheep dog. **Mir hen ken Schof ghat, no hen mir aa ken ~ gebreicht.** We had no sheep, so we didn't need a sheep dog. LRT

Schofscheerdaag, *m* - sheep-shearing day. **Sie hen gsaat, ich soll deheem bleiwe vun de Schul weil's ~ is.** They said I should stay home from school because it's sheep-shearing day. LRT

Schofscheere, *n* - sheep shearing. **Sie yuuse Leckdrick fer ~ heitdesdaags.** They use electricity for sheep shearing nowadays. LRT

schone, *refl* - to take care that one doesn't work too hard. KYG1960

Schoppdach, *n* - shed roof. **Es ~ rinnt.** The shed roof is leaking. LRT

Schoppe, *m* - neck. **am ~ nemme** - to take good hold of a person (by the neck). KYG1961

Schpaal, *m* - chip of stone. KYG1886. **Sell sin Schtee ~.** Those are chips of stone. LRT

Schpaltgscharr, *n* - splitting tools. KYG2035. **En Ax is en ~.** An ax is a splitting tool. LRT

schpankich, *adj* - <*Engl* **1** spunky, brave, spirited, daring. **Seller Buh is en ~ Ding, er**

browiert eenich eppes. That boy is a spunky thing, he'll try anything. **Er is ~er as er verschtennich is.** He is more daring than he is sensible. LRT. **2** tempered. KYG1982

Schpannsaeg, *f* - wood saw. **Die ~ un der Saegbock gehne zammer.** The wood saw and the sawhorse go together. LRT,4/11/2000

Schpannseel, *n* - tether. KYG1990

Schparreblock, *m* - brake block. **En ~, hatt gschpatt, kann hees warre.** A brake block, used hard, can get hot. LRT

Schparrkett, *f* - brake chain. **En verrissni ~ kennt zimmlich gfaehrlich sei.** A torn brake chain could be pretty dangerous. LRT

Schpeckdief, *n* - telescope. KYG1980

Schpeckdrauwe, *pl* - fox grapes. **Sie saage die Raguune gleiche die ~.** They say raccoons like fox grapes. LRT

schpeddele - to scoff. **Seller Mensch dutt immer ~, un ich bin's leedich.** That person is always scoffing and I'm tired of it. LRT. = **schpodde**

Schpeecht-scharefer, *m* - tool to point spokes. KYG2034. = **Schpeeche-scharefer.** LRT

schpeide, *pp* **gschpeidt** - to regret the loss of. **Es schpeidt mich, as ich mei goldner Ring verlore hab.** I regret the loss of my golden ring. LRT

Schpeidele, *pl* - gore (on a garment). **Sie hot en Laschder ~ im Schtock vun ihrem Gaund.** She has a lot of gores in the skirt of her dress. LRT

Schpeit, *m* - <*Engl* spite, rancor. **Ich will dir ken ~ winsche.** I don't want to wish you any rancor. LRT

Schpenglerei, *f* - **1** the work of a tinsmith. KYG2023. **2** tinsmith's shop. = **Schpenglerschapp.** KYG2024

schpettle - to sneer. **Sell waer net der Tscheck, wann er net bissel ~ daed.** That wouldn't be Jake if he didn't sneer a bit. LRT

Schpielsach, *f* - toy. **Der ganz Wuhnschtubb-bodde waar voll ~e.** The whole living room floor was full of toys. LRT

schpiere - to feel. LRT

Schpiggel, *m* - mirror. **Zu viel in der ~ gucke—was gut dutt sell?** Looking in the mirror too much—what good does that do? LRT

schpinne - to purr. **Harich mol, die Katz is am ~.** Just listen, the cat is purring. LRT

Schpinner, *m* - tendril. KYG1985

schpitze - to sharpen. **die Gatt ~** - to be on one's toes. KYG2030. **Mir sedde paar "pencils" ~.** We should sharpen a few pencils. LRT

Schpitzewettrich, *m* - slender plantain. *Plantago pusilla Nutt.* **Es maag drucke sei awwer der**

~ **waxt doch.** It may be dry but the narrow leafed plaintain grows anyway. LRT

schpitzich, *adj* - pointed, peaked. **Selli Schreibfeddere sin awwer ~.** Those writing pens are really pointed (sharp). LRT. **en ~ Gsicht** - a sharp face. **Kannscht du die Schtickel bissel ~ mache?** Can you make these stakes a bit pointed? LRT

schpodde, *pp* **gschpott** - to make fun of. **Yunger, schpott yuscht, du muscht denk der hatt Weg lanne!** Youngster, just make fun, I guess you'll have to learn (I think) the hard way! LRT

schpoddich, *adv* - mockingly. **Schwetz net so ~!** Don't talk so mockingly! LRT

Schpor, *m, pl* ~e - spur. **Seller Haahne hot ~e lenger as ich sei Lewe gsehne hab.** That rooster has spurs longer than I've ever seen. LRT

schpraddlich, *adv* - walking with the legs spread apart more than usual. **Yunger, laaf net so ~!** Young man, don't walk so sprattled [sprattled is an anglicization of the Dutch word **schpraddlich**]. LRT

schpranze, *refl* - to take a defensive attitude. *cf* **sich uffschpranze.** KYG1960

Schprausack, *m* - chaff sack. **Ich hab sei Lewe net uff me ~ gschlofe.** I have never in my life slept on a chaff sack. LRT

schprenge - to engage in intercourse. LRT

Schprichwatt, *n* - proverb. LRT

Schpriggel, *m* - tilt lath. *cf* **Waggeschpriggel.** KYG2017

Schpringbett, *n* - spring bed. **Sell ~ is mir liewer as wie en Schtrickbett.** I like that spring bed better than a rope bed. LRT

schpringe - 1 to swerve (change course quickly). **2** to run. **Ich kann net schtarick genunk ~ fer uffhalde mit ihm.** I can't run fast enough to keep up with him. LRT. **Heidesdaags duhne die Leit ganz iwwer die Welt schpringe.** Now-a-days the people run all over the world. LRT

Schpringer, *m* - a young boy, toddler. **Sell is vorkumme wie er yuscht en ~ waar.** That happened when he was just a child. LRT. **en gleener ~** - a tiny toddler. KYG2030. **Wie unser Suh yuscht en gleener ~ waar, hot er en Bruch ghat.** When our son was only a small toddler, he had a hernia. LRT

Schpringervieh, *n* - young cattle. **Sie hen ihre ~ naus uff die Weed geduh.** They put their young cattle out to pasture. LRT,4/21/2000

schpringich, *adj* - resilient. **Wann mer darich die Wiss laaft, kann mer schpiere as der Grund ~ is.** When one walks through the meadow, one can feel that the ground is resilient. LRT

Schprings-eeg, *f* - spring harrow. **Selli ~ hot net viel gebrocht uff die Vendu.** That spring harrow did not bring much at the sale. LRT

Schpringwagge, *n* - spring wagon. **Sie hen all sell Gaardeschtofft an der Marick gebrocht uff em ~.** They brought all that garden produce to the market on the spring wagon. LRT

Schpringwasser, *n* - spring water. **Sis ken Wasser besser wie gut ~.** There is no water better than good spring water. LRT

schpritze - to sprinkle (of rain). **Guck mol naus, sis am ~.** Look out there, it's sprinkling. LRT

Schpritzer, *m* - sprinkle (of rain). **Es gebt net viel Rege, sis yuscht en ~.** There will not be much rain, it's only a sprinkling. LRT

Schprosse, *m* - round rung (of a ladder). LRT

Schprung, *m* - leap, spring. **Der Hund hot en ~ gemacht fer der Haas fange, awwer er is em weckkumme.** The dog made a spring to catch the rabbit but it got away from him. LRT

Schpruusbaam, *m, pl* -baem - spruce tree. **Ich mehn die Colorado Schpruusbaem sin so schee.** I think the Colorado spruce trees are so pretty. LRT

Schpruusholz, *n* - spruce wood. **Es wunnert mich wie viel annerscht as ~ is vun Beintholz?** I wonder how much different spruce wood is from pine wood? LRT

Schpuchde, *pl* - jokes, pranks. **So ~ sin kinnisch!** Such pranks are childish! LRT

schpuckich, *adj* - unearthly. **Sell waar awwer en ~i Halloief Nacht.** But that was a spooky Halloween night. LRT

Schpundezappe, *m* - stopper. KYG1889

schraexe - to lean at an angle. **Den Baam misse mir ~ gehich der Wind.** We must lean this tree against the wind. LRT

schranke - to walk uneasily (when sick). KYG2100

schrankle - to walk unsteadily (from weakness). KYG2113

schranklich, *adj* - walking uneasily. **Seller alt Mann laaft arig ~.** That old man walks very uneasily. LRT

Schraub, *f* - screw. **Wann du en ~ do in die Wand drehscht, kenne mir des Pickder uffhenge.** If you put a screw here in the wall, we can hang up the picture. LRT,4/11/2000. **die ~ teit aaziehe** - to draw a screw tight. KYG2016. **Nemm net selli ~, sie is verletzt.** Don't take (use) that screw, it is damaged. LRT. **Ya, des is ariyets en ~ los.** Yes, there is something the matter somewhere. LRT,4/18/2000

schrecklich, *adj* - awful. **Sell is ~ der Weg wie er faahrt.** It is terrible the way he drives. LRT. **Seller Wind Schtarem waar ~.** That wind storm was awful. LRT

Schreibbabier, *n* - writing paper. **Maed, dir hett die Schularewet zu duh un dir hett ken ~, was nau?** Girls, you have all this school work to do and you have no writing paper! What now? LRT,4/18/2000

Schreibdisch, *m* - writing table. **In unserem Haus is der ~ der Kichedisch.** In our house the writing table is the kitchen table. LRT,4/18/200

Schreibschleet, *f* - writing slate. **En ~ is nix waert uni Greid.** A writing slate is worthless without chalk. LRT,4/18/2000

Schreiner, *m* - carpenter. **Seller ~ dutt immer recht gudi Arewet.** That carpenter always does real good work. (His workmanship is always very good.) LRT,4/11/2000

Schreinerkischt, *f* - 1 tool chest. *cf* **Gscharrkischt.** KYG2035. 2 carpenter tool chest. LRT

Schreiwer, *m* - scribe.

Schreiwes, *n* - written agreement. **Sei ~ mehnt nix, wann nix uff em Babier is, as wie sei Naame.** His written agreement is worthless if the paper is blank except for his name. LRT, 4/18/2000

schriefe, *pp* **gschrieft** - *<Engl.* to sheriff, get the sheriff after someone. **Sie hen ihn gschrieft fer sei Taxgeld griege.** They sheriffed him to get his tax money. LRT

Schrift, *f* - Scripture. **epper gelannt in de ~** - theologian. KYG1993. **Die Heilich ~ hot all die Gebode as mir breiche.** The Holy Scriptures have all the commandments that we need. LRT

Schriftlehr, *f* - theology. KYG1994

Schriftler, *m* - theologue. KYG1993

schriftlich, *adj* - according to Scripture. **Fer dei Nochber liewe is ~.** To love your neighbor is scriptural. LRT

schriftmaessich, *adv* - scriptural. **Sei Gebreddich is ~.** His preaching is scriptural. LRT

Schritt, *m, pl* **~e** - pace, step. **Er geht ee ~ uff emol.** He goes one step at a time. LRT. **en ~ nemme** - to take a step. KYG1961. **sei aerschde ~e mache** - to take one's first steps. KYG1962. **Es nemmt meh as ee ~ fer en Meil mache.** It takes more than one step to make a mile. LRT. **den ~ geh** - to walk the pace (of a horse). KYG2159. **Er geht ee ~ uff emol.** He goes one step at a time. LRT

schrittweis, *adv* - step by step. **Er is so langsam un ~ darich der Busch geloffe.** Slowly and step by step he walked through the woods. LRT

Schtaakefens, *f, pl* **~e** - stake and rider fence, zig-zag fence, worm fence. **~e sin arig raar heidesdaags.** Worm fences (made of chestnut wood) are very scarce nowadays. LRT,4/18/2000. **Mer seht ganz wennich ~e heidesdaags.** One sees very few zig-zag fences nowadays. LRT,4/21/2000

schtaakefensich, *adv* - zig-zag. KYG2266

Schtaal, *m* - steel. **Es nemmt guder ~ fer gudi Messere**

mache. Good steel is required to make good knives. LRT

Schtaalkumpanie, *f* - steel company. **Er hot sich neigschafft an de ~, nau hot er sex Daag die Woch Arewet.** He worked his way up with the steel company; now he has work six days a week. LRT,4/11/2000

Schtaalmiehl, *f* - steel mill. **Mei Paep hot aagfange schaffe an die ~ wie er varzeh Yaahr alt waar.** My dad began to work at a steel mill when he was fourteen years old. LRT

Schtaalring, *m* - steel ring. **Sell Halsyoch hot en ~an yederem End.** That neck yoke has a steel ring at each end. LRT

Schtaalwaricks, *n, pl* **-wariyer** - steel works, steel plant. **Die Schtadt Pittsbarig hot als en latt -wariyer ghat.** The city of Pittsburgh used to have a lot of steel industries. LRT

Schtaalwoll, *f* - steel wool. **~ is gut fer die eisne Kessel ausbutze.** Steel wool is good to clean out the iron kettles. LRT. **Mir sedde bissel ~ iwwer selli Schiddelaefer reiwe fer sie glitzere mache.** We should rub a little steel wool over those sled runners to make them shine. LRT

Schtaareschtengel, *m* - tall meadow grasses and weeds. KYG1965

Schtachel, *f, pl* **~e** - thorn, prickle. KYG2001. **en ~ heecher geh** - to go up a notch. **Selli ~e sin awwer en Pein, wann mer sie in die Gleeder grickt.** Those thorns are a real

affliction when one gets them in his clothes. **Seller Roseschtock hot en latt ~e.** That rose plant has a lot of thorns. LRT

schtachle - to attempt to sting. KYG1880

schtachlich, *adj* - thorny. **Selli Roseschteck sin arig schtachlich.** Those rose plants are very thorny. LRT.

schtaerde - < *Engl* to start. **~ schaffe** - to set to work. **Du kannscht ~ der Mischtschpraeher laade.** You can begin to load the manure spreader. LRT

schtalle - to get along together. KYG2030

Schtallwand, *f, pl* **-wend** - wall of stall. **Mir misse die -wend uff-fixe.** We need to repair the stable walls. LRT

schtambe - 1 to tamp (powder in a gun). 2 to tamp (dirt in a posthole). KYG1966. **Ich will seller Fenseposchde gut fescht ~.** I want to tamp that fence post real firmly. LRT

schtamble - to tamp. = **schtambe, nunnerschtambe.** KYG1966

Schtamploch, *n, pl* **-leecher** - hole made in ground by horse's stomping. KYG1886. **An'm Blatz wu Geil oft schtehne, datt kann mer sich druff verlosse, as -leecher sin.** At a place where horses often stand, there one can depend on it, there will be stomp holes. LRT

schtandhafdich, *adj* - sturdy. **Sell is en ~er Disch.** That is a

sturdy table. LRT. **Es nemmt en ~i Fens fer selli Oxe drinhalde.** A sturdy fence is required to keep those steers in. LRT. **Eechebaem sin ordlich ~.** Oak trees are quite stable. LRT

Schtann, *f* - end of a piece of timber. KYG2018

schtannehell, *adj* - starlit. **Sis ~ denowed.** It's starlit tonight. LRT

schtannhell, *adj* - unclouded. = **glaar.** KYG2093. **Guck mol wie schee ~ as der Himmel is.** Look how nice and clear (star-bright) the sky is. LRT

schtannich, *adj* - starry. **Sis schee ~ die Nacht.** It's nice and starry this night. LRT

Schtannriesel! - thunderation! (*interj.*) = **Dunnerwedder!** KYG2011

Schtarem, *m* - storm. **Es Vieh is dodarich gerennt wie en ~.** The cattle tore through here like a storm. LRT

schtareme - to take by storm. KYG1962

schtaremich, *adj* - 1 stormy. **Is des ~ Wedder awwer net eppes?** Isn't this stormy weather something? LRT. **2** tempestuous. KYG1982. **Des waar en ~er Daag.** This was a tempestuous day. LRT

Schtaremwind, *m* - tempest. KYG1982. **Der ~ waar am blose.** The tempest winds were active. LRT

Schtaremwolk, *f* - storm cloud. **Selle waar awwer en schwartzi**

~. That was a black storm cloud. LRT

schtarewe - to die. **bletzlich (unbedenkt, unverhofft) ~** - to die unexpectedly. KYG2101. **Der Nochber is arig unverhofft gschtarewe.** The neighbor died very unexpectedly. LRT

schtarick, *adj* - strong. **Es wunnert em wie seller yung Karl so ~ is warre.** One wonders how that young guy got so strong. **Die hadder as du schaffscht, die ~er as du waert.** The harder you work, the stronger you get. LRT. **~ mache** - to toughen. KYG2042. **Selli Buwe sin ~.** Those boys are strong. LRT

Schtarick, *f* - starch. **Sei Hemm brauch meh ~.** His shirt needs more starch. LRT

schtaricke - to starch. **Die Woch hen mir ken Gleeder zu ~.** This week we have no clothes to starch. LRT

schtaricker mache - to strengthen. **Es nemmt paar Schteiber, sell macht's viel schtaricker.** What's needed are several props that will make it much stronger. LRT

Schtarickungsmiddel, *n* - tonic. KYG2034

Schtarre, *m* - visible part of decayed tooth. KYG2035. **Er hot nix meh im Maul as wie schwatzi ~.** He has nothing left in his mouth but black, decayed stumps of teeth. LRT

Schtarrer, *m* - poker. **Der ~ is verboge gange, nau daed**

mer'n yuscht so gut weckschmeisse. The poker has become bent, and now we'd just as well throw it away. LRT

schtarrkeppich, *adj* - uncooperative. KYG2094. **Yunger, sei net so ~.** Young man, don't be so stubborn. LRT

Schtarrkopp, *m* - stubborn person. **Er will gaar nix duh; er is en rechder ~.** He doesn't want to do anything at all; he is a real stubborn person. LRT

schtattfinne - to take place. = **ablaafe, vorgeh.** KYG1961

schtatze, *pp* **gschtatzt** - to fall from. **Ich bin mol vum Hoiwagge gschtatzt.** I once fell from the hay wagon. LRT

Schtatze, *m* - stub (of a tree), stump. **Sie hen hochi ~ schteh glosst im Welschkannfeld.** They allowed tall stubble to stand in the corn field. LRT = **Schtumpe**

schtauche, *pp* **gschtaucht** - to strain (wrench). **Er hot sei Rick wiescht gschtaucht grickt.** He got his back wrenched (jolted) nastily. LRT. **Halt sell yuscht aa! No grickscht dich in der Bauch gschtaucht!** Just keep that up! Then you'll get jolted in the stomach! LRT. **Sei Unfall mit seinere Kaer hot ihn dod gschtaucht.** His accident with his car wrenched him to death. LRT,4/18/2000

schteche, *pp* **gschtoche** - **1** to stab. **Sie hen ihn in der Buckel gschtoche.** They stabbed him in the back. LRT. **2** to stick. **Ich will's ihm ~.** I'll give him a tip (warning). KYG2024. **Der**

Dokder hot en Nodel in mei Aarem gschtoche. The doctor stuck a needle in my arm. LRT. **3** to sting. **Selli Iem hot dich gschtoche.** You were stung by that bee. LRT

Schtecher, *m* - **1** sting of a bee. KYG1880. **2** the stinger of a bee.

Schteche(s)[1], *n* - sharp pain in general. **Ich wees net was letz is, ich hab der ganze Daag ~ do in meim rechtse aarm ghat.** I don't know what's wrong, I've had stinging pain here in my right arm all day. LRT. **Sell ~ in deine Bruscht kennt dei Hatz sei.** That sharp stabbing pain in your chest could be your heart. LRT

Schteche(s)[2], *n* - stitches in (one's) side. KYG1882. **En latt alti Leit wisse was des ~ is, was sie ebmols ganz iwwer ihre Kareber griege.** A lot of old people know what these stitches are that they sometimes get all over their body. LRT

Schteches[3], *n* - pleurodynia neuritis. **Nau wann ich siwwezich yaahr alt bin wees ich was ~ is.** Now that I am seventy (years old) I know what pleurodynia neuritis is. LRT

Schtechmesser, *m* - sticking knife (in butchering). KYG1878. **Wann mer wees was mer am duh is, nemmt's ken gross ~ fer's Blut laafe mache.** If one knows what he is doing, it doesn't take a big sticking knife to make the blood flow. LRT

schtecke - **1** to stick, set. **Schteck's in dei Sack!** Put it in your pocket. LRT. **Der Glaas-**

schtopper schteckt in selle Weiboddel. The glass stopper is stuck in that wine bottle. LRT. **2** to plant. **Zwiwwle ~ -** to set onions. **Es is Friehyaahr un Zeit fer Zwiwwle ~.** It's spring and time to set onions. LRT.

schtecke bleiwe, *pp* **schtecke gebliwwe** - to be stalled (with a load). **Er hot heemgeh welle in sellem Schneeschtarem, awwer er is schtecke gebliwwe.** He wanted to go home in that snowstorm, but he got stuck. LRT. **Mir sin datt rumgefaahre bis mir schteckegebliwwe sin.** We drove around there until we got stuck. LRT

Schteckebuhn, *f* - pole bean. LRT/Leb.Co.

schteckeschteif, *adj* - stiff as a board. KYG1879

schteckich, *adj* - shooting. **~i Schmatze.** Shooting pains. LRT

Schteddel, *n* - town. **Sell ~ hot etliche gudi Essbletz.** That town has several good eating places (restaurants). LRT. **~ hinausgeh** - to go to the back part of town. **~ nausgeh - 1** to go through town. **2** to go into town. KYG2044

Schteddelbump, *f* - town pump. KYG2044. **Wann's Schteddel en Bump hot, kann mer eenichi Zeit Wasser griege; ich gleich sell.** When a town has a pump, one can get water anytime; I like that. LRT

Schteddelche, *n - dim of* **Schteddel.** town. KYG2043. = **Schteddtli.** Leb. Co./ LRT

Schteddelglarick, *m* - town clerk. KYG2044

Schteddelrutsch, *f* - town gossip. KYG2044

Schtee-arewet, *f* - stone work. KYG1888. **Er schafft in em Bruch un dutt ~.** He works in a quarry and does stone work. LRT

Schtee-breche, *n* - quarrying stone. KYG1886. **Verlenger zerick waar ~ en haddi Arewet.** Years ago, quarrying stone was a tough job. LRT

Schtee-eise, *n, pl~* - iron bar used in quarrying stone. KYG1886. **~ sin gut fer Schtee uffgewichde.** Iron bars are good to force (to leverage) rock upward. LRT

Schteeblatt, *n* - large, flat stone. KYG1886. = **Flachschtee.** LRT

schteeblind, *adj* - stone-blind. = **schtockblind.** KYG1886

Schteebloder, *f* - stone blister. KYG1886

Schteebohrer, *m* - borer for making holes in stone. KYG1886. **Ebmols muss en Brunnebohrer aa en ~ sei, wann er Felse drefft.** Sometimes a well borer has to be a stone borer if he hits rocks. LRT

Schteebrecher, *m* - stone crusher. KYG1887. **En ~ koscht en latt Geld.** A stone crusher costs a lot of money. LRT

Schteebrick, *f* - stone bridge. KYG1886. **Es nemmt en Schteemauerer fer en ~ baue.** It takes a stone mason to build a stone bridge. LRT

Schteebruch, *m, pl ~brich* - stone quarry. KYG1888. **Deel Schteebrich warre voll Wasser, un no mache sie en guder Blatz fer hiegeh fische.** Some stone quarries fill up with water and then they make a good place to go fishing. LRT

schteedaab, *adj* - stone-deaf. = **schtockdaab.** KYG1887

Schteedrepp, *f, pl ~e* - stone step. KYG1888. **~e sin besser, in viel Wege, wie Holzdreppe.** Stone steps, in many ways, are better than wood steps. LRT

Schteefens, *f, pl ~e* - stone fence. KYG1887. **~e duhne arig langsam weckfaule.** Stone fences rot way (deteriorate) very slowly. LRT. *cf* **Schteemauer**

Schteeg, *f, pl ~e* - stairs. **Yunger, mach dich die ~ nuff graad nau!** Young man, you go up the stairs (to bed) right now! **Die ~ is hinnich selle Dier.** The stairs are behind the door. **All die ~e sedde en Riggel hawwe.** All stairs should have a railing. LRT

Schteegekarepet, *m* - stair carpet. **Der ~ waert hatt gewore.** The stair carpet gets worn hard. LRT

Schteegruck, *m* - stone jug. KYG1887

Schteehacker - stone cutter. **Seller ~ macht scheeni Arewet.** That stone cutter does nice work. LRT

Schteehammer, *m* - stone

hammer. KYG1887. =
Schteemanwerkhammer.

schteehatt, *adj* - hard as stone.
KYG1886. [I'd rather say: **so
hatt wie'n schtee.** Hard as a
stone. LRT]

Schteehaufe, *m, pl* **-heife** - pile
of stone. KYG1886. **Uff die
Bauereie heidesdaags seht mer
nimmi viel -heife.** On farms,
now-a-days one doesn't see
many stone piles. LRT

Schteehitt, *f* - stone cabin.
KYG1887

Schteekeidel, *m* - stone wedge.
KYG1888

Schteekohle, *pl* - stone coal.
KYG1887

Schteemaurer, *m* - stone
mason. *cf* **Rauhmaurer,
Schteemeeschder.** KYG1887

schteene - to remove from fruit.
Kann ~ - to remove stones of
fruit. KYG1886. **Kannscht du
helfe die Kasche ~?** Can you
help remove the stones from the
cherries? LRT

schteene, *adj* - stone. =
schteenich. KYG1886

schteenich, *adj* - stony.
KYG1888. **Sell Feld is ~.** That
field is stony. LRT

schteeniche, *pp* **gschteenicht** -
to throw stones at. KYG1886.
**Die Buwe waare schlecht, sie
hen die Hinkel gschteenicht.**
The boys were bad, they stoned
the chickens. LRT. **Er waar an
die Vendu gange, un uff em
Weg heem hen paar Buwe ihn
gschteenicht.** He had gone to

the sale, and on his way home a
pair of boys threw rocks at him.
LRT. **Selli schlechde Buwe hen
sell glee Maedli gschteenicht.**
Those bad (misbehaved) boys
stoned (threw stones at) that
little girl. LRT.

Schteeroi, *f* - stone row fence.
KYG1888

Schteeschlidde, *m* - stone sled.
KYG1888. **~ sin aa ebmols
Mischtschlidde.** Stone sleds are
also sometimes manure sleds.
LRT

Schteeschpaale, *pl* - clumps of
stone. LRT

Schteeschteeg, *f* - stone stile.
**En ~ iwwer en Fens seht mer
net oft.** One doesn't see a stone
stile to cross a fence very often.
LRT

Schteeschwamm, *m* - rock
tripe. = **Felseschwamm. En ~ is
nix viel wert.** A rock tripe is not
worth much.

Schteet-tax, *m, pl* **~e** - state tax.
**Ich bin froh as der ~ net
heecher is.** I'm glad the state tax
isn't any higher. LRT

Schteetbressent, *f* - state prison.
Sie hen ihn fatt in die ~ geduh.
They put him away in the state
prison. LRT

Schteetweg, *m, pl* **~e** - state
highway. **Unser ~e sin ordlich
gut heidesdaags.** Our state
highways are in pretty good
condition now-a-days. LRT

Schteewagge, *m, pl* **-wegge** -
wagon rigged for hauling stones.
KYG1886. **-wegge misse
schtandhaft gebaut sei.**

Wagons rigged to haul stones
must be built sturdily. LRT

Schteewaref, *m* - stone's throw.
KYG1888

schteh - to stand. **net gut ~ -** to
be in financial straits. **Sei
Bissniss schteht net arig gut.**
His business is not in very good
standing. LRT. **Wie schtehscht
du mit ihm alleweil?** How do
you stand with him these days?
LRT. **im Weg ~ -** to thwart.
KYG2012. **~ net in meim Weg,
wann ich schaffe will.** Don't
stand in my way, when I want to
do work. LRT. **Die Uhr schteht.**
The clock has stopped.
KYG1889. **Die Uhr is ~
gebliwwe.** The clock stopped.
LRT. **hinnich eppes ~ -** to stand
behind something. KYG2099.
**Ich hab's Kaundi gfrogt fer
uns en neie Schtross mache;
schteht dir Leit mir dehinner?**
I asked the County to make us a
new road; will you folks support
me? LRT

schtehle - to steal. **Es siwwet
Gebott saagt, mer soll net ~.**
The Seventh Commandment
says thou shalt not steal. LRT

Schtehler, *m, pl* **~** - stealer. **~
will ich kenner.** A stealer I do
not want. LRT

Schtehlerei, *f* - thievery.
KYG1997. **Wie bringt mer en
End zu daere ~?** How does one
bring an end to this thievery?
LRT

schtehleswaert, *adv* - worth
stealing. KYG2251. **~, ich wees
nix wie sell.** Worth stealing, I
know nothing like that.
LRT,4/18/2000

schteibere, *refl* - to refuse to do something. **Seller Mann schteibert sich immer, wann mer'n frogt fer eppes duh.** That man always refuses when one asks him to do something. LRT

schteif, *adj* - **1** stiff. **Sis Zeit as mir der Dokder rufe fer den ~e Gaul.** It's time we call the veterinarian for this stiff horse. LRT. **2** tense, stubborn. KYG1986. **Er is ~gnickisch.** He is stiff necked (stubborn). LRT. **Mei Hals is bissel ~ de mariye.** My neck is a bit stiff this morning. LRT

schteif mache - to stiffen. KYG1879. **Mach dei Aarem schteif.** Stiffen your arm. LRT

schteifgschtarickt, *adj* - stiffly starched. KYG1879. **Die Mamm hot mei Hemmer zu ~.** Mother starched my shirts too stiffly. LRT

schteifhalsich, *adj* - stiff-necked. **Er is en ~er, schtarrkeppicher Mensch.** He is a recalcitrant, stubborn person. LRT

Schteifheit, *f* - stiffness. *cf* **Wasserreh.** KYG1879

Schteifkett, *f, pl* ~e - stay chain. **Wann die Geil bissel wild sin, hett mer besser ~e.** If the horses are a bit wild, one had better have stay chains. LRT

Schteigbiggel, *m* - stirrup. **En ~ is abgerisse vun seim Saddel.** A stirrup is torn off on his saddle. LRT

Schteigdreppe, *pl* - stone steps for mounting horse. =

Schteigschtee. KYG1888

Schtellbord, *n* - top board (on a farm wagon). KYG2037

schtelle, *pp* **gschtellt** - to set. **Mir hen zwee Falle gschtellt.** We set two traps. LRT

schtelle, *refl* - to stand still. **Schtell dich!** - Hold still! (said to a cow while milking). KYG1880. **Kuh, wann ich dich melke soll, dann schtell dich!** Cow, if you want me to milk you, then stand still! LRT

Schteltz, *f, pl* ~e - stilt. KYG1880. **Seller yung Mann laaft gut uff ~e.** That young man walks well on stilts. LRT

schtempe, *pp* **gschtempt** - to affix a postage stamp. **Hoscht du seller Brief gschtempt?** Did you stamp that letter? LRT

schtende - to stand. **sei Grund ~** - to take a firm position. KYG1961

Schtengel, *m* - plant stem. LRT. = **Blanzeschtamm**

Schteppe, *n* - stitching. KYG1883

Schtettler, *m, pl* **-leit** - townsman. KYG2044. **Die ~ hen drei Kariche.** The townspeople have three churches. LRT

Schtibbli, *n* - *dim* of **Schtubb.** small room. LRT/Leb

Schtich, *m, pl* ~ - stitch. **Es hot fimf ~ genumme fer sei Schlitz zunaehe.** It took five stitches to close his slit. LRT. **Sie hen ihm im ~ gelosst.** They left him in

the lurch. LRT. **~ halde** - to hold tally. KYG1966. *Proverb:* **En zeitlicher ~ schpaart neine.** A stitch in time saves nine. LRT

schtichle, *pp* **gschtichelt** - to hint (in an insinuating manner). **Du bischt immer am ~, awwer ferwas?** You are always hinting, but for what? **Er hot gschtichelt, er daed sie vielleicht heiere.** He hinted that perhaps he might marry her. LRT. = **fetzle**

Schtickel, *m, pl* ~ - stake. **Wie viel ~ nemmt's fer en Zelt uffhewe?** How many stakes does it take to hold up a tent? LRT

Schtickelfens, *f* - stockade. KYG1883. *cf* **Schtaagefens** - post and rider fence. LRT

schtickerich, *adj* - **1** thick and sticky. KYG1995. **2** consisting of many pieces. **Seller Deppich waar arig ~.** That quilt consisted of many pieces (patches). LRT

schtickich, *adj* - stuffy. **Mach's Fenschder uff, es schpiert ~ dohin.** Open the window, it feels stuffy in here. LRT

schtickle - to do patchwork. = **schtickere.** [**schtickere (schtickle)** and **gwilde,** *qv,* are the two steps in making quilts.] LRT

Schtickli, *n* - *dim* of **Schtick.** a little piece. **Darf ich en ~ Kaes hawwe?** May I have a little bit of cheese? **Darf ich en ~ Babier hawwe?** May I have a scrap of paper? LRT

schtickweis, *adv* - piecemeal.

Er hot sei Arewet so ~ geduh grickt. He got his work done piecemeal. LRT

Schtiefbruder, *m, pl* **-brieder** - step-brother. **Esel sin -brieder zu die Geil.** Mules are stepbrothers to the horses. LRT

Schtiefdaadi, *m* - step-father. **~ odder net, er is mei Daadi.** Stepfather or not, he is my father. LRT

Schtiefeldre, *pl* - step-parents. **En latt Leit hen ~.** Lots of people have step-parents. LRT

Schtiefkind, *n* - step-child. **Seller Mann gleicht sei ~.** That man likes his step-child. LRT

Schtiefsuh, *m* - step-son. **Er is schtolz mit seim ~.** He is proud of his step-son. LRT

schtiffle, *pp* **is gschtiffelt** - to walk stiffly (as is wearing boots). **Ich bin darich der Dreck gestiffelt in meine neie Schtiffel.** I waded through the mud in my new boots. LRT

schtill, *adv* - quiet, still, yet. KYG1880. **Die Kinner waare der ganz Owed schee ~.** The children were nice and quiet all evening. LRT. *cf* **als, als noch, noch, doch**

schtillhalde - to hold still. KYG1880. **Halt dich schtill!** Hold still! LRT

schtillschteh - to stand still. KYG1880. **Schteh schtill, so as ich dei Schuh binne kann.** Stand still so I can tie your shoes. LRT

Schtimm, *f* - voice. **dicki ~**

throaty voice. KYG2008. **Er hot en diefi ~.** He has a deep voice. LRT

schtimme - to tune (any instrument). KYG2074. **Mir hen unser Glafier ~ glosst.** We had our piano tuned. LRT

Schtimmgawwel, *f, pl* **~e** - tuning fork. KYG2074. **Mer muss gut acht gewwe uff ~e.** One must take good care of tuning forks. LRT. = **Schtimmschtock**

Schtimmrecht, *n* - right to vote. **Er is alt genunk fer sei ~ hawwe.** He is old enough to have the right to vote. LRT

Schtimpel, *n* - small remainder. **Es waar ee ~ vun eenre Roll Dachbabier iwwerich gwest.** There was one remnant of one roll of roofing paper left over. LRT

Schtinkbock, *m* - **1** stink pot. **2** stinkbug. = **Schtinkkeffer.** KYG1881

schtinke - to stink. **nooch eppes ~** - to stink of something. KYG1881. **Sell schtinkt zu arig fer mich.** That stinks too bad for me. LRT

Schtinker, *m* - term of opprobrium for person. KYG1881. **Seller Buh is en ~, er hot der Hund losgelosst.** That boy is a stinker, he let the dog loose. LRT

schtinkich, *adj* - smelly, stinking. **Sell Briwwi waar ~.** That outhouse was smelly. LRT. **die ~schde Siggeretts** - the stinkiest cigarettes. KYG1881. **Zu mir is nix ~er as en**

Restaurant voll Siggerettraucher. To me there is noting more stinky than a restaurant full of cigarette smokers. LRT

Schtippel, *m* - tipple. KYG2024

Schtippelschtang, *f* - tipstaff (in a drama). KYG2025

Schtitz, *f* - top hat. KYG2038

Schtitzhut, *m* - stove pipe hat, top hat. **Ich gleich ihn sehne mit seim ~ aa.** I like to see him wearing his stove pipe hat. **Sei ~ Hut is verhaffdich glitzerich.** His top hat is really shiny. LRT

schtiwwle - to walk stiffly (as if wearing boots). KYG2158. = **schtiffle**

schtock-englisch, *adj* - thoroughly English. KYG2001

schtocke - **1** to make a stack. **Mir duhne all des Schtroh ~.** We are stacking all this straw. LRT. **Wann die Scheier voll is, misse mir's Schtroh ~.** If the barn is full, we'll have to stack the straw (out in the field). LRT. **2** to walk rapidly with a cane. KYG2159

Schtocker, *m* - stacker (ricker at thrashing). **Er is der ~.** He is the straw stacker. LRT

schtockschtill, *adj* - absolutely still. KYG1880

schtoddere - to stammer. **Ebmols dutt er so schlimm ~, mer kann ihn schier gaar net verschteh.** Sometimes he stammers so badly, one can hardly understand him. LRT

Schtoffel, *m* - dim of **Christopher.** KYG2283

Schtofft, *n* - stuff. **All des ~ was mir uff em ewwerscht Schpeicher hen, misse mir los warre.** All this stuff that we have in the attic, we need to get rid of. LRT

schtolpere - to trip, stumble. KYG2062. **En latt Leit ~ iwwer selli hoch Diereschwell.** Many people stumble over that high doorsill. LRT

schtolperich, *adj* - prone to stumble. **Des is en ~ Eck.** This is a corner where one is prone to stumble (due to the clutter). LRT

Schtoppelfeld, *n* - stubble field. **Sell waar als en Weezefeld, nau is es en ~.** That used to be a wheat field; now it's a stubble field. LRT

Schtorbank, *f* - store bench. KYG1890. **Ich hab en ~ gsehne as mol en Karichebank waar.** I saw a store bench that once was a church bench. LRT

Schtorbankunnerhewer, *m* - person who "holds down" a bench in a country store. (*facet* for those who loaf in store.) KYG1890

Schtorbax, *f, pl* ~**e** - store box. KYG1890. **Ich duh mei Schuh in's Kemmerli in die ~e wu sie drin kumme sin.** I put my shoes (away) in the closet in the store boxes in which they (originally) came. LRT

Schtorbill, *f* - store bill. KYG1890

Schtordor, *n* - store door.

KYG1890. **Eb die Schtore air-conditioning ghat hen, hen die Schtordiere aa Mickediere ghat.** Before the stores had air conditioning, the store doors also had fly-screened doors. LRT. = **Schtordier**

Schtorfenschderli, *n* - small store window. **Epper hot sell ~ verbroche.** Someone broke that little store window. LRT

Schtorglarick, *m* - store clerk. **Fer ~ sei is ken Suddelarewet.** Being a store clerk is not dirty (wet) work. LRT,4/11/2000

Schtorhalderei, *f* - storekeeping. **Die ~ nemmt en latt Zeit.** This storekeeping business takes a lot of time. LRT

Schtorhaus, *n* - storehouse. KYG1890

Schtorkipper, *m* - storekeeper. **Mei Grempaep Peiffer waar en ~.** My grandfather Peiffer was a storekeeper. LRT

Schtorkuche, *m, pl* ~ - store-bought cake. KYG1890. **Deel ~ sin recht gut.** Some store bought cakes are real good. LRT

Schtorsach, *pl* ~**e** - store wares. **Die Fraa is heemkumme mit em Kareb voll ~e.** My wife came home with a basket full of wares (store merchandise). **Die beschde ~e sin die was mer esse kann.** The best store wares are the edible ones. LRT

Schtortee, *m* - store-bought tea. KYG1974. **~ soll gut sei fer em.** Store-bought tea is supposed to be healthful. LRT

schtodderich, *adv* - stutteringly.

Er schwetzt so ~. He talks so stutteringly. LRT

Schtowwerichkeit, *f* - stubbornness. **Sei ~ verzannt mich bissel.** His stubbornness angers me a bit. LRT

Schtowwerkopp, *m* - stubborn head. **~, Schtarrkopp, Bullkopp, hees ihn was du witt, ich gleich ihn doch.** ~, Schtarrkopp, Bullkopp, call him what you will, I like him anyway. LRT

schtowwrich, *adj* - refractory. **Er is en ~er Bullkopp.** He is an obstinate, bull-headed person. LRT

Schtraahle, *m, pl* ~ - **1** stroke of lightning. **Mer hot Helling gsehne un Dimmle gheert, awwer mer hot ken ~ gsehne. Der Gwidderschtarem waar zu weit weck un mir hen ken Regge grickt.** One could see flashing and hear the thunder, but one could see no lightning streaks. The thunderstorm was too far away and there was no rain. **2** a flash. **3** a bolt. LRT

schtraalich, *adj* - radiant. **Sell Wedderleeche den Owed waar awwer ~.** That lightning this evening was really radiant (bolts everywhere). LRT

Schtraam, *m, pl* **Schtraeme** - shaft of light. **Ich wunner wu seller hell ~ beikummt.** I wonder where that shaft of light is coming from. LRT. *cf* **Helling**

schtrack, *adj* - straight. **Er is en ~er, gut-guckicher, yunger Kall.** He is a straight, good-looking fellow. LRT

schtracks, *adv* - straightway. **Er is graad ~ zu die Dier neigeloffe.** He walked straightaways through the door. LRT

schtraeppe - to strop (a razor). **Der Balwier dutt sei Balwiermesser ~.** The barber strops his straight razor. LRT

schtraff, *adj* - stiff. = **schtarr, schteif.** KYG1879

Schtrang¹, *m, pl* **Schtreng** - trace (part of harness). **iwwer der ~ hacke (schlagge)** - to kick over the traces. = **iwwer die Schnur hacke.** KYG2045. **Wann mer en Gaul eischpanne will, muss mer der ~ uff yeder Seit feschthenke.** In order to hitch a horse, one has to hook fast the trace on each side. LRT

Schtrang², *m, pl* **Schtreng** - 1 thread put up in skeins and hanks. KYG2003. **Sie hot heit paar Schtreng Gaarn gekaaft.** Today she bought a few skeins of yarn. LRT. **2** trace. **Er hot ewwe mol widder iwwer die Schtreng ghackt.** Once again he jumped over the traces [of a horse; of an errant husband.] LRT,4/18/2000

schtratze - to strut. **Der Weg wie er schtratzt, kann mer sehne as er en schtolzer Mann is.** The way he struts, one can see that he is a proud man. LRT

schtraube - to ruffle. **Seller Haahne dutt immer sei Feddere ~, wann er bissel bees watt.** That rooster always ruffles his feathers whenever he becomes a bit angry. LRT

schtrawwle, *pp* **gschtrawwelt** - to struggle. **Mit Ernscht hot er gschtrawwelt.** He struggled in earnest. LRT

Schtreech¹, *m* - blow. **En ~ uff die Naas dutt weh.** A blow on the nose hurts. LRT

Schtreech², *m* - stroke. **aus ~ sei** - to be out of tune. KYG2074. **Die Uhr hot ee ~ gschlagge. Mehnt sell as es ee Uhr is?** The clock struck one stroke. Does that mean that it's one o'clock? LRT

Schtreefe, *m* - stripe. **Er hot en ~ Blut uff seine Schtann.** He has a stripe of blood on his forehead. LRT

Schtreefgaarn, *n* - two-handed net (for use under stream banks). KYG2085

schtreefich, *adj* - 1 striped. **Sie hot en ~er Rock aa.** She is wearing a striped coat. LRT. **2** striated. **Ihre Kieh sin rot ~.** Their cows are red-striped. LRT. **3** streaky. **Sell Aaschtreiches guckt ~.** That painting (paint job) looks streaky. LRT

schtreichle - to pat, stroke. **Er gleicht sei Hund ~.** He likes to stroke his dog. LRT

schtreidich, *adj* - having a falling out. **Die Nochbere sin ~ warre, no is alles zu die Hund gange.** The neighbors had a falling out and then everything went to the dogs. LRT

Schtreiss, *pl* - plumes on a lady's hat. **Sie hot ihre Hut uffglaade ghat mit alle satt ~; mer hot schier net gwisst, eb's Umgraut waar adder was.** She had her hat loaded with all kinds of plumes; one hardly knew whether it was weeds or what. LRT

Schtreissel, *n, pl* **Schtreisslin** - little tassel (*dim.* of **Schtreiss**). KYG1972. **Sell Graas, weil mir's net gemaeht hen, hot nau Sume Schtreisslin.** That grass, because we didn't mow it, now has small seed tassels. LRT

Schtreit, *m* - strife. **Ich wees net was es gebt, sis so en ordlicher ~ in selle Familye.** I don't know what's going to happen, there is quite some strife in that family. **Sie hen zu viel ~ in selle Familye.** There is too much strife in that family. LRT

schtreng, *adj* - strict. *cf* **arig aernscht, hatt, schtrickt. Seller Mann waar immer arig ~ mit seine Buwe.** That man was always very strict with his boys. LRT

Schtrengli, *n* - string. **Es hot en glee ~ Neez rausghunge.** There was a small string of thread hanging out. LRT

schtrichweis, *adv* - in streaks. **So ~ hot selli Familye recht hatt Glick ghat.** In streaks that family had real bad luck. LRT

schtrichweis, *adv* - 1 by narrow sections. **2** for short periods of time. **Mer hot ihn yuscht so ~ heere kenne.** One could only hear him for short periods of time. LRT

Schtrick, *m* - rope. **en gschtreckder ~** - a tight rope. KYG2016. **Heb der ~, so as der Baam net der letz Weg fallt!**

Hold the rope, so that the tree doesn't fall the wrong way! LRT

schtricke, *pp* **gschtrickt - 1** to mend. **2** to knit. LRT

Schtrickschtrump, *m* - unfinished stocking. KYG1883, KYG2016

Schtrimperei, *f* - stocking business. KYG1883

schtrimpfiessich, *adv* - in stocking feet. KYG1884. **Geh net ~ naus uff die Bortsch, sie is nass.** Don't go on the porch in your stocking feet, it is wet. LRT

Schtrimpflicke, *n* - stocking mending. KYG1884. **Wann die Schtrimp ken Lecher hen, brauch mer sie net flicke.** If the stockings have no holes, one doesn't need to mend them. LRT

schtrippe - to strip. **Des Yaahr duhne mir's Welschkann ~ vum Schtock.** This year we are husking the corn from the stalk. LRT

Schtrippschtubb, *f, pl* **-schtuwwe** - stripping room (in tobacco shed). **-schtuwwe hen die menscht Zeit en Offe.** Stripping rooms generally have a stove. LRT

Schtritzbix, *f* - squirt gun. **Die Kinner gleiche schpiele mit selle ~.** The children like to play with that squirt gun. LRT

schtritze - to squirt. **Er dutt die Millich graad vun die Kuh in's Maul ~.** He squirts the milk right from the cow into his mouth. LRT

Schtritzschuss, *m* - syringe-shot. **Der Dokder hot mir en ~ gewwe.** The doctor gave me a syringe-shot. LRT

Schtroh, *n* - straw. *cf* **Langschtroh** - straw of rye thrashed with flail. **gewarrt ~** - tangled straw as it comes from the thrasher. KYG2006. **~ waert gyuust fer Schtrohhiet mache un Vieh un Geil schtraehe.** Straw is used to make straw hats and to bed cattle and horses. LRT

Schtrohbank, *f, pl* **-benk** - straw cutter. **-benk koschde en latt Geld heidesdaags.** Straw cutters (benches) are expensive (antique value) now-a-days. LRT

Schtrohbett, *n, pl* **~er** - straw bed. **Schtroh-un-Schtrickbedder sin altfrenkisch.** Straw and rope beds are old-fashioned. LRT

Schtrohblumm, *f, pl* **~e** - straw flower. **Gedrickeldi ~e sin schee.** Dried straw flowers are lovely. LRT

Schtrohdach, *n, pl* **-decher - 1** straw roof. **Schtrohdecher sin raar heidesdaags.** Straw roofs are scarce now-a-days. LRT. **2** thatched roof. KYG1992

Schtrohfareb, *f* - straw-color. **~ is en satt Gehl.** Straw color is a shade of yellow. LRT

Schtrohgawwel, *f, pl* **-gawwle** - straw fork. **~e sin greeser wie Mischtgawwle.** Strawforks are bigger than manure forks. LRT

Schtrohhaufe, *m* - heap of straw. **Wann mer Schtroh**

brauch is en gleener **~ besser wie ken ~.** If one needs straw, a little heap of straw is better than no heap of straw. LRT

Schtrohhoke, *m* - straw hook. **~ kumme hendich nei fer en latt Sache duh an die Bauerei rum.** Straw hooks come in handy to do a lot of things around the farm. LRT

Schtrohhut, *m, pl* **-hiet** - straw hat. **Deel amische Mannsleit sin bissel annerscht alleweil, sie duhne -hiet draage im Winder.** Some Amish men are a bit different now, they wear straw hats in the winter. LRT

schtrohich, *adj* - strawy. **Der Mischt is awwer ~.** The manure is strawy. LRT

Schtrohkareb, *m, pl* **~** - straw basket. **~ sin aa bissel raar alleweil.** Straw baskets are also a bit scarce now-a-days. LRT

Schtrohsack, *m* - straw mattress, straw tick. **Ich hab sei Lewe net uff meim ~ gschlofe.** Never in my life have I slept on my straw mattress. LRT

Schtrohscheier, *f* - straw barn. **Wann mer en ~ hot, brauch mer ken Schtrohschtock mache.** If one has a straw barn, there is no need to make a straw stack. LRT

Schtrohschtaab, *m* - straw dust. **Wann die Dreschmaschien gut schafft, sett mer net viel ~ hawwe.** If the thrashing machine works well, one shouldn't have much straw dust. LRT

Schtrohschtock, *m* - straw stack. **Die Nochbere hen en**

hocher ~. The neighbors have a high straw stack. **Ich daed saage, seller ~ is hoch genunk.** I'd say that straw stack is high enough. LRT

Schtrohwisch, *m* - wisp of straw. **Kannscht du mir en ~ lange so as ich den Schmutz abbutze kann?** Can you hand me a wisp of straw so I can wipe off this grease? LRT

Schtrooss, *f* - street. **Mir wuhne yuscht iwwer die ~ vun die Karich.** We just live across the street from the church. LRT. **immer uff der ~ leie** - to be going all the time. KYG2019. **Yunger, du settscht net allfatt uff die ~ leie.** Young man, you should not be hitting the road (street) all the time (or gadding about). LRT

Schtrooselicht, *n, pl* ~er - street light. **Sell Schteddel hot scheeni ~er.** That town has nice street lights. LRT

Schtrumpbandel, *m* - stocking garter. = **Schtrimpbandel.** KYG1884

schtruppich, *adj* - tousled. = **schtruwwlich.** KYG2042

Schtruwwelkopp, *m* - tousle-headed man, child. KYG2042. **Er is immer en ~.** The hair of his head is always disheveled. LRT

schtruwwlich, *adj* - uncombed. KYG2093. **Sellem hellkeppiche Buh sei Haar dutt gern ~ warre.** That blonde boy's hair becomes uncombed easily. LRT

schtruwwlich, *adj* - unkempt. *cf* **schlappich, zoppich.**

KYG2106. **Sei Haar is immer ~.** His hair is always unkempt. LRT

Schtudie´res, *n* - studying. **Sei ~ waar ihm hatt gange.** His studies were hard for him. LRT

Schtulgang, *m* - stool (discharge of bowels). KYG1888. **Sauergraut gebt deel Leit loser ~.** Sauerkraut gives some people loose bowels. LRT

Schtumbe, *m* - stump. **um der ~ schwetze** - to talk around the stump. KYG1965. **En ~, die recht Heech, macht en guder Hackglotz.** A stump, the right height, makes a good chopping block. LRT

Schtumber, *m* - stomper (for tamping earth). KYG1886. = **Schtamper.** LRT

Schtumberopper, *m* - stump puller. **En ~ muss gewaldich sei.** A stump puller must be powerful. LRT

Schtumbeschenzel, *n* - stub-tail (of a rabbit). **Mir hen mol en Kaader ghat as ken Schwanz ghat hot, mir hen ihn der Schtumbi gheese.** We once had a tomcat that had no tail; we called him stumpy. LRT

Schtumbeschteddel, *n* - ✥ Fredericksburg, Leb. Co., PA. **Ich hab faddich gemacht in de Hochschul in ~.** I completed highschool in Fredericksburg. LRT,4/21/2000

schtumbich, *adj* - stocky. *cf* **glenner, dicker Mann** - stocky man. KYG1884

Schtumbschwanz, *m* - bob-tailed cat or dog. LRT

schtumm, *adj* - tongue-tied. KYG2034

schtump, *adj* - stagnant. **Ich bin noch net wacker, mei Gedanke sin bissel ~.** I'm not yet awake, my thoughts are a bit dull. LRT

Schtunn, *f* - hour. **alli ~** - all the time. KYG2019. = **Schtund.** [Leb. Co.]. **Ich sing zum Harr, "Ich Brauch Dich alli Schtund."** I sing to the Lord, "I Need Thee Every Hour." LRT

schtuppe, *pp* **gschtuppt** - to stub. **Er hot sei grosser Zehe gschtuppt.** He stubbed his big toe. LRT

Schtutz, *m* - push, shove. **Ich hab net gwisst as er hinnich mir waar bis er mir en ~ gewwe hot.** I didn't know he was behind me until he gave me a shove. LRT

schtutze - to butt, bump. LRT

Schuck, *m* - short downpour of rain in a gust of wind. **Seller ~ Regge hot schur net lang uffghalde.** That short burst of rain surely didn't last long. LRT. **Seller ~ Regge hot mich verschtaunt.** That short downpour of rain surprised me. LRT

schucke - to toss. *cf* **en Ball nuffschmeisse.** KYG2040

Schucke, *n* - tossing. KYG2040

schuckweis, *adv* - for short periods of time. **So ~ hen mir der ganz Daag Regge ghat.** For short periods of time we had rain all day. LRT

Schuhbascht, *f* - shoe brush. **Ich yuus die ~ fer mei Schuh schee glitzerich mache.** I use the shoe brush to make my shoes nice and shiny. LRT

Schuhbax, *f, pl* **~e** - shoe box. **Viel vun meine Schuh sin weckgschtort in die ~e, wu sie drin kumme sin.** Many of my shoes are stored away in the boxes in which they came. LRT

Schuhbendel, *m* - shoe lace. **So viel vun die yunge Leit schpringe heidesdaags rum in ihre Schuhe un hen die ~ net gebunne.** So many young people run around nowadays with their shoes untied. LRT

Schuhbendli, *n, pl* **~n** - shoe lace. **Die ~n bleiwe net gebunne.** The shoe laces won't remain tied. LRT

Schuhgratzer, *m* - shoe scraper. **Du kannscht der Dreck vun deine Schuh abgratze datt am ~.** You can scrape the mud off your shoes there at the shoe scraper. LRT

Schuhledder, *n* - shoe leather. **Ich gleich Schuh as schee weech ~ hen.** I like shoes that have nice soft leather. LRT

Schuhleescht, *m* - shoe last. **So dann un wann finn ich noch Not fer en ~.** Still now and then I find a need for a shoe last. LRT

Schuhlumbe, *m* - shoe rag. **Datt is en ~, butz dei Schuh!** There's a shoe rag, clean your shoes! LRT

Schuhnaggel, *m, pl* **-neggel** -

shoe nail. **Schuhneggel sin bissel raar heidesdaags.** Shoe nails are a bit rare nowadays. LRT

Schuhschnall, *f* - shoe buckle. **Mach dei ~ zu.** Close your shoe buckle. LRT

Schuhsohl, *f, pl* **~e** - shoe sole. **Ich muss mei Schuh zum Schuhmacher nemme. Ich hab die ~e darichgeloffe.** I must take my shoes to the cobbler. I have worn the soles out. LRT [Leb. Co.]

Schul, *f, pl* **~e** - school. **~ halde** - to teach school. **Wann mer en aldi ~ nunnerreisst, muss mer Blatz finne fer die Schuler.** If one tears down an old school building, one must find a place for the pupils.

Schul halde - to teach. **Er guckt zu yung fer Schulhalde.** He looks too young to teach school. LRT. **Er halt Schul in Yarick.** He teaches school in York. = **lehre.** *cf* **lanne.** KYG1975. **~ is haddi Arewet.** Teaching school is hard work. LRT

Schul-esse, *n* - school lunch. **In die alde Daage waar's ~ im Kessel.** In the olden days the school lunch was in the kettle (lunch pail). LRT

Schulbuch, *n, pl* **Schulbicher** - schoolbook. **Die alde deitsche Schulbicher sin mir arig lieb.** The old German schoolbooks are very dear to me. LRT. **En gut ~ is en latt Geld waert.** A good text book is worth a lot of money. LRT

Schulbuh, *m, pl* **Schulbuwe** -

schoolboy. **Mer mehnt es kennt net sei was fer Schpuchde as Schulbuwe ebmols abziehe.** One can hardly believe the pranks that schoolboys pull off sometimes. LRT

Schuld, *f* - blame, fault. **Sis sei eegni ~.** It's his own fault; he's to blame. LRT

Schuldaag, *m, pl* **~e** - schoolday. **Die ~e warre lang wann die Schuler sich net bedraage.** The schooldays get long if the schoolchildren do not behave. LRT

schuldere - to assume responsibility. **Sell is meh as ich ~ kann.** That is more than I can shoulder. LRT

Schuler, *m* - student, scholar, pupil. **Yungi Schuler sin bleed/ sie kumme doch vun weit un breed.** Young students are so shy, they come from far and wide. LRT

Schulgeld, *n* - tuition. KYG2072. **Die Schuler hen en Esse gemacht fer en hunnert Leit fer ~ sammle.** The students served a meal for 100 people to raise tuition money. LRT

Schulgrund, *m* - school ground. **Wie ich aagfange hab in die Schul geh, waar unser Hof graad newich em ~.** When I started school, our yard was right beside the school ground. LRT

Schulhaus, *n* - schoolhouse. **Unser Mt. Zion ~ waar en zwee-schtuwwich, zwee-schteckich Gebei.** Our Mt. Zion schoolhouse was a two-room, two-story building. LRT

Schulhaus-uhr, *f, pl* ~e - schoolhouse clock. **Unser Schul hot zwee Schtubbe un zwee ~e ghat.** Our school had two rooms and two schoolhouse clocks. LRT

Schulhof, *m* - school yard. **Unser ~ hot die Zoar Ludderisch Karich ihre Geil- un-weggli Shed uff die Owedseit ghat.** Our school yard had the Zoar Lutheran Church's horse and buggy shed on the west side. LRT

Schuling, *f* - schooling. = **Lanning. ~ is gross notwennich fer Kinner.** Schooling is of great importance for children. LRT

Schulmeeschder, *m* - teacher. = **Lehrer. KYG1975. Mei ~n hot mich Englisch lerne misse.** My (elementary) teacher had to teach me English. LRT

schun, *adv* - already. **~ e Weil -** for some time. **Mir hen nau ~ e Weil gheert as der Tschecki die Maed gleicht.** We've heard for some time now that Jakey likes the girls. LRT

schunneweil, *adv* - for some time. KYG2019. **Ya, sell waar ~ am aa geh.** Yes, that's been going on for some time now. LRT

schunscht was - something else. **~ soll mer duh?** What else shall one do? LRT

schunscht, *adv* - at other times. = **sunscht. KYG2020. Was ~ hett ich duh selle?** What else should I have done? **~ Zeide**

hedde sie der Barigweg genumme.** At other times they would have taken the mountain road. LRT

Schuppe, *f* - dandruff. = **Schippe. Ich het liewer Schippe uff meim Kopp as wie Hundsfleh.** I'd rather have dandruff on my head than dog fleas. LRT

Schuss, *m* - shot. **Er is ken ~ Pulfer waert.** He's not worth a shot of gun powder. LRT, 4/18/2000

schussweis, *adv* - by jerks. **So ~ schafft er wie en Elefant!** By jerks, he works just like an elephant. LRT

schwachrot, *adj* - pale red. **Schwatzrot is mir liewer wie ~.** I prefer dark red to pale red. LRT

schwachsinnich, *adj* - weak in thought. = **schwach in seine Gedanke. KYG2002. Der Weg wie er gschwetzt hot, hot mer denke misse as er bissel ~ is.** The way he talked one had to think he is a bit weak-minded. LRT

Schwador´, *f* - ☉ Swatara Creek, Leb. Co., PA. KYG2281

schwaerme - to swarm. KYG1978. **Die Ieme sin am ~.** The bees are swarming. LRT

Schwalmenescht, *n* - swallow's nest. **Die Scheierschwalme sin am Neschdet baue.** The barn swallows are building nests. LRT

Schwammbax, *f* - tinder box. KYG2022

schwammich, *adj* - quaggy. **Des Weedschtick is ~; wann's zu nass is, misse mir die Kieh in de Scheier losse.** This pasture field is quaggy; when it's too wet, we must keep the cows in the barn. LRT

schwanke - to sway. **Der Gaul hot Bissel gschwankt un no is er umgfalle.** The horse swayed a bit and then he fell over. LRT

schwankich, *adj* - swaying. **Die Baem waare ~ datt im Wind.** The trees were swaying there in the wind. LRT

Schwammkaader, *m* - womanizer. **Vun yungem uff waar er ewwe en ~.** From his youth he really was a womanizer. LRT

Schwanz, *m* - tail. **Die Kuh hot ihre ~ geschwenzelt.** The cow switched her tail. LRT

schwanze, *pp* **gschwentzt -** to dock an animal's tail. **Die Schoflin sedde immer gschwentzt sei.** The lambs should always be docked. LRT

Schwanzfedder, *f, pl* **-feddre -** tail feather. **Die Fassande hen scheeni -feddre.** The pheasants have nice tail feathers. LRT

Schwanzleng, *f* - tail length. **Wann mer sich an die Kuh hockt fer sie melke, is die ~ net arig lang.** If one sits by the cow to milk her, the tail length is not very long. LRT

Schwanzrieme, *m* - tail strap (in horse harness). KYG1960. **En ~ as zu katz is, macht em Gaul sei Schwanz nuff in de Heh schteh.** A tail strap that is too short causes the horse's tail to stand up.

Schwanzschtick, *n* - tail piece. KYG1960

schwareme - to swarm. **Die Ieme sin am ~.** The bees are swarming. LRT

Schwatzdann, *f* - black thorn. KYG2001

schwatzrot, *adj* - dark red. **~ is mir liewer wie schwachrot.** I prefer dark red to pale red. LRT

Schwatzwalnissbaam, *m, pl* -**baem** - black walnut tree. KYG2161. **Selli Harebschtgewebwarem gleiche die -baem.** Those fall web worms like the black walnut trees. LRT

Schwatzweschp, *f* - common wasp. KYG2169

Schweizer, *adj* - Swiss. **Die ~ sin gudi Uhremacher.** The Swiss are good clockmakers. LRT

Schweizerkaes, *m* - Swiss cheese. **Kaes unni Lecher is ken ~.** Cheese without holes is not Swiss cheese. LRT

schwemme, *pp* **gschwemmt** - to flood. **Der ganz Schwamm waar gschwemmt.** The whole meadow was flooded. *cf* **iwwerschwemme.** LRT

schwenke, *pp* **gschwenkt** - to wave. **Die Kinner hen die Faahne darich die Luft gschwenkt.** The children waved the flags through the air. LRT

schwenzle - to switch the tail.

Die Kieh ~ fer die Micke yaage. The cows switch their tails to chase the flies. LRT

schwenzlich, *adj* - switching (of a mare that is inclined to switch the tail). **Ya, selli Marr is immer so ~.** Yes, that mare is always switching her tail. LRT

Schwerneeder, *m* - son-of-a-gun. **Er is en ~ vun me Mensch.** He is a remarkable person. LRT

Schwernot, *f* - dire need. **Dich soll (doch) die ~ griege!** The deuce take you! = **Dich soll die Grenk hole! Das dich der Guckuck hett!** KYG1963

schwetze - to talk. **~ sachdich** - to talk in a subdued voice. **Yunger, nau schwetz sachdich!** Young man, now talk quietly. LRT. **Ich will hoffe, ich kann immer gut ~ fer unser Parre.** I hope I can always speak in recommendation of our pastor. LRT. **Er schwetzt yuscht so in eem Leier.** He speaks in a monotone. LRT. **~ wehe** - to speak of, about. **Kannscht du ~ zu uns wehe Deitsche Awwerglaawe?** Can you speak to us about Pennsylvania German superstition? LRT. **Es is net zu ~ dewehe.** It is unutterable. KYG2115. **Yunger, mir hen nix fer ~ dewehe.** Young man, we have nothing to talk about. LRT. **gross ~** - to talk big. **devun (dewehe) ~** - to talk about. **darich der Hut ~** - to talk through one's hat. KYG1964

Schwetzerei, *f* - talking. KYG1965

Schwetzfescht, *n* - talking festival. KYG1965

Schwetzmaschien, *f* - talking machine. KYG1965

Schwimmblatz, *n* - swimming hole. **Unser ~ hen mir Kesselloch gheese.** Our swimming hole was called "Kesselloch" (kettle hole). LRT

Schwindlereibabier, *n* - worthless stock. KYG1883

schwinge, *pp* **gschwunge** - 1 to swing (without footing). **Datt hot er ghunge, sei Fiess hen frei in de Luft gschwunge.** There he was hanging, his feet were swinging clear in the air. LRT. 2 to swing (at a ball). **Er hot an der Balle gschwunge, awwer he hot en verfehlt.** He swung at the ball, but he missed it. LRT

Schwingwarick, *n* - tow. = **Warick.** KYG2042

Schwitz, *m* - sweat. **Der ~ is ihm abgloffe.** The sweat rolled off of him. LRT

schwitze - to sweat. **Wann mer schaffe will, muss mer ewwe ~.** If one wants to work, one has to sweat. LRT

schwitzich, *adj* - sweated, sweaty. **Er riecht ~.** He smells sweaty. LRT

Schwiwwelschtul, *m* - swivel chair. **Ich gleich der ~ vanne an meim Schaffdisch.** I like the swivel chair in front of my worktable. LRT

Schwob, *m, pl* **Schwowe** - *lit* Swabian. term of ridicule.

156

Seckel, *n* - scrotum. **Wann die Sei net gschnidde sin, sin die Balle im ~.** If the hogs have not been castrated, the testicles are in the scrotum. LRT

Seckelbruch, *m, pl* **-brich** - scrotal hernia. **Wann ich en Bruch hawwe sett, dann wett ich liewer en Nawwelbruch hawwe as wie en ~.** If I were to have a hernia, I'd rather have an umbilical hernia than a scrotal hernia. LRT

Seef, *f* - soap. **Ich hab noch nie ken ~ gekocht.** I have never boiled soap. LRT

Seefbax, *f* - soap box. **Die ~ is voll Seef.** The soapbox is full of soap. LRT

seefe, *pp* **gseeft** - to soap. **Eb du selli dreckiche Hosse wesche duscht, sedde sie gut gseeft sei.** Before you wash those dirty trousers, they should be well soaped. LRT. **Seef dei Hend gut.** Soap your hands well. LRT

Seefeschissel, *f, pl* **-schissle** - soap dish. **Alligebott sett selli ~ gebutzt sei.** Every now and then, that soap dish should be cleaned. LRT

seefich, *adj* - soapy. **Sell Wasser daerf mer net drinke, es is ~.** We may not drink that water, it is soapy. LRT

Seefkessel, *m* - soap kettle. **Mer kocht ken Fleesch in me ~.** One doesn't cook meat in a soap kettle. LRT

Seeflaag, *f* - soap lye. **~ is schtarick Schtofft.** Soap lye is

pretty strong stuff. LRT

Seel¹, *f* - soul. **Meiner ~ des muss geduh warre.** Surely this must be done. LRT

Seel², *n* - tie of a flail. KYG2014

seene - to strain (milk). **Mir misse immer unser Millich ~ (odder seihe).** We must always strain our milk. LRT

sehne - to see. **Er seht dezu as sell geduh waert.** He will see to it that it gets done. LRT

sehneswaert, *adv* - worth seeing. KYG2251. **Selli scheene alde Kaere sin ~.** Those handsome old cars are worth seeing. LRT,4/18/2000. **Selli Kunschtlerei is ~.** That artistry is worth seeing. LRT

sei losse - to let be as it is. **Loss es sei wie's is.** Let it be as it is. LRT

sei, *poss adj* - his. **Selli Grummbeere sin sei, eb er sie hawwe will odder net.** Those potatoes are his, whether he wants them or not. LRT

Seidebabier, *n* - tissue paper. KYG2026

Seideblatt, *n* - trace of heavy harness. KYG2045

Seidel, *m* - tankard (for beer). KYG1967

Seidemiehl, *f* - silk mill. **Mei Freind hot als in re ~ gschafft.** My friend used to work in a silk mill. LRT

Seider, *m* - cider. **Essich waar mol ~.** Vinegar once was cider.

LRT. **Der ~ schafft.** The cider is turning. KYG2079. **Der ~ is am schaffe.** The cider is fermenting. LRT

Seideschteche, *n* - stitches in (one's) sides. KYG1882. **Selli Buwe duhne immer schpringe bis sie's ~ griege.** Those boys always run until they get side stitches. LRT

Seidewewer, *m* - silk weaver. **Er waar en ~.** He was a silk weaver. LRT

Seierei, *f* - obscene talk. KYG1964. **Sell is awwer 'n ~.** That is such a mess. LRT

seierlich, *adj* - tart. = **scharef, sauer.** KYG1971

Seifass, *n* - hog barrel. **Ebmols wees mer net was im ~ is.** Sometimes one doesn't know what is in the hog barrel. LRT

Seifresse, *n* - unappetizing meal. KYG2090

Seifuder, *n* - hog feed. LRT

Seihduch, *n, pl* **-dicher** - cloth for straining. **Wie ich yung waar hen mir nimmi -dicher gyuust, mir hen** filter pads **gyuust.** When I was young we no longer used filter clothes, we used filter pads. LRT

Seihe-eemer, *m* - straining bucket. **In meine Zeit waare die ~ nimmi gyuust.** In my time the straining buckets were no longer used. LRT

Seihickernuss, *f* - pig hickory nut. LRT

Seikarebs - mammoth pumpkin.

LRT

Seikopp, *m* - crude, unmannerly person. KYG2108. **Er is en ungebutzter ~.** He is a crude, unmannerly person. LRT

Seiriesel, *m, pl* ~ - pig snout. **Saag was du witt, awwer die ~ mache gut Esses.** Say what you like, but pig snouts make good eating. LRT

Seischtall, *m* - hog house. LRT

Seischtick, *n* - two-edged knife (for bleeding hogs). KYG2085. . = **Seischtechmesser.** LRT

Seischwaard, *f, pl* ~e - swine skin. **Die ~e sin noch Bissel haarich.** The swine skins are still a bit hairy. LRT

Seitbordschupplaad, *f, pl* ~e - sideboard drawer. **~e sin ball immer voll.** Side board drawers are usually full. LRT

seitdem, *adv* - since then. = **vun sellem ab.** KYG1993. **~ as mir zwee Kaere hen, geht alles viel besser.** Since we have two automobiles, things are going much better. LRT

Seitdier, *f* - side door. **Unser ~ watt ganz wennich gyuust.** Our side door is used very little. LRT

Seitsack, *m, pl* -seck - side pocket, cargo pants. **Viel vun unser Buwe hen Hosse mit grosse Seitseck.** Many of our boys have cargo pants with large side pockets. LRT

Seitsaddel - side-saddle. **~ reide** - to ride side-saddle. **Weibsleit gleiche ~ reide.** Women like to ride side-saddle. LRT

Seitschtrooss, *f, pl* ~e - side street. **In grosse Schtedt sin ~e notwennich.** In large cities, side streets are necessary. LRT

seitwegs, *adv* - sideways. **Sei Kaer is ~ gehich uns zu rutsche kumme.** His car came sliding sideways towards us. LRT

Seitztaun - ⊕ Lebanon, PA. KYG2275

seiwerlich, *adj* - tidy. KYG2014. **Nau is er dod, awwer er waar immer en ~er Mensch.** Now he is dead (and gone), but he was always a person who was an advocate of cleanliness (tidiness). LRT

Seiyoch, *n* - yoke put on hogs. KYG2263

Selaat', *m* - salad. = **Zelaat. Ich gleich ~, wann die Selaatbrieh bissel Seideschpeck drin hot.** I like salad when the salad dressing has a bit of bacon in it. LRT

Selaat'brieh, *f* - salad dressing. **Ich gleich Selaat, wann die ~ bissel Seideschpeck drin hot.** I like salad when the salad dressing has a bit of bacon in it. LRT

selde, *adv* - infrequently. KYG2103

seldsam, *adj* - unaccountable. KYG2090

sellemno, *adv* - according to that. KYG1992. = **sellemnooch.** [Leb. Co.]

sellemnooch, *adv* - according to that. **~ breiche mir nimmi meh kaafe.** According to that, we'll no longer need to buy more. LRT. = **sellemno**

sellemol(s), *adv* - that time. KYG1991. **~ hen sie en Haufe gyuusdi Gleeder gekaaft.** That time they bought a pile of used clothes. LRT. **~ wie sie Vendu ghat hen, waar's awwer hees.** That time when they had a sale, it was hot. LRT. **~ hen sie alles verkaaft an de Vendu.** At that time they sold everything at the auction. LRT

Selleri, *m* - celery. **wilder ~** - tape grass. *Vallisneria americana Michx.* = **wilder Sellerich, wilder Zellerich.** KYG1969. **Ich gleich Zellerich un Pederli in meine Suppe.** I like celery and parsley in my soups. LRT

selleweg, *adv* - that way, in that manner. KYG1991. **Grickt alles Leckdrick im Haus, ~ breicht dir ken Kohle meh kaafe.** Have everything electrified in the house, that way you won't need to buy coal any more. LRT

selli, *pl* - **1** those. **~ waare die Daage.** Those were the days. KYG2002. **2** that. **~ Kuh gebt en latt Millich.** That cow gives (produces) a lot of milk. LRT

selwertgemacht, *adj* - self-made. **Sei ~i Uhr is schee.** His self-made clock is handsome. LRT

selwert - self. LRT/Leb

senkel, *adj* - perpendicular. **Mei Gremmpaepp hot als gsaat: "Alles is winkel, plamm un ~!"** My grandfather used to say: "Everything is square, plumb and perpendicular." LRT

Senkloch, *n, pl* **-lecher** - sinkhole. **Kallickschteebodde hot immer Sinklecher.** Limestone ground always has sink holes. LRT

senkrecht, *adj* - plumb. LRT

Sensewaref, *m, pl* ~**e** - snathe. ~**e sin bissel grumm un graad.** Scythe snathes are a bit crooked and straight. = **Nibb.** LRT

Sepp, *m* - *dim* of **Joseph.** KYG2284. = **Seppi**

Setzet, *f* - setting (of eggs). = **Setzent. En ~ is die menscht Zeit dreizeh Oier.** A setting of eggs is usually thirteen in number. LRT

sexeckich, *adj* - six-cornered. **Was ~ is, is aa sexseidich.** What is hexagonal is also six-sided. LRT

sexfiessich, *adj* - six-footed. **Umense sin ~.** Ants are six-footed. LRT

sexmol, *adv* - six times. **Epper eppes ~ saage sett genunk sei.** To tell someone something six times should be enough. LRT

sexseidich, *adj* - six-sided. **Was sexeckich is, is aa ~.** What is hexagonal is also six-sided. LRT

sexyaehrich, *adj* - six years old. **Er is en ~er Buh.** He is a six year old boy. LRT

sibbe - to screen. **Die Hembierekanne sett mer vun die Brieh ~.** The raspberry seeds should be sieved from the juice. LRT

sich selwert, *pron, reflex, emph* - himself. **Er kann achtgewwe uff sich selwert!** He can take care of himself. LRT

sicher, *adj* - **1** safe. **2** sure. **Bischt du ~?** Are you sure? LRT

sicher, *adj* - safe. **Is alles ~?** Is everything safe (secure)? LRT

sie, ihne, *pers pron* - them. **Ich hab sie gsehne.** I saw them. **Ich hab ihne es Buch gewwe.** I gave them the book. **zu ihne** - to them. KYG1993. **Ya, die Kinner, mir hen ihne alles gekaaft as sie breiche.** Yes, the children, we bought them everything that they need. LRT

sie, *pers pron* - they. **~ selwer** - they themselves. KYG1995. **~ selwert hen all die Arewet geduh.** They themselves did all the work. LRT

Siessappel, *m, pl* **-eppel** - sweet apple. **Mir breiche -eppel so as mir siessi Schnitz mache kenne so as mir Schnitz un Gnepp esse kenne.** We need sweet apples so we can make sweet snitz so we can eat snitz and gnepp. LRT

Siessgrummbierblanze, *pl* - sweet potato plants. **Die ~ sin geblanzt.** The sweet potato plants have been planted. LRT,4/18/2000

Siessgrummbiererank, *f, pl* ~**e** - sweet potato vine. **So lang wie die ~e warre, wunnert's em as siess Grumbiere aa waxe kenne.** As long as sweet potatoes become vines, one wonders how the sweet potatoes can grow as well. LRT

Siessgrummbiereschtick, *n* - sweet potato patch. **Ihre ~ hot vier Roihe, baut dreissich Fuuss lang.** Their sweet potato patch has four rows about thirty feet long. LRT

Siesskasch, *f, pl* ~**e** - sweet cherry. **Ich gleich ~e, es macht mir nix aus eb sie schwatz, weiss, odder rot sin.** I like sweet cherries, it doesn't matter to me whether they are black, white, or red. LRT

Siesskascheboi, *m, f* - sweet cherry pie. **Ich hab sei Lewe ken ~ gesse.** I have never in my life eaten a sweet cherry pie. LRT

Siffer, *m* - drunk. **Fer sei ganz Lewe lang waar er ewwe en ~.** For his whole life he was indeed a drunk. LRT

Silwerbabier, *n* - tinfoil. **Mir hen als ~ uffghowe un hen's uff Balle gewickelt.** He used to save tinfoil and wrapped it on balls. LRT

Sindeschuld, *f* - penalty. If we hurt ourselves due to something stupid that we had done, Mom would say: **"Sell is dei ~!"** [That is your penalty for sinning.] LRT. **Sell is dei ~.** That (what has happened to you) is the result of your sinning. LRT

Sindewelt, *f* - world of sin. **Alli Mensche helfe mit de ~.** Each person helps to add to the sins of the world. LRT,4/11/2000

Singern, *f* - songstress. **Sie is en ordlich gudi ~.** She is a pretty good songstress. LRT

Sinn, *m* - sense. **im ~ hawwe** -

to have on one's mind. LRT

sinnbildisch, *adj* - typical. = **vorbildich.** KYG2087

Sitzblatz, *m, pl* -**bletz** - seat. **Die Boss hot ken leeri -bletz meh.** The bus has no more empty seats. LRT

sitzebleiwe - to remain seated. **Wann du nix schunscht zu duh hoscht, dann bleib yuscht sitze.** If you don't have anything else to do, then you can just remain seated. LRT

Sitzfleesch, *n* - "flesh to sit on." **Er hot ken ~.** He can't sit still. KYG1880

so - so. ~ **Dings** - things like that. **un ~ desgleiche** - and such as that. KYG1992. ~ **de gleich** - things like that. [Leb. Co.]. **Mir hen Buhne Sume un ~ de gleich heemgebrocht fer in der Gaarde duh.** We brought bean seed and the like home for the garden. LRT

Socke, *m* - **1** foot of stocking. = **Schtrumpsocke.** KYG1883. **2** stocking feet. KYG1884

sohle - to sole (a shoe). **Kannscht du mei Schuh ~?** Can you sole my shoes? LRT

Sohl-ledder, *n* - sole leather. **Wu kann mer gut ~ finne?** Where can one find good sole leather? LRT

Soldaa´deblummeschtrauss, *m* - scarlet sage plant. LRT

Soldaad´egleeder, *pl* - soldier's uniform. ~ **gucke immer gut.** Soldier's uniforms always look good. LRT

Soldaat´, *m* - soldier. **Bischli-Gnippli waar en ~ im Zwedde Weltgrieg.** C.R.B. was a warrior (soldier) in World War II. LRT

Solkiblug, *m, pl* **Solkiblieg** - riding plow. **Sie hen als gsaat, as Solkiblieg fer fauli Leit sin.** They used to say that riding plows are for lazy people. LRT

Sootbax, *f, pl* ~**e** - seed box. **Sei Drill sett greeseri ~e hawwe.** His drill should have bigger seed boxes. LRT

suckle - to suck. **Sell Kalb gleicht em der Daume ~.** That calf likes to suck one's thumb. LRT

Suddelarewet, *f* - dirty (wet) work. **Fer Schtorglarick sei is ken ~.** Being a store clerk is not dirty work. LRT,4/11/2000

suddre - to smolder. **Sell Feier vun geschder is als noch am ~.** That fire from yesterday is still smoldering. LRT

Sumebuchzeit, *n* - seed catalog time. **Ich gleich immer wann es ~ is. Sell mehnt Winder is glei verbei.** I always like when it's seed catalog time. That means the winter will be over soon. LRT

Sumesaeher, *m, pl* ~ - seed sower. **Die ~ sin draus in de Felder.** The seed sowers are out in the fields. LRT

Summ, *f* - sum. **Selli Erebschaft waar en recht grossi ~.** That inheritance was a real large sum. LRT

summerfleckich, *adj* - freckled. **Wie kummt's as die**

rothaariche Leit so ~ sin? Why is it that the red-haired folks are so covered with freckles? LRT

Sunndaagesse, *adj* - Sunday meal. **Was heescht du en ~?** What do you call a Sunday meal? LRT

Sunndaags, *f* - Sunday rest. **~ is der Daag fer em sei Ruh griege.** Sunday is the day for one to get his rest. LRT

Sunndaagsbreddich, *f* - sermon for Sunday service. **Es nemmt der Parre baut acht Schtund fer sich rischde fer sei ~ gewwe.** It takes the pastor about eight hours to prepare his Sunday sermon. LRT

Sunndaagsgaund, *m, pl* -**geind** - dress worn on Sunday. **Ihre -geind sin all schwatz un weis.** Her Sunday dresses are all black and white. LRT

Sunndaagsgleeder, *pl* - Sunday clothes. **Ihre ~ sin immer so schee gebiggelt.** Her Sunday clothes are always so nicely ironed. LRT

Sunndaagshemm, *n, pl* ~**er** - Sunday shirt. **Sei Fraa dutt immer sei ~er so schee gewesche un gebiggelt halde.** His wife always keeps his Sunday shirts washed and ironed so nicely. LRT

Sunndaagshosse, *pl* - Sunday britches. **Sei ~ sin schwatz.** His Sunday trousers are black. LRT

Sunndaagschulpicknick, *m, f* - Sunday school picnic. **Mir hen immer en gudi Zeit an die ~.** We always have a good time at the Sunday school picnic. LRT

sunndaagsich, *adj* - pertaining to Sunday. **Was geht dann aa as du heit (Mittwoch) so ~i Gleeder aahoscht?** What is the going on that you are wearing such Sunday clothes today (Wednesday)? LRT

Sunndaagsschul, *f* - Sunday school. **Die ~ fangt aa am halwer Zehe.** The Sunday school begins at nine thirty. LRT

Sunndaagsschulbuch, *n, pl* -bicher - Sunday school book. **Ihre -bicher sin baut ausgewore, sie breiche nei-i.** Their Sunday school books are about worn out, they need new ones. LRT

Sunndaagszeiding, *f* - Sunday newspaper. **Unser ~ kummt immer frieh mariyets.** Our Sunday newspaper always arrives early in the morning. LRT

Sunneblicker, *pl* - sporadic spots of sunlight on cloudy days. **Deheem hen mir als gsaat, "~, Regge schicke."** At home we used to say, "sporadic sunshine sends forth rain."

Sunneblumm, *f, pl* ~e - sunflower. **Guck yuscht mol, ihre ~e sin sex Fuuss hoch.** Just look, their sunflower plants are six feet tall. LRT

Sunneblummesume, *n* - sunflower seed. **Die Veggel gleiche ihre ~.** The birds like their sunflower seeds. LRT

Sunnefinschdernis, *f* - solar eclipse. **Es kennt ordlich dunkel warre, wann die Sunn in die ~ geht.** It could get pretty dark if the sun goes into a solar

eclipse. LRT

Sunnefisch, *m, pl* ~ - sunfish. **Die ~ hen scheeni gehli Beich des Yaahr.** The sunfish have nice yellow bellies this year. LRT

Sunneglesser, *pl* - sunglasses. **Sie hot ~ aaghat.** She was wearing sunglasses. LRT

Sunneschtraal, *m, pl* ~e - sunbeam. **Guck mol, die ~e sin am Wasser ziehe.** Look (once), the sunbeams are drawing water. LRT

Sunne-uffgang, *m* - sunrise. **Sie waare do vor ~.** They were here before sunrise. LRT

Sunnunner - sundown. **Yungi, dir misst deheem sei bis ~.** Young people, you will need to be home by sundown (sunset). LRT

Suppekessel, *m* - soup kettle. **Unser ~ is nie net gross genunk.** Our soup kettle is never large enough. LRT

Suppeleffelvoll, *m* - tablespoon-full. **Ich will en ~ vun sellem Epplesaes versuche.** I want to taste a tablespoonful of that applesauce. LRT

Suppeschissel, *f* - tureen. KYG2042. **Die menschde ~e hen en Deckel.** Most tureens have a lid. LRT

Suppleffel, *m* - tablespoon. **~ sin zu gross fer gleeni Kinner.** Soup spoons are too large for small children. LRT

Suss, *f* - *dim* of **Susanna.** KYG2286

Talyen´ner, *m* - Italian. KYG2274

Tammkatznode, *pl* - tomcat notes (*facet.*). KYG2033

Taunschipp, *n* - *<Engl* township. KYG2044.

Taunschipp-affis, *f* - township office. KYG2044

Taunschipp-lumbe, *m, pl* ~ - township rags. KYG2044

Taunschipp-weg, *m, pl* ~e - township road. KYG2044. **Es ~ hot en Affis un gebt Acht uff die ~e.** The township has an office and takes care of the township roads. LRT

taxbaar, *adj* - taxable. KYG1973. **Es sin net viel Sache as net ~ sin.** There are not many things that are not taxable. LRT. **Ich bin froh as die Ess-Sache net ~ sin.** I'm glad that food items are not taxable. LRT

Taxbezaahler, *m* - taxpayer. KYG1974. **Leit as net ~ sin, sin arig raar.** People that are not tax payers are very scarce. LRT

Taxbill, *f* - tax bill. KYG1973. **En ~ griege is ke Schpass.** Getting a tax bill is no fun. LRT

taxe - to tax. KYG1973

Taxeinemmer, *m* - tax collector. = **Taxhewer, Taxkolleckder** [Leb. Co. LRT]. KYG1973

Taxerei, *f* - everlasting taxing. KYG1974

taxfrei, *adj* - exempt from tax. =

zollfrei. KYG1973. **Mer wunnert yuscht was es nemmt fer eppes ~ mache.** One just wonders what it takes to make something tax exempt. LRT

Taxgeld, *n* - money for taxes. KYG1973

Taxlischt, *f* - tax list. KYG1974

Teckscht, *m* - text. KYG1990. **Kannscht du selli alt Deitsch Schrift ~ lese?** Can you read that old German hand written text? LRT

Tee, *m* - tea. **im ~ sei** - to be tipsy. = **im Darr sei, im Dau sei, en Kapp uff hawwe, zu viel in der Naas hawwe, wennich in de Schnut hawwe, wennich gsoffe sei.** KYG2025. **Die gwixde Gsundheitsleit saage ~ soll gsund sei fer em.** The keen healthcare people say that tea (drinking) is supposed to be healthful. LRT

Teeblatt, *n, pl* -**bledder** - tea leaf. KYG1975. **Ich gleich so dann un wann Sallwei -bledder tschaae.** I like to chew sage tea leaves, now and then. LRT

Teeblettche, *n* - tea saucer. = **Teeblettli** [Leb. Co. LRT]. KYG1977

Teegscharr, *n* - tea set. KYG1977

Teehaffe, *m* - teapot. = **Teekann.** KYG1976

Teekessli, *n, dim* of **Teekessel** - little tea kettle. KYG1975. **En kupper ~ is schee.** A little copper tea kettle is pretty. LRT

Teekoppli, *n* - tea cup [Leb. Co. LRT]. = **Teekoppche.** KYG1975

Teekoppvoll, *m* - teacupful. = **Teekopplivoll** [Leb. Co. LRT]. KYG1975

Teeleffel, *m* - teaspoon. KYG1978

Teeleffelvoll, *m* - teaspoonful. KYG1978. **Es nemmt drei ~ fer en Suppeleffel voll mache.** It takes three teaspoons to make a table spoonful. LRT

Tellefon, *m,f* - telephone. **Der ~ geht.** The telephone is ringing. KYG1979. **Wann der ~ ringt, sett mer en antwadde.** If the phone rings, one should answer it. LRT

Tellefonposchde, *m* - telephone pole. KYG1980

Temaets´, *f* - common tomato. *Lycopersicum esculentum Mill.* = **Bammerans, Bommerans, Bummerans, Gummerans, Tomaddis.** *cf* **Gehltomaets, Liewesappel.** KYG2032

Temaets´blanz, *f* - tomato plant. KYG2032. = **Tomaetsblanz.** LRT

Temaets´brieh, *f* - tomato juice. KYG2032. = **Tomaetsbrieh.** LRT

Temaets´roi, *f* - tomato row. KYG2032. = **Tomaetsroi.** LRT

Temaets´saess - tomato sauce. KYG2032. = **Tomaetssaess.** LRT

Tempel, *m* - temple. KYG1982

Tempelgebei, *n* - temple building. KYG1983

tempere, *refl* - to be temperate. KYG1982

Temperenz-breddicher, *m* - temperance preacher. KYG1982

Temperenz-red, *f* - temperance speech. KYG1982

Tenor, *m* - tenor (voice). KYG1986. **Er dutt ~ singe.** He sings tenor. CRB. **Ich hab immer Bass gsunge bis unser Karichkor en ~ gebreicht hot, no hab ich ~ gsunge.** I always sang bass until our church choir needed a tenor, then I sang tenor. LRT

Teschdament, *n* - (New) Testament. **Nei Teschdament.** *cf* **Alt ~.** KYG1989. **Mir sedde en B-B-B Nei ~ Iwwersetzing hawwe.** We should have a Buffington-Barba-Beam New Testament translation. LRT

Textbuch, *n* - textbook. KYG1990. **Die Textbicher sin immer so deier.** The textbooks are always so expensive. LRT

Till, *m* - *dim* of Tilghman. KYG2287. = **Tilli**

Tinktur´, *f* - tincture. KYG2022. **~ vun Eiodein macht die Waarze weckgeh.** Tincture of iodine takes away warts. LRT

tirann´isch, *adj* - tryannical. KYG2087

toole - to toll. **Wann der Mensch wu gschtarewe is 50 Yaahr alt waar, hot die Glock 50 Mol gschlagge (getoolt).** If the person who died was 50 years old, the bell struck 50 times. LRT

Trocke, *n* - truck farming. KYG2067

Tschaerli, *m* - <*Engl.* Charley *dim* of Charles. KYG2283

tschaerre, *pp* **getschaerrt** - to put up in jars. **Sie hen die Gummere getschaerrt.** They put the cucumbers up in jars. LRT

Tschessi, *m* - Jesse. **epper ~ gewwe - 1** to give a sound paddling. **2** to give a sound scolding. LRT. **Ich hab ihm ~ gewwe.** I gave him heck. LRT

tschickere, *pp* **getschickert** - to cultivate. **Er hot die Lott getschickert mit em Eegeilstschicker.** He cultivated the lot (garden plot) with the one-horse cultivator. LRT

Tschunse - ✪ Jonestown, Leb. Co., PA.

uffbasse - 1 to pay attention. **Yunger, du daedscht besser ~!** Young fellow, you had better pay attention! LRT. **2** to take care. *cf* **sarye, Acht gewwe.** KYG1960

uffbaue - to build up. **Was umfallt, muss mer ewwe widder ~.** What falls down has to be rebuilt again. LRT

uffbleiwe - to remain open. **Deel vun die Ess-sach-Schtore bleiwe vier-un-zwanzich Schtund der Daag uff.** Some of the grocery stores remain open 24 hours a day. LRT

uffbluge, - to turn with a plow.

LRT

uffbome - to wind up warp on cylinder. KYG2165

uffbreche, *pp* **uffgebroche** - to break up. **Die Bissniss is uffgebroche.** That business went into bankruptcy. LRT

uffbreddiche - to talk something up. KYG1965

uffbringe, *pp* **uffgebrocht** - KYG2117. to bring up, mention. **Es macht em schier narrisch wann er so dummi Sache uffbringt.** It almost drives one crazy, when he brings up such dumb things. LRT. **Sie bringe immer Sache uff as mer net heere will.** They always bring up (mention) things that one doesn't want to hear. LRT

uffbrockle - to break up and soak (as bread in milk). **Du kannscht Brot ~.** You can break up bread. LRT

uffdenke, *pp* **uffgedenkt - 1** to think up. KYG1998. **Was hett dir uffgedenkt?** What did you think up? LRT. **2** to untwine. = **uffwickle.** KYG2114

uffdrehe, *pp* **uffgedreht** - to turn up. KYG2078. **Es sin en latt Leit uffgedreht fer die Versammling.** A lot of people turned up for the gathering (meeting). **Mer wees net was es naegscht uffdreht.** One never knows what will develop next. LRT. = **nuffdrehe, ruffdrehe, uffschlagge**

uffeegne - "to own up," admit. **Zu so eppes wett ich gaar net ~.** I would not want to admit to such a thing. LRT

uffeidere - to become enlarged (as a cow's udder). **Die Kuh grickt glei en Kalb—guck mol wie sie am ~ is.** The cow will soon calve—look how her udder is enlarging. LRT

uff-faahre, *pp* **uffgfaahre** - to rise up in anger. **Uff ee Mol is er uffgfaahre, ich hab net gwisst was am aageh waar.** All of a sudden, he rose up in anger, I didn't know what was going on. LRT

uff-falle - to cause an open wound by falling. KRG2251

uff-fasse, *pp* **uffgfasst** - to place in bags. **Hett dir der Weeze uffgfasst?** Did you bag the wheat? LRT

uff-feiere, *pp* **uffgfeiert** - to fire up. **Sunndaagoweds hen mir immer die Schuleffe uffgfeiert.** Sunday evenings we always fired up the school stoves. LRT

uff-fiedre - to use up (fodder). KYG2117. **Well, es Welschkannlaab is schier gaarli all uffgfiedert warre.** Well, the cornfodder was nearly all fed. LRT

uff-flicke - to patch up. LRT

uff-frische - to refresh. **Wann mer de Blumme bissel Wasser gebt, sell frischt sie uff.** If one gives the flowers a little water, that freshens them up. LRT

uff-un-ablaafe - to promenade. **Im Summer duhne die Buwe und die Maed viel uff-un-ab do bei uns verbei laafe.** In the summertime the boys and girls walk back and forth (by here) a lot. LRT

uffgeblose, *adj* - bloated. **Sis en doder Raguun dattdrunne newich de Schtrooss, un weil's so hees is, is er gross ~.** There is a dead racoon down there beside the road, and since it's so hot, it's really bloated. LRT

uffgebroche, *adj* - **1** insolvent, "broke." **Der Weg wie er sei Bissniss gschprengt hot, is es ken Wunner as sie ~ is.** The way he ran his business, it's no wonder it became insolvent (went broke). LRT. **2** ulcerated. **uffgebrochni Haut** - ulcerated skin. KYG2088. **Oi guck mol, selli wiescht Pock is ~.** Oi look, that ugly pimple has opened. LRT

uffgeh - 1 to rise (of the sun). **Die Sunn is am ~.** The sun is rising. LRT. **2** to open. KYG2099. **Ya, die Dier is uffgange.** Yes, the door has opened. LRT

uffgemacht, *adj* - made up, unfounded. **en ~er Rumor.** KYG2103

uffgemundert, *adj* - encouraged. **Sich ~ halde, sell macht em gsund.** To keep oneself in a positive state of mind, that keeps one healthy. LRT

uffgeraahmt, *adj* - tidy. KYG2014. **Des is awwer en scheeni uffgeraahmdi Schtubb.** But this is a neat orderly room. LRT. *cf* **nett, niedlich, sauwer, uffgschlickt**

uffgewwe, *pp* ~ - to give up. KYG2263. **Er hot sei Arewet in de Inschurens-Bissniss ~.** He gave up his work in the insurance business. LRT. **net ~ -**

to be unflinching. KYG2102. **Yunger, schlack nei, un geb net uff.** Young man, strike in (be the aggressor) and don't give up. LRT. *cf* **eidraage, weiche**

uffgriege - to cause to rise. **Es is Zeit fer sell Maedel ~, sie muss in die Schul geh.** It's time to get that girl up (out of bed), she must go to school. LRT

uffgritzle - to use up in scribbling. KYG2117. **Die Kinner hen alles uffgegritzelt ghat, mer hot nix meh lese kenne.** The children had scribbled all over everything, nothing was readable anymore. LRT

uffgschlosse, *adj* - unlocked. **en uffgschlossni Dier -** an unlocked door. KYG2107. **Die Dieb hen ken Druwwel ghat fer alles schtehle, sie hen en uffgschlossni Dier ghat.** The thieves (robbers) had no trouble stealing everything, they had an unlocked door. LRT

uffhalde, *pp* **uffghalde - 1** to delay. **Well, ich denk mir misse unser Schwetze uffheere, ich will dich net ~.** Well, I guess we'll have to quit talking, I don't want to delay you. LRT. **2** to hold up. **Ich wees as die Memm dich deheem hawwe will, un ich will dich net ~.** I know your mother wants you to come home and I don't want to hold you up. LRT. **All die Kaere uff de Schtrooss hen uns uffghalde.** All the cars on the road (*i.e.* the traffic) held us up (delayed us). LRT,4/18/2000. = **uffhewe**

uffhalde, *refl* - to spend time. **sich bei der Maed ~ -** to spend time with the girls. KYG2019.

Yunger, hald dich yuscht bei die Maed uff bis du die <u>recht</u> finnscht. Young man, you just spend time with the girls until you find the <u>right</u> one (to marry). LRT

uffheere - to quit, stop work. **Du hoscht hatt genunk gschafft heit; du darfscht nau ~.** You worked hard enough today; you may quit now. LRT

uffhelle - to clear off (as the weather). **Sis am ~!** LRT

uffhewe - to save. **Heb en Galle vun de Fareb uff, mer wees nie net wann mer bissel brauch.** Save a gallon of the paint, one never knows when a bit is needed. LRT. *cf* **aushalde, zerickhalde**

uffhuddle - to tangle. *cf* **verhuddle, verwickle, warre.** KYG1967

uffhunze, *pp* **uffghunzt -** to waste. KYG2170. **Sie hen en ganzer Daag uffghunzt.** They wasted a whole day. LRT

uffkehre - to sweep up. **Kannscht du den Dreck ~?** Can you sweep up this dirt? LRT

uffkumme, *pp* **is ~ - 1** to recover from illness. **Sie is ~ vun ihre Granket.** She recovered from her illness. **2** to rise (of the sun). **Die Sunn is am ~.** The sun is rising. **3** to spring up. **Der Graas-sume was mir gsaeht hen in der Hof is am ~.** The grass seed which we sowed in the yard is springing up. LRT. **4** to come up, rival. **Nix kann ~ dezu.** It is unrivaled. = **Es hot ken**

Gleiches. KYG2111. **Was kummt's naegscht uff?** What will develop next? LRT

ufflaafe, *pp* **uffgeloffe** - to swell. **Dei Beh sin uffgeloffe.** Your legs are swollen. LRT

ufflege, *pp* **uffgelegt** - to lay up (a wall). **Die Mannsleit hen die Mauer uffgelegt.** The men laid up the (foundation) wall. LRT

ufflese - to read up on. **Wann mer die Zeiding grickt, kann mer ~ vun die Neiichkeide.** If one gets the newspaper, one can read up on the news. LRT

ufflosse - to stop, let up. *cf* **aahalde** - to continue or keep up. LRT. = **abbreche, uffheere, schtill schteh, schtoppe.** KYG1889. **Es losst net uff.** It is unremitting. KYG2110. **Der Regge will yuscht net ~.** The rain just won't quit. LRT

uffmache, *pp* **uffgemacht - 1** to make up, reconcile. **Die Buwe waare am fechde, awwer sie hen widder uffgemacht.** The boys were fighting, but they made up again. **Selli ganz Gschicht hot er ~, sis nix waahr.** He made up that whole story, nothing is true. LRT. **2** to open. **sei Meind ~** - to make up his mind. **widder ~** - to reopen. **Er hot sei Schtor widder uffgemacht.** He reopened his store. LRT

uffnemme - to take up. **~ mit -** to take up with. KYG1963

Uffnemmer, *m* - person who raked and tied after grain was cut. KYG2015

uffreene - to rein up a horse. **En**

Gaul muss lanne schtill schteh, schunscht kann mer'n net ~. A horse must learn to stand still, else one cannot rein him up. LRT

uffreisse - to tear open. KYG1976. **Kannscht du mir den Brief ~?** Can you tear open this letter for me? LRT

uffrichdich, *adj* - upright. **Der Grabbschtee schteht ~.** The tombstone is standing erect. LRT

uffriehre - to stir up. **Loss es yuscht uff zu ihm, er kann blendi Druwwel ~.** Just let it up to him; he can stir up plenty of trouble. LRT. **Der Mosch kocht nau schund fer paar Schtund, mir sedde'n bissel ~.** The mush has cooked for several hours now we should stir it up. LRT

uffriehrisch, *adj* - rebellious. KYG1882. **Sei net so ~ !** Don't make such a fuss! **Ich wees net was am aageh waar. Die Sei waare der ganze Daag ~.** I don't know what was going on. The hogs were disturbed the entire day. LRT

uffrolle - to unroll. = **abrolle.** KYG2111. **Tschecki, kannscht du seller Bendel ~, so as mir en weckduh kenne?** Jakey, can you roll up that cord, so we can put it away. LRT

Uffruhr, *m, f* uproar. **So en ~ hab ich noch nie net gsehne ghat.** Such an uproar I had never seen before. LRT

uffruhrisch, *adj* - tumultuous. KYG2074. **Ei, des waar awwer schund en arig ~ Wese.** Oh, my this has already been a very

tumultuous matter. LRT

uffsaege - to saw up. **Ich saeg des Schtick Holz uff in gleeni Schticker.** I'll saw this piece of wood into small pieces. LRT

uffschaffe, *pp* **uffgschafft** - to stir up, upset. **Die Leit waare arig uffgschafft wehe daere Schiesserei in die Schul.** The people were very upset about this shooting incident in the school. LRT. **Selli granke Kinner hen awwer ihre Memm uffgschafft ghat.** Those sick children really worked up their mother emotionally. LRT,4/11/2000

uffschaffe, *refl, pp* **uffgschafft** - to work oneself up. **Er hot sich recht uffgschafft grickt ghat.** He had gotten himself all worked up (frustrated). LRT

uffscheine - to shine up (one's shoes). **~, ya, des dutt mer mit de Bascht.** Shine up (one's shoes), yes, one does this with a brush. LRT

uffschiesse, *pp* **uffgschosse** - to shoot up rapidly. **Seller Yunger is schnell uffgschosse.** That young man grew up very rapidly. **Mer mehnt des Welschkann waer yuscht iwwernacht uffgschosse wie des.** It seems like this corn just shot up like this overnight. LRT

uffschittle - to shake up. *cf* **uffriddle. En latt Sadde Medizin soll mer recht gut ~, eb mer sie nemmt.** A lot of kinds of medicine one is supposed to shake up really well before taking them. LRT

uffschlafe - [*facet*] to thaw out

(of musical sounds from a horn on a cold morning). KYG1992

uffschlicke - <*Engl* to slice up, to tidy. *cf* **uffraahme**. KYG2014

uffschliesse, *pl* **uffgschlosse** - to unlock. KYG2107. **Wie sie die Kischt uffgschlosse hen, hen sie en latt Sache gfunne.** When they unlocked the chest, they found a lot of things. LRT

uffschlitze - to slit open. **Fer ausfinne was letz waar hen sie der Maage ~ misse.** In order to find out what the trouble was, they had to slit open the stomach. LRT

uffschmeisse, *pp* **uffgschmisse** - to throw open. KYG2009. **Er waar grank, un er is net besser warre bis er uffgschmisse hot.** He was sick, and he didn't improve until he vomited. LRT

uffschmutze - to slick up. **So as die Flinde net roschde, sett mer sie bissel ~.** In order to keep the guns from rusting, one should slick them up a bit. LRT

uffschnappe - to tilt up. KYG2017. **Geb acht selli Kellerdier is uffgschnappt.** Be careful the cellar door is tilted up. LRT

uffschneide - to cut up. **eppes dinn ~** - to cut something thin. **Ich gleich die Gummere recht dinn blettlich ~.** I like to cut up the cucumbers in thin slices. LRT

uffschniere - to unlace. KYG2107

uffschpanne, *pp* **uffgschpannt**

- to open an umbrella. KYG2089. **Sie hen's Zelt uffgschpannt.** They set up the tent. LRT

uffschparre, *pp* **uffgschparrt** - to open. **es Maul ~** - to yawn. **In de Halbschtund as mir do ghockt hen, hot sie ihre Maul en dutzend Mol uffgschparrt.** In the half hour that we have been sitting here, she yawned a dozen times. LRT,4/18/2000

uffschpiele - to wash dishes. **Sis Zeit fer Gscharr ~.** It's time to wash the dishes. LRT

uffschpringe, *pp* **is uffgschprunge** - to burst open. **Die Wassermelone sin uffgschprunge.** The watermelons burst open. LRT

uffschtarre - to stir. **Wann mer die Kohle bissel uffschtarrt, no watt's Feier recht hees.** If one stirs the coals a bit, then the fire gets really hot. LRT

uffschteche - to open with a pointed instrument. **Wann mol en Gschwaer en gehler Kopp hot, no is es Zeit fer en ~.** Once a boil has a yellow head, it is time to open it with a pointed instrument. LRT

uffschteh - 1 to arise. **Sis nein Uhr, Zeit as du uffschtehscht.** It's nine o'clock, time that you get up (out of bed). LRT. **2** to stand up. **3** to advocate. **Ich will net ~ fer sell.** I don't want to be an advocate of that cause. LRT

uffschtelle - 1 to stop in at an inn. **~ fer Middaag esse** - to stop in for the noon meal. PB,6/26/25. **2** to set up. **Wer nix ~ kann, kann aa nix baue.** He

who can't set anything up, can't build anything either. LRT

uffschticke (fer) - <*Engl* to stick up for (one's part). KYG1878. **Er is en guder ehrlicher Buh. Mer kann immer ~ fer ihn.** He is a good honest boy, one can always stick up for him (defend him). LRT

uffschwetze - 1 to talk someone into something. KYG1964. **2** to talk up (to a person). KYG1965

uffsetze, *pp* **uffgsetzt - 1** to set up (drinks). **Geschder hoscht du's uffgsetzt fer mich, heit is es mei Zeit.** Yesterday you set it up for me, today it's my turn. **Wann du un dei Freind noch em Wattshaus kumme den Owed, duhn ich eich's bissel ~.** If you and your friend come to the inn (tavern) tonight, I'll give you a little treat. LRT. **2** to give a treat (Leb Co). **Do is wennich eppes fer dich, ich will dir's ~.** Here is a little something for you, I want to give you a treat. LRT. **3** to stack up. **Die Kinner hen die Blacks uffgsetzt.** The children stacked up the blocks. LRT

uffsuche, *pp* **uffgsucht** - to search for, to look up. **Er hot all sei Voreldere uffgsucht.** He looked up all of his ancestors in a genealogical study. LRT

ufftrimme - <*Engl* to trim up. KYB2062. **Wie der Tscheck un die Kaet gheiert hen, hen die Nochbere ihre Kaer alles uffgetrimmt ghat.** When Jake and Kate were married, the neighbors had really trimmed up their car. LRT

uffwareme - to warm up. **Du**

kannscht sell Hinkelbottboi was iwwerich waar vun geschder ~. You can warm up that chicken potpie that was left over from yesterday. LRT

uffweeche - to soften by soaking. **Eb mer darri Buhne kocht, sett mer sie fer sex Schtund ~.** Before one cooks dried beans, they should soak for about six hours. LRT

uffweise, *pp* **uffgewisse** - to show up. **Es Wedder waar wiescht un's hot niemand uffgewisse fer die Karich.** The weather was bad and no one showed up for church. *cf* **uffdrehe.** LRT

uffwenne - to turn hay. KYG2077. = **wenne**

uffwesche, *pp* **uffgewesche** - to clean. **Sie hen die ganz Kich uffgewesche.** They washed up the whole kitchen. LRT

uffwesche, *refl* - to wash up. *cf* **sich fege, nuffschwemme.** KYG2167. **Well, sis baut Zeit fer esse, mir daede uns besser ~.** Well, it's just about time to eat, we had better wash up (our hands and faces). LRT

Uffweschkiwwel, *m* - wash-up bucket. KYG2169. **Der ~ is am rinne.** The wash-up bucket is leaking. LRT

uffwische, *pp* **uffgewischt** - to wipe up. **Ich hab all seller Dreck uffgewischt.** I wiped up all that dirt. LRT

uffyoche - to yoke up. KYG2263

uffyuuse - <*Engl* to use up.

KYG2117. **Wie sie faddich waare mit ihrem Deppich, hen sie alli Blacke uffgeyuust hat.** When they were finished with their quilt, they had used up every patch. LRT

uffzaehle, *pp* **uffgezaehlt** - to tabulate. **Mir hen uffgezaehlt wie viel Leit as an die Gemee waare.** We tabulated how many people were at church. LRT

uffziehe, *pp* **uffgezoge** - to raise (a family). **Selli Familye hot 16 Kinner uffgezoge.** That family raised 16 children. LRT

Uhrebutzer, *m* - jeweler. **Seller ~ is sei Geld waert.** That jeweler is worth his money. LRT

umbatzle - to tumble over. = **umschtatze.** KYG2073. **Der Wind hot geblose un all die Blumme uff die Bortsch sin umgschtatzt.** The wind blew and all the plants on the porch tumbled over. LRT

umbennich, *adj* - overpowering. **Er is en ~er Mann.** He is an overpowering man. LRT

umbluge - to turn with the plow. KYG2078. = **unnerbluge.** LRT

umfalle, *pp* **umgfalle** - to tip over. *cf* **umschmeisse.** KYG2024. **Der Schtamm vun sellem Baam waar faul un endlich is er umgfalle.** The trunk of that tree was rotten and finally it fell over. LRT

umherlaafe, *pp* **umhergeloffe** - to wander around. **Er is umhergeloffe wie en Blinder.** He wandered around like a blind one. LRT

umkehre - to turn about. = **rumdrehe, rumkehre, sich umwenne.** KYG2078. = **umdrehe.** LRT

umkumme, *pp* **is ~** - to perish. **Fimf Mannsleit sin ~ in sellem Feier.** Five men died (perished) in that fire. LRT

umlege, *pp* **umgelegt** - to lay on the other side, to lay down or over. **Sie hen die Leeder umgelegt.** They laid the ladder down or over on the other side. LRT

umleidlich, *adj* - unpleasant. **Kinner, selli Yacht is mir ~.** Children, that noise is unpleasant for me. LRT

umsaege - to saw down. **der Baam ~** - to saw the tree down. LRT

umschiewe, *pp* **umgschowe** - to push over. **Die yunge Ketzer hen paar Graabschtee umgschowe.** The young scoundrels pushed a few tombstones over. **Der Graabschtee ~ odder umschmeisse.** LRT

umschtilpe - to turn upside down. KYG2078

umschtoosse - to unsettle, to knock over or over throw. *cf* **wanke, vum Blatz bringe.** KYG2113. **Die Bulle hen sell Fass umgschtoosse.** The bulls upset that barrel. LRT

unaagenehmlich, *adj* - unpleasant. *cf* **unblessierlich, ungemietlich, widderwaddich.** KYG2109

unaaschtendich, *adj* -

unbecoming. = **ungeziemt.** KYG2091. **Sell is en ~er Gaund fer selli Frau.** That's an unbecoming gown for that woman. LRT

unaenlich, *adj* - unlike. = **ungleich.** KYG2107

unaerdlich, *adj* - unearthly. *cf* **schpuckich.** KYG2100

unappeditlich, *adj* - unappetizing. KYG2090. **Selli Ess-Sache gucke mir ~.** Those foods look unappetizing to me. **Seller Geruch is ~.** That smell is unappetizing. **Seller Hinkelmischt datt vanne iwwer der Hof zoddle guckt an riecht so ~.** Spreading that chicken manure over the front lawn looks and smells so unpleasant. LRT

unbaremhatzich, *adj* - unmerciful. = **hatthatzich.** KYG2108

Unbaremhatzichkeet, *f* - unmercifulness. KYG2108.

unbaschdich, *adj* - uncivil. KYG2093

unbedenkt, *adv* - unthinkingly, without thinking. **~ saage** - to say thoughtlessly. KYG2113. **Geschder hen mir ~ Bsuch grickt.** We had an unexpected (didn't think about it, it was a surprise) visit yesterday. LRT. = **unbedacht, unnebedenkt.** PB,7/6/25. **Mer muss sich schemme wie des ~ vorkumme is.** One needs to be ashamed how this happened without thinking. LRT

unbeholfe, *adj* - unhandy. = **unhendich, unschicklich.**

KYG2103

unbekehrt, *adj* - unconverted. KYG2094. **Heit sin en latt Leit bekehrt warre an de Karich, awwer es sin noch blendi as ~ sin.** Today there were a lot of people converted at the church, but there are still plenty (of folks) who remain unconverted. LRT

unbekimmerlich, *adj* - unconcerned, uncaring. **Ferwas sett mer so ~ sei?** Why should one be so unconcerned? LRT. **Sell waar ihm en gross ~ Wese gewest.** That was a matter of total unconcern to him. LRT

unbekimmerlich, *adv* - unconcerned, uncaring. **(die Bledder in de Biewel) so ~ drehe** - to thumb through (the Bible). KYG2010.

unbenaamt, *adj* - unnamed. KYG2108. **Des Kind was do vergrawwe is, waar dod gebore un es waar ~.** The child that is buried here was stillborn and was unnamed. LRT. = **ungenannt**

unbennich, *adj* - unmanageable. KYG2108. **Seller Buh is ~, sie wisse gaar net, was zu duh mit ihm.** That boy is unmanageable, they don't know what to do with him. **Ihre Buwe sin immer so ~.** Their boys are always so unruly. LRT. = **wiescht, wild**

unbewegt, *adj* - unmoved. KYG2108. **Sei Fraa is gschtarewe un er waar ganz ~.** His wife died and he was totally unmoved. LRT

unblessierlich, *adj* - unpleasant. **Selli Yacht waar mir arig ~.**

That noise was very unpleasant to me. LRT

unbrofittlich, *adj* - unprofitable. KYG2110. **Sei Bissniss waar ~ un is futsch gange.** His business was unprofitable and it went belly-up. LRT. *cf* **unwaertvoll**

undankbaar, *adj* - ungrateful. KYG2103. **Selli Leit hen en latt Hilf grickt awwer sie waare ~.** Those people got a lot of help but they were ungrateful. LRT

undenklich, *adj* - unthinkable. KYG2113

unendich, *adj* - unending. KYG2101. **Seller Daag wu's football Schpiel waar, waar en unendlichi Roi Kaere am Haus verbeigange.** That day of the football game, an endless row of cars passed the house. LRT. = **endlos, unendlich**

unerheert, *adj* - unheard of. *cf* **unerlebt.** KYG2104

unerlaabt, *adj* - not permitted. **Fer yaage geh Sunndaags is ~.** To go hunting on Sundays in not permitted. LRT

unerwaart, *adj* - unaware. = **unversehne.** KYG2091

unewe, *adj* - undulating, uneven. KYG2100. **Die Leit gleiche net wann der Karichhof ~ is.** The people don't like when the cemetery is uneven. LRT. = **hiwwlich**

unfaeh'ich, *adj* - unable. KYG2089

unfehlbaar, *adj* - unfailing.

KYG2101. **Es macht nix aus was seller Yunge browiert, er is die menscht Zeit ~.** It doesn't matter what that young man tires, he rarely fails. LRT

unfreindlich, *adj* - unkind. = **net baremhatzich.** KYG2106. **Er macht immer so'n wiescht Gsicht un guckt so ~.** He always makes such an ugly face and looks so unfriendly. LRT

unfruchtbaar, *adj* - unfruitful. KYG2103. **Sei Arewet waar ~.** His work was unfruitful. LRT

ungebacke, *adj* - lacking common sense. **Er is en alder ~ner Geesbock.** He's an old goat, lacking common sense. LRT

ungebascht, *adj* - unbrushed. KYG2092

ungebleecht, *adj* - unbleached. KYG2092

ungebodde, *adj* - unbeaten. KYG2091. **Die Ringkemfer an unser Schul sin so weit des Yaahr ~.** The wrestlers at our school are undefeated so far this year. LRT

ungebutzt, *adj* - uncleaned. KYG2093. **Er is en ~er Seikopp.** He is an unclean pig head. LRT

ungelannt, *adj* - untutored. = **net gelannt.** KYG2114. **Er schickt sich immer so ~ aa.** He always acts so untrained. LRT

Ungelegenheit, *f* - circumstance. **in ~ kumme** - to come into untoward circumstances. KYG2114

ungeloffe, *adj* - untrodden. **en ~r Weg** - an untrodden path. KYG2114

ungemei, *adj* - uncommon. = **ungewehnlich.** KYG2094

ungerechderweis, *adv* - unjustly. KYG2106

ungerecht, *adj* - unjust. = **unrecht, unrechtschaffich, net recht.** KYG2106

Unglaawe, *m* - unbelief. KYG2091. **Sei ~ is wie en Granket zu ihm, er will jeder Mensch nix glaawe.** Unbelief is like a disease to him, he doesn't want to believe anybody anything. LRT

Unglaawer, *m* - unbeliever. KYG2091. **Sie sin all Grischde in seine Familye, awwer er is en ~.** All the members in his family are Christian (believers), but he is an unbeliever. LRT

unglaawich, *adj* - disbelieving. **en ~er Mensch** - an unbelieving person. *cf* **en unglaawener Mann.** KYG2091l. **Ya, er is en ~er Mensch.** Yes, he is a disbelieving person. LRT

ungleich, *adj* **1** unequal. *cf* **unewe.** KYG2101. **Alle Backeschtee in sellem ganze Haus gucke ~.** Each brick in that whole house look dissimilar. LRT. **2** unlike. **Selli Brieder sin arig ~.** Those brothers are very unlike (one another). LRT

unglicklich, *adj* - unlucky. KYG2108. **Es scheint er is immer so en ~er Mensch.** It appears that he is always such an unlucky (unfortunate) person.

LRT

Unglicklichkeit, *f* - misfortune. **In allem ~, waare mir net deheem, wie sie do waare fer uns bsuche.** Of all misfortune, we were not home when they were here to visit us. LRT

Unglicksdaag, *m* - unlucky day. KYG2108. **Der Daag wie ihre Scheier nunnergebrennt is, waar en ~ fer die ganz Nochberschaft.** The day their barn burnt down was unlucky for the whole neighborhood. LRT

Ungraut, *n* - **1** weeds. **~ sin eenichi Blanze as am waxe sin wu sie net sedde.** Weeds are any plants that are growing where they shouldn't be. **Ihre Gaarde is immer voll ~.** Their garden is always full of weeds. LRT. **2** undisciplined youth. KYG2099.

ungscheit, *adv* - unwisely. **Yunger, du schicksch dich awwer ~ aa.** Young man, you are acting very unwise. LRT

ungschicklich, *adv* - tactless. **Schick dich net so ~ aa.** Don't act so tactless. LRT

ungsund, *adj* - unwell. **Fer so hatt schaffe is ~.** To work so hard is not healthful. LRT

unheilich, *adv* - unhallowed. KYG2103. **Sich so aaschicke is ~.** To act like that is unhallowed. LRT

unleidlich, *adj* - unbearing. = **umleidlich.** KYG2091

unmanierlich, *adv* - unmannerly. **Er schickt sich so**

~ **aa.** He acts so unmannerly. LRT

unmechdich, *adj* - unconscious. KYG2094. **In sellem Unfall is er aus de Kaer gschmisse warre; er waar baut en Schtund uumechdich gewest.** In that accident, he was thrown from the car; he was unconscious for about an hour. LRT. = **uumechdich**

unnadierlich, *adj* - unnatural. KYG2109. **Schnee im Yuli is ~.** Snow is July is unnatural. LRT

unnebedenkt, *adv* - unintentionally. KYG2105

unnedarich, *adv* - through below. KYG2008. **Die Radde sin ~'s Welschkannheisli gschprunge.** The rats ran under (through beneath) the corn crib. LRT

unnedraus, *adv* - down country. **Sie hen ganz ~ im Land gewuhnt.** They lived way down in the country. LRT

unneedich, *adj* - unnecessary. KYG2109. **Sell laut Gegreisch is ~.** That loud screaming is unnecessary. LRT

Unneedichkeet, *f* - unnecessariness. KYG2109. Leb. Co. ~keit.

unneher, *adv* - along the bottom. **Schreib dei Naame ~.** Write your name along the bottom. LRT

unnenei, *adv* - in under. KYG2095. **Sie hen sell Fleesch ~ in der Backoffe geduh.** They put the meat down in the bottom of the oven. LRT

unneraerdisch, *adj* - underground. KYG2096

unnerbreese - to undervalue. KYG2098

Unnerdaan, *m* - underling subject. KYG2097

unnerdricke - to stifle. *cf* zerickhewe. KYG1879

Unnergang, *m* - undoing. KYG2099. **Selli eent satt Medizin waar sei ~.** That one kind of medicine was his undoing. LRT

unnergeh, *pp* is unnergange - **1** to set (of the sun). **Die Sunn geht unner.** The sun is going down. **2** to go down, to sink. **Dreed net in sell Eis datt, du gehscht unner.** Don't step into that ice, you will sink. **3** to undergo. **Sie sin en latt hatt Glick unnergange.** They underwent a lot of bad luck. LRT

Unnergewicht, *n* - underweight. KYG2099. **Selli Seck Aarensche sedde vier Pund wiege, awwer sie sin all ~.** Those bags of oranges are supposed to weigh four pounds, but they are all underweight. LRT

Unnergleeder, *pl* - underclothes. KYG2096. **Mei verrissni ~ sin mir umleidlich.** My torn underwear is uncomfortable. LRT

Unnergrund, *m* - subsoil. **Der ~ is viel besser wie ken Grund.** The subsoil is much better than no soil. LRT

Unnergrundweg, *m* - tunnel.

KYG2074

Unnerhecke, *pl* - underbrush. **Sei Weg darich die ~ mache.** To thread one's way through the underbrush. KYG2004. = **Unnerholz.** KYG2095

Unnerhemm, *n* - undershirt. KYG2097. **Sell ~ is rot, un es sett weiss sei.** That undershirt is red and it should be white. LRT

unnernemme - to undertake. KYG2098. **Sell is meh Arewet as ich ~ will.** That is more work than I want to undertake. LRT

Unnernemmung, *f* - undertaking. = **Vornemmes.** KYG2098

Unnerrees, *m* - tail race. KYG1960

Unnerrock, *m* - **1** under jacket. KYG2096. **2** underskirt. = **Unnerschtock.** KYG2097. **De Fraa ihre ~ is zu lang; er hengt unnich ihrem Gaund raus.** My wife's petticoat is too long; it hangs out from under her dress. LRT

unnerschetze - to underrate. = **zu gering aaschlagge.** KYG2097

unnerschlechdich, *adj* - undershot. KYG2097

unnerschreiwe, *pp* **unnerschriwwe** - to undersign. KYG2097. **Sei Mom hot ihm sei Lanning unnnerschriwwe.** His mother undersigned his education. LRT. *cf* **unnerzeechne**

unnerscht, *adj* - the lowest. **Sis en Loch am ~e Paert vun die**

170

Fens. There's a hole in the lowest part of the fence. LRT

unnerschtecke - to tuck under (as end of band in tying grain). KYG2072

unnersewwerscht, *adv* - upside down. **Mir hen sell Fass ~ gedreht.** We turned that barrel upside down. LRT

unnersuche, *pp* **unnergsucht** - to research., investigate **Sache ~** - to conduct research. **Ich hab's gedichdich unnergsucht, awwer ich hab nix gfunne.** I researched it thoroughly, but I found nothing. LRT

unnersuche, *refl* - to try. = **browiere, versuche.** KYG2071

unneruff, *adv* - **1** (coming) up the road. **2** (coming) up the rear. **Sie wuhne datt drunne, un allegebott kumme sie ~ fer uns sehne.** They live down there and every now and then they come up the road to see us. LRT. **3** up from below. KYG2116. **Die Warem sin ~ zugraddle kumme vum Keller.** The worms came crawling up from the cellar. LRT

unnerverkaafe - to undersell. = **wollfeiler [= welfler. LRT], verkaafe.** KYG2097

unnerwehe losse - to refrain from. **Des Umgangwese misse mir ~.** This sex thing we've got to refrain from. LRT

unnerwegs, *adv* - on the way. **~ losse** - to stop. KYG1889. **~ kennt dir schtoppe un "Hello" saage.** On your way, you can stop and say "Hello." LRT

Unnerwelt, *f* - underworld. KYG2099

Unnerzug, *m* - undercurrent. KYG2096

unni, *prep* - without. **~ Geld geht mer net weit.** Without money one won't get very far. LRT

unnich, *prep* - under. **~ Elt** - under age. = **unne, unner.** *cf* **drunner** - under it. KYG2095. **Duh selli Bax unnich dei Bett.** Put that box under your bed. LRT

unrecht, *adj* - tort. KYG2040. **Sell waar en ~ zu sellem Mann.** That was an injustice to that man. LRT

Unrot, *m* - undesirable person or animal. KYG2099

Unruh, *f* - unrest. KYG2110. **Grieg macht viel ~.** War creates much unrest. **So en ~ will ich sei Lewe nimmi sehne.** Such unrest I don't ever want to see in my whole life. LRT. = **Uffruhr.** KYG2075

Unruhzeit, *f* - time of unrest. KYG2110. **Griegszeit is aa ~.** Wartime is also a time of unrest. LRT

unsauwer, *adj* - unclean. = **dreckich, unrein, net sauwer.** KYG2093

unschuldich, *adj* - innocent. **Ya, du bischt ~.** Yes, you are innocent. LRT

unsicher, *adv* - dangerous, unsafe. LRT

unsri, *f* - *poss pron* - ours.

Hoscht du selli 1928 Chevy Kaer gsehne,? Sell waar ~. Did you see that 1928 Chevy automobile? That was ours. LRT

unverbrennt, *adj* - unburnt. KYG2092

unverdeelt, *adj* - undivided. KYG2099. **Mir daede gleiche eier ~i Acht hawwe.** We'd like to have your undivided attention. LRT

unverdient, *adj* - undeserved. KYG2099. **Sellem Kind sei Bletsching waar ~.** That child's spanking was undeserved. **Sei grosser Unglick is ~.** His great misfortune is unmerited. LRT

unverdraeglich, *adj* - unbearable. KYG2091

unverdrosse, *adj* - unawed, undeterred. KYG2091

unverennert, *adj* - unchanged. KYG2093. **Ich hab mei Backebuch verlore ghat, un wie ich's widder gfunne hab, waar's ~.** I had lost my wallet, and when I found it again, it was unchanged. LRT

unvergesslich, *adj* - unforgettable. KYG2102. **Wie die Memm 80 Yaahr alt waar, hen mir en scheeni Versammling ghat fer sie; sell waar ~.** When mother was 80 years old, we had a nice gathering (party) for her; it was unforgettable. LRT

unvergunnich, *adj* - uncharitable. KYG2093

unverhiedlich, *adj* - unavoidable. KYG2091. **Alt waare is ~.** Getting old is unavoidable. LRT. = **unverhietlich**

unverhoffdich, *adj* - unintentional. KYG2105. [We rarely use **un-**, but instead **net**. LRT. Apply to all of the following words.]

unverhofft, *adj* - unannounced (of guests). KYG2090. **Geschder hen mir ~ Bsuch grickt.** Yesterday we got unexpected guests. LRT

unverleglich, *adj* - undeniable. *cf* **Es hot net verleegelt sei kenne.** It was undeniable. KYG2095. **Die Yunge hen die Schaade geduh ghat; es waar ~.** The young ones had done the damage; it was undeniable. LRT

unverletzt, *adj* - unhurt. KYG2104. **Mir hen alles gut bedracht un mir hen nix ~ gsehne.** We examined everything well and we found everything unhurt. LRT

unvermixt, *adj* - unmixed. KYG2108. = **net vermixt.** LRT

unversalze, *adj* - unsalted. KYG2111. = **net unversalze.** LRT

unverschrocke, *adj* - undismayed. = **unverzaagt.** KYG2099. = **net verschrocke.** LRT

Unverschtand, *m* - lack of common sense. **Was fer ~ is dann sell?** What lack of common sense is that? **Schick dich net so dumm aa, sell is yuscht ~.** Don't act so stupid, that is just ignorance (lack of understanding). LRT

unverschteert, *adj* - undisturbed. KYG2099. **Des Haaseyaage waar Schpass heit; die Haase waare ~.** This rabbit hunting was fun today; the rabbits were undisturbed. LRT

unverschtennich, *adj* - not understanding. KYG2098. **Die Yunge waare awwer ~ heit.** The young fellows were really unruly today. LRT

unversehne, *adj* - unprovided, unaware. KYG2110. = **net versehne. Des Geil schlachde fer die zaahme eigschparrde Fix fiedere, waar mir ganz ~.** I was not at all aware of this butchering horses to feed the domesticated caged foxes (grown for their furs). LRT

unversichert, *adj* - unprotected. KYG2110. = **net versichert.** LRT

unversucht, *adj* - untried. = **unbrowiert.** KYG2114. = **net versucht, net browiert.** LRT

unverwelklich, *adj* - unwitherable. KYG2116. = **net verwelklich.** LRT

unverzaagt, *adv* - **1** fearlessly. **Seller Hund is so ~ druffhiegange.** That dog went about it without fear. **2** undismayed. **Die Geil hen yuscht ~ datt gschtanne.** The horses just stood there without any disturbance. LRT

unvorsichdich, *adj* - disregarded. KYG2110. = **net vorsichdich.** LRT

unwaahr, *adj* - untrue. *cf* **falsch.** KYG2114. = **net waahr.**

LRT

unwaahrscheinlich, *adv* - unlikely. KYG2107. = **net wahrscheinlich.** LRT

Unwaerdichkeet, *f* - unworthiness. KYG2116

unweislich, *adj* - unwise. *cf* **ungscheit.** KYG2116

unweltlich, *adj* - unworldly. KYG2116

unwillens, *adv* - unwilling. = **unwillich, net willens.** KYG2115

unwillkumm, *adj* - unwelcome. KYG2115. = **net willkumm.** LRT

unwissend, *adv* - unknowingly. = **unwissentlich.** KYG2107

unwohl, *adj* - unwell. = **ungsund.** KYG2115. = **net wohl.** LRT

unzaehlich, *adj* - unnumbered. KYG2109

unzeidich, *adj* - untimely. KYG2114

Unzucht, *f* - unseemliness. KYG2112

unzufridde, *adj* - dissatisfied. **Ferwas bischt du so ~?** Why are you so dissatisfied? **Es macht nix aus was mer dutt fer ihn, er is immer ~.** It doesn't matter what one does for him, he is always unsatisfied. LRT. = **net zufridde.** KYG2111

Ursach, *f* - reason. **Es is ken ~ devor.** It is unwarrantable. KYG2115. **Es hot niemand**

gewisst fer was as er sell geduh hot, er hot ken ~ gewwe kenne. No one knew why he did that, he could give no reason. **Die ~ as ich net an die Versammling waar, waar as ich grank waar.** The reason that I was not at the gathering was that I was sick. LRT

uumechdich, *adj* - unconscious. LRT. = **unmechdich**

Vaddel, *m* - quarter. **der ~ nemme** - to take advantage of. KYG1960

Vaddeldaalerschtick, *n* - 25¢ piece. KYG2082. **En ~ is nimmi genunk fer der Fon yuuse.** A quarter (a 25¢ piece) is not enough anymore to use the phone. LRT

vaddelhaft, *adv* - taking advantage of another. KYG1963

vannedraus, *adv* - out front. **Datt ~ schteht en Hasch.** Out front there stands a deer. LRT

vanneherschpringe - to run ahead. **Ich gleich wann die Hund ~.** I like when the dogs run ahead. LRT

vanneherreide, *pp* is **vannehergeridde** - to ride in advance. **Die Pollies sin vannehergeridde.** The police rode ahead. LRT

vannenausbezaahle - to pay in advance. **Wann's en Yaahr nemmt, bis sie unser Schank mache kenne, dann sedde mir nix ~ breiche.** If it will take a year before they can get to making our cupboard, then we should not need to pay anything in advance. LRT

vannenausdenke, *pp* -gedenkt - to think ahead. KYG1998. **Sie hen nie nix vannenausgedenkt odder geplaant.** They never thought or planned anything ahead. LRT

vannenaussaage, *pp* **vannenausgsaat** - to tell in advance. KYG1981. **As mer net datt laafe sette, sell hen sie uns vannenausgsaat ghat.** They had told us in advance that we should not walk there. LRT. = **vorhersaage**

vannenausschicke, *pp* **vannenausgschickt** - to send on before. **Ich hab ihm lang vannenaus Watt gschickt ghat, as ich net kumme kann.** I had sent him word long ago that I could not come. LRT

vannenausschwetze - to talk of what one will (not) do in the future. KYG1965

vannenaussehne, *pp* **vannenausgsehne** - to see in advance. **Mer hot ~ kenne as er verliere daed.** One could see in advance that he was going to lose. LRT

vannenuff, *adv* - up by the front way. KYG2116. **Du kannscht do vanne am Hof nuff-faahre.** You can drive up here in front of the yard. LRT

vardem, *adv* - before this. = **devor**. KYG1999. **Davor, hen immer die Vorb(e)reiting Samschdaag Oweds ghat.** Formerly they always held a preparatory service on Saturday evenings (prior to Communion Sunday). LRT

varderhand, *adv* - ahead of

time. **net ~ geblaant sei** - to be unpremeditated. KYG2110. **Hoscht du sell ~ gewisst?** Did you know that beforehand? LRT

vaschichfalle, *pp* is **vaschichgfalle** - to fall forward. **Er is vaschichfalle.** He fell over forward. LRT

Vedderschteddel, *n* - near the center of town. KYG2043

vellich, *adj/ adv* - true to type. KYG2068. **Vellichi sin sell?** Which ones are they? LRT

vendere - to take a guess. KYG1961

Venduschreiwer, *m* - sale clerk. **Sie hen gsaat, sie kenne em ~ sei Gschreib net lese.** They said thay can't read the sale clerk's writing. LRT,4/18/2000. **Er is en ~.** He is a sale clerk. LRT

veraer´gere, *pp* **veraergert** - to worsen. **Sie hen gschafft un gschafft, awwer sie hen yuscht alles veraergert.** They worked and worked, but they just made everything worse. LRT

veral´dert, *adj* - timeworn. KYG2021

verbab´ble, *refl* - to talk too long. = **sich verblaudre**. KYG1964

verbadd´ere, *pp* **verbaddert** - to perplex, disturb. **Es waar en grossi Versammling un er waar der Schwetzer, awwer er hot vergesse, was er saage hot welle. Sell hot ihn awwer verbaddert.** It was a large gathering and he was the speaker, but he forgot what he wanted to say. That really perplexed him. LRT

verbam´ble, *pp* **verbambelt** - to squander (money; time). **Sie sedde blendi Geld hawwe, wann sie's net all verbambelt hedde.** They should have plenty of money if they had not squandered it. LRT. **Zeit ~ (verbemble)** - to kill time. KYG2019. **Fer selli Leit all zammer bringe uff eemol, duht zu viel Zeit verbambele.** To bring all those people together at one time, is a waste of time. LRT

verbapp´le, *refl, pp* **verbappelt** - **1** to blurt out. = **sich verblatsche, sich verblaudre. Er dutt sich immer so ~.** He always blurts out things he should not. LRT. **2** to talk too long. KYG2034. **Die Versammling waar voll Harrlichkeit bis Deel's verbappelt hen.** The meeting was filled with joy (and happiness) until some talked too much (and too long). LRT

verbei´nemme - to take past. KYG1963

verbei´schtolbere, *pp* **verbeigschtolbert** - to stumble past. **Er is an die Dier verbeigschtolbert.** He stumbled past the door. LRT

verbeisse, *pp* **verbisse** - to crush with the teeth. KYG1978. **Der Hund hot sell Hinkel alles verbisse ghat.** The dog had bitten (and crushed) that chicken terribly. LRT

verbei´faahre - to drive by or past. LRT

verbei´laafe - to walk past.

KYG2159. **Ya, du kannscht yuscht an daere Arewet ~, ich geb nix drum.** Yes, you can just walk by this work, I don't care. LRT

verbei´rolle - to roll by. **Selli alt Kaer rollt allegebott do verbei.** That old car rolls by here every now and then. LRT

verbei´schnieke, *pp* **is verbeigschniekt** - to sneak past. **Die Buwe sin do am Haus verbeigschniekt.** The boys sneaked here past the house. LRT

verbess´ere, *refl* - to improve upon oneself. **Wann mer hatt genunk browiert, kann mer sich ~.** If one tries hard enough, one can improve oneself. LRT

verbie´de, *pp* **verbodde** - to prohibit. **Ich hab yaage welle uff ihre Felder, awwer sie hen mir's verbodde.** I wanted to hunt on their fields, but they prohibited it. LRT

verbie´ge, *pp* **is verboge** - to bend out of shape. **Wann em sei Brill alles verboge is, daed mer sie besser yuscht so gut weckschmeisse.** When one's glasses are all bent out of shape, one might as well throw them away. LRT

verbin´ne - to untie. *cf* **losbinne, losmache, uffmache.** KYG2114

verblie´he, *pp* **verblieht** - to be past blooming. **Die Blumme sin verblieht.** The flowers are past their bloom. LRT

verbren´ne - **1** to burn. **es Maul ~** - to speak at the wrong time.

KYG2019. **Er schwetzt immer, wann er net sett un verbrennt sei Maul.** He always talks and says things he shouldn't say (burns his mouth). **Sie hen seller ganz Haufe Gfrees verbrennt.** They burnt that whole pile of trash. LRT. **2** to burn badly. KYG2256. **Yunger, nau du muscht achtgewwe, seller Kaffi is hees; du verbrennscht dei Maul.** Young one, you need to be careful, that coffee is hot; you'll burn your mouth badly. LRT,4/18/2000

verbutzt´ - stunted. **Selli Busslin gucke bissel ~.** Those kittens look a bit stunted. LRT

verdan´ke, *pp* **verdankt** - to have to thank for. KYG1990.

verda´rewe - to spoil. LRT

verdascht´, *adj* - thirsted. KYG1999. **Er waar schlimm ~** He was in dire straits because of thirst. LRT

verdasch´de, *pp* **is verdascht** - to die from thirst. KYG1999. **Er is verdaschdt.** He died of thirst. LRT

verdee´le, *pp* **verdeelt** - **1** to divide and share. **Es kann verdeelt sei.** It is separable. **Dir Kinner misst die Kichlin ~.** You children must share the cookies. **2** to divide into parts. LRT

verden´ke - to take amiss. KYG1963

verdil´liche, *pp* **verdillicht** - to stamp out. **Selli Giftranke hen mir mol endlich verdillicht.** We have finally eradicated that poison ivy. LRT

174

Verdinscht´, *m* - pay, salary. **Die Woch waar sei ~ greesser wie gwehnlich.** This week his earnings were larger than usual. LRT

verdollt´, *adv* - deucedly. **Er hot ihre en ~er Schtooss gewwe.** He gave her a heck of a push. LRT

verdrau´(n)ensvoll, *adj* - trusting. = **zudrauisch.** KYG2070. **Er is en ~er Mensch.** He is a trustworthy person. LRT

Verdrau´e, *n* - reliance. **Deel Leit duhne gaar ken ~ in seller Mann.** Some people put absolutely no trust in that man. LRT. = **Zuverdraue**

verdreck´e, *refl* - to soil one's clothing. **Wann du dich net ~ witt, dann daedscht besser im Haus bleiwe.** If you don't want to dirty yourself, then you had better stay in the house. LRT

verdre´de - to trample. **Noch die Vendu waar der Hof alles ~.** After the sale, the yard was all trampled. LRT

verdreht´, *adj* - twisted. **Die Darem sin ~.** The intestines are twisted. KYG2084. **Sei Daerem sin ihm ~ warre.** His intestines became twisted. LRT

verdreh´e, *pp* **verdreht** - to be confused, *i.e.* turned around. **Bis er faddich waar schwetze, hot er alles verdreht ghat.** By the time he was finished talking he had confused everything. LRT

verdreh´e, *pp* **verdreht** - to cause pain by twisting. **Ei, du Gott nochemol, hab ich awwer mei Buckel verdreht.** Oh, my God, did I ever twist my back (it really hurt). LRT,4/18/2000

verdreh´e - to turn the wrong way. KYG2077

verdrick´e, *pp* **verdrickt** - to mash. **verdrickdi Grummbiere** - mashed potatoes. **Du kannscht die Grummbiere ~.** You can mash the potatoes. LRT

verdrip´pelt, *adj* - trampled. **Noch die Vendu waar der Hof alles ~.** After the sale the yard was all trampled. LRT. *cf* **verdrede**

veree´niche, *pl* **vereenicht** - to unite. = **eenich mache.** KYG2106. **Sie waare all mitnanner eenich.** They were all united with one another. LRT

veree´nicht, *adj* - united. **Vereenichde Brieder** - United Brethren. **die Vereenichde Schtaade** - the United States. KYG2106

veren´nere - to change. **sich net ~** - to be unchangeable. KYG2093. **Wann alles so gut geht, was wett mer ~?** When everything goes so well, what would one want to change? LRT

verfau´le, *pp* **verfault** - to rot away. **Der ganz Kareb voll Grummbiere waar verfault.** The whole basket of potatoes was rotted. LRT

verfech´de, *refl, pp* **verfochde** - to be involved in quarrels. **Er un sei Aldi hen sich verfochde bis sie nimmi beinanner bleiwe hen kenne.** He and his wife were continually involved in quarrels until they could no longer stay together. LRT

verfeh´le - to miss. **Wann sie yaage gehne, dutt er immer eppes ~.** When they go hunting, he always misses something. LRT

Verfieh´rer, *m* - seducer. **Der ~ is net sei Salz in der Supp wert.** The seducer is not worth the salt in his soup. LRT

verfieh´re - to seduce, to mislead. *cf* **aapacke. Du muscht net dei Kinner ~.** You must not mislead your children. LRT

verfin´gere, *pp* **verfingert** - to smudge with the fingers. **Die Kinner hen die Fenschdere in die Diere alles verfingert ghat.** The children had the windows in the doors all smudged. LRT

verfleck´e, *pp* **verfleckt** - to stain, soil, spot.. **Selli Bluing hot sei Hemm alles verfleckt.** That bluing put a stain all over his shirt. LRT

verflickt´, *adj* - mended many times. **Sie sin reich, weil er immer ~i Hosse aa hot.** They are rich because he always wears trousers that have been patched many times. LRT

verfoch´de, *adj* - disputatious. **verfochtni Leit** - quarrelsome folks. KYG2164. **Mit so verfochdeni Leit will ich nix zu duh hawwe.** I don't want anything to do with such fighting people. **Selli Haahne sin verfochtni Dinger.** Those roosters are critters prone to fight. LRT

verfran´zelt, *adj* - worn to

fringes. **Guck mol datt, sei Hossebeh is alles ~!** Look there, his pants leg is all frayed. LRT,4/18/2000

verfres´se, *pp* **verfresst** - to squander on food. **Die Keffer hen unser Blummschteck alles ~.** The beetles really riddled our flower plants. LRT

verfro´re, *adj* - frozen. **Sie is en ~nes Ding.** She is a really sensitive person to the cold. LRT

verfug´gere, *pp* **verfuggert** - to waste. KYG2170. **Sie hen all ihre Geld verfuggert.** They squandered all their money. LRT

vergaf´fe, *pp* **vergafft** - to make a slip of the tongue. **Desemol hot sie die Waahret bissel vergafft.** This time she stretched the truth a bit, by a slip of the tongue. LRT

vergaf´fe, *refl, pp* **vergafft** - to be mistaken. **Er hot sich vergafft; er hot gemehnt, es waar en Fisch, awwer es waar en Ool.** He was mistaken; he thought it was a fish, but it was an eel. LRT

vergeb´ens, *adv* - unavailing. = **vergeblich.** KYG2090

vergeh, *refl* - to dissolve. LRT

verglenn´ere, *pp* **verglennert** - to make smaller. **Sie hen die Pickders verglennert.** They reduced the size of the photos. **Mir hen die Schreiner grickt fer unser Bank ~.** We got the carpenters to make our bench smaller. LRT

vergnodd´le, *refl, pp*

vergnoddelt - to become entangled in frustration. **Wie sie sell gheert hot vun sellem Buweschtreech, hot sie sich ganz vergnoddelt.** When she heard of those boyish pranks, she became all entangled in frustration. LRT,4/11/2000

vergraa´we, *pp* **~** - to bury. **Sie hen der Hund ~.** They buried the dog. LRT

vergrat´ze, *pp* **vergratzt** - to spoil by scratching. = **verschinne. Selli Hecke hen ihm sei Kaer alles vergratzt.** Those bushes really scratched up his car. **Mit seim Schuppkarich hot er mei neie Kaer vergratzt.** He scratched my new car with his wheelbarrow. LRT

vergraun´ze, *refl* - to complain irritably. **Vergraunz dich doch net so!** Don't be so irritable! Don't be such a constant complainer! LRT

vergrisch´e, *adj* - prone to scream (of a child). **Selli Yunge sin en ~ni Drupp.** That is a screaming bunch of kids. LRT. **Sell Kind is en ~ glee Ding.** That child is a screaming little thing. LRT

vergroozt´, *adj* - moldy. **Die Schunke sin ~.** The hams are moldy. LRT

vergrum´pelt, *adj* - crumpled. **Sell Babier waar so ~, mer hot's net lese kenne.** That paper was so crumpled, one couldn't read it. LRT

verguck´e, *pp* **verguckt** - to get the wrong impression from looking at something. **Er hot**

des ganz Ding verguckt. He got the wrong impression from the whole thing. LRT,4/18/2000

verhau´se, *pp* **verhaust** - **1** to keep an untidy house. KYG2114. **2** to spoil, destroy. **Der Schtarem hot alles dorum verhaust.** The storm destroyed everything around here. LRT

verheilt´, *adv* - spoiled by tears. **Er hot sich so ~ ghat, sei Gsicht waar ganz rot.** He had cried so much, his face was all red. LRT

verhenk´e, *pp* **verhenkt** - to bedeck with ribbons, jewelry, etc. **Die Weibsleit hen sich awwer ordlich verhenkt ghat mit alli sadde Sache.** The women really had themselves decorated with all sorts of things. LRT

verhit´ze, *refl* - to become overheated. **Im Aagscht nemmt's net lang fer sich ~.** In August it doesn't take long to overheat oneself. LRT

verhock´e, *pp* **verhockt** - to reset, relocate. **der Leinschtee ~** - to reset a line stone. **Mir hen sei Graabstee verhockt.** We have relocated his tombstone. LRT

verhop´ple, *refl* - to get one's feet tangled. KYG1967

verhung´ere - to starve. **En latt aaremi Kinner duhne alle Daag ~ ganz iwwer die Welt.** A lot of poor children starve to death every day all over the world. **Es waer Zeit as ich eppes gesse hab, ich waar schier gaar verhungert.** It was time that I had eaten something,

I was almost starved. LRT

veriw´wer, *adv* - over, past. **Ich bin froh as die Leckshen ~ is.** I'm glad the election is over. LRT

verkat´ze, *pp* **verkatzt** - to cut short. **Sie hen's Singes an die Versammling verkatzt.** They cut short the singing at the gathering. LRT

verkol´lebiert, *adj* - thunderstruck. = **gewiddergschlagge.** KYG2012

verkutz´le - to make untidy. KYG2114

verlaa´fe, *refl, pp* **verloffe** - to go astray. **Yunger, ~ dich.** Young man, get out of the way. **Er hot sich verloffe.** He took a walk (and disappeared). **Du kannscht dich yuscht ~.** You can just get the heck out of here. LRT

verlan´ge - to want. **Der Eppelsaesskuche is so gut, un du verlangscht en net?** The applesauce cake is so good, and you don't care for any? LRT

Verlan´ge, *n* - want. KYG2162

verlan´ne - to unlearn. KYG2107

verlap´pe - to muff, miss. **Mir hen Bsuch ghat awwer mei aldi hot'n verlappt.** We had company but my wife missed it. LRT

verlau´se losse - to let run down. **Sie hen ihr Haus yuscht ~ geh glosst.** They just allowed their house to run down. LRT

verlech´ere, *pp* **verlechert** = to put holes in. **Die Schiessmannsleit hen sell Schtick Blech ordlich verlechert.** The target shooter men put lots of holes in that piece of tin. LRT

verlecht´, *adj* - parched with thirst. = **verlechert.** KYG1999

verleeg´le - to repudiate. **Mir wisse all was er geduh hot, awwer er verleegelt es ewwe yuscht.** We all know what he did, but he just denies it. LRT

verle´ge, *pp* **verlegt** - to mislay. **Ich hab mei Hendsching verlegt—ich wees gaar net wu ich sie hie geduh hab.** I mislaid my gloves—I have no idea where I put them. LRT

verleh´ne - to let, rent. **widder ~ -** to sublet. **Sie hen die Bauerei verlehnt.** They rented the farm out. LRT

verleng´ere - to prolong. **Mer kann die Arewet ~, wann mer sich alle paar Minudde uff's Hinnerdeel hockt.** One can prolong the work if one sits on his backside every few minutes. LRT

verlee´de - to tire of. KYG2025

verlier´e, *pp* **verlore** - to loose. **en Watt ~ -** to let a naughty word slip out. **Er hot all sei Geld verlore.** He lost all of his money. LRT

verlog´e, *adj* - mendacious. **Sie hen mir gsaat as er en verlogner Mensch is.** They told me he is a mendacious person. LRT

verlos´se, - to leave. **Sei Fraa hot ihn verlosse.** His wife left him. LRT

verluschdie´re, *refl* - to relish. **Er dutt sich immer ~, awwer deel Leit hasse fer ihn sehne kumme.** He always has a ball (a good time), but some people hate to see him come. LRT

vermaric´ke, *pp* **vermarickt** - to notice. **Ich hab vermarickt as du bissel laahm gehscht.** I noticed that you are going a bit lame. LRT

vernaeh´e, *pp* **vernaeht** - to use up in sewing. **Sie hot ihre Neez all vernaeht.** She used up all her thread in sewing. LRT

vernag´gele, *pp* **vernaggelt** - to fasten down with more nails than are needed. **Sie hen awwer des Dach vernaggelt!** They used far too many nails in nailing on this roof. LRT

verneww´le - to get tipsy. = **sich bedrinke.** KYG2025

vernich´de - to destroy. KYG2099. **In re alde Karich sett mer nix ~.** One should not destory a thing in an old church. LRT

vernum´me, *adj* - understood. KYG2098. **Ich hab ~ ghat er waert en Parre, awwer er is net.** I had understood he was a pastor, but he is not. LRT

verpef´fert, *adj* - spoiled with too much pepper. **Wie mei Fraa noch mei Maedelfreind waar, hab ich re mol heemgemachdi Brotwascht gewwe. Paar Yaahr nochdem as mir gheiert waare, hot sie mir gsaat, "Selli**

Wascht waar ~!" When my wife was still my girl friend, I once gave her some of our homemade sausage. Several years after we were married she told me, "That sausage was peppered too heavily!" LRT

verpiss´e, *refl* - to soil by urinating. **Lach net so hatt, du meechscht dich ~.** Don't laugh so hard, you'll wet your pants. LRT

verreg´gere, *pp* **verreggert** - to be spoiled by rain. **Alles was sie heit duh hen welle is verreggert gange.** Everything they wanted to do today was spoiled by the rain. LRT

verreis´se, *pp* **verisse** - to tatter, rend asunder. KYG1972. **Seller glee Buh hot die Zeiding alles verrisse ghat.** That little boy had torn the newspaper to shreds. **Du kannscht selli Babiere ~, mir breiche sie nimmi.** You can tear those papers to bits, we don't need them anymore. LRT

verrenke, *pp* **verrenkt** - to twist. **Er hot sei Handgelenk ~.** He sprained his wrist. LRT

verrenkt, *adj* - twisted. **en ~er Fascht.** KYG2084

Verren´king, *f* - twist (of limb, body). **Die ~ vum seim Gniegwareb hot ihm en latt Schmatze gewwe.** The dislocation of his knee joint gave him a lot of pain. LRT

verrieh´re, *pp* **verriehrt** - to mix by stirring. KYG1882. **Sie hen alles verriehrt ghat, mer hot net gwisst was was waar.** They had everything all stirred

up, one hardly knew what was what. LRT

verrunz´le, *pp* **verrunzelt** - to wrinkle. KYG2255. **Dei Hosse sin alles verrunzelt.** Your trousers are all wrinkled. LRT,4/18/2000

Versamm´ling, *f* - meeting, gathering. **Im Yaahr 2000 waar die siwweunfuffzichscht PA Deitsch ~ ghalde in Lykens, PA.** In the year 2000, the 57th PA Dutch gathering was held in Lykens, PA. LRT,4/18/2000

versa´riye - to provide for. **Seller Mann dutt gut ~ fer sei Famillye.** That man provides well for his family. **Wann sie en Esse hen an die Karrich, dutt selli Fraa alles ~.** When they have a meal at the church, that lady cares for everything. LRT

versau´e, *pp* **versaut** - to dirty. **Du hoscht awwer dei Hosse versaut!** You have certainly dirtied your pants! LRT

verscharr´e - to scatter by scratching. **Wann mer net Acht gebt, duhne die Hinkel alles ~.** If one is not careful, the chickens will scratch and scatter everything. LRT

verscheecht´, *adj* - terrified. **Die Katze waare ganz ~.** The cats were really terrified (scared). LRT

verschenk´e, *pp* **verschenkt** - to give away. **Mir hen ken Eppel meh; mir hen sie all verschenkt.** We have no more apples; we gave them all away. LRT

verschen´ne - to mar, scratch.

Duh sell net ~! Don't mar that! LRT

verschies´se, *pp* **verschosse** - 1 to riddle by shooting. **Wann die Haase so wiescht verschosse sin, no wett ich sie liewer net esse.** If the rabbits are badly shot up, I'd rather not eat them. **2** to use up in shooting. = **weckschiesse.** LRT

verschie´we, *pp* **verschowe** - to scramble. **die Kalenner ~** - to scramble the almanacs. **Bis sie faddich waare, hen sie alles verschowe ghat.** By the time they were finished, they had scrambled everything. LRT

verschin´ne, *pp* **verschunne** - 1 to skin. KYG1976. **Wu hoscht du dei Gnie so verschunne?** Where did you skin your knee like that? **2** to scratch, scuff. = **gratze, vergratze. Bis der Daag rum waar, hot er sei neie Schuh alles verschunne ghat.** Till the day was out, he had his new shoes all scratched up. **Wann du der Hof maehscht, geb Acht as du net selli Baemlin verschinnscht.** When you mow the lawn, be careful you don't scuff the bark of those small trees. LRT

verschlag´ge, *pp* **~** - to smash. **In seim Unglick hot er sei Kaer alles ~.** In his accident he really smashed his car. LRT

verschlap´pe - to mess up. **O, guck mol, ich duh mei Gaund ~; ich muss en Schatz aaschpelle.** Oh look, I am messing up my dress; I must pin on an apron. LRT. **Duh dei Schatz aa. Du witt net dei Gaund ~.** Put your apron on, you don't want to mess up your dress. LRT

verschlaw´were, *refl* - to soil one's clothing by slobbering. **Wann sell Kind sich so ~ dutt, dann misst dir em en Schlawwerduch aaduh.** If that child slobbers like that, then you will need to put a bib on it. LRT

verschlec´ke - to lick all over. **Der Hund verschleckt em ganz iwwer, wann mer en losst.** The dog licks all over you if you let him. LRT

verschlen´kere - to waste. *cf* **verschwenne, verschwende, weckbamble.** KYG2170

verschlimm´ere, *pp* **verschlimmert** - to worsen. **Sie hen sellre Familye der Verdrau gewwe fer sell Haus uff-fixe Geld-frei, awwer sie hen yuscht alles verschlimmert.** They gave that family the trust of fixing up that house rent free, but they just allowed it to worsen in condition. LRT,4/18/2000

verschlit´ze, *pp* **verschlitzt** - to slit up. **Er hot sei Yaaghosse alles verschlitzt.** His hunting pants are all slit up. LRT

verschlo´fe, *refl* - to oversleep. **Wann ich en Weckuhr hett, daed ich mich net immer ~.** If I had an alarm clock, I wouldn't always oversleep. **Er is en ~ner Ding.** He is a sleepy head. *cf* **Schlofkopp.** LRT

verschmac´ke - to take a taste. KYG1972. **Do verschmack mol die Grumbiere un saag mir was sie noch breiche.** Here taste these potatoes and tell me what they still need. LRT

verschmeis´se, *pp* **verschmisse - 1** to smash by throwing. **Die Buwe hen sell Fenschder alles verschmisse mit Schtee.** The boys had smashed up that window by throwing stones. **2** to litter excessively. **Die Yunge hen der ganz Hof verschmisse ghat mit blechni Kanne.** The young men had thrown tin cans all over the yard. LRT

verschmie´re, *pp* **verschmiert** - to smear. **Er hot sei Gleeder alles mit Fareb verschmiert ghat.** He had smeared paint all over his clothes. **Ei du Liewer, du hoscht awwer dei Maul verschmiert!** Oh, my dear, you have really messed up your mouth. LRT

verschmut´ze, *pp* **verschmutzt** - to soil with grease. **Sell Waggeraad hot net all der Schmutz grickt, du hoscht aa dei Hosse verschmutzt.** That wagon wheel didn't get all the grease, you have also gotten some on your pants. LRT

verschnee´-e - 1 to become snowbound. **2** to spoil by snowing. **Die Versammling is verschneet gange.** The meeting was canceled because of snow. LRT

verschnipp´le - to snip to bits. **Do, Maed, is en Scher, dir kennt des Babier alles ~.** Here, girls, is a pair of scissors, you can snip this paper to bits. LRT

verschoss´e, *adj* - shot away, shot to pieces. **Selli Buwe hen die Fenschder scheiwe alles ~ ghat.** Those boys had the window panes shot to pieces. LRT

verschpae´de, *refl* - to be behind time. *cf* **sich verseime.** KYG2019

verschprung´e, *adj* - split open. **Die Wassermeluune waare alles ~.** The watermelons were all split open. LRT

verschrec´ke - to terrify. *cf* **vergelschdere.** KYG1989. **Sell hot uns awwer verschreckt wie seller Block im Keller gebroche is.** That really terrified us, when that girder broke in the cellar. LRT

verschrei´we, *pp* **verschriwwe** - to prescribe. **Der Dokder hot mir mei Medizien verschriwwe.** The physician prescribed my medicine. LRT,4/18/2000

verschtam´pe, *pp* **verschtampt** - to trample. **Die Kieh hen sei ganz Arebele-schtick alles verschtampt.** The cows trampled to ruin his whole strawberry patch. LRT

Verschtand´, *m* - **1** common sense. KYG2098. **Hoscht du ken ~?** Don't you have any common sense? **2** understanding. **Sei ~ vun seim Handwarick is gut.** The understandings of his trade is good. LRT. *cf* **Verschtendnis.**

verschtaun´lich, *adj* - surprising. **Sache wie sell kenne arig ~ sei.** Things like that can be very surprising. LRT

verschtech´e, *pp* **verschtoche** - to pierce with a lot of holes. LRT

verschten´nich, *adj* - respectable. = **geschtimiert.**

Yunger, nau sei ~, ich will schtolz sei mit dir. Young man, behave yourself (act respectable), I want to be proud of you. LRT

verschte´che - to sting (full of holes). KYG1880

verschtic´ke, *pp* **verschtickt** - to strangle. **Er is dod, weil er verschtickt is.** He is dead because he suffocated. LRT

verschtic´ke, *refl* - to strangle. **Yunger, fress net selli heese Peffer, du verschtickscht dich.** Young man, don't eat those hot peppers, you'll strangle yourself. **Geb Acht datt drunne in sellem Loch, du kenntscht dich ~.** Be careful down there in that hole, you could suffocate. LRT

verschtimm´le, *pp* **verschtimmelt** - to mutilate. **Mei Urgrossdaadi hot als Fense gfixt, awwer er hot sie yuscht alles verschtimmelt.** My great-grandfather used to fix fences but he just messed them up. LRT

verschtohl´nerweis, *adv* - underhandedly. KYG2096

verschtoppt´, *adj* - stopped up. KYG1889. **Die Ablaafpeif is ~.** The drain pipe is stopped up. LRT

verschtop´pe - **1** to stop a hole. **2** to stop (a leak). KYG1889

verschtruww´le - to tousle. KYG2042. **Der Wind hot ihm die Haar alles verstruwwelt ghat.** The wind had really disheveled his hair. LRT

verschwap´pe, *pp* **verschwappe** - to trade off. **Sie hen ihre aldi Kaer verschwappt uff en neie.** They traded their old car for a new one. LRT

verschwee´re, *pp* **verschwore** - to swear. **Er hot sich verschwore ghat.** He had committed himself under oath. LRT

verschwet´ze - to talk into. = neischwetze. KYG1964

verschwin´ne, *pp* **verschwunne** - to disappear. **Des waar als en Baam do, awwer der is verschwunne.** There used to be a tree here, but it has disappeared. LRT

verschwit´ze, *pp* **verschwitzt** - to soil by sweating. **weschnass verschwitzt** - sweated through and through. **Du hoscht zu viel Gleeder aa, du bischt yo alles weschnaas verschwitzt.** You've got too many clothes on, you are soaking wet with sweat. LRT

verschwit´ze, *refl, pp* **verschwitzt** - to perspire. **Yunger, du hoscht dich awwer verschwitzt; du settscht net so hatt schaffe.** Young man, you have really perspired. You should not work so hard. LRT

verseh´ne - to provide for someone. **Die Mamm dutt immer die Kinner gut ~.** Mom always provides well for the children. LRT

versei´me, *refl, pp* **verseimt** - to be late. **Er hot sich verseimt.** He is tardy. **Sie hen sich verseimt un waare net datt am nein Uhr wie sie sei hedde**

selle. They ran late and were not there at nine o'clock, as they should have been. LRT

versich´ere - **1** to guarantee. *cf* **epper** (*dat.*) **gut sei fer eppes (devor)** - to guarantee someone something. KYG2165. **2** to insure. **Sie hen ihre Haus gut versichert ghat, wie's nunner gebrennt is.** They had their house well insured when it burnt down. LRT

Versich´ering, *f* - insurance. KYG2166. **Do in unserem Land sin die ~ Bissnisse wunnerbaar gross.** Here in our country (USA), the insurance businesses are huge. LRT

versin´diche, *refl, pp* **versindicht** - to sin. **Ya, er hot sich versindicht.** Yes, he did commit sin. = **sindiche.** LRT

versoh´le - to flog thoroughly. *cf* **darichweeche.** KYG2001

versoh´le, *refl* - to begrime one's trousers. KYG2065

Versuch´ing, *f* - temptation. KYG1983. **Der Deiwel wees wie er uns in die ~ nemme kann.** The devil knows how to tempt us. LRT

Verun´glickde, *pl* - unfortunate people. KYG2102. **Die ~ hen alles verlore im Feier.** The unfortunate people lost everything in the fire. LRT

verwach´e - to be unable to sleep. KYG2090

verwat´zelt, *adj* - closely rooted. **Der Grund um seller Schtock waar ganz ~.** The ground around that plant was closely rooted. LRT

verwax´e, *pp* ~ - to grow out of. **Er hot sei Gleeder ~.** He grew out of his clothes. LRT

verweech´e, *pp* **verweecht** - to become too soft. **Selli Buhne hen zu lang gekocht, sie sin ganz zu verweecht.** Those beans have cooked too long, they have gotten much too soft. LRT

verwei´le, *refl, pp* **verweilt** - to pass the time. **Fraa, ich will hoffe, du kannscht dich ~, wann ich fer paar Woche net deheem bin.** Wife, I hope you can pass the time if I am not at home for several weeks. **Er hot sich paar Daag verweilt bei seine Schwogersleit.** He tarried for several days with his in-laws. LRT

verwelk´e, *pp* **verwelkt** - to wither. **Selli Blummeschteck gucke awwer verwelkt.** Those flower plants look withered. LRT

verwet´ze, *refl* - to bedraggle one's clothes with mud. LRT

verwex´le¹ - to mix up. **Des is en Schand wie unser Kinner immer ihre Gleeder verwexselt griege.** It's a shame how our children always get their clothes mixed up. *cf* **wexle**. LRT

verwex´le² - to take for another. KYG1962

Verwick´lung, *f* - tangle. KYG1967

verwick´elt, *adj* - involved. **net ~** - unembarrassed. KYG2100.

Er waar alles ~ mit selle Schtorbissniss. He was all involved in that store business. LRT

verwick´le, *pp* **verwickelt** - 1 to wrap up. KYG2252. **Sie hen sellem Yunge sei Beh alles verwickelt ghat.** They had thoroughly bandaged that young man's sore (injured) leg. LRT,4/18/2000. 2 to become entangled. **Geb Acht, selli Kuh kennt sich in sellem Droht ~, no hen mir Druwwel.** Take heed, that cow could become snarled in that wire, then we've got problems. LRT

verwieh´le, *pp* **verwiehlt** - to root over. **Die Sei hen der ganz Hof verwiehlt ghat.** The hogs had rooted up the whole yard. LRT

verwisch´e, *pp* **verwischt** - to catch somebody doing something he should not be doing. **Sie hen die Buwe verwischt am Drugs verkaafe.** They caught the boys selling drugs. LRT

veryaa´ge, *pp* **veryaagt** - to chase in all directions. **Die Hinkel waare ganz veryaagt.** The chickens were chased all over the place. LRT

verzaeh´le - to recount. **Verzaehl mir mol die Gschicht.** Tell me the story. LRT

verzannt´, *adj* - angry. **gschwind ~ sei** - to be a sorehead. **Sell hot mich ~.** That made me angry. LRT. = **en Schpaa uff de Axle draage** - to carry a chip on the shoulder. KYG1990

verzann´lich, *adj* - producing anger. KYG2071. **Was er geduh hot, waar ~!** What he did caused others to become angry! **Iwwer ee Weil is des awwer en ~ Wese warre.** After a while this really became a disturbing matter. LRT. *cf* **griddlich**

verzap´pe - to tap out. KYG1969. **Daedscht du mir gern en Glaas Seider ~?** Would you please tap a glass of cider for me? LRT

verzie´he, *pp* **verzoge** - to warp. *cf* **wickle**. KYG2165. **Die Keller Dier is awwer verzoge.** The cellar door is really warped. LRT

verzop´pe - to pull to pieces. LRT

verzuck´e, *refl, pp* **verzuckt** - to shrug. **Er hot sich gaar net verzuckt.** He did not even shrug his shoulders. *cf* **unbekimmerlich schiddle.** LRT

verzwan´ne - to twist. = **verdrehe, verrenke, verzwaerne.** KYG2084

verzwar´ewle - to blow into tangles. KYG1967

verzwen´ge, *pp* **verzwengt** - to force something out of shape. **Sie hen gschowe an sellem Dor bis es ganz verzwengt waar.** They pushed on that gate until it was all twisted out of shape. LRT

Viehabzieher, *m* - cattle skinner. **Er is en guder ~.** He is a good cattle skinner. LRT

viel, *adj* - much. **Es is net ~**

dezu. It is trivial. KYG2063. **Es mehnt net ~ zu mir.** It doesn't mean much to me. LRT

vierbeenich, *adj* - four-legged. **Mir sedde froh sei, as mir so viel ~i Gediere hen.** We should be glad that we have so many four-legged animals. LRT

Viereck, *n* - square. **Sei ~ is net ganz winkel.** His square is not quite true. LRT

viereckich, *adj* - square. **En ~i Moddel hot aa vier Seide.** A square mold also has four sides. LRT

viert - fourth. **zu ~ (dritt) geh** - to go four (three) at a time. KYG2019. **Sell is es ~ Mol as sie sell geduh hen.** That is the fourth time that they did that. LRT

voraa'kumme - to thrive. KYG2007. **Selli zwee Bauere-Familye kumme recht gut aa.** Those two farm families are really thriving. LRT. *cf* **waxe, zunemme, gut gerode, gut waxe, zu Gnaade kumme**

vorbei'reide, *pp* **is vorbeigeridde** - to ride past. **Er is an unserem Haus vorbeigeridde.** He rode past our house. LRT

vorbei'renne, *pp* **is vorgeigerennt** - to rush past. **Sie waare in so me Huddel, sie sin yuscht vorbeigerennt.** They were in such a hurry, they just rushed by. LRT

Vorbereiding, *f* - preparation service (before Holy Communion). **Fer lenger hen mir immer die ~e**

Samschdaagoweds ghat. Years ago we always had the Preparatory Services Saturday evenings. LRT

vorbringe - to propose. **Heit hen sie en Blaan vorgebrocht.** Today they brought forth a plan. LRT

vorbringe - to bring forth. **viel ~** - to yield good results. KYG2263

vordrehe - to turn ahead. **die Uhr ~** - to set a clock ahead. **Friehyaahrs duhne mir die Uhre en Schtund ~.** In the spring we turn the clocks ahead one hour. **Mit unser narrischi Zeit, dreht mer die Uhr vor im Friehyaahr.** With our crazy time (daylight saving time) the clock is turned forward in the spring. LRT

vorduh - to put ahead (of other tasks). **Deel Arewet sett mer immer ~.** Some chores should always be given priority. LRT

Vorgang, *m* - lead. **~ mache (nemme)** - to take the lead. KYG1961

vorhawwe - to undergo verbal, public examination. KYG2096

vorlosse - to permit to come to the front. **Die Eifiehrer duhne die Glieder ~ fer's Nachtmohl nemme.** The ushers allow (lead) the church members to go forward to take Holy Communion. LRT

vornemme, *refl, pp* **vorgenumme** - to resolve. **Ich hab mir vorgenumme, mir daede sell nimmi duh.** I have resolved not to do that anymore.

LRT

vorreedich, *adj* - in store. KYG1890

vorrutsche - to slip, slide ahead. **Seller Buh dutt immer ~, wann er uff die Karichebank hockt.** That boy always slides forward when he sits on the church pew. LRT

vorschmeisse, *pp* **vorgschmisse** - to reproach with. **Ich hab gemehnt, es daed niemand wisse, was ich geduh hab, awwer er hot mir's vorgschmisse.** I thought no one had known what I had done, but he accused me of it. LRT

vorschpringe, *pp* **is vorgschprunge** - to run ahead. **Wie immer, er is vorgschprunge.** As always, he ran ahead. LRT

vorschtelle, *refl* - **1** to resist the temptation. KYG1983. **2** to imagine. **Ich kann mir gaar net ~ was sell gekoscht hot.** I can't imagine what that cost might have been. LRT

Vorsinger, *m* - song leader. **Selli Karich hot immer en ~ ghat.** That church always had a song leader. LRT

vorsitze, *refl* - to take a seat up front. **Yunger, sitz dich vor.** Young man, you take a seat up front. LRT

vun, *prep* - from. **~ yeher** - from olden times. KYG2020. **Ya, sell kummt ~ yeher.** Yes, that comes form olden days. LRT

vun(e)nannerkumme, *pp* **~** - to become separated. **Zwee**

Gleecher vun de Kett sin ~.
Two links of the chain separated. LRT

vun(e)nannerhalde - to keep separated. **Die Hinkel un die Haahne ~** - to keep the hens and the roosters separated. LRT

Waahl, *f* - choice. **uff die ~ schteh** - to be undecided. = **in der ~ schteh.** *cf* **Er is uff der Schnepp.** He is undecided. KYG2095

waahr, *adj* - true. = **gedrei, recht, richdich, trei.** KYG2068. **Ich will yuscht heere was waahr is.** I only want to hear what is true. LRT

waahrhaft, *adj* - truthful. = **waahrhafdich.** KYG2071. **Mer wunnert fer was as mer schwetze sett vun "~", wann's der eesichscht Weg is as mer sei sett.** One wonders why one should talk about being "truthful" when it's the only way one should be. LRT

Waahrheit, *f* - truth. **die deitschi ~** - the plain, unvarnished truth. KYG2070. **Alles as mir gheert hen heit waar fer schur die ~.** Everything we heard today, surely was the truth. LRT

waahrsaage - to tell someone's fortune. KYG1980. **Ich kann dir nix ~.** I can't forecast anything for you. LRT

Waahrscheinlichkeit, *f* - probability. LRT/Leb.Co.

Waarhaus, *n* - warehouse. *cf* **Schtorhaus.** KYG2164. **Die gleene Schtore griege ihre Sache aus de Waarheiser.** The

little stores get their merchandise (stock) out of the warehouses. LRT

waarme, *refl* - to warm oneself. = **waerme.** KYG2164.

waarmhatzich, *adj* - warmhearted. KYG2164. **Sie is en ~i Fraa.** She is a warm-hearted wife. LRT

Waarz, *f, pl* **~** - wart. KYG2166. **Soll ich dir weise wie selli ~ abzubinne?** Should I show you how to tie off that wart? LRT

waarzich, *adj* - warty. KYG2166. **Sei Aagdeckel is awwer ~.** His eyelid is really warty. LRT

Waasem, *m* - grassy surface, sod. KYG2075. **Unser Hof hot guder ~.** Our yard has good sod. LRT

Wacke, *f* - stone. KYG1886

wacker, *adj* - awake. **Bischt du ~?** Are you awake? LRT

wackle - to teeter. **vaschich un hinnerschich ~** - to teeter back and forth. KYG1978. **Geb Acht, du bischt am hinnerschich un vaschich ~.** Be careful, you are teetering backwards and forwards. LRT

wacklich, *adj* - wobbly. **Q: Wie bischt du? A: Oh, so wie die Ende, immer mit zwee Beh, awwer ebmols bissel ~.** How are you? Oh, always on two legs like the ducks, but sometimes a bit wobbly. LRT

Waddefresser, *m* - word processor, term coined by C.R.

Beam, *ca.* 1980.

Waddefresserwese, *n* - personal computer technology. **Ya, ich denk des ~ is lanneswaert.** Yes, I think this P.C. technology is worth learning. LRT,4/18/2000

Wadding, *f* - wording. **Deel vun selle ~ in sellre Gschicht sin mir net bekannt.** We are not familiar with some of the wording in that story. LRT,4/11/2000

Waerdaag(s)hemm, *n* - workday shirt. **Hot er en nei ~?** Does he have a new work shirt? LRT, 4/11/2000

Waerdaagsgleeder, *pl* - weekday clothes, workday clothes. LRT

Waerming, *f* - warmth. = **Waerme.** KYG2165. **Die ~ vun dem Offe waert em glei zu viel.** The warmth of this stove soon gets to be too much. LRT

waert, *adj* - worth. **Was is die Arewet ~?** What is the fee for this work? LRT,4/18/2000

Waerwel¹, *m* - middle of the skull. **Er hot en bludder Blacke graad am ~ vun seim Kopp.** He has a bald spot right on the center of his head. LRT

Waerwel², *m, pl* **~e** - larva of the warble fly. KYG2166

Wagge, *m* - wagon. **dreischpennicher ~** - three-horse wagon. KYG2005

Wagge-lann, *f, pl* **~e - 1** thill. KYG1997. **2** shaft. **Mer kann ken grosser Gaul in selli ~e**

schpanne. One can't hitch a big horse in those shafts. LRT

Waggenaggel, *m* - pin of doubletree. LRT

Waggereef, *m* - wagon tire. KYG2025. **Der ~ is runnergfloge.** The wagon wheel rim flew off. LRT

Wallem, *m, pl* **Wallme** - heaped row (of hay). **Es Hoi duhne mir immer in langi Wallme reche.** We always rake the hay into long, heaped rows. LRT

Walli, *m* - *dim* of Walter. KYG2287

wallixe - to wallop. KYG2160

Wallniss-schtumbe, *m* - walnut stump. KYG2161. **Wie lang nemmt's fer en ~ weckfaule?** How long does it take for a walnut stump to rot away? LRT

Walme, *pl* - windrows. **Wie daed mer Hoi mache unni ~?** How would one make hay without windrows? LRT

Walniss-schaal, *f, pl* **~e** - walnut shell. KYG2161. **~e mache en hees Feier.** Walnut shells make a hot fire. LRT

Walnissdramm, *m* - walnut steeped in spirits. KYG2161

walnissgehl, *adj* - walnut-yellow. KYG2163

Walnissholz, *n* - walnut wood. KYG2161. **~ macht en scheeni Kischt.** Walnut wood makes a lovely chest. LRT

Walnisskann, *f, pl* **~e** - walnut kernel. KYG2161. **Ich hass ~e**

wann sie Schaale drin hen. I hate walnut kernels that have shells (in and among them). LRT

Walnissland, *n* - land on which walnut trees grow. KYG2161

Walnissrinn, *f* - walnut bark. KYG2161. **Die ~ macht gut Feierholz.** The walnut bark makes good kindling. LRT

Walnuss, *f* - walnut. *Juglans, sp.* (NECr,SESr). = **Walniss** (elsewhere). KYG2161. **Grossi Walniss Bleck sin en latt Geld wert.** Big walnut logs are worth a lot of money. LRT

Walz, *f, pl* **~e** - roller for plowed field. **Die hilzne ~e sin ewwe noch die beschde.** The wooden rollers are still the best ones. LRT

Walzergang, *m* - waltz step. KYG2162

Wammes, *m* - blouse, jacket. **Sis bissel kiehl draus, daedscht besser dei ~ aaduh.** It's a little cool outside, you'd better wear your jacket. LRT

Wammes-aremel, *m* - jacket sleeve. **Dei ~ is verrisse.** Your jacket sleeve is torn. LRT

Wandbopp, *f* - wallflower. = **Lo(f)geige, Lovgeige.** KYG2160

Wanddeppich, *m* - tapestry. KYG1969

wandere - to wander. *cf* **rumdowe, rumlaafe, rumwandre, umherlaafe.** KYG2162

Wanderei, *f* - wandering. KYG2162

Wanderluscht, *f* - wanderlust. *cf* **Wunnerfitz.** KYG2162

wanke - to be unstable. KYG2113

wankle - to totter. KYG2040

wanne, *pp* **gewannt** - to warn. **Yunger, du waarscht gewannt.** Young man, you were warned. LRT

Wanning, *f* - warning. KYG2165. **uhne ~** - unawares. **Yunger, hoscht du selli ~ gheert?** Young man, did you hear that warning? **Ganz uff ee mol, unni ~ hot er en latt Hatzdruwwel ghat.** All of a sudden, without warning, he had a lot of heart trouble. LRT. = **Waerning**

warefle - to throw dice. = **hossle.** KYG2009

Warem, *m* - worm in a mill (as kind of conveyer). **Was dreibt der ~ in sellere Maschien?** What drives the (conveyer) worm in that machine? LRT,4/18/2000

wareme, *refl* - to warm oneself. KYG2164. **Tschump mol en dutzed [Leb. Co. = dutzend] mol nuff un nunner un warem dich.** Jump up and down a dozen times and warm yourself. LRT. **Sis kalt datt draus, kumm rei ins Haus un waarem dich bissel.** It's cold out there, come in the house and warm (up) a bit. LRT

Waremli, *n, pl* **~n** - little worm. **Die ~n sin all verkaaft.** All the little worms have been sold. LRT/Leb,4/11/2000

Waremloch, *n, pl* -lecher - worm hole. **Es sin an latt -lecher in sellem Holz.** There are a lot of worm holes in that wood. LRT,4/18/2000

Warewel, *m* - **1** turn button. = **Driller.** KYG2078. **2** twirl. = **Waerwel.** KYG2083

waricke, *adj* - made of tow. KYG2042

Warickzeich, *n* - tool. KYG2034

Warrant, *f* - <*Engl* warrant. **en ~ rausgriege** - to swear out a warrant. KYG2165

Waschtfillsel, *n* - sausage stuffing meat. **Seifleesch macht gut ~.** Pork makes good sausage stuffing meat. LRT

Waschtschtoppedaag, *m* - stuffing sausage day. **Heit waar ~.** Today was sausage stuffing day. LRT

Wasser, *n* - water. **Es ~ rollt vun de Ende.** The ducks shed water. LRT

Wasserloch, *n* - "a neat little fishing hole. We also had one we called **es Kesselloch.**" LRT

Wasserreh - limp stiffness (from drinking cold water or from swelling). KYG1879

Wasserschpritz, *f* - squirt. **Er is en gleeni ~.** He is a little squirt [said of a tiny boy]. LRT

Wassersimpel, *m* - temberance crank. KYG1982

Wassersucht, *f* - dropsy. LRT

Watt, *n, pl ~e* - word. **Sie hen ihm ~ gschickt ghat, awwer er hot sich aagschickt as wann er gaar nix gwisst hot.** They had sent him word, but he acted as though he knew nothing. **sich uff sei ~ verlosse** - to trust another's word. KYG2070. **Mir sin uff sei Watt gange.** We trusted in his word. **Was waar sell ~, was er gsaat hot?** What was that word he used? LRT, 4/11/2000. **sei ~ nemme devor** - to take one's word for something. KYG1962. **epper an seim ~ nemme** - to take someone at his word. KYG1963

Wattschaft, *f* - tavern. KYG1973. = **Watthaus. Der Tschon Schmidt is der Eegner vun sellem Wattshaus.** John Schmidt is the owner of that tavern. LRT

Wattshausbortsch, *f* - tavern porch. KYG1973. **Sie hen scheeni Schtiel uff ihre ~.** They have nice chairs on their tavern porch. LRT

Watzele, *pl* - tooth roots. **Die Backezaeh hen so viel as vier odder meh ~.** Molars have as many as four roots or more. LRT

watzle - to take root. KYG1961

watzlich, *adj* - full of roots. **Wu kumme all die Watzele bei? Der Grund is iwwerall ~.** Where do all these roots come from? The ground is full of roots everywhere. LRT

Waxlicht, *n, pl ~er* - taper (lighter). KYG1969. **~er uff Grischtdaagsbaem kenne arig gfaehrlich sei.** Wax tapers

(candles) on Christmas trees can be very dangerous. LRT

Webzeddel, *m* - warp. = **Wewerzeddel, Zeddel.** KYG2165

Weck, *m, pl ~* - bun-like yeast cake. KYG2260. **Sie hen gudi ~ an de Karich gemacht.** They made good buns at the church. LRT,4/18/2000

weckbemble - to fool away time. KYG2019. = **bamble.** Leb. Co./ LRT. **Seller Yunge dutt zu viel Zeit ~.** That young man fools away too much time. LRT

weckbleiwe - to remain at a distance. **Wann sie sich so aaschicke welle, dann bleiwe mir yuscht weck.** If they want to act like that, then we'll just keep our distance. LRT

weckdappe, *pp* **weckgedappt** - to trudge away. KYG2068. **Ich denk er hot nix heere welle, fer sell is er weckgedappt.** I guess he didn't want to hear anything, that's why he trudged away. LRT

weckesse, *pp* **weckgesse** - to eat down quickly. **Sis nix meh uff em Disch; sie hen alles weckgesse.** Nothing remains on the table; it's all been eaten away quickly. LRT

weckfange, *pp* **weckgfange** - to snatch away. **Mir hen die Radde weckgfange, eb sie Schaade duh hen kenne.** We caught the rats away before they could do any damage. LRT

weckgratze - to scratch away. **Kannscht net selli Waarz ~?**

Can't you scratch that wart away? LRT

weckhalde, *refl* - **1** to seclude. **2** to keep away. **Der Offe is hees, halt dich weck.** The stove is hot, keep away (from it). LRT

weckhalde - to ward off. **Die Hund duhne die Grundsei vun unser Bauerei ~.** The dogs keep the ground hogs away from our farm. LRT

weckkehre, *pp* **weckgekehrt** - to sweep away. **Sie hen der Dreck all weckgekehrt.** They swept all the dirt away. LRT

wecklaafe, *pp* **weckgloffe** - to walk away. **Die Weibsleit sin yuscht do weckgloffe, ich wees net wu sie hiegange sin.** The women just walked away from here, I don't know where they went. LRT

weckmaehe - to remove by mowing. **Kannscht du sell Umgraut an de Fens nooch ~?** Can you mow away those weeds along the fence? LRT

wecknemme, *pp* **weckgenumme** - to remove. **Selli Benk uff de Bortsch hen sie weckgenumme.** They removed those benches from the porch. LRT,4/18/2000. = **fattnemme, runnernemme.** KYG1962

weckreisse, *pl* **weckgerisse** - to tear down (a building). KYG1976. **Sie hen die Scheier weckgerisse.** They tore the barn down. LRT

weckroppe - to remove by plucking. **Kannscht du sell Umgraut an de Fens nooch ~?**

Can you pluck away those weeds along the fence? LRT

weckroschde, *pp* **weckgeroscht** - to rust away. **Es is weckgeroscht, so as mer nix meh sehne hot kenne.** It had rusted away so that nothing more could be seen. LRT

wecksaege - to saw away. **Saeg selli Nescht weck, sie sin zu naegscht am Haus.** Saw those branches off, they are too close to the house.

weckschaffe - to get rid of. **Der Schnee misse mir ~. Mariye is die Leicht.** We must get rid of the snow. Tomorrow is the funeral. LRT

weckscheie, *refl* - to shrink from. **sich ~ vor epper** - to shy away from someone. **Sie duhne sich ~.** They shy away. LRT

weckschere - to cut away. **Deel vun die Mannsleit sedde deel vun ihre Haar ~.** Some men should cut away some of their hair. LRT

weckschidde - to pour away. LRT

weckschiewe - to shove away. **Kannscht du seller Schtuhl vanne an die Dier ~?** Can you push that chair away in front of the door? LRT

weckschlagge, *pp* **weckgschlagge** - to knock away. **Schlack die Mick weck!** Knock that fly away! LRT

weckschmeisse - to throw away. **Mir misse die faule Eppel ~.** We have to throw the rotten apples away. **Wann du sell net**

gleichscht, dann schmeiss es weck. If you don't like that then throw it away. LRT

weckschnarre - to jerk away. LRT

weckschpringe, *pp* **is weckgschprunge** - to skedaddle. **Es waar ihm bang er greecht Schlaeg, no is er weckgschprunge.** He was afraid he'd get a spanking, then he ran away. LRT

weckschridde - to step away. **Wann du seller Geruch net gleichscht, dann schritt yuscht weck.** If you don't like that odor, then just step away. LRT

weckschtecke - to put in a safe place. **Schteck sell Geld weck, so as niemand es seht.** Put that money away so that no one sees it. LRT

weckschtecke - to stow away. LRT

weckschtelle - to set away. = **wecksetze. Duh die Heffe ~ bis mariye frieh.** Set these crocks away until tomorrow morning. LRT

weckschtolpere - to stumble away. **Sis ball Zeit as du dich do weckschtolperscht.** It's about time you stumbled away from here. LRT

weckschtoosse - to push away. **Kannscht du seller Glumpedreck ~?** Can you push away that clump of dirt? LRT

weckschtore - to store away. KYG1890. **Schtor dei Windergleeder weck.** Store your winter clothes away. LRT

weckschwemme, *pp* **weckgschwemmt** - to wash away. **Sell Hochwasser hot paar Baem weckgschwemmt.** That high water washed away a few trees. LRT

weckwesche, *pp* **weckgewesche** - to sweep away (action of flood water). **Es Hochwasser hot all der Sand weckgewesche.** The high water washed all the sand away. LRT. *cf* **hieschwemme, weckschwemme.** KYG2167. **Sell Hochwasser hot ihre vedderschder Hof weckgewesche.** That high water (flooding) washed away their front lawn. LRT

weckwuppsche, *pp* **weckgewuppscht** - to jerk away. **Yuscht so uff eemol waar's weckgewuppscht.** All of a sudden it was jerked away. LRT

Wedder, *f* - weather. **Ich gleich des schtaremich Wedder net.** I don't like this stormy weather. LRT. **Es ~ guckt net gut.** The weather is unfavorable. KYG2102. **Ich gleich's Wedder wu mer Schnee grickt im Winder.** I like the weather, where it snows in the winter. LRT. **rauh, kalt ~** - cold, unpleasant weather. KYG2109. **Sis ewwe Winder un sell mehnt's ~ is rauh un kalt.** Of course it's winter, and that means the weather is raw and cold. LRT

Wedderbatt, *m* - resistance. *cf* **Weddersteh. Nemm dei ~!** Take your stand (of resistance)! **Yunger, du muscht dei eegner ~ nemme.** Young fellow, you must stand in your own defense. LRT

Wedderbording, *f* - siding (of a house). **Die ~ sett aagschtriche sei.** The siding should be painted. LRT

wedderdappe - to walk up against. = **wedderlaafe.** KYG2159. **Er is wedder sell Fass gedappt wie en Gsoffner.** He walked against that barrel like a drunk. LRT

wedderhalde, *pp* **wedderghalde** - to sustain one's part. **Er hot wedderghalde bis sie ihn vergraawe hen.** He resisted until his death (until they buried him). LRT

Wedderleechschtraahle, *m* - stroke of lightning. **Sell waar awwer en heller ~.** That was a bright stroke of lightning. LRT

wedderschiewe - to push against. **Du kannscht die Wand net weckschiewe, es macht nix aus wie hatt as du wedderschiebscht.** You can't push the wall away; it doesn't matter how hard you push against it. LRT. **Kannscht du der Disch wedder die Wand schiewe?** Can you push the table against the wall? LRT

wedderschmeisse - to throw against. KYG2009. **Schmeiss nix datt wedder, sell is Glaas.** Don't throw anything against there, that is glass. LRT

wedderschteh, *pp* **weddergschtanne** - to be opposed to something. = **degehe sei. Sie hen en nei Feierhaus baue welle, awwer es hen zu viel Leit weddergschtanne.** They wanted to build a new firehouse but there were too many people opposed. LRT

wedderschteibere, *refl* - to oppose stubbornly. **Ya, schteiber dich yuscht wedder, ich geb nix drum.** Yes, you can just stubbornly oppose, I don't care. LRT

weech, *adj* - soft, tender. **~ mache** - to soften. **Seller Balle is ~.** That ball is soft. LRT. **~ Fleesch** - tender meat. KYG1984. **Sell Fleesch hot lang genung gekocht, sis schee ~.** That meat has boiled long enough, it's nice and tender. LRT

weech-hatzich, *adj* - tender-hearted. KYG1984. **Es nemmt net viel fer sie heile mache, sie is arig ~.** It doesn't take much to make her cry, she is very tender-hearted. LRT

Weechholz, *n* - soft wood. **Sell is ~, wann mer en Naggel datt neigloppt, un's dutt net gern schpalde.** That is soft wood, if you drive a nail into it, and it's not likely to split. LRT

weechmeilich, *adj* - tender-mouthed. KYG1985

weechschaalich, *adj* - soft-shelled. **Mer kann gut wisse as eier Hinkel ken Oischderschaale griege, so ~ wie eier Oier sin.** One can well know that your chickens don't get any oyster shells, as soft-shelled as your eggs are. LRT

Weedfeld, *n, pl* **~er** - pasture field. **Die ~er sin nimmi so gross, as sie als waare.** The pasture fields are not as large as they used to be. LRT

Weezeboddem, *m* - soil adapted for growing wheat. **Ya, sell is**

guder ~. Yes, that is good wheat soil. LRT

Weezekann, *f, pl* **~e -** seed of wheat. **Is es net en Wunner was en gleeni ~ duh kann, wann sie uff der Bodde fallt?** Isn't it a wonder what a small wheat seed can do when it falls on the ground? LRT

Weezeschacke, *n* - wheat shocking. **Wann mer am ~ is, un mer hot en diefer Nawwel, un mer grickt Weezegraane in den Nawwel, no is der Deiwel los.** If one is shocking wheat, and one has a deep navel, and one gets wheat awns in his navel, then the devil is loose. LRT

Weg, *m* - way. **zerickgeh iwwer der ~, as mer kumme is -** to retrace one's steps. **Kumm graadeswegs!** Come right now! LRT. **uff der ~ sei -** to be on your way (somewhere). LRT,4/11/2000. **zu ~e bringe -** to accomplish a task. KYG1972. **Waert dir um der Weg gewest, wann mir gschtoppt hedde letscht Mittwoch?** Would you have been home, if we had stopped (at your home) last Wednesday? LRT

Wegschteier, *m* - ability to walk erect. **Er hot sei ~ verlore.** He lost his balance, was unable to walk. (He was intoxicated.) LRT. **Er is so schwach, er hot der ~ nimmi.** He is so weak he is hardly able to walk. KYG2159

weh, *adj* - sore. **Du hoscht en schwatz un bloher Blacke datt uff deim Aarem, dutt's ~?** You have a black and blue mark there on your arm, does it hurt? = **~er**

Blacke, eppes ~es. LRT

Wehaag, *n* - sore eye. **Hoscht du en ~?** Do you have a sore eye? LRT

wehduh, *pp* wehgeduh - to injure, hurt. **Dutt dei Aarem weh?** Does your arm hurt? **Ich hab mei Fuuss wehgeduh iwwer'm Holzhacke.** I hurt my foot while chopping wood. LRT,4/18/2000

wehe, *prep* - regarding. **Nau ~ daere Fecht, was kannscht du mir saage?** Now about this fight, what can you tell me? LRT

Wehes, *n* - sore. **Was hoscht du ~ an deim Aarem?** What is the sore on your arm? LRT, 4/18/2000

Wehhals, *m* - tonsilitis. *cf* **Halsweh, roher Hals.** KYG2034

Wehmaul, *n* - sore mouth. **Was? Du hoscht en ~, well, dann halt dei Maul.** What? You have a sore mouth, well, then keep it shut. LRT

wehre, *refl, pp* **gwehrt -** to resist. **Er hot sich gwehrt.** He resisted. LRT

Wei, *f* - wine. **Ich gleich Drauwewei.** I like grape wine. LRT

wei!, *interj* - then! KYG1993

weiderreeche - to reach further. **Em Hund sei Kett waar lenger, as ich gemehnt hab un no hot er ~ kenne, as ich gemehnt hab.** The dog's chain was longer than I thought it was

and therefore he could reach further than I thought. LRT

Weil, *f* - while. **selli ~ -** during that time. KYG1991. **Die ganz ~ as die yunge am rumschpringe waare, waar ihre Paep deheem am schaffe.** The whole while (time) that the boys were gadding about, their dad was home working. LRT

Weili, *n* - *dim* of **Weil.** a little while. **en glee ~. Bleib yuscht en glee ~, no sehnscht vielleicht en glee Geili.** Stay just a little while, then perhaps you'll see a little horse. LRT

Weis, *f* - tune. **Nau welle mir singe, weescht du die ~?** Now we want to sing. Do you know the tune? LRT. **en ~ hawwe -** to carry a tune. KYG2074. **Selli ~ is mir net bekannt.** I don't know that tune. LRT

Weischtee, *m* - cream of tarter. = **Weiss-schtee.** KYG1971

Weissbeint, *f* - white pine. LRT/Leb.Co.

Weisskopp, *m* - tow-headed child. KYG2043. **Der ~ Buh hot gfrogt fer en Glaas Wasser.** The tow-headed boy asked for a glass of water. LRT

Weisswalniss, *f* - white walnut. *Juglans cinerea L.* = **Budderniss, Eelnuss, Eelwalniss.** KYG2161

Weisswalnissbaam, *m* - white walnut tree. = **Eelnussbaam, Eelwalnissbaam.** KYG2161

weit, *adv* - far. **~ eweck -** remote. **Bleib ~ weck so as nix dich drefft.** Stay far away so that nothing hits you. LRT

Welschhaahnekopp, *m* - turkey gobbler head. KYG2076

Welschhinkel, *n* - female turkey. *cf* **Welschhaahne.** KYG2075. **En gschlacht ~ as baut zehe Pund wiegt, macht en schee Esse.** A dressed turkey hen that weights about ten pounds makes a nice meal. LRT

Welschhinkelbruscht, *f* - turkey breast. KYG2075. **En ~ hot ganz bissel Fett.** A turkey breast has very little fat. LRT

Welschkannbaschder, *m* - corn shucker. **Ya, er is en guder ~.** Yes, he is a good corn husker. LRT

Welschkannfaahne, *f* - tassel (of corn). KYG1972. **Sis yuscht hinne im Juli un mer seht schund ~ so rum her.** It's only late July and one already sees tassels (of corn) here and there. LRT

Welschkanngrutze, *pl* - corn cobs. **~ sin net viel Geld waert.** Corn cobs are not worth much money. LRT

Welschkannroi, *f, pl* **~e** - row of corn. **Des Feld is voll ~e.** This field is full of rows of corn. LRT

Welschkannschaeler, *m* - corn sheller. **Unser ~ hot mer immer vun Hand drehe misse.** We always had to turn our corn sheller by hand. LRT

Welschkannschipp, *f* - corn scoop. **Ich gleich en ~ fer mei Schnee scheppe.** I like a corn scoop to shovel my snow. LRT

Welt, *f* - world. **Die ~ muss em verleed sei.** We are sick of the world. **Die ~ is mir verleed.** I am discouraged with the world. LRT

Weltdeel, *n* - section of the world. **Do in dem ~ schwetze mir Deitsch.** Here in this part of the world we speak (PA) German. LRT,4/11/2000

welterlich, *adv* - terribly. **Die letschde Paar Daage hot's ~ geregert.** The last few days it rained terribly. = **wedderlich.** LRT

Weltfriede, *m* - world peace. **Gebt's sei Lewe ~?** Will there ever be world peace? LRT, 4/11/2000

Weltgedob, *n* - world turmoil. **Sis immer ~!** There is always unrest somewhere in the world. LRT,4/11/2000

Weltgrieg, *m, pl* **~e** - world war. **Unser Nochbersbuh is umkumme im Zwedde ~.** Our neighbor boy was killed in World War II. LRT,4/11/2000. **Ich will hoffe mir sehne nix meh wie die Weltgriege eens un zwee.** I hope we don't see anything like World Wars I and II. LRT

weltlich, *adj* - temporal. *cf* **zeitlich.** KYG1983. **Die Yunge sin arig ~ heidesdaags.** The young folks are very temporal (worldly) now-a-days. LRT. **Er will yuscht ~ sei; er will nix zu duh hawwe mit Gott.** He just wants to be worldly; he doesn't want to have anything to do with God. LRT,4/11/2000

Weltlichkeit, *f* - worldliness.

Sei ~ dreht en latt Leit ab. His worldliness turns a lot of people off. LRT/Leb,4/11/2000

Weltluscht, *f* - worldly pleasure. **~ is net all schlecht.** Worldly pleasure is not all bad. LRT, 4/11/2000

wenne - to turn (the sod)(hay). = **wende.** KYG2077. **Wann Hoi druff geregert waert, no muss es die menscht Zeit gewennt sei.** If hay is rained on, it usually has to be turned. (tedded). LRT. *cf* **uffwenne.** KYG1978. **Des Hoi misse mir ~ eb mir's in die Scheier duhne.** We will need to ted this hay before we can put it in the barn. LRT

wennich, *adv* - little. **~ gschpassich** - somewhat peculiar. **~ schwerlich** - somewhat heavy. **Er schickt sich immer ~ gschpassich aa.** He always acts somewhat peculiar. LRT

Wennschtecke, *m* - turning stick (in butchering). KYG2079. **En ~ is notwennich fer die Seidaerem butze so as mer sie yuuse kann fer Wascht mache.** A turning stick is necessary to clean hog intestines, so that they can be used to make sausage. LRT

Wesch, *f* - wash. **~ ausringe** - to wring out the wash. KYG2166. **Mir hen en grossi ~ heit.** We have a big wash (laundry) today. LRT

Wesch-schissel, *f* - washbasin. KYG2167. **En ~ macht en gudi Wasserschissel fer die Hund.** A wash basin makes a good water dish for the dogs. LRT

Wesch-schteiber, *m* - wash line prop. = **Wesch-schtang.** KYG2168. **~ sin net immer notwennich wann mer gudi Poschde un Leine hot.** Wash line props are not always necessary if one has good posts and lines. LRT

Wesch-schtend, *m* - washstand. KYG2169. **Unser Grosseldre hen en ~ gyuust.** Our grandparents used a wash stand. LRT

Wesch-schtendschupplaad, *f* - washstand drawer. KYG1269. **Ich bhald mei Weschlumbe in de ~.** I keep my wash cloth in the wash stand drawer. LRT

Wesch-schtubb, *f, pl* - **schtuwwe** - washroom. KYG1269. **Ihre Haus hot ken ~.** Their house has no (laundry) room. LRT

Weschausdreher, *m* - wash wringer. = **Weschringer.** KYG2169

Weschbank, *f* - bench for washtub. KYG2169. **Unser ~ sett frisch aagschtriche sei.** Our bench for the wash tub needs a new paint job. LRT

Weschbleh, *f* - wash bluing. = **Weschbloh.** KYG2167

Weschblock, *m* - washing stool. KYG2166

Weschbohl, *f* - washbowl. KYG2167. **Selli ~ in de Baadschtubb is zu glee.** That washbowl in the bathroom is too small. LRT

Weschboiler, *m* - wash boiler. (Cr,Cl,Dn,Lr,Ln,Nd,NWSl). =

Weschbeiler (Cbs,Cn,NWLh, Emy,SESr,NESr,Un), **Weschzuwwer** (Elh), **Weschkessel** (Mn,NMy), **Waschboiler** (SWMe, SEYk), **Eisekessel** (SEYk), **Dampkessel, Wasserboiler.** KYG2167. **Seller ~ is zu schwer fer die Weibsleit, wann er voll is mit Wasser.** That wash boiler is too heavy for the women when it is full of water. LRT

Weschbord, *n* - washboard. KYG2167. **Dreckichi Gleeder wesche mit'nı ~ is haddi Arewet.** Washing dirty clothes with a wash board is hard work. **Mir duhne unser Wesches uff'm ~.** We do our washing on a washboard. LRT

Weschbordreiwer, *m* - washboard rubber. KYG2167

Weschdaag, *m* - washday. KYG2167. **Bei uns is Muundaag ~.** With us Monday is washday. LRT

Wescherei, *f* - confounded washing. KYG2168. **Die ~ alli Mundaag macht em ebmols bissel umleidlich.** This confounded washing every Monday makes one a bit uncomfortable at times. LRT

Weschfraa, *f* - washer-woman. = **Weschern.** KYG2168. **Wann du eppes wisse witt wehe deine Weschgleeder, muscht ewwe die ~ froge.** If you want to know something about your wash clothes, you'll have to ask the washer-woman. LRT

Weschhaus, *n* - wash house. = **Weschheisel, Wesch-schendi.** KYG2168. **Ihre ~ waar aa ihre**

Butscherhaus. Their wash house was also their butcher house. LRT

Wesching, *f* - washing. = **Wesche.** KYG2168

Weschkareb, *m, pl* -**karewe** - wash basket. KYG2167. **Sie hot en alder heem-gemachder ~ mit vier gleeni hilzni Fiess.** She has an old homemade wash basket with four small, wooden feet. LRT

Weschkessel, *m* - wash kettle. KYG2168

Weschkich, *f* - wash kitchen. KYG2166

Weschlein, *f* - wash line. = **Wesch-seel.** KYG2168. **Die Mamm waert bees, wann die ~ nunnerreisst, wann sie voll ghengt is mit Gleeder.** Mom gets angry when the wash line tears down, when it's loaded with clothing. LRT

Weschleinschteiber, *m, pl* ~ - wash line prop. **Die Weibsleit yuuse nimmi so viel ~, wie sie als hen.** The women don't use as many wash line props as they used to. LRT

Weschlumbe, *m* - washcloth. KYG2167. **Der ~ is voll Lecher, mir breiche en neier.** This wash cloth is full of holes, we need a new one. LRT

Weschlumbedaag, *m* - Thursday after Ash Wednesday. KYG2012

Weschmaschien, *f, pl* ~e - washing machine. KYG2166. **Die neie ~e hen ken Ringers meh.** The new washing machines no longer have wringers. LRT

Weschmaschienringer, *m* - clothes wringer. **En ~ is ken Blatz fer em sei Finger neigepetzt griege.** A wringer is no place to get one's finger pinched into. LRT,4/18/2000

weschnass, *adj* - soaking wet. **Er hot gschafft bis er ganz ~ gschwitzt waar.** He worked until he was soaking wet with perspiration. LRT

Weschpedeiwel, *m* - male wasp. KYG2169

Weschpenescht, *n* - wasp's nest. KYG2169. **Es waar en ~ in unserem Baam.** There was a wasp's nest in our tree. LRT

Weschpeneschttee, *m* - wasp's nest tea. KYG2169

Weschpeschtecher, *m* - wasp's sting(er). KYG2169. **Wann der ~ unnich deine Haut henge bleibt, meechscht du Druwwel hawwe.** If the wasp stinger gets stuck under your skin, you may have trouble. LRT

Weschpeweiwel, *n* - female wasp. KYG2169

Weschposchde, *m, pl* ~ - wash line post. KYG2168. **Letscht Summer hen mir unser ~ aagschtriche.** Last summer we painted our wash line posts. LRT

Weschringer, *m* - wash wringer. **Maedli, du muscht achtgewwe as du net dei Finger in der ~ grickscht.** Little girl, you must be careful not to get your fingers into the

wash wringer. LRT

Weschwasser, *n* - water used or to be used for washing. KYG2168. **Fer schpaarsam sei, kann mer's ~ yuuse fer's Gaardesach wessere.** To be conservative (saving) one can use the wash water to water the garden plants. LRT

Weschzuwwer, *m, pl* -ziwwer - wash tub. **Langi Yaahre zerick waare die Weschziwwer vun Holz gemacht.** Many years ago the wash tubs were made of wood. LRT

Wese, *n* - matter. **waerdens ~!** - confounded thing! KYG1998

wessere, *pp* gewessert - to water. **Hoscht du die Blanze gewessert?** Did you water the plants? LRT

wettre - to thunder and lighten. KYG2011

wetze - **1** to whet (hone). **Mei Sens is schtump, ich muss sie ~.** My scythe is dull, I need to whet (hone) it. LRT. **2** to rub together with a swishing noise (as trousers legs). **So grossi Hossebeh misse schur ~.** Such large pants legs surely must rub noisily. LRT

wewe, *pp* gewowe - to weave. **Selli Fraa hot schund en latt scheeni Sache gewowe.** That woman has already woven a lot of nice things. LRT,4/18/2000

Wewwi, *m* - sore (in speaking to children). **Oh mei liewes Kind, hoscht du en ~?** Oh my dear child, do you have a sore (boo-boo)? LRT

Wexel, *n* - small change. **Kannscht du mir ~ gewwe fer en zehe Daalernot?** Can you give me small change for a ten dollar bill? **Ennich-epper as eppes zu duh hot mit Geld muss wisse wie mer ~ macht.** Anyone who has anything to do with money must know how one makes change. LRT

Wickel, *m* - **1** roll of hair. **am ~ nemme** - to take by the hair. KYG1962. **2** something that has been wound around. **Was fer'n ~ is dann sell?** What kind of a wound around affair is that? LRT

wickle - to wrap. **sich aus eppes ~** - to wriggle out of a tight spot. KYG2016. **Sie hen Yesus in en Windelduch gewickelt un hen ihn in en Fuderdrog gelegt.** They wrapped baby Jesus in swaddling cloth and lay him in a manger. LRT

widdergebore sei - to be reborn. **Deel Leit welle nix heere vun ~.** Some people don't want to hear about being born again. LRT

widderhole - **1** to repeat. **Kannscht du mir sell ~?** Can you repeat that for me? **2** to fetch again. **Mir sin kumme fer Karepse ~.** We came to fetch pumpkins again. LRT

widdersaage - to repeat. **Kannscht du sell ~, ich hab dich net geheert.** Can you repeat that, I didn't hear you. LRT

widderschtandlos, *adj* - unopposed. KYG2109

widdersehne - to see again.

Kumm, mir welle dich ~.
Come, we want to see you again.
LRT

Widderwaddichkeit, *f* -
unpleasantness. =
Unblessierlichkeit. KYG2109

widderzammebringe - to
reunite. **Alle Yaahr duhne mir
die Freindschaft ~.** Each year
we reunite the relatives. LRT

Wies, *f* - *dim* of Louisa. **Mir
hen die ~ Kann vun der Rot
Kuh gekennt, wu mir glee
waare.** We knew of Louisa
Kern of Red Run, when we were
little. CRB

wieschderlich, *adv* - very badly.
**Der Yarick hot sei gleener
Bruder ~ abgezankt.** George
upbraided his little brother very
badly. LRT

wiescht, *adv* - ugly. **Schick dich
net so ~ aa!** Don't act so ugly!
LRT

wieschtgaschdich, *adj* -
extremely nasty. **Yunger, sei
net so ~.** Young man, don't be
so down right nasty. LRT

Wille, *m* - will. **um ihre ~ -** for
her sake. **Um ihre ~ hen sie es
geduh.** They did it for her sake.
LRT

Wille, *m* - will. **Er hot en ~
gemacht.** He was testate.
KYG1989. **Hot er en ~ ghat
wie er gschtarewe is?** Did he
have a will when he died (was
he testate at his death)? LRT

Wind, *m* - wind, knowledge. **~
griege vun eppes -** to be
secretly informed of something.
**Sie hot ihn verlosse, is sell

recht? Mir hen bissel ~ ghat
vun sellem.** She left him, is that
correct? We caught wind of
that. LRT. **~ fasse -** to take a
second breath. KYG1960

Windbeidel, *m* - an
undependable person. KYG2095

Winderreddich, *f, pl* ~ - winter
radish. **Ich hab immer ~ besser
gegliche wie Summerreddich.** I
always liked winter radishes
better than summer radishes.
LRT

Winderzwiwwel, *f* - top onion.
Allium proliferum. KYG2038.
**Die ~ griege ken Sumekepp;
sie griege Kepp mit gleeni
Zwiwwlin drin.** The winter
onions don't get seed heads; they
get heads with little onions in
them. LRT

windich, *adj* - squally. **Sis so ~,
es Laab vun die Baem is schier
all weckgeblose.** It's so windy
that the foliage from the trees is
nearly all blown away. LRT

Windwarwel, *m* - whirlwind,
tornado. KYG2039.**Der ~ hot
der Wagge umgschmisse.** The
whirlwind upset the wagon.
LRT

winkel un senkel, *adj* - plumb.
LRT: Grandfather used to say:
"Winkel un senkel!"

Winkeleise, *n* - carpenter's
square. **En Schreiner kann net
viel duh unni en ~.** A carpenter
can't do much without a try
square. LRT

Winkeleise, *n* - (carpenter's) try
square. KYG2071. **Leg's ~
driwwer, no weescht eb's
Winkel is odder net.** Lay the

try square over it, then you will
know if it's square or not. LRT

winnisch, *adj* - warped.
KYG2165. **Des feicht Wedder
hot die Dier ~ gemacht.** This
damp weather warped the door.
Selli Dier guckt ~ zu mir. That
door looks warped to me. LRT

winsche - to wish. **Ich winsch
dir gut Glick!** I wish you well.
LRT,4/18/2000

Winsche, *pl* - wishes. **Ich geb
dir mei beschdi ~!** I give you
my best wishes! LRT

Wippli, *n* - small switch, whip.
**Yunger, wann du dich net
bedraagscht, grickscht du des
~ uff dei Hinnerdeel.** Young
man, if you don't behave, you'll
get this little whip on your
behind. LRT

wisse - to know. **Mer kennt net
wisse.** There's no telling.
KYG1981

wissewaert, *adv* - worthy of
knowing. **Wann's net ~ is,
dann will ich's aa net wisse.** If
it isn't worth knowing, then I
don't want to know it.
LRT,4/18/2000

Woch, *f, pl* ~e - week. **alle drei
~e -** tri-weekly. KYG2063. **Sell
waar die ~ wu die
Freindschaft heem kumme
waare.** That was the week when
the relatives had come home.
LRT

Woch, *f* - week. **die ~ -** this
(last) week. KYG2000. **Die
(letscht) Woch hen mir zu viel
Versammlinge ghat.** This (last)
week we had too many
meetings. LRT

192

Wolfzaeh, *pl* - oversized teeth. KYG1978

woll, *adv* - I suppose it is. KYG2068. **Des is woll der Weg wie es sei sett.** I suppose this is the way it should be. **Ich denk sell waar ~ der Weg as mir's hawwe hedde selle.** I suppose that is well the way we should have it. LRT

Woll, *f* - wool. **Mir misse die Schof scheere, mir breiche die ~.** We need to shear the sheep, we need the wool. **Ya, sie hen die ~ iwwer sei Aage gezoge.** Yes, they pulled the wool over his eyes. LRT,4/11/2000

Wollefliess, *m* - woolen fleece. **Ich will die ~ kaafe, was dir vun eem Schof abgshore hett.** I want to purchase the woolen fleece that you've shorn from one sheep. LRT,4/11/2000

Wollewwerschteddel, *n* - ✪ Mt. Aetna, Leb. Co., PA.

wollfelguckich, *adj* - cheap (in appearance). KYG1973. **Selli Valentine** decorations **sin ~.** Those Valentine decorations are tawdry looking. LRT

Wollgaarn, *n* - worsted. KYG2250. **Sei Wammes is vun ~ gemacht.** His jacket is made of worsted (fabric). LRT,4/18/2000

Wollhensching, *pl* - woolen gloves. **Die ~ halde em sei Hend schee warem.** The woolen gloves keep one's hands nice and worm. LRT,4/11/2000

Wollhut, *m* - woolen hat. **Sei schwatzer ~ waar net wolfel.** His black woolen hat was not

cheap. LRT,4/11/2000

wollich, *adj* - woolen. **Sell is en scheeni ~i Deck.** That is a nice woolen blanket. **Seller Yunge will immer sei brau ~ Hemm aaduh.** That young man always wants to wear his brown woolen shirt. LRT,4/11/2000

Wollrock, *m* - woolen coat. **Wann's so kalt is, kann mer froh sei, as mer'n ~ hot.** When it's this cold, one can be glad one has a wool coat. LRT,4/11/2000

Wollsack, *m* - woolen bag. **Der ~ is voll.** The wool sack is full. LRT,4/11/2000

wu, *rel pron* - that. **Die Desks, ~ (as) net abgfinnischt waare.** The desks that weren't finished. KYG1992. **Sie wuhne am Blatz ~ em Tscheck sei Grosseldre mol gewuhnt hen.** They live at that place where Jake's grandparents once lived. LRT

wu-anne, *adv* - where to. = **wuhie.** KYG2027. **Wu sette mir des anne duh?** Where should we put this? LRT

Wuhnblatz, *m* - residence. **Sell is ihre ~.** That is their residence. LRT

Wunnerfitz, *n* - curiosity. **Es ~ hot ihn grickt.** He was consumed by curiosity. KYG2162. **Der ~ blogt ihn.** Curiosity is getting the best of him. LRT

Wunners, *pl* - great shakes. *cf* **Er is en Ratt draa.** He is some shakes at it. **Sie hen ~ gemacht wie schee as er gsunge hot.** They marveled at how

beautifully he sang. LRT

wunnerswaert, *adv* - worthwhile. KYG2251. **Ihre Gutmehnichkeit is immer so ~.** Her kindness is always so admirable. LRT,4/18/2000

wunslich, *adj* - smooth, soft (of young animals). **Die Busslin sin awwer ~.** The kittens are really smooth and soft. LRT

wunzich, *adj* - tiny. KYG2024. **Sell is en ~ glee Wutzli.** That is a tiny little piglet. LRT

Wut, *f* - madness, anger. **So ~ hab ich sei Lewe net gsehne.** Such anger I have never seen. LRT

yaage - to hunt. **en Haas ~** - to hunt a rabbit. KYG

Yaaghosse, *pl* - hunting pants. **Er hot sei ~ alles verschlitzt.** His hunting pants are all slit up. LRT

Yaahr, *n* - year. **des ~** - this year. KYG2000. **Was gebt's Neies des ~?** What new (things) can we expect this year? LRT

Yaahrbuch, *n* - yearbook. KYG2260. **Deel vun die Sache in ihrem ~ kann mer net lese.** Some of the things in their yearbook are illegible. LRT,4/18/2000

yaahrelang, *adv* - **1** for many years. **Fer ~ hen mir sie net gsehne ghat.** For many years we had not seen them. LRT,4/18/2000. **2** year long. **Ihre Arewet halt's ganz ~ (Yaahr rum).** Their work lasts the whole year long (whole year round). LRT,4/18/2000

Yaahreszeit, *f* - season. = **Zeit vum Yaahr.** *cf* **Yaahrgang. Harebschts is mei liebschdi Zeit vum Yaahr.** Fall is my favorite time of the year. LRT

yaahreweis, *adv* - **1** by the year. **Er dutt die Bauerei ~ lehne.** He rents the farm by the year. **2** annually. **Selli Versammlung hen sie ~.** That gathering is held annually. LRT, 4/18/2000

Yaahrzaahl, *f* - birth year. **Er wees sei ~ net.** He doesn't know the year he was born. LRT, 4/18/2000

yaehrlich, *adj* - yearly. **Mir hen zwee ~i Familye- versammlinge.** We have two family gatherings each year. LRT,4/18/2000

Yaerdschtecke, *m* - yardstick. **Wie ich in die Schul gange bin, hot die Schulmeeschdern immer'n ~ hendich ghat.** When I went to school, the teacher always had her yardstick handy (for whippings). LRT,4/18/2000. = **Yaardschdecke**

Yammer, *m* - misery. **Ei du ~ yeh nochemol, ferwas gehscht du net heem?** Oh my sakes, why don't you go home? **Oh ~ yeh nochmol, was fer Elend hen sie nau?** Oh my sakes, what misery are they into now? LRT

Yammerdaal, *n* - ✪ Vale of Tears, located just north of Clay, Lanc Co., PA. CRB. *cf* **Saeglochgrick**

Yarick, *m* - York. = **Yaerick**

yaunze - to yelp. KYG2262

yeher, *adv* - from the remotest times and places. **Er is vun ~ beikumme un des wees ken Mensch wu.** He came from no one knows where. LRT

Yess, *f* - tantrum. **in re ~** - in a tantrum. KYG1969. **Er is en e ~ kumme.** He flew into a rage. KYG1981

Yochbord, *n* - yoke put on oxen horn. KYG2263

Yohannes, *m* - John. **~ 3:16 is so en Haaptschrift in die Biewel.** John 3:16 is an important passage in the Bible. LRT

Yohannes, *m* - [St.] John. **im ~ bleiwe** - to stick to the subject. KYG1878

Yoli, *m* - *dim* of **Joseph.** KYG2285

Yoni, *m* - *dim* of **Jonathan.** = **Yones.** KYG2285

Yuchenblessier, *f* - youthful pleasure. KYG2265

Yugendluschdichkeit, *f* - youthful mirth. LRT/Leb.Co.

yung, *adj* - young. **Oh, fer widder ~ sei!** Oh, to be young again! LRT

Yunger, *m* - young fellow. **mei ~** - my son. **Ferwas saagt er zu ihm "Yunger," er is yo schund fuffzich Yaahr alt.** Why does he say to him "young fellow," he already is fifty years old. LRT

Yunionsoldaat, *m* - Union soldier. KYG2105

Yuschdiss, *m* - <*Engl* justice,

squire. **Der ~ gebt acht uff so Sache.** The squire takes care of such things. LRT

Zaah, *m, pl* **Zaeh** - tooth. **hinnerschder ~** - back tooth. **en beeser ~** - an aching tooth. **vedderer (vedderschder) ~** - front tooth. **aagefaulder ~** - decayed tooth. **hohler ~** - hollow tooth. **wacklicher ~** - loose tooth. KYG2035. **en ~ fille** - to fill a tooth. **die Zaeh blicke (blecke)** - to show the teeth. **Mei Zaeh hen uffenanner geggleppert.** My teeth chattered. KYG2036

Zaahblicker, *m* - toothpick. = **Zaeheblicker, Zaehebutzer, Zaeheschtarrer.** KYG2036. **Sei Fraa gleicht net wann en ~ aus seim Maul schteckt.** His wife doesn't like when a toothpick protrudes from his mouth. LRT

Zaahgeropp, *n* - tooth-pulling. KYG2036. **Des ~ waert als wennicher.** Having teeth pulled is on the decline (since the use of fluorine). LRT

Zaahgschwaer, *m* - ulcer at a tooth. KYG2088. **En ~ is ken Schpass.** An abscessed tooth is no fun. LRT

Zaahlaad, *f* - jawbone, gums, tooth socket. KYG2037. **Mei falschi Zaeh mache mei ~ weh!** My false teeth make my gums sore! LRT. [In Leb. Co., we usually called this the gums, but occasionally, we called the gums **Zaahfleesch**, *qv*. LRT]. = **Zahnfleesch**

zaahne - to shed teeth. KYG1979

Zaahropper, *m* - tooth

extractor. = **Zaehropper.** KYG2036. **Deel Zaehdokder gleiche net Zaeh roppe.** Some dentists don't like to pull teeth. LRT

Zaahschmatze, *pl* - toothache. = **Zaahweh.** KYG2036

Zaahwatzel, *f* - tooth root. KYG2036

Zaahweh, *n* - toothache. **Fer ~ hawwe is ken Schpass.** To have a tooth ache is no fun. LRT

zaart, *adj* - tender. **Selli Eppel sin schee ~.** Those apples are nice and tender. LRT

Zacke, *m* - = tooth. *cf* **Zackche,** *dim of* **Zacke.** KYG2035

zacklich, *adj* - scalloped. **Mir hen sell Dischduch ~ gemacht.** We made the tablecloth (edges) scalloped. LRT/Leb

zaeh, *adj* - tough. KYG2042. **Die Haut uff dem Hinkel is ~.** The skin on this chicken is tough. LRT

Zaeh, *pl* - teeth. **falschi ~** - set of false teeth. = **Reef, Blaade.** KYG1978. **Er hot zwee ~ as er roppe losse muss.** He has two teeth that he needs to have pulled. LRT

Zaehbascht, *f* - toothbrush. = **Zaahbascht.** KYG2036. **Unser Zaehdokder gebt uns oftmols en ~ fer nix.** Our dentist frequently gives us a toothbrush for free. LRT

Zaehbulwer, *n* - tooth powder. = **Zaehpulfer.** KYG2036. **~ verkaaft net zu gut heidesdaags.** Tooth powder

doesn't sell too well now-a-days. LRT

Zaehche, *n* - *dim of* **Zaeh.** toothie. KYG2036

Zaehglepperes, *n* - chattering of teeth. KYG2036

Zaehgnaersche, *n* - gnashing of teeth. KYG2036

Zaehichkeit, *f* - toughness. KYG2042

zaehle, *pp* **gezaehlt** - to presume, expect, reckon. **Es is so gezaehlt.** It is so presumed. LRT. **Yonnie, ich zaehl sell is so.** Johnny, I reckon that is so. LRT

Zaehropperei, *f* - business of pulling teeth. KYG1978. **Zidder as mir so viel Fluorine yuuse, is die ~ nimmi was sie mol waar.** Since we use so much fluorine, the business of pulling teeth is not what it once was. LRT

Zaertlichkeit, *f* - tenderness. KYG1985

zamme-schteh - to stand together. **Wann dir zammeschteht, grickt dir's geduh.** If you stand together, you'll get it done. LRT

zammebacke - to stick together (in cooking). KYG1878

zammebappe - to stick, paste together. = **zammeschtecke, zammeschticke.** KYG1878. **Kannscht du des un sell vunnanner mache, sie sin zammergebappt?** Can you separate this and that, they are stuck together? LRT

zammebhalde - to keep together. KYG2030. **Ich will hoffe sie kenne die Familye ~.** I hope they can keep the family together. LRT

zammeblaudre - to talk together. = **zammeschwetze.** KYG1965

zammebleiwe, *pp* **zammergebliwwe** - to remain together. **Die Gemeesleit sin all zammergebliwwe.** The church members all stayed together. LRT

zammedrehe - to twist together. KYG2084. **Mer dutt der Droht ~ fer sell feschtmache.** One secures that by twisting the wire together. LRT

zammeduh - to put together. **Kannscht du selli Raetzel widder ~?** Can you put that puzzle together again? LRT. **Mer kann viel Kieh ihre Millich ~ un niemand wees der Unnerschitt.** One can put the milk of many cows together and no one can tell the difference. LRT

zammefaahre, *pp* **zammegfaahre** - to start from fright. **Ich hab noch nie nix so gesehne ghat, wie's die Memm zammegfaahre is.** I never saw anything like it, the way mother was shocked from fright. LRT

zammefeddle, *pp* **zammegfeddelt** - to string up. **Sie hen alles zammegfeddelt ghat.** They had strung everything together. LRT

zammefiege - to fit together. = **in enanner mache.** KYG2030

zammefliege, *pp* **is zammegfloge** - to smash together. **Die zwee Kaere sin zammergfloge un ee Mensch waar dod.** The two cars smashed together and one person was dead. LRT

zammehocke, *refl* - to sit together. **Ya schur, dir kennt eich ~.** Yes, surely you can sit together. LRT

zammelege, *pp* **zammegelegt** - to contribute jointly. **Die Gemeensglieder hen en Haufe Geld zammegelegt, Gott sei Dank!** The church members jointly contributed a pile of money, thank God! LRT

zammenaggele, *pp* **zammegenaggelt** - to nail together. **Sie hen selli Bord zammegenaggelt.** They nailed those boards together. LRT

zammenemme - to take together. KYG1963

zammepacke, *pp* **zammegepackt** - to pack the ground (by a heavy rain). **Der Regge hot der Grund hatt zammegepackt.** The rain really compacted the soil. LRT

zammereche - to rake together. **Ich rech die Bledder zamme.** I'll rake the leaves together. LRT

zammereide, *pp* **is zammegeridde** - to ride together. **Mir hen net genunk Geil fer uns all ~.** We don't have enough horses for all of us to ride together. LRT

zammerleere - to pour from one container to another. LRT

zammeschaffe - to work together. **~ mehnt viele Hend macht leichdi Arewet.** Working together means many hands make light work. LRT,4/11/2000

zammeschnalle - to strap together. **Schnall selli zwee Geil zamme, no hoscht en Paar.** Strap those two horses together and you've got a pair (of horses). LRT

zammeschparre - to pen up together. **Ya, mer kann die Hinkel un die Haahne ~.** Yes, one can pen the hens and the roosters together. LRT

zammeschpelle - to pin together. = **zuschpelle.** KYG2030

zammewatzle, *pp* **zammegewatzelt** - to have roots intertwine. **Selli Blumme waare alles zammegewatzelt gewest.** Those flowers were all rooted together. LRT

zammewatzle, *pp* **zammegwatzelt** - to have roots intertwine. **Selli paar Schteck datt in sellem Haffe sin alles zammegwatzelt.** Those few plants in that crock have their roots intertwined. LRT

zammewickle, *pp* **zammegewickelt** - to wrap together. **Wie des gross Esse verbei waar, hen die Weibsleit all die dreckiche Dischdicher zammegewickelt un hen sie heemgenumme fer sie wesche.** When this large dinner was over, the women wrapped together all the dirty tablecloths and took them home to wash them. LRT,4/18/2000

Zang, *f, pl* **~e** - tweezer. KYG2081

Zankes, *n* - upbraiding. KYG2117

Zann, *m* - resentment, anger. = **Zaern. Sei ~ hot ewwe iwwergenumme.** His resentment took control. LRT. **Sei ~ verschreckt deel Leit.** His anger frightens some people. LRT,4/11/2000

zannich, *adj* - prone to anger. **Yunger, sei net so ~!** Young man, don't be so angry! LRT, 4/18/2000. = **zannlich**

zannlich, *adj* - irritable, prone to anger. **Sei net so ~!** Don't be so irritable! LRT. = **zannich**

Zapper[1], *m* - tug (as fish tug on a line). KYG2072

Zapper[2], *m* - tapster. KYG1970. **Er is en Bier ~.** He is a beer tapster. LRT

Zarefer, *m* - wrangler. **Seller Mann is immer en ~.** That man is always one to argue. LRT, 4/16/2000. *cf* **zarefe**

zarre - to tug. = **ziehe, hatt ziehe.** KYG2072

zawwlich, *adj* - wiggling. **Mer hen gemehnt die Sau waar dod, awwer sie is als noch ~.** We thought the pig was dead but it is still wiggling. LRT

Zeck, *f* - tenacious pesty person. KYG1983

Zeddel[1], *m* - tag. **Seller ~ uff sellem Rock weist as er net deier is.** That tag on that coat shows that it is not expensive.

LRT

Zeddel², *m* - ticket. **En ~ fer sell Football Game koscht dreissich Daaler.** A ticket for that football game costs $30. LRT,4/18/2000

Zeddel³, *m* - warp (in carpeting). KYG2165

zedre - to trill (of birds). KYG2061

Zeeche, *pl* - signs of the zodiac.

Zehe Gebodde, *pl* - the Ten Commandments. KYG1983. **Mer muss meh duh as yuscht die ~ lese.** One must do more than just read the Ten Commandments. LRT

Zehe-acker-riewe-feld, *n* - ten acre beet field. KYG1984

Zehe-daaler-not, *f, pl* **~e** - ten-dollar bill. KYG1985. **Ich hett gern zwee scheeni nei-ie ~e fer meim Kindsbuh gewwe fer Grischtdaag.** Please, I'd like two nice ten dollar bills to give my grandson for Christmas. LRT

zehe-penni, *adj* - ten-penny. KYG1986. **En ~ Naggel is en Schpeik.** A ten-penny nail is a spike. LRT

Zehe-sent-schtemp, *m,f* - ten-cent stamp. KYG1984. **En ~ is net genunk heidesdaags.** A ten cent stamp is not enough now-a-days. LRT

zehe-yaehrich, *adj* - ten-year-old. KYG1987. **~ is en scheeni Elt.** Ten-year-old is a nice age. LRT

Zehedel, *n* - tenth. KYG1986. **Yuscht ee ~ vun selle Gediere sin gsund.** Only one-tenth of those animals are healthy. LRT

Zeheder, *m* - **1** the figure ten. KYG1983. **2** ten-dollar bill. KYG1985. **Do is en fuffzich Daalernot, ich hett gern fimf ~.** Here is a fifty dollar bill, please may I have five 10-dollar bills? LRT

Zehegwaartschtenner, *m* - ten-quart can. KYG1986. **En ~ is yuscht was mir breiche fer sell.** A ten-quart can is just what we need for that. LRT

zehemol, *adv* - ten times. KYG1983. **~ dreissich is dreihunnert.** Ten times thirty is 300. LRT

Zehenaggel, *m, pl* **-neggel** - toe nail. KYG2030. **Wann die Zeheneggel fungus hen, gucke sie net schee.** If the toe nails have fungus, they are not pretty. LRT

Zeichniss, *n* - testimonial. **~ abgewwe** - to give testimony. KYG1989. **Sei ~ hot mich denke mache.** His testimonial made me think. LRT

Zeide, *pl* - times. **haddi ~** - hard times. **vor ~** - in olden times. = **vor alders.** KYG2020. **Die erschde paar Yaahre vum 1930 waare haddi Zeide.** The first few years of the 1930s were tough times. LRT

zeideweis, *adv* - periodically. **So ~ griege mir en latt Hilf.** Periodically we get lots of help. LRT

zeidich, *adj* - **1** seasonable. **2**

ripe. **Die Biere sin ~, es is Zeit fer sie roppe.** The pears are ripe, it's time to pick them. LRT

zeidiche - to ripen. **Die Sunn duht alles schneller ~.** The sun ripens everything faster. LRT

Zeit, *f* - time. **die ~ saage -** to tell time. KYG1981. **Weescht du was ~ as es is?** Do you know what time it is? LRT. **die ~ nemme -** to take the time. KYG1962. **fer'n katzi ~ -** temporarily. KYG1983. **Fer en katzi ~ hen mir unser Ess-Sache grickt fer nix.** Temporarily we got our food for nothing (free). LRT. **bei ~ -** at the appointed time. **en bissi ~ -** a busy time. **die narrisch ~ -** Daylight Saving Time. **zimmlich gudi ~ -** a pretty good time. **epper en scheeni ~ weise** - to show someone a good time. **en ariye ~ -** a hard time. **Es is hoch ~.** It is high time. **zu seinre ~ -** in his time. KYG2018. **en ~ her -** for some time now. = **en ~ lang. an die rechde (zu rechder) ~ kumme -** to come in the nick of time. **die ~ vum Yaahr -** this time of the year. **gehich ~ -** against time. **~ sei fer** - to be time to. **~ halde -** to keep time. **~ mache -** to make time. **sich ~ nemme -** to take time off. KYG2019. **Es is unni ~.** It is timeless. KYG2020. **die ~ biede** - to bid the time of day. **Der alt Mann datt die Schtrooss drunne hot mir die ~ gebodde.** The old man down the street there bid me the time of day. LRT

Zeitgeischt, *m* - spirit of the time. KYG2019

Zeitlang - longing. **~ griege fer epper -** to long for someone.

KYG2019. *cf* **Es is mir ~ warre.** It took too long, I got bored. LRT

zeitlich, *adv* - in time. = **in Zeit, bei Zeit, in Zeit, rechtzeidich, uff Zeit.** KYG2019. **Er waar ~ do.** He was here promptly. LRT

Zeitsfrog, *f* - a question of time. KYG2019

Zeituhr, *f* - time clock. KYG2020. **Die Schaffleit misse immer neidricke an de ~, wann sie an die Arewet gehne.** The employees always have to punch in at the time clock, when they go to work. LRT

zeitweis, *adv* - for a time. KYG2018. **So zeideweis hot's schwer runner gemacht (gereyert).** At times it rained heavily. LRT. = **zeiteweis**

Zelt, *n, pl* **~er** - tent. KYG1986. **Wu kann mer grossi ~er kaafe.** Where can you buy big tents? LRT

Zeltduch, *n* - tent cloth. KYG1986. **En ~ muss Wasser hewe.** A tent cloth must be water-proof. LRT

Zelthaus, *n* - tent. KYG1986

Zenkrin, *f* - termagant, a quarrelsome woman, a shrew. = **gross-gfressich Weibsmensch.** KYG1988

Zeppli, *n* - *dim* of **Zappe.** LRT/Leb.Co.

zerecht´bringe - to set in order. **Sache ~** - to set things in order. = **Sache in Adder duh. Mariye fangt die Schul aa, no sedde mir alles ~ kenne.** Tomorrow

school starts, then we should be able to set everything in order. LRT

zerecht´mache - to adjust. KYG2061. **Sie hen ihn zu viel getschaertscht ghat fer sei Schtorsache, awwer sie hen's ihm zerechtgemacht.** They had charged him too much for his store merchandise, but they made an adjustment. LRT

zerick´binne, *pp* **zerickgebunne** - to tie back the off-side horse. KYG2015. **En wusslicher Newegaul muss gut zerickgebunne sei.** A frisky side horse must be tied back real well. LRT

zerick´dappe, *pp* **zerickgedappt** - to trudge back. KYG2068. **Er is datt hinnich die Scheier zerickgedappt.** He trudged back there behind the barn. LRT

zerick´denke - to think back. **Ferwas will mer ~? Mer kann nix verennere.** Why should one think back? One can change nothing. LRT

zerick´drehe - to turn back. **die Zeeche uff de Uhr ~** - to turn back the hands of a clock. KYG2077. **Mit unser narrischi Zeit dreht mer die Uhr zerick im Harebscht.** With our crazy time (daylight saving time) the clock is turned back in the fall. LRT

zerick´haltend, *adj* - undemonstrative. = **schei.** KYG2095

Zerick´henkrieme, *m* - tie-back strap. = **Zerickbinnrieme.** KYG2015

zerick´mache - 1 to remove straw to the rear when thrashing. KYG2006. **2** to be back (on time). **Yunger, mach dich zerick vor halb Nacht.** Young man, you be sure to be back before midnight. LRT

zerick´maule - to talk back. = **zerickschwetze.** KYG1964

zerick´nemme - to take back. KYG1962

zerick´schmeisse - to throw back. KYG2009. **Geh darich die Grummbiere, un die was zu glee sin, schmeiss sie zerick.** Go through the potatoes. Throw the ones that are too small back. LRT

zerick´schneide, *pp* **zerickgschnidde** - to top (a plant). KYG2037. **Die Baemlin vanne am Haus duhne mir zerickgschnidde halde.** We keep the shrubbery, in front of our house, cut back. LRT

zerick´schteh - to stand back. **Schteh zerick, so as du net weh geduh waerscht.** Stand back so you don't get hurt. LRT

zerick´bezaahle - to pay back. **Vorher hoscht du mir Geld gewwe ghat fer paar Sache kaafe, awwer mir hen nix gebreicht. Nau will ich dich ~.** Earlier you had given me money to buy a few things, but we didn't need anything. Now I want to pay you back. LRT

zerick´bleiwe, *pp* **is gebliwwe** - to stay back or behind. **"Bleib zerick!" hot er gegrische.** "Stay back!" he shouted. **Bleib zerick, der Bull meecht dich renne.** Stay back, the bull might ram you. LRT

zerick´dreiwe, *pp* **zerickgedriwwe** - to repulse. **Noch em Feier, hen sie die Kieh zerick in die Scheier gedriwwe.** After the fire, they drove the cows back into the barn. LRT

zerick´duh - to put back. **Wie er im Schtor waar, hot er eppes aus me Fass genumme, no hen sie ihm gsaat er soll's ~.** When he was in the store, he took something out of a barrel, then they told him to put it back. **Tschanni, sell is net fer dich; du muscht es ~.** Johnny, that's not for you. You must put it back! LRT. = **zerickschtelle, zericksetze.**

Zerick´fall, *m* - relapse. **Sie hen gemehnt, er is iwwer sei Bruschtfiewer, awwer er hot en ~ ghat.** They thought he was recovered from his pneumonia, but he had a relapse. LRT

zerick´geh - to go back. **Geh zerick, un saag sell widder, ich hab dich net verschtanne.** Go back and say that again, I didn't understand you. LRT

zerick´gnarre - to give a surly answer. **Yunger, du settscht net so ~.** Young man, you should not answer in such a surly way. LRT

zerick´griege - to recover, get back. **Selli Gleeder waare mir gschtole gwest, awwer ich hab sie zerickgrickt.** Those clothes were stolen from me, but I got them back. LRT

zerick´halde - to restrain. = **zerickhewe. Es sin zwee**

Schuler as mir ~ misse fer en Yaahr. There are two students that we have to hold back for a year. LRT

zerick´hocke, *refl* - to sit back. **Du kannscht dich ~ un waarde.** You can sit back and wait. LRT

zerick´kaafe, *pp* **zerickgekaaft** - to repurchase. **Yaahre zerick hab ich seller Gaul verkaaft, awwer no schpaeder hab ich ihn zerickgekaaft.** Years ago I sold that horse, but then later I bought it back. LRT

zerick´kumme - to come back, return. **Sie hen verlosse ghat, awwer sie sin widder ~.** They had departed but they returned again. **Zwee Yaahr in Florida waar genunk, es waar Zeit fer ~.** Two years in Florida were enough, it was time to come back. LRT

zerick´nemme - to recant, take back. **Sell hett ich net saage selle, ich nemm's zerick.** I should not have said that, I'll take that back. **Mir nemme alles zerick was dir net yuuse kennt.** We'll take back everything that you can't use. LRT

zerick´reeche - to reach back. **Mit seine lange Aerem hot er ~ kenne.** He could reach behind him with his long arms. LRT

zerick´reide, *pp* is **zerickgeridde** - to ride back. **Wann dir hiereide hett kenne, dann sett dir aa ~ kenne.** If you could ride there, you should also be able to ride back. LRT

zerick´rufe - to call back. **Selli**

Kaere hen Fehler, sie rufe sie zerick bei de Dausende. Those cars have defects, they are calling them back by the thousands. LRT

zerick´schelde - to scold in return. **Wann du net gleichscht, was er dir gsaat hot, dann kannscht du ihn vielleicht bissel ~.** If you don't like what he said to you, perhaps you can scold him back a bit in return. LRT

zerick´schicke - 1 to remand. **2** to remit. **3** to repatriate. **Ich gleich, wann ich en Buch kaaf, un wann ich's net gleich, as ich's ~ darf.** I like when I buy a book (and have it sent to me), and if I don't like it that I may send (or take) it back. LRT

zerick´schicke - to send back, return. **Wann'd des Buch net gleichscht, dann schick's zerick.** If you don't like this book, then send it back. LRT

zerick´schlagge, *pp* **zerickgschlagge** - to strike back. **Sie hot ihn gschlagge, no hot er sie graadeswegs zerickgschlagge.** She hit him, then he hit her right back. LRT

zerick´schprenge, *pp* **zerickgschprengt** - to cause someone to beat a hasty retreat. **Er hot sei Backebuch verlore ghat. Sell hot ihn graad zerickgschprengt fer's Suche.** He had lost his wallet. That caused him to run right back in search of it. LRT

zerick´schridde - to step back. **Schritt zerick, der Dampf vun dem Kessel grickt dich!** Step back, the steam from this kettle will get you. LRT

Zerick´sehne, *n* - hindsight. **Vaerschichsehne is besser wie ~.** Foresight is better than hindsight. LRT

zickzack, *adv* - zig-zag. = **schtaakefensich.** KYG2266

ziddere - to quiver, quake. **Tschecki, was is letz? Du zidderscht wie en Blaat im Wind.** Jaky, what's wrong? You are shaking like a leaf in the wind! LRT

Zidderli, *m* - pig's feet jelly. LRT/Leb.Co.

ziehe, *pp* **gezoge - 1** to ring a church bell. = **die Glock ~. Yaahre zerick hot mei Daadi oft die Karicheglock gezoge.** Years ago my dad often rang the church bell. LRT. **2** to pull. **Garick ~** - to uncork. KYG2095. **en Lein unnich's Watt ~** - to underline a word. KYG2097. **Ich gleich sehne wann die Fisch beisse un duhne der Garick unnich's Wasser ~.** I like to see when the fish bit and pull the cork (floater) under the water. LRT

Ziel, *n* - purpose, aim. **Was is dei ~?** What is your aim? LRT

ziele - to take good aim. **Ziel net, wann du net schiesse witt.** Don't aim if you don't want to fire. LRT

Zieraat, *f* - trinket. KYG2062

Ziggel, *m* - tile. KYG2017. **Langi Yaahre zerick waar die Zoar Ludderisch Karich in Mt. Zion Leb. Co. PA, die Ziegel Kirche (Ziggel Karich) gheese.** Many years ago Zoar Lutheran Church in Mt. Zion, Lebanon County, PA was called

"**die Ziggel Karich**" ("the tile church"). LRT

Ziggelbrennerei, *f* - tile works. KYG2017

Ziggeldach, *n* - tile roof. KYG2017. **En rot ~ guckt schee.** A red tile roof looks attractive. LRT

Ziggelroi, *f* - row of tiles. KYG2017

Zindloch, *n* - touch hole (on gun). = **Zindpann.** KYG2041

zingle - 1 to give a tingling sensation. **Ich wees net was letz is un ferwas as es so zingelt in meim Aarem.** I don't know what is wrong and why I have this tingling sensation in my arm. LRT. **2** to wag the tongue. KYG2034. *cf* **glingle, zwitzere.** KYG2022

zinke, *adj* - zinc. **en zinkne Iwwerlaad** - zinc coffin. KYG2266

Zinke, *pl* - prongs. **Selli Gawwel hot scheeni langi ~.** That fork has nice long prongs. LRT

zinne, *pp* **gezinnt** - to tin. **Sell Schtick Eise hen sie gezinnt.** They tinned that piece of iron. LRT

zinnich, *adj* - tinny. = **blechich.** KYG2023

Zion - ✪ Zionsville, PA. KYG2282

Zionsbrieder, *pl* - United Zion's Children (religious denomination). KYG2266

zittre - to trill (of birds). =

drillere, drilliere. KYG2061

Ziwwerbinner, *m* - tub cooper. KYG2071

Ziwwerche, *n* - small tub. KYG2071. = **Ziwwerli.** Leb. Co. **Selle gleene hilzne Ziwwerlin sin en latt Geld wert.** Those little wooden tubs are worth a lot of money. LRT. = **Ziwwerli**

zollfrei, *adj* - toll-free. KYG2032

Zollhaus, *n* - toll house. KYG2032

Zollikoffer, *m* - name of a prayer book. KYG2266

Zollkolleckder, *m* - toll collector. KYG2031

Zoppe, *m* - tatter. = **Huddel, Zoddel.** KYG1972

Zopplein, *f* - check line. LRT

Zoppziggel, *m* - check rein. **Sell Paert vun em Geilsgschaar heest mer en ~.** That part of a horse harness is called a checkrein. LRT

Zott, *f* - spout of teapot. KYG1976

zottlich, *adj* - shaggy, ragged, tattered. *cf* **lumpich, verrisse.** KYG1972. **Dei Gleeder gucke ordlich ~.** Your clothes look quite tattered. **Sei Kutt guckt awwer ~.** His jacket really looks shaggy. LRT

zowwle - to pull someone's ears. = **epper die Ohre ~.** LRT

zu, *adv* - too. *cf* **aa, dezu, dergleiche. ~ erbarmlich** - too bad. = ~ **schlimm.** ~ **gross** - too big. ~ **gut** - too good. KYG2034

zu, *prep* - to. ~ **all vun uns** - to all of us. ~ **sich selwer** - to him/herself. = **draa, aa, gehe, noch, uff, um.** KYG2027. **Sie hot's ~ sich selwert ghalde.** She kept it a secret. LRT

zubinne, *pp* **zugebunne** - to tie shut. **die Seck ~** - to tie bags. KYG2015. **Hoscht du die Weezeseck zugebunne?** Did you tie the wheat sacks shut? LRT

zubleiwe - to remain closed. **Schliess die Dier odder sie bleibt net zu.** Lock the door or it won't stay shut. LRT

zubleschdere - to cover with plaster. **Tschannie, ich wott du daedscht sell Loch ~.** Johnny, I wish you would plaster that hole shut. LRT

zublose, *pp* **is zugeblose** - to blow shut (of road with snow). **Ya, die Schtrosse sin zugeblose.** Yes, the roads are blown shut. LRT

zuborde, *pp* **zugebordt** - to board shut. **Wann so en Schtarem kummt, daed mer besser die Fenschdere ~.** When there's such a storm coming, one had better board the windows shut. LRT

Zucht, *f* - noise, racket. **So'n ~ is genunk fer em narrisch mache.** Such noise is enough to drive one crazy. LRT

zucke, *pp* **gezuckt** - **1** to quiver. **Wie er am Blut gewwe waar, hot er gezuckt, no hot die Fraa Druwwel ghat die Oder finne.** When he was giving blood, he

quivered and the woman had trouble finding the vein. LRT. **2** to twitch. **Wann die Maed Lecher in die Ohre gemacht griege, deife sie sich net ~.** When the girls have their ears pierced, they may not twitch or jerk. LRT

Zuckerarebs, *f* - sugar pea. **~e, leicht gekocht mit Bissel Budder, mache gut Esses.** Sugar peas, lightly cooked, with a little butter, make good eating. LRT

Zuckerarebs, pl - **~e,** *f* - sugar pea, snow pea. LRT

zuckerich, *adj* - sugary. **Ebmols wann der Hunnich zu lang schteht, watt er ~.** Sometimes when the honey stands too long, it gets sugary. LRT

Zuckerkichli, *n, pl* **~n** - sweet cake. **Ihre ~n sin immer so gut.** Her sugar cookies are always so good. LRT

Zuckermaul, *n* - person with sweet tooth. KYG2035

zuckich, *adj* - twitchy. KYG2084. **Die Sau is noch net ganz dod, sie is noch bissel ~.** The hog isn't totally dead, it is still a bit twitchy. LRT

zudecke - to cover with hoe in planting. LRT

zudrehe - to turn shut. **Dreh der Wasserzappe zu.** Turn off the water faucet. LRT

zudrehe - to turn off (a spigot). KYG2077. **Kannscht du seller Deckel ~?** Can you turn that lid shut? LRT

zudricke - to squeeze shut.

Drick dei Aag zu. Close your eye. LRT

zu dritt, *adv* - triple. **Sie waare ~ gebore.** They were born triplets. KYG2062. **Sie sin ~ in die Karich gange.** The three of them went to church. LRT

Zuflucht, *f* - refuge. **Bekimmer dich net, dei ~ is immer do.** Have no concern, your refuge is always here. LRT

zufrid´de, *adj* - satisfied. **gut ~ mit sich selwert sei** - to be smug. **Wann du ~ bischt, dann mache mir's so.** If you are satisfied, we'll do it that way. LRT

Zug, *m, pl* **Zieg** - sweep (of wind)

zugleich´, *adv* - at the same time. *cf* **debei, denewe.** KYG2019. **~ as mir deheem am butschere waare, hen sie sich geblessiert in Deitschland.** At the same time we were butchering at home, they were taking pleasure in Germany. LRT

zugreife - to take hold of. KYG1961

zuheele - to heal (up). **Seller Schnitt is am ~.** That cut is healing up (shut and forming a scab). LRT

zukumme, *pp* **is ~** - to regain consciousness. **Ya, uumechdich waar er, awwer er is widder ~.** Yes, he was unconscious, but he regained his consciousness. LRT

zumache - to shut, close. **Mach die Dier zu.** Close the door. LRT

201

zumauere, *pp* **zugemauert** - to wall up. KYG2160. **Er hot selli Lecher zugemauert.** He walled up those holes. LRT

Zunaame, *m* - surname. **Sei ~ is Teufel. Mer wunnert wu so Naame beikumme.** His surname is Teufel. One wonders where such names come from. LRT

zunaehe, *pp* **zugenaeht** - to sew shut. **Deel Leit sedde ihre Maul zugenaeht hawwe.** Some people should have their mouths sewn shut. LRT

Zung, *f* - tongue. **sei ~ verliere** - to be tongue-tied (remain silent). **en schteifi ~ hawwe** - to be tongue-tied (to have an abnormality). KYG2034. **Wann er schwetzt, heert mer as eppes letz is mit seine ~.** When he talks, one hears that there is an abnormality with his tongue. LRT

zuscheppe - to shovel shut. **Schepp sell Loch zu.** Fill that hole with dirt (using a shovel). LRT

zuschiewe - to push shut. **Schieb die Dier zu.** Push the door shut. LRT

zuschlagge, *pp* **zugschlagge** - 1 to help a blacksmith in welding a tire. KYG2025. **2** to slam shut. **Seller Yunge hot die Dier zugschlagge.** That young man slammed the door shut. LRT

zuschmiere, *pp* **zugschmiert** - to smear shut (cracks with plaster). KYG1889. **epper** (*dat.*) **die Aage ~** - to blind someone to the truth. KYG2071. **Selli Lecher uff em Bodde hen sie zugschmiert.** They smeared

those holes on the floor shut. **Selli paar Riss datt in de Wand—kannscht du sie ~?** Those few cracks there in the wall, can you close them with plaster? LRT

zuschpelle - to pin together. **Wann die Gleeder ken Gnepp hen, no muss mer sie zuschpelle.** If the clothes have no buttons, then they have to be pinned (shut or together). LRT

Zuschtand, *m, pl* **Zuschtende** - state, circumstance. **Sell is awwer Schaad, fer sich in so schlechdi Zuschtende finne.** That is a pity to find oneself in such bad circumstances. LRT

zuschtoppe - to stop up. KYG2016. **Selli Raddelecher sedde mir ~.** We should stop up those rat holes. **Seller Fudersack hot en Loch, kannscht's ~ mit bissel Schtroh?** That feed sack has a hole, can you stop it with a little straw? LRT

zuschwemme, *pp* **zugschwemmt** - to cover with silt, mud. **Die Schtrooss waar zugschwemmt.** The road was covered with mud. LRT

Zuverdraue, *n* - trust. = **Verdraue.** KYG2070

zu verdraue - to be trusted. **Er is net ~.** He is not to be trusted (or depended on). LRT

Zuwwerdaub, *f, pl* **-dauwe** - tub stave. KYG2073

Zuwwervoll, *m* - tubfull. KYG2072. **Sie hen en ~ Fisch heemgebrocht vum See.** They brought a tub full of fish home from the ocean. LRT

zuziehe - to pull tight. KYG2016. **Die Vorhanger do in die Schtubb misse mir ~, weil's zu hell is.** The curtains here in the room need to be drawn shut, because it's too light (in here). LRT

zwaar, *advbl.* - 'Tis true. KYG2026. **Ya, ~ du hoscht recht.** 'Tis true, you are right. LRT

zwanne - to twist (yarn). = **zwaerne.** KYG2084

Zwannraad, *n* - twisting wheel. = **Zwaernraad.** KYG2084

zwanzich - twenty. **in die ~** - some twenty. KYG2082. **Sie hen ihm in die ~ Daaler gewe.** They gave him some twenty dollars. **Mir hen so in de ~ Bendi-Hinkel un Haahne.** We have some 20 Bantam hens and roosters. LRT

Zwanzichdaalernot, *f* - $20 note. KYG2082. **En ~ geht nimmi so weit as sie als is.** A twenty dollar bill isn't worth what it used to be. LRT

zwanzichmol, *adv* - twenty-fold. KYG2082. **Muss ich dir's ~ saage?** Must I tell you 20 times? LRT

Zwanzichschdel, *n* - twentieth. *cf* **zwanzichscht.** KYG2082

zwanzichscht, *adj* - twentieth. **Des is es ~ Schtick vun daere Raetzel.** This is the twentieth piece of this puzzle. LRT

zwanzichyaehrich, *adj* - twenty-year-old. KYG2082. **Is des awwer net eppes, nau hen mir en ~er Buh?** Isn't this something, now we have a twenty-year-old son? LRT

Zwarickax, *f, pl* ~**e** - twibill ax. KYG2082. ~**e kenne bissel gefaehrlich sei.** Twibill axes can be a bit dangerous. LRT

Zwariwel, *m* - turnbuckle. KYG2078

zwedde, *refl* - **1** to happen twice. KYG2082. **2** to become two years old. KYG2086. **Wann eppes sich ~ dutt, is es ewwe in die Roi fer sich dridde.** If something occurs twice, it is in line to occur thrice. LRT

zweddens, *adv* - secondly. = **im zwedde Blatz. Die Reis waar schee, awwer im erschde Blatz, sie hot en latt Geld gekoscht, un im zwedde Blatz, mir waare zu en langi Zeit vun heem gewest.** The trip was nice, but in the first place, it cost a lot of money, and in the second place, we were away from home for too long a time. LRT

zwee - two. ~ **vunne** - two of them. KYG2084. **in ~** - in two pieces. **en Wochner ~** - in two weeks (or so). **so'n Uhre ~** - about two o'clock. **in ~ breche** - to break in two. KYG2085. **Sell guckt wie guder** candy, **ich nemm zwee vunne.** That looks like good candy, I'll have two (of them). LRT

zwee-erlee, *adv* - in two sorts. KYG2085

zwee-schteckich, *adj* - two-storied. **Unser Mt. Zion Schulhaus waar en zwee-schtuwwich, ~ Gebei.** Our Mt. Zion schoolhouse was a two-roomed, two-storied building. LRT

zwee-stuwwich, *adj* - two-roomed. **Unser Mt. Zion Schulhaus waar en ~, zwee-schteckich Gebei.** Our Mt. Zion schoolhouse was a two-roomed, two-storied building. LRT

zwee-yaehrich, *adj* - two-years-old. KYG2085. **Sell ~ Buwli is uns oh so lieb.** That little two-year-old boy is so dear to us. LRT

zweebehnich, *adj* - two-legged. *cf* **zweenich.** KYG2086. **Vergess net, Mensche sin yusht ~.** Don't forget, humans have only two legs. LRT

Zweebuschelsack, *m* - two-bushel bag. KYG2085. **En ~ voll Weeze is blendi schwer fer mich.** A two-bushel sack filled with wheat is plenty heavy for me. LRT

zweedottrich, *adj* - having two yolks. KYG2263

zweefach, *adj* - twofold. KYG2085. **Die Ursach fer die Versammling is ~.** The reason for this meeting is twofold. LRT

zweefarewich, *adj* - two-colored. KYG2085. **Holschtee Kieh sin ~.** Holstein cows are two-colored. LRT

zweefeischdich, *adj* - two-fisted. KYG2085. **Er is en ~er Mensch.** He is a vigorous, viral person. LRT

Zweegeilsbauerei, *f* - two-horse farm. KYG2086. **~ hot nix zu duh mit wie viel Acker as die Bauerei hot, yuscht wie viel Geilschtell as die Scheier hot.** A two-horse farm has nothing to do with the number of acres the farm has, only how many horse

stalls the barn has. LRT

Zweegeilslein, *f* - two-horse line. KYG2086. **En ~ macht's hendich fer en Zweegeilsfuhr faahre.** A two-horse line makes it convenient to drive a two-horse team. LRT

Zweegeilswagge, *m* - two-horse wagon. KYG2086. **En Zweegeilsbauerei hot schur genunk en ~.** A two-horse farm, sure enough has a two-horse wagon. LRT

zweegsichdich, *adj* - two-faced. KYG2085. **Sis ebmols hatt fer bekannt warre mit ~i Leit.** Sometimes it's hard to get to know two-faced people. LRT

zweehendich, *adj* - two-handed. KYG2085. **Sell is en ~i Arewet.** That job requires two hands. LRT

zweemol, *adv* - twice. *cf* **zwettmol.** KYG2082. **Sell is es zwett Mol as ich ihn gsehne hab.** That is the second time that I saw him. LRT

zweereddrich, *adj* - two-wheeled. ~ **Dreckkarich** - two-wheeled dump cart. KYG2086. **Mir sin noch em Schteddel gange mit de ~ Gick.** We went to town with the two-wheeled sulky. LRT

zweeschpennich, *adj* - two-horse. KYG2085

zweeschteckich, *adj* - two-storied. KYG2086. **Sell ~ Gebei in de Mitt vum Schteddel is nunnergebrennt.** That two-story building in the middle of town burnt down. LRT

zweeseidich, *adj* - two-sided.

KYG2086. **Wann eppes ~ is, mehnt's: eens odder's anner.** If something is two-sided, it means: it is one or the other. LRT

zweesitzich, *adj* - two-seated. KYG2086. **En ~ Waegli is oftmols zu glee fer deel Famillye.** A two-seated buggy is oft times too small for some families. LRT

zweeyaehrich, *adj* - two-years-old. **Ya, der Tscheck is nau ~.** Yes, Jake is now two years old. LRT,4/18/2000

Zweeyaehricher, *m* - two-year-old child. **En Zweeyaehriches kann schund en latt Wadde saage.** A two-year-old child can already say many words. LRT,4/18/2000

zweezinkich, *adj* - two-pronged. **Zwee- un drei-zinkichi Gawwele yuust mer fer Fruchtgarwe schmeisse.** One uses two and three-pronged (tined) forks to throw grain sheaves. LRT

Zwelfdel, *n* - twelfth. KYG2081. **En ~ vun me Dutzend Oier is ee Oi.** A twelfth of a dozen of eggs is one egg. LRT

Zwelfder, *m* - the number 12. KYG2081. **Er hot grossi Fiess, er brauch en ~ Schuh.** He has big feet, he need a (size) 12. LRT

zwelfmol, *adv* - twelve-fold. KYG2081. **Am Halbnacht schlackt die Uhr ~.** At midnight the clock strikes 12 times. LRT

zwett - second. **der ~ Grischtdaag** - the second day of Christmas. LRT

zwettglennscht, *superl adj* - next to smallest. **Er is der ~ vun de Buwe.** He is next to the smallest of the boys. LRT

zwicke - to pinch. LRT

Zwickel, *m* - fool, clown. **en elender ~** - miserable little thing. **= en elender Gweckel.** KYG1997

zwidderich, *adj* - shimmering (tremulously). **Mei Aage sin ~.** My eyesight is unclear. LRT *cf* **zwitscherich**

zwiggere - to twitter. KYG2084

zwillere - to warble. *cf* **zwitschere.** KYG2163. **Harich mol wie seller Voggel zwillert.** Listen how that bird is warbling. LRT

zwillich, *adj* - twilled. **Er hot en ~er Rock aa.** He has a twilled (cotton cloth) coat on. LRT

Zwillich, *m* - twill. KYG2083

Zwilling, *pl* - twins. **Siamesische ~** - Siamese twins. **Der Terry un der Jerry sin ~.** Terry and Jerry are twins. LRT

Zwillingbopplin, *pl* - **1** twin boys. KYG2083. **2** twin babies. **Die ~ waare 20 Minude vun nanner gebore.** The twin babies were born 20 minutes apart. LRT

Zwillingbruder, *m* - twin brother. KYG2083. **Er hot en ~, awwer sie gucke gaar net gleich.** He has a twin brother, but there is absolutely no resemblance between them. LRT

Zwillingkinner, *pl* - twin children. KYG2083. **Selli Famillye hot zwee paar ~.** That family has two sets of twin children. LRT

zwischedarich, *adv* - right through between. KYG2009. **Die Kinner sin graad ~ uns grosse Leit gschprunge.** The children ran right through between us adults. **Sie sin ~ die zwee Heiser gfaahre.** They drove right through between the two houses. LRT

zwischedrin, *adv* - in between. **Ich hab datt ~ ghockt.** I sat in between there. LRT

zwischenei, *adv* - between times. KYG2020. **Ich hab en Schtick Fleesch ~ geduh gschwischich zwee Schticker Brot.** I put a piece of meat between two pieces of bread. LRT

zwitzerich, *adj* - tingling. KYG2022. **Mei Aage waare ~.** My eyes were shimmering (I couldn't see clearly). LRT

Zwiwwel, *f, pl* **Zwiwwle** - onion. LRT

204